U.S. National Security and Foreign Policymaking After 9/11

U.S. National Security and Foreign Policymaking After 9/11

Present at the Re-creation

M. Kent Bolton

Rowman & Littlefield Publishers, Inc.
Lanham • Boulder • New York • Toronto • Plymouth, UK

ROWMAN & LITTLEFIELD PUBLISHERS, INC.

Published in the United States of America
by Rowman & Littlefield Publishers, Inc.
A wholly owned subsidary of
The Rowman & Littlefield Publishing Group, Inc.
4501 Forbes Boulevard, Suite 200, Lanham, Maryland 20706
www.rowmanlittlefield.com

Estover Road
Plymouth PL6 7PY
United Kingdom

British Library Cataloguing in Publication Information Available

Library of Congress Cataloging-in-Publication Data

Bolton, M. Kent.
   U.S. national security and foreign policymaking after 9/11: present at the
re-creation / M. Kent Bolton.
      p. cm.
   ISBN-13: 978-0-7425-4847-3 (cloth : alk. paper)
   ISBN-10: 0-7425-4847-3 (cloth : alk. paper)
   ISBN-13: 978-0-7425-5900-4 (pbk. : alk. paper)
   ISBN-10: 0-7425-5900-9 (pbk. : alk. paper)
   1. September 11 Terrorist Attacks, 2001—Influence. 2. National security—
United States. 3. United States—Foreign relations—2001– I. Title. II. Title:
US national security and foreign policymaking after 9/11.
   HV6432.7.B65 2007
   355'.033073—dc22   2007007578

Printed in the United States of America

⊗™ The paper used in this publication meets the minimum requirements of
American National Standard for Information Sciences—Permanence of Paper
for Printed Library Materials, ANSI/NISO Z39.48-1992.

Contents

Preface

HYPOTHETICAL

Imagine being a professor with expertise on U.S. national security policy preparing to teach a course on that subject in 1963. Assume, further, that you wished to teach your students about the Cuban Missile Crisis. The Cuban Missile Crisis was a nuclear standoff between the U.S., the USSR, and to a lesser extent, the Cubans, that occurred in October 1962, and the basic information about the standoff would have been public knowledge. For instance, many of your students would have known that President John F. Kennedy announced a public ultimatum to the Soviets in late October 1962. The ultimatum instructed the Soviet première to cease and desist from deploying offensive nuclear weapons on Cuban territory lest war occur. How would our professor prepare herself for her forthcoming course?

Our hypothetical professor might have read in media accounts that something called the Excomm (i.e., the executive committee of the National Security Council) deliberated during the crisis and she therefore would expect that the Excomm would be an important focus for her course. She would naturally have searched for a book or monograph—scholarly or journalistic—that discussed the Excomm of the NSC and the NSC's uses during the Kennedy and previous administrations. She very likely would have discovered that few works existed on the NSC, much less the Excomm. Instead, she would have found a few journalistic accounts that mentioned the NSC or the Excomm, but beyond that she would have found little that explained the NSC (and the Excomm of the NSC) and how it functioned during the missile crisis.

Our professor would have persisted. Perhaps she would have found the 1947 National Security Act (NSA) that created the NSC (as well as other national security institutions). Finding the 1947 NSA, she would have discovered how critical the legislation was in creating what became the Excomm during the missile crisis. That would have led her to a number of additional questions. Who worked for the NSC and from where did they come? Who comprised the NSC membership? Why? Why was Kennedy's NSC configured differently than President Eisenhower's in the fall of 1956 when Eisenhower confronted the Suez-Sinai debacle and the Soviets' heavy-handed intervention in Hungary simultaneously? Wondering how the NSC might have evolved since the previous year's debacle known as the Bay of Pigs, she might have decided to compare the Kennedy administration's deliberations during the missile crisis with deliberations during the Bay of Pigs.

In preparing for her course, our professor may well have established that a focus of analysis rarely written about in the media or in academe was, nevertheless, seemingly critical to U.S. policymaking. Presuming she was a careful scholar, she would have discovered that a report (the Jackson Committee report on the NSC) had criticized President Eisenhower's NSC just a couple of years earlier. Consequently, she would have been interested in studying the Jackson report for its recommendations. She would have likely discovered that President Kennedy had consciously changed his NSC from the Eisenhower template Kennedy inherited. By this point, our professor would have determined that no scholar or journalist could fairly or comprehensively have analyzed U.S. national security policy (or the Cuban Missile Crisis) without understanding how the NSC fitted into the complex puzzle of policymaking.

Along the way our professor might have discovered that the Excomm's composition included Secretary of Defense Robert S. McNamara and Secretary of State Dean Rusk and that McGeorge Bundy (Kennedy's "NSC advisor") was also included as was the president's brother, Attorney General Robert F. Kennedy. She would recognize that by virtue of its membership, the NSC "principals" necessarily represented multiple executive branch agencies: the Department of Defense, the Department of State, the NSC, the Department of Justice, and perhaps others. She would therefore attempt to determine who, at lower levels, was involved and what routines existed allowing interdepartmental communications to flow from the various executive agencies to the NSC and *vice versa*, from the president in NSC principals meetings back to the department secretaries. Surely she would have discovered that the intelligence community was the eyes and ears of the NSC, and she would have wished to learn more about it. This would have led her to examine the Central Intelligence Agency (also created by the 1947 NSA), but since the military services had their own intelligence collection, she would have probably thought it important to consider intelligence beyond the CIA. She would probably have become frustrated multiple times at the lack of scholarly treatment of the NSC and how integral it had become to U.S. national security policymaking.

FOLLOWING 9/11 AND ITS IMMEDIATE AFTERMATH

Though somewhat exaggerated, the hypothetical posed was where scholars and journalist found themselves in December 2004! Certainly, articles and books had been written following 9/11 about President Bush's "war cabinet," an ad hoc configuration of the NSC principals. Furthermore, scholars, journalists, and the attentive public learned throughout 2003 and 2004 that major reorganizations and changes were being considered for America's national security institutions (the NSC, the intelligence community, and the way the two interacted), which had served America well over the Cold War. One may have unearthed newspaper articles—in what follows we unearthed many—but apart from the ad hoc journalistic coverage, no textbooks, monographs, or scholarly articles existed as yet detailing the fundamental changes that occurred to America's foreign policy and national security decision-making institutions since 9/11, specifically the major legislation known as the Intelligence Reform and Terrorism Prevention Act. Since the tragedy of 9/11, multiple postmortems examining intelligence and policymaking failures were conducted in the U.S. and as many reports were issued, most recommending major reorganization. Some of the most important ones were published in a Herculean effort to make sure America was ready for the next 9/11—or at least more ready. Incredibly, during a hotly contested presidential election year, a number of factors, forces, and influences converged resulting in that legislation; the legislation will likely affect U.S. foreign and national security policy for a generation or more. Its 1947 sibling affected those same policies for some two generations.

In the spring of 2005, I was scheduled to teach a course I have taught several times. The course focused on the America's National Security Council and its role in national security and foreign policy decisionmaking. As I contemplated how I had taught the course in the past, I realized that fundamental changes had occurred since I had last taught the course; I therefore set about to find scholarship that explained those changes. I well understood that in 1947 as the Cold War began, Congress passed and President Truman signed the National Security Act (1947) creating the National Security Council, the Central Intelligence Agency, the unified defense department, and a host of new Cold War institutions, procedures, and processes. Though rarely written about, at least in scholarly publications, the NSC was well-known to me from graduate school days and my doctoral dissertation research. In December 2004, the Intelligence Reform and Terrorism Prevention Act (IRTPA) was signed into law. Just as the 1947 NSA created new institutions, the IRTPA created the office of the director of national intelligence (ODNI and DNI respectively). The IRPTA created other new institutions: the National Counterterrorism Center (NCTC), the National Counterproliferation Center (NCPC), and the Joint Intelligence Community Council (JICC), which now interacts with the NSC. The IRTPA made the newly created DNI an NSC "principal," an important policymaking position. Given how important the NSC principals have become, what's truly remarkable is how little has been written specifically about them. Understandably, I found nothing but newspaper articles that discussed the new DNI.

Beyond the NSC principals, many of America's most well-known agencies and bureaus, the FBI and the CIA for instance, have fundamentally been reorganized since 9/11 for a new mission in a new world of transnational and other non-state threats. The FBI, while still America's premier crime fighting agency, has been reoriented considerably to prevent another 9/11. The CIA, whose director (Director of Central Intelligence or DCI) formerly existed in law as the head of all intelligence products for the president, has been supplanted in those duties by the DNI. The DNI is now authorized to redirect intelligence priorities and budgets of the fifteen disparate intelligence collection and intelligence analysis agencies. While the CIA remains the center of Human Intelligence, that is, espionage and spying, it answers to the DNI, at least by law. A new cabinet agency, the Department of Homeland Security (DHS), was created, having cannibalized some twenty-plus bureaus and agencies that formerly existed in other executive departments of the federal government. How President Bush receives his nearly daily intelligence briefings and sets policy as well as how future presidents will do the same has been fundamentally altered by the IRTPA. Intriguingly, just as so few Americans understood the creation of the NSC and CIA in 1947—as anecdotally evidenced each time I taught my NSC course—relatively few Americans today know more about the IRTPA and the reorganizations it mandated for America's national security institutions and policies.

In a sense this book is about two simple ideas. The first idea is the myth that politics stops at the water's edge. The aphorism is intended to suggest that when it comes to foreign policy, or more particularly, America's foreign and national security policy, only America's "national security interests" matter. The stakes are accordingly considered too high to allow domestic politics to interfere, and policymakers therefore check their egos, their agendas, their parochial interests, at the door of the center of policymaking, the NSC principals committee. The myth is probably the result of a simpler time when America was not a hegemonic power, a time when America's role in the world was minimal and when America could afford to follow an isolationist posture in global affairs. As most Americans intuitively understand, politics does not stop at the water's edge. On the contrary, all sorts of domestic sources influence and shape U.S. policymaking. Though it may be intuitive to many, it is seldom well-understood by the public, even the attentive public. And that is the second idea on which this book turns.

If many Americans understand that U.S. domestic politics affects U.S. national security, why is it that most Americans cannot identify the National Security Council or other parts of the bureaucracy regularly affected by domestic politics? Why do so few books systematically consider the same? Why can so few Americans speak intelligently about how domestic politics affects national security? To the extent that discussions of the effects of domestic politics on national security and foreign policymaking exist at all, they are typically discussed pejoratively. Radio talk show hosts, opinion columnists, and pundits of virtually every political stripe decry how their political opponents are beholden to special interest groups, how a president with whom a particular pundit takes issue consults opinion polls in policymaking, and so on. But the interactions between domestic politics and national security is complex and daily; nor is it always a negative thing in a pluralistic society.

Domestic politics affect U.S. national security policy and they do so consistently, irrespective of political party, from the most prosaic of foreign and national security policymaking to the most critical. The very pundits who decry it count on it. Their livelihoods are materially affected by the sway their opinions have on U.S. policymaking, both public and foreign. This book therefore seeks to consider important domestic sources as well as external sources of U.S. national security policymaking in a particularly important period of world history. America is currently involved, for better or worse, in a foreign policy gamble: the gamble that Western democracy may be exported to the non-Western world and that doing so is integral to fighting America's Sunni-Salafi extremist enemies, the ideological-cum-theocratic transnational entities that attacked the United States on September 11, 2001.

America and its policymakers have toyed with the notion of making democracy an explicit foreign policy goal for decades, if not longer. However, until recently, democracy and pluralism have been ideals the U.S. preferred: values that underlay its foreign policy goals rather than explicit objectives. Today, America has troops in at least two Muslim countries, Afghanistan and Iraq. America has its troops in other Muslim and non-Muslim countries, including, importantly, multiple countries in the Horn of Africa, and perhaps with good reason. Billions of dollars have been spent on the gamble and thousands of lives have been lost in its implementation. The implications are difficult to overstate. Additionally, partly as a result of these interventions and partly as a result of a host of domestic influences, the very institutions, processes, routines, and actors that have dominated U.S. foreign policy since the beginning of the Cold War (1947) are being affected by these decisions and the gamble. We attempt to present a coherent examination of some of the external and domestic sources that have resulted in these monumental changes.

The book is organized in what we hope is a logical and coherent way. Chapter 1 introduces the topics briefly discussed in the preface. Some U.S. foreign policy history is considered for context. In chapters 1 through 3, we define important concepts for analytic purposes. We specify indicators of those concepts, for instance, independent and dependent variables. We discuss what others have called America's Cold War consensus and we provide a conceptual/theoretical and methodological framework and explain how we will employ it in subsequent chapters. In chapter 4, using excellent secondary sources (and a few primary ones), we explore the U.S. National Security Council and its evolution from Truman to George W. Bush. Two or three recent books have presented comprehensive analyses and histories of the NSC, one published in 2005. Our intention in chapter 4 is not to recreate the wheel. Rather, it is to summarize the research of others and to present what we call the president-NSC-policymaking model, the basis of which was created in law by the National Security Act of 1947. Since it was signed into law (summer of 1947) it has evolved into the highest level of foreign and national security policymaking. In presenting the NSC, we also render graphically each administration's president-NSC-policymaking model. In chapter 4 we briefly consider some important amendments to the 1947 NSA including the 1949 reorganization and the 1986 Goldwater-Nichols Act. In chapter 5, we present President George W. Bush's version of the president-NSC-policymaking model until the IRTPA became law.

In chapters 6, 7, and 8 we employ the framework articulated earlier to consider critical external, governmental, and societal inputs or sources that cause U.S. foreign policy to be what it is at a given time. We argue that a particular configuration of those finite clusters of inputs caused U.S. national security and foreign policymaking to *change* following 9/11. Those three chapters then lead toward chapter 9, in which the legislation we believe represents the first significant change since the 1947 National Security Act is examined carefully. The external, governmental, and societal inputs discussed in previous chapters are linked to specific changes that the IRTPA amended in the original 1947 National Security Act. The IRTPA created a host of new bureaucracies, institutions, procedures — very much as did the 1947 NSA — that one must understand in order to comprehend how America's national security institutions have fundamentally been altered. Finally, our conclusions are presented in chapter 10.

CHAPTER 1

Introduction

We have set for ourselves a rather peculiar combination of objectives. First, in the following pages we attempt to create a conceptual framework for analyzing U.S. foreign policy. The conceptual framework owes a debt to James Rosenau and other comparative foreign-policy analysis scholars. Other scholars have presented different theoretical and conceptual frameworks. This book may be distinguished by, among other things, the particular framework employed: the comparative foreign-policy analysis framework and the theories that the framework suggests. Second, we examine the behemoth institutional complex of governmental bureaucracies and agencies, all of which determine, create, and implement U.S. national security policy. It is these institutions, procedures, and processes, which are necessary to direct massive enterprise such as U.S. foreign policy and national security policy, that are our analytic focus. Specifically, we examine the National Security Council—the primary locus of U.S. foreign policymaking—and other institutions created by the 1947 National Security Act to thwart the USSR. The National Security Council—or a part of it we call the president-NSC-policymaking model—is our primary unit of analysis for the comparisons we make throughout. We therefore define and conceptualize the president-NSC-policymaking model, created by the 1947 National Security Act and its subsequent amendments. Since 9/11 the new legislation in the Intelligence Reform and Terrorism Prevention Act, which became law in December 2004, has *substantially* altered the way the NSC interacts with the entire U.S. intelligence community and how the latter functions. Thus, a principal focus here is to examine what caused those changes—what external-systemic, societal, and governmental inputs resulted in the IRTPA.

Near the end of World War II, U.S. policymakers in both the executive and legislative branches came to realize several important features about global politics and the systemic balance of power that caused them to change the trajectory of U.S. foreign policy, something that had previously changed only incrementally since the origins of the republic. Important summits were held at the end of World War II by the victors in order to administer the areas left in shambles by the war. The three main summits were held at Potsdam, Yalta, and Tehran. There the victors, including the U.S. and its then-ally, the Soviet Union, ostensibly agreed to terms by which the victors would administer over the results of World War II's devastation for roughly a period of two years. At the end of the administrative period, U.S. policymakers believed—perhaps hoped is more accurate—that most of the nation-states in question would have had the chance to rebuild their basic infrastructures and would be prepared to hold elections whereby their future leaders and governance systems would be established, more or less democratically. When democratic governance did not emerge uniformly, the U.S. believed its erstwhile ally, the Soviet Union, was largely responsible for the lack of democratic governance. U.S. policymakers therefore came to regard the Soviet Union as a *tyrannical* threat bent on world domination and thereby antithetical to America's own security interests. As we will demonstrate, U.S. policymakers nearly always view the world in terms of *political freedom and liberty* versus its opposite *tyranny*, and have done so since America's emergence as a democratic republic.

Consequently, a Cold War consensus formed among U.S. policymakers across the respective branches of the government that ultimately formed a bipartisan consensus toward what was perceived widely as Soviet tyranny. The Cold War consensus took for granted that the Soviet Union was an existential threat to world stability, democratic governance, and the capitalist economic system the U.S. hoped would emerge in World War II's wake. The main objective of the Cold War consensus became thwarting the Soviet Union and its central-command economic system. Because U.S. policymaking institutions created by America's constitution were deemed inadequate to the task, the executive and legislative branches agreed to create a new constellation of executive institutions in order to contain Soviet tyranny. The policy was *containment of Soviet tyranny* and a collection of new agencies were created in order to implement America's containment policy.

Together, these realities on the ground led to an extraordinary event in America's history as a republic and as its then relatively short history as one of the world's two superpowers. The event was the passage of the 1947 legislation known as the National Security Act (the 1947 NSA). Since we will discuss it in more detail elsewhere, here we consider the 1947 NSA only in passing. The 1947 NSA created the National Security Council (destined to become the central locus of U.S. national security decision making), the U.S. Department of Defense, America's Central Intelligence Agency and other critical institutional infrastructure that would subsequently become America's national security state or *Pax Americana*. The 1947 NSA fundamentally altered U.S. foreign policy. Importantly, thereafter the U.S. jettisoned its former isolationist orientation toward global politics. Moreover, following the 1947 NSA the U.S. president was given important new authorities and powers that did not exist in the U.S. Constitution per se. The U.S. Constitution simply delineated the president as the commander in chief of the U.S. military (Article II, Section 2). Congress was tasked with declaring war and funding the commander in chief in his Constitutional prerogative, thereby preventing the presidency from ever becoming too powerful (i.e., tyrannical) and prohibiting a president from taking America to war without the agreement of Congress.

The 1947 National Security Act was not only a historically important piece of legislation, it created over time a reliable template of policymaking that attempted to foresee potential challenges the U.S might face as it contained the Soviet Union. The 1947 NSA therefore gave the president control over the U.S. National Security Council (NSC) and created what eventually became known as the National Security Council advisor (NSC advisor). The NSC advisor has at times been more influential than either the secretary of state or the secretary of defense. Indeed, the secretary of defense, created in the 1947 NSA and recreated in an amendment to the 1947 NSA, the 1949 Reorganization Bill, was then seen as a bureaucratic weakling compared to the secretary of state. In time, the secretary of defense would become more powerful, bureaucratically, than virtually any other cabinet secretary. The NSC advisor too would become extremely important to U.S. national security policymaking throughout and after the Cold War. The 1947 NSA (and its amendments) therefore created two wholly new positions, both of which have become staples in U.S. foreign policymaking and national security policymaking.

In examining the complex of U.S. national security bureaucracies, we will examine the 1947 NSA, its subsequent amendments, and the important institutions the 1947 NSA created. This has been done elsewhere, though comparatively little scholarship exists about the 1947 NSA and the machinery it created, particularly given its extreme importance and centrality to U.S. foreign policy. In 2005, an important history was published that provided a comprehensive examination of the 1947 NSA—David Rothkopf's *Running the World*. Prior to *Running the World*, only a relative few had undertaken works that provided insight into the 1947 NSA and the national security council. (By contrast, myriad books and articles have been written about the CIA, another of the 1947 NSA's creations.) Despite Rothkopf's contribution, such scholarship has been rare. Three other important books had been written about the NSC when we began this book. In 2004, former policymaker Karl Inderfurth and scholar Loch K. Johnson published a significant contribution, *Fateful Decisions*. Previously, near the end of the 1990s, Amy B. Zegart published *Flawed by Design*, another important contribution. Prior to Zegart's book, scholar John Prados published *Keepers of the Keys* in 1991.[1] Apart from these scholarly explorations of the NSC, precious few other scholarly works have examined the 1947 NSA and its various creations systematically or comprehensively.

Here, we will examine the 1947 NSA with a different purpose than Rothkopf's or other examinations of the NSC and the 1947 NSA. Namely, here we examine the 1947 NSA in order to compare it with a recent amendment to the original 1947 NSA, the Intelligence Reform and Terrorism Prevention Act (IRTPA). The IRTPA substantively altered the 1947 NSA, including how the NSC ought to operate in the future, how the CIA ought to be fitted into the reformed intelligence community created by the IRTPA, and how the Department of Defense ought to interact with both the intelligence community and the NSC advisor as well as the newly created director of national intelligence position in the future. Thus, another objective of this book is to compare the 1947 NSA with the 2004 IRTPA, something that has not been attempted elsewhere.

The conceptual definitions and frameworks presented early on provide a simple and natural way in which to compare the 1947 NSA with the 2004 IRTPA in subsequent chapters. The 1947 NSA and the 2004 IRTPA were passed and signed into law in response to two major turning points in U.S. foreign policy: the beginning of the Cold War and the attacks on the U.S. on September 11, 2001. Both instances were *perceived* by U.S.

policymakers as evidence of an expansive new tyranny foisting itself upon the global community. Each presented new problems for U.S. policymakers in its own way. The 1947 NSA was passed in order to give the president the institutional tools and agility to defeat the Soviet Union over the course of the Cold War. That is, the legislation created a complex set of institutions that were conceived of as lending themselves to containing and ultimately defeating the Soviet Union, a traditional state actor, albeit one that was seen as an existential threat to the future of the U.S. Similarly, the 2004 IRTPA was passed to create for the president a complex set of institutions and tools to fight a new transnational phenomenon, the global jihadi hydra, also understandably seen as an existential threat to the U.S. Therefore, a comparison of the two legislative acts is an important and, as yet, unexamined aspect of U.S. national security policy and the institutions that implement these policies.

In the following chapters, a roadmap is followed. First, we consider U.S. foreign policy, how to define it conceptually, and a brief history of it from the origins of the republic to the twentieth century. Next, we present a brief history of the Cold War and its causes, with a view toward setting that important history up for comparisons made in subsequent chapters. While examining both periods, the 1947 NSA is necessarily considered in some detail. In light of the recent scholarship noted above, we will present only brief summaries of each administration, Harry Truman through George W. Bush. However, we also seek to identify the generalizable trends as well as the unique features of each president's NSC and its activities as the principal locus of decision making. At the end of each administration a graphical representation of the particular administration's president-NSC-policymaking model, including the NSC principals and how the president and NSC interacted with other crucial executive agencies, is presented for comparative purposes. It may be used as the unit of comparison (analysis) for each administration from Truman to George W. Bush. Clearly, prior to the 1947 NSA some policymaking structure must have existed so we briefly compare what we call the *president-cabinet policymaking model* with the president-NSC-policymaking model that supplanted it.

In addition to highlighting the similarities and differences in the ways each president has used his president-NSC-policymaking model, a few additional matters will necessarily require attention. Between the origins of the 1947 NSA and its 1949 "reorganization" amendment and the IRTPA

(December 2004), minor modifications have been made to the NSC and the way it interacts with the larger bureaucracy; we will examine those as well. In covering the Cold War and the 1947 NSA we attempt to present a picture of the evolution of the intelligence community from its early origins, as created in the 1947 NSA, to what became some fifteen separate, disparate intelligence agencies, often with missions that overlapped or, worse, worked at cross purposes. We also consider an important but little-known institution, the President Foreign Intelligence Advisory Board (PFIAB), though it was *not* created by the 1947 NSA. While the NSC and how it fits into the president-NSC-policymaking model is the principal focus, it is helpful to understand the intelligence community and other appendages to the NSC and the president-NSC-policymaking model that evolved over the years of the Cold War.

Later, we consider 9/11—an event we define as a foreign policy crisis— and its aftermaths. While 9/11 was a foreign policy crisis, it was also a discrete event. Many of its effects were nearly immediate but its longer-term effects continue to this day, albeit with diminishing influence. In considering 9/11 as a foreign policy crisis and as an external source of U.S. foreign policy change, we also consider the Iraq War as an important external influence of U.S. national security policy. External events, as we will demonstrate, are one of five main clusters of U.S. foreign policy inputs that yield what U.S. national security policy and foreign policy are at given times. Additionally, there are *domestic* sources of U.S. foreign policy—societal inputs, governmental inputs, individual and role inputs—that must be considered as they demonstrably alter U.S. foreign policy on occasion. Typically, U.S. national security policy does not change dramatically from year to year, from president to president, or even over the course of long periods such as from the origins of the republic to the twentieth century or, say, the Cold War. However, infrequently events conspire to cause *fundamental changes* in U.S. national security policy (i.e., the dependent variable or that which we wish to explain in this analysis). One cause of these rare substantive changes is foreign policy crises; thus, we will return to the causal nexus of foreign policy crises multiple times.

Finally, we provide a detailed examination of the IRTPA and the changes that it mandated as well as how those changes have been implemented under President George W. Bush, the president in office over the entire post-9/11 period. In presenting the analysis of the IRTPA, comparisons with the 1947 NSA are made where appropriate. The concluding chapter also makes observations about the future of U.S. foreign policy and the most recent developments, many of which happened while this book was being completed.

NOTE

1. As a professor of political science and global studies I have used each of the aforementioned books in different combinations with additional case studies to teach a course at California State University on U.S. national security institutions and processes. Additionally, I wrote my Ph.D. dissertation for Ohio State University using the National Security Council and "NSC principals" as the units of analysis.

CHAPTER 2

The Rise of America's National-Security State (Pax Americana)

The United States has long championed freedom because doing so reflects our values and advances our interests. It reflects our values because we believe the desire for freedom lives in every human heart and the imperative of human dignity transcends all nations and cultures.

—White House, *The National Security Strategy of the United States of America*, March 2006

U.S. FOREIGN POLICY: ORIGINS OF THE REPUBLIC

Since becoming a republic America has always represented certain preferences and values, which have often been expressed in its foreign policy. The history of the republic's Founding Fathers is largely a history of concerns about how Europeans (and others) might pit one American state against another, thereby employing a strategy of divide and conquer to weaken the young American republic's defenses. The Federalist Papers frequently noted the concerns that John Jay, Alexander Hamilton, and James Madison (the Federalist who agitated for a strong central government) had about foreign interests insinuating themselves into America's politics. Certainly, America's history in the late 1700s and early 1800s gave U.S. policymakers as well as the Founding Fathers reason for concern about a future wherein European powers entangled themselves in America's internal affairs as well as about the consequences of America involving itself in the domestic affairs of others.

Federalist Papers 3, 4, 5, and 6 were particularly illustrative. In Federalist 3, John Jay wrote: "At present I mean only to consider it [security] . . . for the preservation of the peace and tranquility, as well as against the dangers from *foreign arms and influence* . . . Let us therefore proceed to examine whether the people are not right in their opinion that a cordial Union, under an efficient national government, affords them the best security that can be devised against *hostilities* from abroad." In Federalist 4 Jay wrote: "But the safety of the people of America against dangers from *foreign* forces depends not only on their forbearing to give *just* causes of war to other nations, but also on their placing and continuing themselves in such a situation as not to invite hostility or insult; for it need not be observed that there are *pretended* as well as just causes of war." Specifically referring to the American colonists' experiences with the British Crown, Jay wrote in Federalist 5 that the "history of Great Britain is the one with which in general" the young republic was most familiar. "We may profit by their experience without paying the price which it cost them." The lesson John Jay and the Federalists drew from this was that a unified federal government would offer the best protection against Britain and other potential enemies. In Federalist 6, Jay turned his attention to international "factions" which Great Britain or others might use against each other to divide Americans into factions working at cross-purposes.[1]

The new republic's first president, General George Washington, similarly cautioned his countrymen against foreign entanglements. In his farewell address following his two terms, President Washington worried that the new republic would come to harm by intermeshing America's political affairs with others. He suggested what he believed was needed for a "more perfect union" to remain whole. Said former President Washington: "and, what is of inestimable value, [the states] must derive from union an exemption from those broils and wars between themselves, which so frequently afflict neighboring countries not tied together by the same governments, which their own rival ships alone would be sufficient to produce, but which opposite foreign alliances, attachments, and intrigues would stimulate and embitter." Washington next wrote about treaties the United States entered into with both Great Britain and Spain. He noted that America ought not to favor one foreign nation over another, for there may be unanticipated results for U.S. interests. What types of unanticipated results concerned Washington? In a section of his speech worth quoting at length, President Washington offered the following advice to his compatriots about the potential consequences of U.S. entanglements with foreign governments:

> Against the insidious wiles of foreign influence . . . the jealousy of a free
> people ought to be constantly awake. . .
>   The *great rule of conduct for us in regard to foreign nations is in extend-*
> *ing our commercial relations, to have with them as little political connec-*
> *tion as possible.* So far as we have already formed engagements, let them
> be fulfilled with perfect good faith . . . Europe has a set of primary interests
> which to us have none or a very remote relation. Hence [Europe] must be
> engaged in frequent controversies, the causes of which are essentially for-
> eign to our concerns. Hence, therefore, it must be unwise in us to implicate
> ourselves by artificial ties in the ordinary vicissitudes of her politics, or the
> ordinary combinations and collisions of her friendships or enmities . . .
>   Why forego the advantages of so peculiar a situation? Why quit our own
> to stand upon foreign ground? Why, by interweaving our destiny with that
> of any part of Europe, entangle our peace and prosperity in the toils of Eu-
> ropean ambition, rivalship, interest, humor or caprice?[2]

President John Quincy Adams, America's sixth president (1825–1829), neatly captured Washington's counsel against foreign entanglements and the Founders' preference for what became known as "isolationism," a policy whereby America stood as an example to other peoples and governments but consciously chose to stay out of other nations' business. In an 1821 speech, just prior to the Monroe Doctrine, Adams spoke directly of America's foreign policy and the values that animated it.

> [America] has uniformly spoken among [the assembly of nations], though
> often to heedless and often to disdainful ears, the language of equal liberty,
> of equal justice, and of equal rights.
>   [America] has, in the lapse of nearly half a century, without a single ex-
> ception, respected the independence of other nations while asserting and
> maintaining her own.
>   She has abstained from interference in the concerns of others, even when
> conflict has been for principles to which she clings, as to the last vital drop
> that visits the heart . . .
>   Wherever the standard of freedom and Independence has been or shall be
> unfurled, there will [America's] heart, her benedictions and her prayers be.

In perhaps Adams's most famous oratorical embellishment, Adams said: "But [America] goes not abroad, in search of monsters to destroy. She is the well-wisher to the freedom and independence of all. She is the champion and vindicator only of her own. She will commend the general cause by the countenance of her voice, and the benignant sympathy of her example."[3]

THE SHINING CITY ON THE HILL: ISOLATIONISM

America was blessed—some of the Founders apparently believed providentially[4]—with geography that permitted isolationism. On two of America's four sides were oceans so large as to make America a veritable fortress against superior military force. To simplify somewhat, it would be fair to characterize American foreign policy from its origins through the early twentieth century as based on three main tenets: 1) commercial liberalism; 2) what became the Monroe Doctrine (c. 1823), limiting American and European ventures to their respective hemispheres of influence; and 3) isolationism, a strategic orientation that characterized U.S. foreign policy, with few exceptions, until the twentieth century.

Commercial Liberalism: Laissez Faire

Americans valued liberal economics. Borrowed heavily from Europe, the classic European liberal view of economics was laissez faire. Government should involve itself in commercial relations between individuals only as a measure of last resort. Free trade between individuals, merchants, and private interests was deemed desirable. It was largely premised on Ricardo's theory of comparative advantage and Locke's and Mills's philosophizing on the social contract. The former hypothesized that trade between individuals and peoples unhindered by government interference would benefit all parties involved, provided peoples specialized in that in which they had a comparative advantage. Social contract suggested that the governments existed at the peoples' behest; to the extent they ought to involve themselves in people's business at all, it was as a neutral arbiter over disputes involving trade, property, and general security.

The Monroe Doctrine: Respective Spheres of Influence and Security

The Monroe Doctrine (1823), began a series of presidential doctrines in U.S. foreign policy history. The Louisiana Purchase (1803) roughly doubled the size of the United States giving the U.S. strategic depth it previously lacked. President Washington warned his successors that America ought not to conquer lands but acquire them through transactions. The Louisiana Purchase was what Washington had envisioned. Between the Louisiana Purchase and the Monroe Doctrine was the war of 1812, after which America's leaders felt compelled to declare that the United States was permanent; European intrigues would no longer be tolerated. Indeed, America was becoming powerful enough to defend its lands, original and newly acquired by way of the Louisiana Purchase. In December 1823, President Monroe promulgated a three-point program of U.S. foreign policy: henceforth, America was an intact unified nation, from America's perspective, beyond the machinations of Europeans; any attempts by Europe to meddle therein would be considered a national security threat; correspondingly, Europe could expect that America would stay out of Europe's own political and geopolitical intrigues. The Monroe Doctrine's close proximity temporally to the war of 1812 was no coincidence. The American government would no longer submit to European monarchies grabbing land in the New World by dint of superior force. It fitted well with America's preference of isolationism. America intended not to meddle in others' affairs and expected the same in return as a simple matter of reciprocity.

Later, Thwarting Tyranny

Thus U.S. foreign policy from its foundation as a republic (1776) until World War II—some 140 years later—was a simple product of values held by Americans largely rooted in America's origins and represented directly in America's national mythology and ethos. From those values came priorities, what one might call goals and objectives. First, America prioritized the *freedom to sell its goods and services to others*—that meant access to European markets. Second, and clearly related, America's objectives included *freedom of navigation*, so that Americans get their goods to Europe and vice versa. A third objective was *thwarting tyranny*. According to America's mythology, America's democratic principles were thought to be the best organizing principles of governance and requisites of the social contract between Americans and their own government; it was taken for granted that those principles were transferable if not exportable to others. Another goal or objective of early U.S. foreign policy was *peace and prosperity*, a preference in and of itself but also an objective presumed to be the objective of all enlightened peoples. While other specific objectives might be enumerated, these few capture America's national security objectives based on its founding values.

This brief exploration of early America was intended to demonstrate three points. The first point was to link the genesis of American foreign policy, simply and understandably, to its early history, fleeing Europe and European tyrannies. A central premise of this book is that U.S. foreign policy *changed* following World War II as the Cold War commenced. In particular, isolationism as a strategic orientation and objective was forever replaced by internationalism and eventually by what might properly be called interventionism. Second, as U.S. objectives changed following World War II, significant new institutions were created to implement U.S. national security, specifically by the 1947 National Security Act (1947 NSA). The creation of these national security institutions shortly after World War II became the institutional basis of *Pax Americana*, America's national security state, which was erected to resist Soviet Communism, perceived as a dangerous and historic tyranny that threatened America's way of life.

We later argue that 9/11 and its aftermath resulted in similar changes in U.S. national security policy objectives, whose consequences included the institutional changes enacted by the 9/11 and the Robb-Silberman WMD Commissions and memorialized in the Intelligence Reform and Terrorism Prevention Act (the IRTPA). In other words, similar to the 1947 NSA, the IRTPA, which amended the original 1947 NSA, created yet again a set of new institutions to implement America's new national security objectives and empower America's policymakers with tools appropriate for the task in a strange, new international environment in which non-state or transnational actors required special attention while traditional state actors remained threats. We will compare the 1947 NSA with the IRTPA in subsequent chapters.

Third, the brief foreign policy history was intended to suggest a simple conceptual definition of foreign policy and/or national security policy for subsequent use. We repeatedly identified specific concepts in describing

America's early approaches to global politics. Those concepts included goals and/or objectives as well as values. The latter were explicitly linked to America's national mythology and ethos. A third concept of the definition was how America pursued its national security objectives: instruments or tools. From these simple concepts, a conceptual definition for U.S. national security policy may be stated explicitly, one that lends itself to particular theoretical orientations.

U.S. FOREIGN POLICY: A PRÉCIS OF *PAX AMERICANA* IN THE TWENTIETH CENTURY

In the remainder of this chapter, we undertake a fuller examination of U.S. national security in the twentieth and twenty-first centuries. The intent here is to establish the points of comparison of U.S. national security policy as it changed quickly following World War II—a war that, according to U.S. mythology and ethos, America sought to avoid. In fact, according to the worldview most Americans held about their country and how it came to be a superpower—or hegemonic power—America was dragged into World War II against its better judgment. For Americans, Pearl Harbor, December 7, 1941 was a dastardly attack on an America that attempted to stay mostly impartial vis-à-vis fascism and imperialism. That Japan attacked America on that "day of infamy," jibed well with how many Americans—policymakers and the mass public—saw their fateful response to Pearl Harbor and, further, America's full mobilization against a war of aggression launched against a largely innocent America.

During and shortly after World War II America was again called to meet its fate, according to the worldview described. U.S. policymakers ultimately were compelled to protect Europe, Asia, and eventually the international community, against a growing tyranny in the East: Soviet communism. Soviet communism was seen by most Americans as an even more dramatic threat than fascism had been. It required that the United States completely reorient its previous 140-plus years as an isolationist nation. It marked a critical turning point in America's national security history. As is the case with most modern nation-states, such turning points do not happen without consequences and associated costs. Nor can such changes occur without the proper cultural foundations and societal support. Given America's long-standing global orientation of isolationism, U.S. policymakers necessarily had to prepare the way for the American public to accept the dramatic change to America's future orientation of internationalism. In America's case, changing its strategic posture from an isolationist power to an interventionist one—in conflict with the Founders' views of foreign entanglement noted above—required a fundamental and appropriate articulation of America's role in the world that accounted for America's mythology and ethos. The metamorphosis involved a confluence of international external events and a remarkable bipartisan effort. Before that history is recounted, however, an explication of what constitutes U.S. foreign policy and national security policy is required.

U.S. National Security Policy: A Conceptual Approach

U.S. foreign policy has been defined in a variety of ways. Two scholars, the late Eugene R. Wittkopf and Charles Kegley Jr., defined it as follows: U.S. foreign policy is the goals or objectives that U.S. policymakers seek to attain abroad, the values (American ethos) that underlie those objectives and the instruments or tools used to achieve them.[5] Their definition was clearly intended as a conceptual one with three principal concepts: goals and/or objectives, values, and instruments or tools. Employing it, an analyst needs only to articulate America's policymakers' goals and objectives, divine the values represented in those goals, and identify the instruments used to achieve them and to conceptualize U.S. foreign policy. But there is more to their definition than may first meet the reader's eye. For instance, U.S. national security policy is something that is purposive. Policymakers seek particular and specific goals. It is presumed that America's foreign policy reflected certain core values or worldviews—what we simply call *ethos*. Here their definition is accepted and narrowed to the subset of U.S. foreign policy: U.S. national security policy. Hence, U.S. national security policy is the goals U.S. decisionmakers seek to attain abroad to ensure America's national security, the values that give rise to those goals, and the instruments used to achieve them.

Wittkopf and Kegley developed their definition at a time when a subdiscipline within international politics and foreign policy studies enjoyed wide popularity. That subdiscipline was called *comparative foreign policy analysis*. Some of its original practitioners included James Rosenau, Charles Hermann, Maurice "Mickey" East, Pat McGowan, and many others; the Kegley-Wittkopf definition arose from the same milieu. One goal of these scholars was the accretion of generalizable knowledge across a number of foreign-policy actors (states, to be precise). They therefore collected data on multiple state actors over time and subjected their data to empirical examination in order to generate propositions and hypotheses about those actors in international politics. They believed that when their hypotheses were subjected to empirical testing, generalizable knowledge would follow. James Rosenau wrote a particularly important piece on comparative foreign policy analysis during the period in which he argued that all state actors have a finite set of foreign policy inputs (x or independent variables). Rosenau wrote that five clusters of foreign policy inputs produced all states' foreign policy behavior; that is, all states' foreign policy (the y or dependent variable) could be observed as a product of inputs from the same five clusters of independent variables.[6]

The five independent variables (or clusters of variables) were identified as external-systemic, societal, governmental, individual, and role. External inputs were any external stimulus or stimuli to which a government felt the need to respond, or similarly any external event that a government perceived as an opportunity. These included changes in the balances of power external to the state in question, wars and various other conflicts likely to change a given balance, world economic events of import, and so on. The societal cluster included all the various societal forces that affect a given government, its polity, and ultimately its foreign policy behavior. Special interest groups lobby for policy changes and positions, frequently affecting foreign policy. The media present what a nation's people ultimately see of a nation's policymaking and thereby shape what a nation's people think about, if not always what they think exactly. The "CNN effect," now more generalizable as cable, radio, Internet, and "blogosphere" effects, shape how people view their government's policymaking. Election-year politics and the elections cycle itself are included in the societal cluster, as politicians and their supporters take election-year positions that are often different than their positions during non-election years. The government cluster of independent variables was conceived as the effects that the ponderous bureaucracy has in shaping foreign policy. By virtue of sheer size and magnitude, those bureaucracies may create policy impetuses (accelerate one policy over another) or constrain and defeat the objectives of individual policymakers (attenuate one policy versus another). Bureaucracies are characterized by their parochial missions and competition over finite and scarce resources. The individual cluster of inputs is those behaviors that policymaking elites of a nation bring to bear on the bureaucracy. While America's presidents have largely come from similar backgrounds, they bring different life experiences and idiosyncrasies with them into the highest circles of policymaking. Presidents of different generations have different life-shaping events and, consequently, likely bring different analogies and lessons they have learned with them when they enter office. Those differences have the potential, at some times more than others, to affect foreign policy. In addition to the president, other policymaking elites at various times have affected a nation's foreign and national security policy—certain secretaries of state and defense and certain national security council advisors, for instance. Finally, role inputs are nearly the opposite of individual inputs: rather than what idiosyncrasies a particular president brings with him to office, role expectations prescribe certain acceptable behaviors and proscribe unacceptable behavior. These expectations then cause the office to shape the person, more than the reverse.

Rosenau argued that what differentiated one state's foreign policy output from another was the precise composition—the relative weight and influence of particular independent variables—during a given time period *or* over time. To illustrate, consider a government from a Western European nation, the United States, or Canada. It would likely be heavily influenced in the normal course of policymaking by all of the five inputs but especially by societal variables (reflecting the pluralistic system of governance), governmental inputs (due to the complex bureaucracies involved in national security policymaking), and role inputs (the influence of role expectations on policymakers who are accountable to their publics). By contrast, a nation such as Kim Jong Il's North Korea, with an authoritarian one-man or nearly one-man rule, would likely be influenced more by individual inputs and far less shaped by, say, societal inputs. Presumably, Kim Jong Il has interest groups to whom he is beholden in some sense—his million-person-strong military, for example—but North Korea cannot be characterized as pluralistic and, therefore, societal inputs probably exert very little influence on its behavior.

Eugene Wittkopf and Charles Kegley conceptualized Rosenau's "pretheory" as an analytic construct or device that could be used to compare the foreign policies and national security policies of many nation-states (the goal of comparative foreign policy analysts) but also to compare the policy of a single nation-state, the United States, over time. They used the metaphor of a "funnel of causality," in which the reader must conceive in her mind's eye of a funnel that is large at the top but gets smaller at the bottom. Into the funnel, inputs constantly flow; out of the funnel, after processing according to a given situation or time, outputs constantly result. They conceptualized the narrow end of the funnel as *an intervening variable*, something they called *process*. Process represented differing situations and issues at different times.

For instance, most would agree that the Cuban Missile Crisis was a time during which policymaking was very different than, say, during the negotiations over NAFTA as the Cold War neared its conclusion. If so, surely the process differed, and that meant the relative influence of the clusters of independent variables was probably different. The reader might think of the bureaucratically led negotiations that were negotiated over two presidential administrations before NAFTA was signed. The vast foreign policy bureaucracy clearly would have been much more influential in that case than during the Cuban Missile Crisis where a small, exclusive, secret group of policymakers thrashed about for a solution. Another possible process scenario might be an issue area wherein particularly influential policymakers have specialized expertise. Former President George H. W. Bush was a former envoy to the People's Republic of China. When the Tiananmen Square crackdown occurred on his watch, it should not surprise the analyst that President Bush might have considered his own expertise compelling enough to avoid including China experts from, say, the Department of State in particular meetings on how the U.S. ought to have responded to the brutal crackdown in China.

Though Rosenau's framework was not a theory, it is amenable to traditional theories of international politics and comparative foreign policy. The external-systemic cluster, for instance, may easily be conceptualized in terms of a stimulus-response model hypothesized by realpolitik. Briefly, realpolitik conceives of the international system consisting of state actors defined by sovereignty. Sovereignty is not divisible: a government represents a state's sovereignty or else it is not a government. Nor does any higher authority exist above sovereign states. In other words, no supranational entity exists globally to adjudicate the disputes that invariably arise in international politics. Conversely, governments and the states they represent do possess variable power: some states are powerful and others are not. Given those rules, realpolitik predicts that states will engage in "self-help" as the only logical behavior in a system so characterized by international anarchy. Ultimately, the powerful will prevail in most cases and the weak will suffer the indignities the powerful impose on them. Conflict is perpetual as are stratagems such as alliance formation between weaker states to counter more powerful states. Understanding the inner workings of the government (the state)— whether it is characterized by democratic, pluralistic governance or, say, by authoritarian policymakers—is therefore irrelevant for realpolitik: the internal political processes of governments are superfluous for political realists. States are assumed to behave in a unitary fashion, more or less rationally, responding to threats and opportunities as the case may be. An illustrative example would be Graham Allison's model I analysis of the Cuban Missile Crisis.[7]

All the other clusters of independent variables are domestic sources of U.S. national security policy. As such, they are theoretically beholden to neoliberalism. Put simply, the neoliberal alternative to realpolitik conceptualizes a more complex international system than the assumptions of realpolitik allow. Neoliberals agree that the international system is comprised of state actors—and they may well be the most prominent actors in the system—but other important actors exist as well. Non-state actors, for instance, may well be important. Recall America's humanitarian intervention in Somalia near the end of the George H. W. Bush administration. Not only did the U.S. *not* intervene via utility-maximizing self-interest—the intervention was explicitly for humanitarian reasons—Bush may well not have intervened had CNN's cameras not shown the human misery in Somalia repeatedly, creating an impetus for action. The source of the misery was largely a product of tribal and warlord groups (non-state actors) and their attacks on nongovernmental organizations (NGOs, other non-state actors) that were seeking to ameliorate the suffering by Somalis. Clearly, for neoliberals, non-state actors may at times be important actors that realpolitik simply chooses to ignore. Similarly, the assumption of unitary behavior and rational decision making are both problematic for neoliberals.

Additionally, let us pretend temporarily that a state's top policymakers do behave in a unitary fashion and do consider their national security options using some type of cost-benefit analysis. Those top decision makers do not actually implement most of the policies they choose. Rather, the large labyrinth of bureaucracies that are the sine qua non of modern nation-states implement policy. As Graham Allison demonstrated in his organizational and bureaucratic models, a bureaucracy's standard operating procedures may well affect a given policy as it is implemented. Similarly, parochialism and bureaucratic politics affect outcomes. By definition, top policymakers representing their bureaucratic homes, all working for America's general national interests, offer differing options based on the bureaucratic missions they represent. America's defense department might be expected to offer military solutions while its state department might offer diplomatic solutions.

One need not be tethered to a particular theory. In fact, one of the utilities of employing Rosenau's "pre-theory" is that the analyst may deploy various theories depending upon which cluster of independent variables the analyst is examining. More important, for our purposes, is the level of analysis. In what follows, the level of analysis is predominately the NSC principals. Thus, while theory is important, it is often implicit in what follows. Indicators of exogenous variables are explicitly detailed and the primary indicator of the dependent variable, as we demonstrate presently, is the president-NSC-policymaking model.

U.S. foreign policy and its subset, national security policy, may be conceptualized in terms of goals and/or objectives, values or ethos widely held by a people and reflected by those people's policymakers, and the instruments used to achieve those objectives. What caused U.S. foreign policy to be what it was during the Cold War was the process, that is the relative influence of the five sets of inputs or independent variables. That process resulted in a particular output: predominately *containment* of Soviet Communism, *internationalism-interventionism*, some version of the *Monroe Doctrine* updated by Truman's Doctrine, *commercial liberalism*, and so forth. During tense phases of the Cold War, analysts expected that external inputs were extremely important as well as, occasionally, individual inputs, especially during foreign policy crises. During more routine times of the Cold War, characterized by less tension, probably governmental, societal, and role inputs were more important. During specific periods of the Cold War, say every two years during a U.S. midterm election cycle in America's domestic politics, societal inputs might have been especially important. Or during periods wherein especially influential pundits from major newspapers and other media outlets were at their apogees, perhaps persons such as William Safire or Walter Cronkite before they retired, societal influences might have dominated particular time periods. The analyst's task is to be able to identify specific inputs, then consider the process that occurred.

Such a conceptual definition along with the input (independent variables) and output (dependent variables) construct proves particularly useful in dissecting U.S. national security policymaking. Together they provide a utilitarian approach for examining foreign policy across many governments or state actors as well as for one government or state actor over discrete time periods. In what follows, two such discrete time periods are analyzed and compared. The first is the period of time during which the Cold War between the U.S. and its formidable enemy, the Soviet Union, began and ended. The rise of the American national security state (*Pax Americana*) occurred during the time period from shortly after World War II through 1950 when the Korean War began. Many books have analyzed this period, so our presentation values brevity over depth of analysis for the Cold War. The second discrete time period examined is the period that followed September 11, 2001, when America's national security state was attacked by a new external threat: a non-state, transnational network of global jihadis who sought America's destruction and the re-establishment of the historic Islamic Caliphate system where it had once existed.

The historical Islamic Caliphate system, unfortunately, encompassed territory of national-security interest for the U.S. (and the West generally). Existence of the historic Caliphate and Western civilization, therefore, constitute an existential conflict of interest. Many similarities will be discovered between the early Cold War and the early post-9/11 era, including the creation of new and complex foreign policy, national security, and intelligence collection and analysis institutions. Hence, comparing the two periods provides an interesting evaluation of America's goals and objectives, the values that give rise to them, and the instruments used to achieve them during the two periods. That comparison and particularly the procedural and institutional entities created in the latter period are the central focus of the following chapters.

President George W. Bush's National Security Policy

In fall 2002, the Bush administration published *The National Security Strategy of the United States,* December 2002, a document mandated by Congress. The thirty-or-so pages of documents were a compilation of President Bush's speeches since 9/11. In this document, several objectives were highlighted as new objectives in America's national security. The primary objective of the document was the identification of emerging transnational threats, global jihadis, and states that harbor them. In spring 2006, the revision appeared on the White House website. *The National Security Strategy of the United States,* March 2006, is worth considering briefly here. The 2006 version consisted of 54 pages of bulleted lists and headings. It suggested that the Bush administration had learned something in the years since the 2002 version, including a great deal about insurgencies (i.e., the Iraq War). In section one, "Overview," its authors began with:

> It is the policy of the United States to seek and support democratic movements and institutions in every nation and culture, *with the ultimate goal of ending tyranny in our world.* In the world today, the fundamental character of regimes matters as much as the distribution of power among them. The goal of our statecraft is to help create a world of democratic, well-governed states that can meet the needs of their citizens and conduct themselves responsibly in the international system. This is the best way to provide enduring security for the American people.[8]

To illustrate how far the 2006 document had come since the 2002 version, just a brief discussion of the document's sections suffices. The White House included a section on the U.S. as "Champions of Human Dignity," another on "Strengthen Alliances to Defeat Global Terrorism and Work to Prevent Attacks Against Us and Our Allies," and another on "Work with Others to Diffuse Regional Conflicts," suggesting the administration may have learned the value of limited multilateralism since 2002, or the lack of efficacy of unilateralism. Sections reminiscent of the 2002 document such as "Prevent Our Enemies from Threatening Us, Our Allies, and Our Friends with Weapons of Mass Destruction," but also a broadening of traditional national security which included sections on "Ignite a New Era of Global Economic Growth through Free Markets and Free Trade," and "Expand the Circle of Development by Opening Societies and Building the Infrastructure of Democracy," all appeared in the 2006 revision.[9]

Arguably, democratic governance has become an explicit objective of U.S. national security policy. The president's 2006 document on national security made that clear and inarguable. President Bush's proactive commitment to democracy is reflected in the section where the authors wrote: "To protect our Nation and honor our values, the United States seeks to *extend freedom across the globe by leading an international effort to end tyranny and to promote effective democracy.*" Political freedom and thwarting its opposite, tyranny, are particularly though not necessarily uniquely American values reflected historically in U.S. foreign policy and national security policy. *The National Security Strategy of the United States,* March 2006, continued: "All tyrannies threaten the world's interest in freedom's expansion, and some tyrannies, in their pursuit of WMD or sponsorship of terrorism, threaten our immediate security interests as well."[10] While democratic governance has always been a preference and/or underlying value of U.S. foreign policy, we argue it has moved from a value or preference to a formal national security objective. Along the way, we will discover that influential policymakers and academics (neoconservatives) fought a "battle royal" for President Bush's national security agenda and apparently prevailed.

The Iraq War has become extremely unpopular, as the 2006 midterm elections amply demonstrated. Nevertheless, we believe that democracy as a national security objective will likely persist (though it will be subject to ups and downs). As a result of the Iraq War, its neoconservative authors have become somewhat tarnished in 2005–2006. We suspect, however, that while the eagerness of future presidents to foist democracy on others will be tempered, democracy will remain a national security objective. Now that it has been introduced as a U.S. foreign policy and national security objective, it will be difficult for future presidents to dispose of it. If this is true, it will not be the first time. President James "Jimmy" Carter introduced human rights to America's national security agenda and lexicon. Once characterized as naive, human rights have in fact become part of U.S. foreign policy and national security policymaking. Thus, whoever the next president is, whether Democrat or Republican, democracy will remain a part of America's national security objectives. If properly tempered, we can think of far worse objectives for the U.S.

SUMMARY

In this chapter, we established the basis for subsequent analysis by developing five central themes. First, we examined the context of U.S. foreign policy as a new republic at its origins, with a view toward illustrating specific principles of U.S. national security policy. One point was that America's origins—and therefore the mythology that evolved over time about its origins—were relatively unique. From the start, Americans were a collection of races, ethnicities, religions, and cultures that formed an experiment in governance, "a more perfect union." That experiment was based on the social contract, limited government, and traditional European Enlightenment thinking. It was, furthermore, based on a rejection of the tyrannical systems that characterized Europe as the new American republic began. Consequently, Americans embraced an ethos (and underlying mythology) about their new republic which consisted of a beliefs in political freedoms as enshrined in its founding documents. Its Founding Fathers, similarly, represented those beliefs and that mythology.

A second theme was that due to unique circumstances, America was permitted an isolationist orientation, by virtue of geography, as it interacted with the rest of the world in its first 140-plus years of existence. Of course, it did not begin that way. The British, the French, and the Spanish all competed for suzerainty over parts of what became the United States of America. Nevertheless, following the war of 1812, America was more or less a modernizing republic based on these philosophies, myths, perceptions, and realities. *Isolationism* was originally enshrined by the republic's founders and proved a utilitarian orientation that allowed America to evolve, relatively unencumbered, as a great power and eventually as a superpower. As perceived in America's mythology and ethos, America only reluctantly jettisoned isolationism for internationalism and interventionism when it was thrust into international politics following World War II and it only did so because justice in the world required it. America's policymakers perceived themselves as forced to counter the tyranny of the Soviet Union, the other superpower that emerged from the ashes of World War II.

During America's isolationist period, U.S. policymakers were weary of European conquests and balances of power and their attendant political intrigues. American policymakers held that most European governments were characterized by tyranny, with foreign policies based on the needs of the particular tyrant—that is, some monarchy's needs. In such systems, America's founders assumed, the values and objectives of the leaders, not the people, were reflected in European governments' various foreign policy positions and predispositions. Therefore, such foreign nations were deemed undesirable as political partners. Any temporary alliances into which America entered were therefore conceived as short-term expediencies and little else. Trade and economic commercialism rather than strategic alliances was what guided American global behavior during its long isolationist period.

The third theme followed from the second. U.S. global behavior was not only isolationist in its orientation, it explicitly eschewed anything other than economic alliances with European nations. America viewed interactions between Americans and others almost strictly in terms of commercial intercourse. "Trade by all means," it might thus be framed, "but do not get politically entrapped." From the founders to America's first president (President George Washington) to John Quincy Adams and beyond, this represented the essence of America's international relations and diplomacy until the twentieth century.

As the industrial revolution swept Europe, America, and elsewhere, trade of manufactured goods was hastened. As manufactured goods proliferated so too did the number of interactions between America's merchant and ownership classes and their counterparts elsewhere. As the industrial revolution hastened modernity, the oceans that once protected America seemed to shrink. Historically, great European powers were characterized by great fleets of ships, both commercially owned and husbanded by European militaries. As modernity caused the perceived and real shrinkage of the distances that previously protected America's democratic experiment, America's international behavior expanded beyond its earlier limitations. The United States even participated, albeit rarely and on a far-smaller scale, with other great powers in far-flung trade and politics. The changing external international environment caused America to change, however incrementally.

Therefore a fourth theme established was that by the turn of the twentieth century, the United States was rapidly becoming a great power itself. Europe continued to dominate world politics but the United States lagged behind less and less each year. The twentieth century ushered in myriad other changes that affected the U.S. and its international affairs. America's mythology and ethos failed to keep pace with the rapidly changing external environment. By World War I and especially by World War II, America's mythology and ethos finally began to change. By World War II, America's ethos and mythology held that the U.S. had not fundamentally changed; American exceptionalism still characterized the American experiment. Against formidable odds, America saw itself as attempting to remain the "shining city on the hill," and continued to hold itself out as an example for other to emulate. The myth that America had not changed was ultimately shattered by the time of the Pearl Harbor attack. The attack provided the impetus that caused the United States to mobilize into an industrial, military giant, and America's perception of itself changed accordingly. No longer could U.S. policymakers stand by while powerful and brutal agents forcibly changed the international environment. U.S. policymakers came to believe that lest their compatriots' and their own destinies be shaped by others (invariably "others" were conceptualized as tyrants), *America would have to shape the international environment.* While a powerful isolationist segment of America's policymakers and attentive public continued to exist, Pearl Harbor rendered them largely obsolete. America was about to metamorphose into a superpower, the national security state that many of the founders had resisted.

Finally, as America reoriented itself to a rapidly changing world context, World War II ended. It ended in Europe earlier than it ended in the Pacific. The principals in Europe became exhausted and those left standing were the victors. While the allies fought courageously and efficiently, the Russians bore the brunt of the violence that characterized fascism's last gasps. Shortly thereafter, war ended in the Pacific theater as well. However, after some four years of bloody fighting, the war in the Pacific ended by virtue of another American step toward superpower status: America's scientists, who themselves benefited greatly from the industrial revolution and modernity, harnessed the atom. The Manhattan Project successfully developed and tested an atomic weapon. The fission weapon developed represented the capability to alter former balances of power in an instant. After failed attempts by both the allies and the Japanese to arrange a surrender through diplomacy, President Harry Truman deployed two of the most horrible weapons the world had seen in Hiroshima and Nagasaki. World War II ended with a terrible cataclysm.

Near the war's conclusion, the allies came to certain agreements at Tehran, Potsdam, and Yalta. Accordingly, the devastated parts of the world would be administered by allied powers for a discrete period of time, after which they would hold their own elections and rebuild their lives and their systems of governance. America could scarcely have conceived of any nation, under the circumstances, not rebuilding itself, at least to some degree, in America's image. America's policymakers were confident that the most recent war-to-end-all-wars would usher in an era of democratic governance and pluralistic polities. Instead, the Cold War began. Faced so soon after world war with a new and arguably more dangerous tyranny, America now opposed its former World War II ally. Decisions were made on the spot as to how the U.S. would face the Soviet Union in what became the Cold War.

NOTES

1. Mortimer J. Adler, ed., *J. S. Mills*, vol. 40, *Great Books of the Western World* (Chicago: Encyclopedia Britannica, 1996), 30–39 (my emphasis).

2. George Washington, "Transcript of President George Washington's Farewell Address (1796)," http://www.ourdocuments.gov/doc.php?flash=true&doc= 15&page=transcript (accessed December 22, 2005) (my emphasis).

3. John Quincy Adams, "John Quincy Adams on U.S. Foreign Policy (1821)," The Future of Freedom Foundation, http://www.fff.org/comment/AdamsPolicy.asp (accessed January 22, 2006) (my emphasis).

4. Washington too spoke of providence, as did many of the founders. Whether they believed "providence" was related to a God who foreordained the republic is subject to interpretation. To be sure, the oratorical device of "providence" was commonly used in speeches from the period. Mortimer J. Adler, ed., "John Jay, Federalist I and II," in *J. S. Mills*, vol. 40, *Great Books of the Western World* (Chicago: Encyclopedia Britannica, 1996), 30–33.

5. In one of their recent editions, the authors wrote that "[f]oreign policy embraces the goals that the nation's officials seek to attain abroad, the values that give rise to those objectives, and the means or instruments used to pursue them." Eugene R. Wittkopf, Charles W. Kegley Jr., and James M. Scott, *American Foreign Policy* (Wadsworth Publishing, 2002), 14.

6. James N. Rosenau, "Pre-Theories and Theories of Foreign Policy," in *Approaches to Comparative and International* Politics, ed. R. Barry Farrrell (Evanston, IL: Northwestern University Press, 1966).

7. Many versions of realpolitik exist emphasizing one assumption over others. What is important for present purposes is to illustrate that governments (states) will act more or less rationally. In Graham Allison's famous formulation, the author called this the rational model of foreign policymaking. Graham Allison, *Essence of Decision: Explaining the Cuban Missile Crisis* (New York: Little, Brown & Co., 1972).

8. (This document, as with its predecessor, is in Acrobat Reader format and there is a discrepancy between the internal and Acrobat Reader pagination. Both will be provided here.) White House, *The National Security Strategy of the United States*, March 2006, White House, http://www.whitehouse.gov/nsc/2006/nss2006.pdf, 1 (Acrobat Reader pagination, 6) (accessed March 16, 2006). For the previous *National Security Strategy of the United States, December 2002*, see http://www.whitehouse.gov/nsc/nss.pdf.

9. White House, *The National Security Strategy of the United States*, March 2006, White House, http://www.whitehouse.gov/nsc/2006/nss2006.pdf, iii (Acrobat Reader pagination, 4).

10. White House, *The National Security Strategy of the United States, March 2006*, White House, http://www.whitehouse.gov/nsc/2006/nss2006.pdf, 3 (Acrobat Reader pagination, 8).

CHAPTER 3

The Cold War Consensus and the National Security Act

THE COLD WAR CONSENSUS

We noted an important requisite to what became the 1947 National Security Act and the National Security Council (NSC), the unified Department of Defense, the CIA, and other institutions that the act created, at the end of chapter 2. It was a social-cultural consensus that the Soviet Union represented a dangerous tyrannical threat to America's way of life. It included a consensus among policymakers of both major parties, as well as the so-called attentive and mass publics in America. Indeed, a tremendous amount of consensus was necessary for a divided Congress—Republican senator Arthur Vandenberg (MI) ran the U.S. Senate during part of the period—to work closely with a Democratic president, Harry S. Truman, in order for the 1947 NSA to become law. Since we wish to compare the 1947 NSA with the 2004 Intelligence Reform and Terrorism Prevention Act (December 2004), that Cold War consensus is worth our consideration. For comparative purposes, the Cold War consensus may be examined relative to what we consider a similar post-9/11 consensus. Whether in fact a new consensus was created by 9/11 and its aftermath will be a question we will consider in subsequent chapters.

It may be difficult for those who grew up near the end of the Cold War or later to appreciate fully the magnitude of the cooperation that occurred from roughly 1946 through much of the 1950s and well beyond. One phrase characteristic of the time was that when it came to national security, "politics stopped at the water's edge." It meant the following: first, America's system was designed as an adversarial system. The Founding

Fathers clearly valued democratic governance over efficiency. Thus, in terms of public policy, the political process was intentionally made adversarial and confrontations were expected. In fact, such inefficiencies were desirable to prevent unpredictable and dramatic changes in policy. Second, when America found itself under threat of external conquest, the system also presumed that a commonality of purpose would emerge. The rub, of course, was that policymakers in different branches might not perceive external threats equally. If only one branch of government argued that America's existence was threatened, the founders must have presumed that the particular branch of government was necessarily wrong in its perception. Put differently, were the U.S. truly faced with an existential national security threat, surely reasonable people would perceive the threat in reasonably similar ways. Once so perceived, "politics stopped at the water's edge" suggested that all policymakers would check their parochial interests at the door and work together for the good of the republic.

Politics, of course, never wholly stopped at the water's edge. National security policy is a product of objectives and goals that policymakers seek to attain abroad, the underlying values that give rise to those goals, and the instruments used to achieve them. While values are largely generalizable across a people (for example, America's ethos and its underlying mythology), objectives and goals may or may not be. One should expect some variations in terms of precise goals and objectives to exist among policymakers. Instruments, even more, may be expected to inspire disagreements. To illustrate the point, polls showed that many Americans perceived Saddam Hussein as a tyrant whose existence was bad for America and global stability. Moreover, Saddam was nearly uniformly perceived as a threat to an American ally in the region, Israel. One of the underlying values involved in this perception was democratic governance as the best system of governance generally. Most Americans believed that democracy created a marketplace of ideas: the assumption that a marketplace of ideas necessarily led to the best, most rational, most value-maximizing choices over time. The particular objective—well before 2003—was to keep Saddam Hussein's power in check. Put differently and reminiscent of Cold War's jargon, the objective was to "contain" Saddam Hussein. That goal was widely held by the mass public, the attentive public, and policymakers, as demonstrated in polling data in late 2002 and early 2003.

The question became how. What instruments were appropriate to achieve a widely held goal based on generalizable U.S. values? To many if not most policymakers, containment was a natural choice. Many of Washington's policymakers naturally turned to an instrument that had been successful against an exceptionally threatening Soviet state and the ideology that animated it during the Cold War. Further, containment was the choice out of habit. However, others, who are described in subsequent chapters as "neoconservatives," believed that containment was futile. To simplify their argument somewhat, they believed that in a post-9/11 world in which global jihadis sought an apocalyptic conflagration with the West and all non-Muslim peoples—at least those who failed to convert given the chance—containment entailed too many risks. What if, the neoconservatives asked, Saddam Hussein, whom they wrongly but understandably believed was furtively working on weapons of mass destruction, were to share those weapons with global jihadis.[1] Consequently, some policymakers, though they held the same values as others, and essentially the same goals, believed the nature of the threat so compelling that it negated containment as an appropriate instrument. Neoconservatives therefore did what might logically be expected: they revisited their original objective with the understanding that containment was futile and then proceeded to what they reasoned was the next-best alternative. If Saddam could not be contained, then the only prudent thing to do was to remove him from power. Toppling the Hussein dictatorship therefore became the neoconservatives' instrument of choice. Toppling a regime, however, clearly constituted a radical departure from U.S. national security policy.

Of course, this description is a highly simplified version of the actual debates that engulfed Washington D.C.'s policymakers and punditocracy. Its purpose was to demonstrate that national security is always politicized. "Hawks" and "doves" have always existed in America's policymaking circles. Hawks and doves may well seek the same goal or objective; they often differ on how to achieve it. That difference notwithstanding, doves and hawks still represented consensus in terms of U.S. national security objectives. In fact, while many disagreed with the Bush administration's decision to intervene rather than contain Iraq, once decided, most Americans, including even most Americans who had not voted for George W. Bush, rallied around the decisions. The consensus that emerged following 9/11 eventually came to accept the administration's decision to topple the Hussein regime. That the post-9/11 consensus may no longer include the

Iraq War did little to diminish the consensus that developed regarding global jihadis.

That some consensus degraded over time is not surprising. Many factors contributed to its deterioration: evidence that Saddam was not stockpiling weapons of mass destruction and in fact had very little capacity to create such weapons (a justification for dismissing containment), America's steady rate of troops killed and maimed in Iraq, the hints of quagmire reminiscent of the Vietnam era, and the failure to discover connections between Saddam's regime and those who attacked America on 9/11 (another justification for the Iraq War), as well as additional factors. What strikes us as more surprising is how much consensus persisted given those realities. Recent polling data illustrated a lack of confidence in President Bush yet little change in America's fear of another attack in its future by global jihadis. For example, in early 2006, a *Los Angeles Times*/Bloomberg poll found "a majority still willing to take tough steps to reduce the risk of terrorism—including surrendering some of their civil liberties and supporting military action against Iran if it continues to advance toward developing nuclear weapons." The same poll found that only 31 percent of Americans polled believed they were better off due to Bush's policies [in Iraq]; some 62 percent believed the nation needed "to move in a new direction" to counter the jihadis.[2] Americans continued to believe the threat was real.

Thus is the complexity of consensus. America is a nation characterized by pluralistic or democratic governance. To some extent, therefore, U.S. national security policy is inevitably derived from the democratic process. In one sense, American national security policy might be conceived as the product of 300 million, or some subset thereof, different objectives changing constantly as the accretion from each of the individual's objectives changed over time and were eventually reflected in policymaking outcomes. We, however, chose to define national security differently. While reflective of different American perspectives, the definition we used suggested that U.S. national security policy results from the goals and objectives U.S. policymakers seek to attain abroad. Clearly, this reduces the millions to a very small portion of that number. Individual Americans' goals and objectives are presumably reflected in their policymakers' goals and objectives. Were it not so, those policymakers—at least those who are elected—would not remain in office for long. Through the ballot box Americans reflect their goals and objectives in the policymakers they elect, and the policymakers they elect associate themselves with particular policy choices, ultimately subjecting the policymaker to the accountability of the electorate. And George W. Bush was reelected despite the Iraq War! (Though the 2006 midterm elections demonstrated just how unpopular the Iraq War was.) It would not be unusual, particularly given the durable nature of "values," for most Americans' values to be reflected in U.S. policy despite the inevitable politicization that subsequently occurs.

Thus we return to the issue of consensus and how it is reflected in U.S. national security policy. Historically, America's commercial liberalism, belief in democratic governance, desire for peace and prosperity, and many other values were reflected in American national security policy. For its first 140-plus years, those values were reflected in American national security policy. The times and the context of those times permitted a U.S. national security strategy of isolationism to maximize American goals and values. But as we described, that changed dramatically after World War II. The question remains, which values and objectives were reflected in U.S. policy as the United States emerged a superpower following World War II?

The answer is that an interesting reflection of America's goals and objectives changing in response to a vastly changing international environment emerged quickly following the war's end. Prior to the end of World War II, America had never been a superpower or even been considered a "great power." In short order, that perception changed. America was left relatively intact after World War II, both commercially and militarily. Though a world war, the "world" in the late 1930s and early 1940s did not necessarily include the United States as particularly important strategic territory.[3] Following World War II, America changed from a country far away from the center of politics, art, science, philosophy, diplomacy, and warfare, to a nation at the very nexus of all those areas, emerging as one of the most powerful nations on earth. America mobilized in what can only be described as an unprecedented feat. Quickly, the United States became the protector of Europe, hitherto the center of post-Enlightenment world power and history. One external factor that drove this dramatic change was America's collective recognition of a threat, or tyranny, to put in uniquely American terms. President Franklin D. Roosevelt perceived the threat of a tremendous tyranny in European fascism and Japanese imperialism, but other American policymakers and the American public did not perceive those threats until the Pearl Harbor attack of December 7,

1941. Had the Japanese known what their attack would unleash in America, they may never have tried their desperate gambit. But they did. The result helped build an American empire that would thereafter determine the fates of the very peoples who attacked the U.S.

During the period of America's involvement in World War II, Americans underwent a dramatic societal transformation. American values changed little: a nation's values are typically unusually resistant to change. Nevertheless, America gradually became a superpower during those years. As the U.S. mobilized, the American public, the attentive public, and policymakers eventually began to perceive their role in the world differently. Hitherto America's role had more or less been perceived by Americans as that of the "shining city on the hill." As such, while America *represented* freedom, democratic governance, and commercial liberalism, it did little to proselytize actively on behalf of those ideals globally. Rather, it sat as an example for the world to observe. Those wishing to follow America's example were certainly encouraged to do so and were considered allies; those who chose not to follow America's example were pitied as unenlightened thinkers. Rarely, however, had America gone out "in search of monsters," as John Quincy Adams so aptly put it. World War II and its aftermath changed America's core belief from that of being able safely to avoid monsters to that of necessarily pursuing such monsters (tyrannical regimes) to protect America's very existence. This rather dramatic change required the emergence of the Cold War consensus.

Cold War Consensus

The old consensus that revolved around isolationism was supplanted by a new consensus that accepted that America had come of age. Having come of age during a time of paroxysms of violence, yet having survived the violence relatively well, Americans began to accept they had global responsibilities. Policymakers, the attentive public, and with time most Americans came to believe that in order to protect America's unique system of governance domestically, threats from abroad could no longer be ignored. The past two world wars aptly demonstrated the consequences of tyrannical regimes foisting their own interests onto their neighbors. While seas obviously separated the U.S. mainland from the arenas in which such conflicts historically occurred, those same oceans no longer protected America from the consequences. What began as a European quarrel perforce became an American problem; what began as imperial ambitions in Asia, became America's travails. The global economy as well as the global balance of power made it so. From America's own perspective (based on America's founding mythology and ethos) America must henceforth shape external events lest those events shape America's destiny!

In short, a new consensus of American *internationalism* was born out of two world wars in the twentieth century. Consensus may be a nebulous concept, as demonstrated in Richard Melanson's *American Foreign Policy Since the Vietnam War: The Search for Consensus from Richard Nixon to George W. Bush*. For Melanson, the Cold War consensus included policy consensus, essentially a shared worldview (what we have called ethos) among the policymaking elites and perhaps the attentive public. Cultural consensus, another requisite of the overall Cold War consensus in Melanson's view, consisted of broad public approval. Finally, Melanson argued that procedural consensus was required—essentially, consensus in Congress and between the executive and legislative branches. Together these three types of consensus formed what Melanson called the Cold War consensus. Others have wrestled with consensus as well. Kegley's and Wittkopf's *American Foreign Policy* also argued that a Cold War consensus existed following World War II and developed into generalizable goals ("tenets") of U.S. foreign policy during the Cold War. Others have either explicitly or more often implicitly targeted consensus as indicative of America's Cold War security policies. Leslie Gelb's and Richard Betts's excellent book on the Vietnam War argued that America's Cold War consensus inevitably led to the Vietnam War.[4] That others have wrestled with defining consensus makes our job here considerably simpler. Here, we define consensus as broadly held views about America's role in the world including policymakers of both parties (what might be called U.S. foreign policy orthodoxy), the attentive public, those few persons who move in and out of policymaking positions or hold important positions in media and think tanks, and broad public support regarding America's appropriate role in international politics.

The three World War II summits convened near the war's end were previously noted. The victors divided up the war-torn parts of Europe and Asia for administrative purposes. Once the war was officially concluded, the Soviets, the British, the French, and the Americans (as well as the Chinese to a lesser extent) moved into their respective administrative areas. America's understanding was that following two years of help and administration by the allies, elections would be held. For America, elections were and still are the exemplar of democracy. Hence, as the Cold War commenced, events conspired to shape what became America's Cold War consensus. First, President Harry Truman declared the Soviets had violated solemn pledges they made at those summits. Second, the British announced to their counterparts in the United States that, despite their agreements, the British could no longer sustain their presence and administration over Greece. Coupled with suspect Soviet behavior in and around Turkey, this became the Turkey-Greece affair that so troubled U.S. policymakers. America would necessarily have to replace the British lest the Soviets take even fuller advantage of the postwar chaos. The Truman Doctrine and the Marshall Plan both resulted from these events, signaling the beginning of a new consensus. Third, by 1948, when the Berlin airlift began, Prime Minster Winston Churchill had given his "iron curtain descending" speech and President Truman his "Truman Doctrine" speech. When the Soviets blocked allied access to the partitioned Berlin, the U.S. and the Soviets nearly went to war over it. The solution was the American airlift of food and medicines into the sectors from which they were being kept. Fourth, a civil war broke out in China between the Chinese Communist Party and the Kuomintang (or nationalists), ending with the former victoriously declaring the People's Republic of China and the latter fleeing for their lives to neighboring Formosa (Taiwan) by 1949. To U.S. policymakers, the attentive public, and the mass public, Chinese communists' victory spelled disaster, since they perceived China (referred to in the idiom of the early Cold War as Red China) as little more than the lapdog of the Soviets (a misperception, as time proved). Therefore, from the U.S. perspective, a Communist monolith now reached from eastern Europe to east Asia. Fifth, and arguably the final impetus to America's emerging Cold War consensus, was the outbreak of the Korean War. In June 1950, North Korea's communist forces made a daring blitzkrieg across the parallel—jointly accepted by the victors of World War II—dividing North from South Korea. Together, and over so short a time period, these events collectively forged a Cold War consensus that characterized U.S. national security policy and how America broadly perceived its role in what was widely perceived as a radically new international political environment.

Elsewhere, we shall examine foreign policy crises with special attention to the process associated with them. It is therefore unnecessary to delve into the precise criteria here. However, the reader should understand that a foreign policy crisis is an event that represents a high threat to the policymakers and/or their country. It is an event with a short decision time; that is, policymakers perceive themselves to have a short time in which to respond before the situation changes, and quite possible worsens. Finally, a foreign policy crisis is an event that takes policymakers by surprise. With the possible exceptions of the Korean War's beginning as North Korea launched its strike against the south, as well as China's entry into the war on behalf of North Korea in the fall of 1950, the above events did not constitute a foreign policy crisis according to the definition we use. Nevertheless, the events seemed to come at policymakers in rapid succession and at least some of the events caught America's foreign policy decision makers unaware. Consequently, this series of events that began the Cold War was perceived by policymakers collectively as crisislike. Policymakers perceived the events of 1946–1950 as somewhat similar to a foreign policy crisis despite the fact that the events did not meet the precise definition. It is important that the reader understands the distinction between the 1946–1950 period and the immediate post-9/11 period. The former was a perceived crisislike atmosphere and the latter was a bona fide foreign policy crisis. We will return to the issue of foreign policy crises in some detail later.

Crises, and even events approximating them, are potentially extraordinarily important events. A foreign policy crisis has been demonstrated empirically to be a unique decision-making setting.[5] The reason is simple and straightforward. Namely, during crises policymakers are compelled to improvise and rely far less on the vast bureaucracy that typically backstops policymakers. Contingency plans are unavailable due to failure to anticipate the event. Having so little time in which to make decisions, policymakers are forced to convene in smaller groups of decision makers, again excluding the larger bureaucracy, with all its specialized functions and knowledge as well as all its parochial views and potential obstacles. The importance of high threat should be self-evident. Were it not for high threat, the other issues would become more or less moot. For now, suffice it to note that the events of 1946–1950 were perceived as constituting grave threats to President Truman and his key decision makers. It is precisely during such times that change in U.S. foreign policy is most likely. Crises are rare events, to be sure; when they occur, the opportunity for individual policymakers to change U.S. national security policy's trajectory is distinct from all other situational contexts.[6] That policymakers do not always avail themselves of the opportunities afforded them by crises does not lessen the extremely critical nature of crises.

By the 1950s, U.S. foreign policy changed from its historical isolationist stance to one of internationalism, or more properly interventionism. That change was made possible, as noted above, by the confluence of events as the Cold War escalated in earnest. President Truman, as noted, declared the Truman Doctrine. His words demonstrated the urgency with which he and other U.S. key policymakers saw the looming existential contest with the Soviets.

> At this present moment in world history nearly every nation is confronted with alternative ways of life. And the choice is too often not a free one. One way of life is based upon the will of the majority, free institutions, representative government, free elections, guarantees of individual liberty, freedom of speech and religion, and freedom from political oppressions.

The second way of life was based "upon the imposition of the will of a minority upon a majority, upon control of the press and other means of communication by a minority, and upon terror and oppression," he continued. After distinguishing between two stark alternatives, President Truman then promulgated what thereafter became known as the Truman Doctrine: "I believe that it must be the policy of the United States to give support to free peoples who are attempting to resist subjugation by armed minorities or outside forces. It must be our policy to assist free peoples to work out their own destiny in their own way." President Truman's doctrine changed the trajectory of U.S. foreign policy from its first 140 years of isolationism to interventionism. He continued. "It is imperative to our security that we help the Greek nation to preserve its free institutions."[7] By referring to "outside forces," President Truman referred directly and unambiguously to the Soviets. Henceforth, U.S. national security policy would take on the responsibility of ensuring that the choice of alternative ways of life for others would be made under conditions America perceived as free from minority or outside forces.

During the history of U.S. national security policy—including most of the Cold War and the time since—the U.S. Congress has not sat awestricken by a president (save a couple of notable exceptions) as the president decided by fiat the future course of U.S. national security. Congress has an equal, perhaps more than an equal, set of foreign policy prerogatives delineated in the U.S. Constitution (Article I). But these were not normal times. They were the beginning of the Cold War. Tensions were extraordinarily high, the American people were quite willing to give the president very wide berth, and Congress became a willing accomplice. From the top policymakers of both parties, to the attentive public, to the mass public, the following tenets of U.S foreign policy emerged by the early 1950s.

First, America had the moral and material wherewithal to prevent Soviet tyranny from overtaking countries in Europe and elsewhere. Second, the United States would enforce its will that peoples under threat of subjugation and oppression—as the U.S. defined it—would be protected from armed minorities internally, but also from hostile Soviet tyranny externally. Third, that doing so would require large sums of money spent to defend free peoples globally through vast military means when necessary and through economic and diplomatic means when possible. In short, America would contain Soviet tyranny. Fourth, while the Monroe Doctrine continued to proscribe Europeans (now read Soviets) and others from meddling in the Western hemisphere, the U.S. would no longer act as though bound by the Monroe Doctrine. The world had effectively become the Western hemisphere for the U.S. Fifth, nuclear weapons would be used on the Soviets if necessary—early on to compel, subsequently to deter. This was the Cold War consensus formed in the late 1940s and early 1950s. And with few exceptions it remained U.S. policy over the length of the Cold War. Following the Cold War's end in 1991, the same consensus more or less held and was simply aimed at new potential tyrannies as they appeared from time to time. Those tyrannies became jingoistic, chauvinistic, nationalist regimes that were perceived as oppressing others (such as the former Yugoslavia) and, in 1993, terrorism. However, in abeyance of clearly identified tyranny, U.S. security policy drifted and cast about during the 1990s with each new tyranny replaced by another as it appeared on the horizon. Until 9/11, the Cold War consensus was relatively intact; what it lacked was a clear and demonstrable tyranny on which to focus. Once that tyranny became clear to nearly all Americans and others on 9/11, America returned to its recurrent search—its search for an appropriate role in the new complex global environment.

Empirical Indicators of America's Cold War Consensus

Though the Cold War consensus was described above and other scholars have similarly written about it, empirical evidence of its existence is persuasive. The bureaucracy cannot exist without a trace of its existence being left in records such as appropriations. If the Cold War consensus we have described in fact existed there should be a good deal of appropriations data demonstrating that it was funded year after year. Moreover, the data should be fairly consistent over the time frame we posited: namely, as the Cold War began and as it continued over five Democratic administrations (the Truman, Kennedy, Johnson, Carter, and Clinton administrations) and five Republican ones (the Eisenhower, Nixon, Ford, Reagan, and George H.W. Bush administrations). The data should also show continuity from congress to congress irrespective of which party controlled the legislature.

We have already examined the multiplicity of events that began the Cold War. We noted that these events collectively were perceived by policymaking elites *and* average Americans as indicative of the Soviets' expansionist tendencies. Hence, both policymakers and the mass public perceived the world as a dangerous place where America's survival was not guaranteed. Consequently, policymakers created new institutions (the 1947 NSA being the basis of many) for the purposes of winning or simply surviving the Cold War. Among other things the 1947 National Security Act created the unified defense department, the National Security Council, the CIA, and what became a complex array of intelligence collection and intelligence analysis agencies. The budget of many of these institutions was classified, so we will focus on the unified defense department's appropriations.

We further argued that following the Soviet Union's demise, bureaucratic inertia, and the public's comfort level with the Cold War mentality (after two generations, the Cold War was all many Americans had known of global politics) obviated new and creative thinking following the Cold War to replace the Cold War consensus. Rather than thinking anew about what new threats might emerge, most of American society and America's policymaking elites continued thinking about that with which they had grown so comfortable. To be clear, we are not faulting Presidents George H. W. Bush, Bill Clinton, or George W. Bush. Absent the 9/11 attacks (or some other bona fide foreign policy crisis), the sheer size of the bureaucracy and the power of role expectations of behavior associated with particular public offices (role theory) coupled with the lack of imagination from the punditocracy and other factors, would have produced more continuity with only incremental change. It may seem strange to suggest that no new thinking occurred late in the Cold War or after the Soviets' ultimate demise. Indeed, new thinking proliferated. However, new thinking was not taken very seriously. It was often criticized as being naive and wishful thinking. Societal and governmental inertia were more powerful than academics publishing treatises on the peace dividend or global warming or some other notion of threat. Therefore, while academics, think-tank policymakers, and pundits of many stripes published and circulated recitations of new global threats to the United States, the U.S. government and societal forces coupled with lack of imaginative leadership, absent some dramatic event, resulted in the continuation of the Cold War consensus despite the fact that the Soviet Union ceased to exist.

Bureaucratic Indicators: Defense Spending as
Illustrative of the Cold War Consensus

Following the Soviet Union's eventual collapse, U.S. policymakers searched for new monsters (global tyrannies) on which to focus America's vast military and national security empire. Following World War II and at other critical junctures in its history when the global environment has presented them with change, Americans and their policymakers have searched for an appropriate role in world politics. Following the first Twin Tower attacks (roughly one month following President Clinton's inauguration), the aftermath of 40-plus years of the Cold War focused Americans' attention elsewhere yet again and, importantly, away from the looming jihadi challenge. During the Cold War, the Soviet Red Army enforced Soviet "buffer" states and their allegiance in the Soviet Bloc. While doing so, the stultifying effects of the Soviet Red Army produced an added value (certainly not fully appreciated until it ceased to exist) of preventing nationalism, separatism, irredentism, and other parochial forces from tearing unnatural creations (e.g., Yugoslavia) apart. Once the Soviet Union ceased to thwart these centrifugal forces, the forces returned. Recall in particular how former Yugoslavia broke into pieces beginning in 1991 and piece-by-piece thereafter. First Slovenia and Croatia broke away from the Serbian-controlled confederation. Next came Bosnia-Herzegovina, ending with

Kosovo. U.S. national security policy under President Clinton, and the policies of other institutions such as the EU and the United Nations, understandably shifted their focus to the death and mayhem that accompanied the disintegration of failed states. Unfortunately, as policymakers focused their attention and resources in former Yugoslavia and elsewhere, too few resources were devoted to the rise and proliferation of the global jihadis.

The net result was that inertia rather than change dominated. American society and America's national security state had grown comfortable with generations of the Soviet threat, so it was relatively easy for both to accept that other threats loomed. Accordingly, the peace dividend never materialized. Similarly, the Cold War consensus remained intact even without a single overarching tyranny on which to focus. Rather, the tyranny *du jour* became the focus, whether it was nationalism's remnants from the Cold War, poorly-understood jihadi forces, or something else entirely. Overall, the military was not refitted to meet the needs of newly anticipated threats on the horizon; therefore, bureaucratic inertia guaranteed that the vast sums of money America spent on defense against the Soviet Union continued to be spent, by and large, after its demise.

A critical indicator of the Cold War consensus, therefore, is America's defense spending (and other national security spending) during the Cold War years versus the decade between 1991 and 2001. For instance, following the disintegration of the Soviet Union, with an appropriate time lag for fiscal-year appropriation cycles, the defense appropriation for the U.S. military should show a significant decline during the 1990s. While some decline is evident, it is also evident that this decline was: a) not particularly significant (given that the Soviet Union actually ceased to exist); and b) quite short-lived. The following graphic illustrates the point. The average appropriation, computed in constant 2000 dollars for the Cold War years (say 1950–1991) was $319.500 billion. The average defense spending for 1991–2001 (the post–Cold War, pre-9/11 period), in the same constant dollars, was $308.545 billion.

Let us recall that President George H. W. Bush was elected president in 1988, inaugurated in January 1989, and served as commander in chief until January 1993. Notwithstanding the above graphical representation of defense appropriations, the average amount of the defense spending appropriations signed by President Bush (41) during the 1989–1993 period was $352.750 billion, certainly higher than the entire period between the

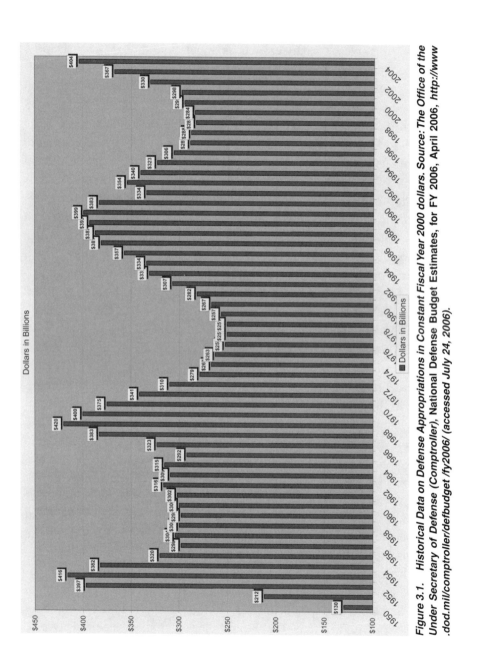

Figure 3.1. Historical Data on Defense Appropriations in Constant Fiscal Year 2000 dollars. Source: The Office of the Under Secretary of Defense (Comptroller), National Defense Budget Estimates, for FY 2006, April 2006, http://www .dod.mil/comptroller/defbudget /fy2006/ (accessed July 24, 2006).

end of the Cold War and the 9/11 attacks, a period in which Americans were supposed to be the beneficiaries of a peace dividend.[8] What strikes us as surprising is how little President Clinton reduced defense spending even when no clear tyranny existed for America to thwart.

Indeed, defense spending appeared to bottom out in 1995–1996. Following those relatively lower spending years, spending in constant 2000 dollars dipped below $300 billion. (The average of fiscal years 1948 through 2001 was $309.074 billion.) However, it began to increase again in 1999 and through 2001. If fact, using the defense department's own appropriations data (all in constant 2000 U.S. dollars), the trend of upward spending was clear. For instance, consider the defense appropriations from the same source beginning with the end of the Cold War (say 1991) through the end of the Clinton administration's second term (2001, the last Clinton-submitted budget). The average for the years 1991–2001 was a robust $308.550 billion, computed in constant 2000 U.S. dollars.

By comparison, consider the post-9/11 Bush administration's appropriations. First, it must be noted that the defense department's comptroller office estimated fiscal years 2005 onward in their 2006 publication. Those estimates were parsimonious, to put it charitably. For instance, for fiscal years 2005 and 2006 the comptroller's office estimated the defense budget at $405 billion and $382 billion respectively. Actual spending, including supplemental budgets, was higher, as reported yearly in the major newspapers as the appropriation process went from the Office of Management and Budget (OMB) to the House of Representatives to the Senate and back to the OMB where the president eventually signed the appropriation into law. To illustrate, in 2005 the fiscal year 2006 appropriation for defense worked its way through the aforementioned processes. What the comptroller estimated as $382 billion for fiscal year 2006 was reported as totaling some $445 billion including one supplemental but excluding at least one other supplemental worth roughly $80 billion.[9] Of course, those data were reported in current dollars (i.e., 2005 dollars) and not corrected for inflation. However, even if the data were corrected for inflation (converted into constant 2000 U.S. dollars) the estimate fell well short of the actual amount appropriated. In fact, the actual appropriation was about 16.5 percent higher than the comptroller's estimate, *ceterus peribus*. Moreover, we have found no reliable way to know which supplemental appropriations were and were not included over variable time periods. Indeed, a cynic might be tempted to think that the government routinely confuses which supplemental appropriations are included in a particular year's appropriations. Nevertheless, spending appears to be quite a lot higher than the comptroller's estimates.

Societal Indicators of the Cold War Consensus

For the first couple of years following 9/11 one could find numerous reports of American unity with respect to the issue of the global war on terrorism, as the administration then called it. Since then, the war on terror has experienced several name changes: from "the global struggle against violent extremism" (in late 2005 when Karen Hughes returned to the administration), to "the long struggle against terror" (the U.S. military's 2006 report). Whatever one wished to call it, Americans rallied around the administration even if they had not voted for or supported President Bush's policies before 9/11. As public opinion soured over the Iraq War, it became difficult to separate the two issues in many Americans' minds. A few observations may be made, however. The Pew Charitable Trust published telling research comparing the Vietnam and Iraq Wars. It demonstrated that in contrast to the Vietnam War where "the difference of opinion between Republicans and Democrats about Vietnam never exceeded 18 percentage points," the Iraq War divided "America along partisan lines in a way that Vietnam never did." Pew's survey found "that 73% of Democrats" believed that military action in Iraq was the wrong decision, "compared with just 14% of Republicans—a gap roughly three times as great as the largest partisan gap in opinions about Vietnam." Pew also noted that three years earlier "the public judged Bush's performance on Iraq largely on the original decision to go to war. But today, perceptions of progress in Iraq and views of the likelihood for success are far more influential." Pew's survey demonstrated clearly that the Iraq War, and not the war against global jihadis, was hurting the president. For instance, "views on whether taking military action in Iraq was the right or wrong decision have remained unchanged over the past year, opinions about how the war is progressing are not fixed, and are causing a greater *drag* on the president's approval ratings." The Pew survey explicitly concluded that "Bush's recent slide in the polls reflects growing public doubts about Iraq." That is, the Iraq War was hurting the administration's approval ratings, both on personal and job performance, yet consensus that formed shortly after 9/11 was still considerable and bipartisan.[10]

Clearly, the main problem with polling data, then, was that the Iraq War had caused a "drag" on the president's personal approval and job approval. Many Americans simply did not differentiate between the two enough for the difference to be captured in the admittedly blunt instrument of polling data.[11] It therefore became relatively difficult to demonstrate that the societal consensus created after 9/11 continued to shape foreign policy and policymakers. However, in late 2003 (admittedly before public opinion over Iraq began to plummet demonstrably), one study conducted by the American Enterprise Institute (AEI) hinted that societal consensus continued despite the difficulties that continued in Iraq. In September and October of 2003, the insurgency had begun to become evident to all but the most obtuse of the Iraq War supporters. Author Karlyn H. Bowman (AEI, Public Policy), wrote the following about American public opinion based on her extensive research. It is worth quoting at length for proper context. Her findings demonstrated that:

> Americans are never spoiling for a fight. But once convinced of the justness of a cause, they are resolute. They give their Presidents considerable latitude in the conduct of foreign policy once a basic level of trust has been established. The magnitude of the 9/11 attacks, the personal response of President Bush and the response of his team gave the administration instant credibility in an area where the President previously had average marks. Since the start of the military campaign in Afghanistan on October 7, 2001, *large majorities of Americans have been supportive of the Bush administration's actions in the war on terrorism*. The proportion of Americans that believes the United States is winning the war against terrorism, however, has fluctuated. Americans expect this struggle to be a long one. Three questions asked by the Pew Research Center—one in October 2002 and two in April 2003—show that majorities of Americans believed, both before and after the war in Iraq, that it would help in the war against terrorism.[12]

Thus, societal indicators portrayed the same consensus or societal inertia that was formed following the trauma of 9/11. When society believed their leaders were moving the country in the wrong direction, unsurprisingly, polling data reflected that belief.

Finally, recall the summer 2005 London "Tube attacks." Jihadis in London detonated multiple bombs, nearly simultaneously, that understandably panicked many Britons on July 7, 2005. Two weeks later some copycat Islamists (thought probably not jihadis) attempted a second attack that failed to affect London materially but likely exacerbated the fear already felt by many Britons. A week thereafter, jihadis attacked Sharm el-Sheikh, an Egyptian Red Sea resort. In a second Pew study, this one from 2005, the researchers found "President Bush's approval ratings have shown modest improvement" as a result of the London bombings, as they did following the Madrid bombing on March 11, 2003. Interestingly, though only 62 percent of the respondents interpreted the London July 7 attacks as a clash between the West and Islam (the so-called clash of civilizations) "a sizable number of those who say the attacks represent[ed] only a limited conflict today believe it will grow into a major world conflict in the future (25 percent of the general public)."[13]

In short, though the Iraq War has soured public opinion as reflected in the midterm elections (2006), a distinction must be made between those who have lost faith in the Iraq War and those who continue to believe that America shall remain a future target of global jihadis. That the Iraq War has been explicitly compared to the Vietnam War may be appropriate in the proper context. For instance, we suspect that once the "fiasco," as one author recently called it, in Iraq is stabilized and America's military is used to protect America from future jihadi attacks, the same sort of consensus that survived the Vietnam War will survive Iraq.

SUMMARY

Here we elaborated on the definition of U.S. national security and foreign policy presented in chapter 2. We also built on the previous chapter's brief history of U.S. foreign policy to develop thematic tenets of U.S. foreign policy as America became a hegemonic power early in the Cold War, one of two superpowers left standing as World War II's devastation finally ended. We documented what we and others have called the Cold War consensus and we illustrated its existence with data from public opinion polling data as well as defense appropriations data that demonstrated that however isolationist American had once been, from 1950 forward, that isolationism was permanently replaced by internationalism.

By design, America's institutions are not subject to radical and erratic changes. Rather, change typically occurs incrementally over long time periods. However, on rare occasion, more dramatic changes do occur in the institutions, bureaucracies, and agencies that create and implement U.S.

national security policy. Hence, the importance of foreign policy crises was briefly addressed in this chapter. We briefly introduced the exceptionally important—yet poorly understood—National Security Act (NSA of 1947) and a couple of the foreign policy, national security, intelligence-collection, and intelligence-analysis institutions, procedures, and processes created to thwart the Soviet Union during the Cold War.

NOTES

1. This is for illustrative purposes only. First, the neoconservative view was somewhat oversimplified. Second, a logical flaw seemed evident to this author both at the time and currently. Namely, however evil Saddam Hussein proved himself repeatedly—and to be sure, he had proved himself evil—why on earth would he ever share such weapons with jihadis bent on attacking the U.S. and its allies, as that would invariably lead to his own destruction? Whatever else one wishes to think about Saddam Hussein, he also proved time and again that his own survival was his preeminent priority.

2. Ronald Brownstein, "Bush's Ratings Sink, but Trust Remains," *Los Angeles Times*, January 27, 2006. http://www.latimes.com/news/nationworld/nation/la-na-poll27jan27,0 ,510814.story?coll=la-home-headlines. In particular, see the "Information Box" at the bottom of the piece.

3. One prominent example of a geostrategic theory of international politics around the turn of the twentieth century was Sir H. John Mackinder's "heartland theory." Sir Mackinder was a British geographer who wrote a paper entitled "The Geographical Pivot of History," which was published in 1904. Mackinder's thesis suggested that the control of Eastern Europe was vital to control of the world as follows: who rules East Europe commands the heartland; who rules the heartland commands the world-island; who rules the world-island commands the world. The United States was conspicuously absent from Mackinder's strategic pivot, relegated merely to the world islands.

4. Richard A. Melanson, *American Foreign Policy since The Vietnam War: The Search for Consensus from Richard Nixon to George W. Bush* (New York: E.H. Sharpe, 2004); Eugene R. Wittkopf, Charles Kegley, Jr., and James M. Scott, *American Foreign Policy*, 6th ed.; Leslie H. Gelb and Richard K. Betts, *The Irony of Vietnam: The System Worked* (Washington, DC: The Brookings Institution, 1979).

5. Charles F. Hermann, *Crises in Foreign Policy* (Indianapolis, IN: Bobbs-Merrill Publishing, 1969). See also M. Kent Bolton, "*Pas de Trois*: The Synergism of Surprise, Threat, and Response Time and its Effects on U.S. Foreign Policy Behavior," *Conflict Management and Peace Science* 18, no. 2 (2001): 175–212.

6. Charles F. Hermann, "International Crisis as a Situational Variable," in *International Politics and Foreign Policy*, ed. James Rosenau (New York: The Free Press, 1969), 409–421.

7. Harry S. Truman, "Suggested Draft of the President's Message to Congress on the Greek Situation, March 7, 1947" (Truman Doctrine Documents, Truman Presidential Museum and Library, Independence, MO, 1947), http://www.trumanlibrary.org/whistlestop/

study_collections/doctrine/large/documents/index.php?pagenumber=6&documentid =39&documentdate=1947-03-07&studycollectionid=TDoctrine&groupid= and http:// www.trumanlibrary.org/whistltop/study_collections/doctrine/large/documents/index.php ?pagenumber=5&documentid=39&documentdate=1947-03-07&studycollectionid =TDoctrine&groupid= (accessed in February 2005; reviewed in March 2006)

8. All the defense appropriation data comes from the Office of the Under Secretary of Defense (Comptroller), *National Defense Budget Estimate for FY 2006* (Washington, DC: 2006), http://www.dod.mil/comptroller/defbudget /fy2006/ (accessed July 24, 2006). All dollars are constant 2000 dollars.

9. Defense appropriations for the fiscal year 2006 that began in October 2005 were reported throughout the calendar year. The eventual amount was reported in fall just before fiscal year 2006 began. See Liz Sidoti, "Senate Votes to Give Bush More War Funds," *Washington Post*, October 7, 2005, http://www.washingtonpost.com/wp-dyn/content/article/2005/10/07/AR2005100700202.html; and Associated Press, "Senate Approves $50 Billion for War Efforts," *Los Angeles Times*, October 8, 2005, http://www.latimes .com/news/nationworld/world/la-fg-iraqbill8oct08,1,6709172.story?coll=la-headlines-world. For some of the obfuscation with supplementals see Shailagh Murray, "House Approves War Funding," *Washington Post*, March 17, 2005, http://www.washingtonpost .com/wp-dyn/articles/A40248-2005Mar16.html; Richard Simon, "House Approves $82-Billion War Spending Bill," *Los Angeles Times*, May 6, 2005, http://www .latimes.com/news/nationworld/nation/la-na-spend6may06,1,5546810.story?coll =la-headlines-nation; Associated Press, "$82 Billion OK'd in Emergency Spending," *Los Angeles Times*, May 11, 2005 http://www.latimes.com /news/nationworld/nation/ la-na-spending11may11,1,6383767.story?coll=la-headlines-nation; Jonathan Weisman and Shailagh Murray, "Congress Approves $82 Billion for Wars," *Washington Post*, May 11, 2005, http://www.washingtonpost.com/wp-dyn/content/article/2005/05/10/ AR2005051001145.html; and David Kirkpatrick, "Congress Approves Financing to Fight Wars and Terrorism," *New York Times*, May 11, 2005, http://nytimes.com/2005/ 05/11/politics/11spend.html.

10. Pew Charitable Trusts, *Analysis: The Iraq-Vietnam Difference* (Pew Charitable Trusts, 2006), http://www.pewtrusts.com/ideas/ideas_item.cfm?content_item_id=3368& content_type_id=18&issue_name=Public%20opinion%20and%20polls&issue=11&page =18&name=Public%20Opinion%20Polls%20and%20Survey%20Results (my emphasis).

11. To be sure, the Bush administration initially attempted to conflate 9/11 with what became the Iraq War. As shall be discussed in the chapter on the Iraq War as a source of U.S. foreign policy and national security policy, the White House conducted a campaign of misdirection—and that is a charitable assessment—in which the perpetrators of 9/11 were repeatedly linked to Saddam Hussein in the run up to the Iraq War and in the 2004 presidential election cycle. Ironically, when opinions on the Iraq War headed south so did opinions on the president, making him a victim of his campaign's own success. However, the post-9/11 consensus, as shall be demonstrated repeatedly in subsequent chapters, is largely still intact.

12. Karlyn H. Bowman, *America after 9/11: Public Opinion on the War on Terrorism and the War with Iraq* (American Enterprise Institute for Public Policy, 2003),

http://www.ciaonet.org/wps/bok01/; for her full findings, see http://www.ciaonet.org/ wps/bok01/bok01.pdf (accessed May 18, 2006) (my emphasis).

13. Andrew Kohut and Carroll Doherty, "Bush Approval Rises Modestly: Tempered Public Reaction To London Attacks" (Pew Research Center for the People and the Press, 2005), http://www.pewtrusts.com/pdf/PRC_terror_0705.pdf (accessed May 18, 2006).

CHAPTER 4

The National Security Act and National Security Institutions

THE 1947 NATIONAL SECURITY ACT AND ITS CENTRALITY TO U.S. FOREIGN POLICY

The National Security Act of 1947 (the 1947 NSA) was drafted for a multiplicity of reasons. Perhaps foremost among them was that the conclusion of World War II left the global system's balance-of-power environment irreversibly changed. Europe was no longer the center of international politics, finance, art, science, and diplomacy; Europe lay in ruins. Europe's rich history, of course, had not changed. But physically, Europe had: Europe's infrastructure was in a shambles. Consequently, Europe was perceived by American policymakers as vulnerable to Soviet Russia's expansionism. Russia had been seen historically by many Western Europeans, historically, in rather condescending terms; it was the backwater of Europe where feudalism was the rule rather than the exception. It was perceived, further, as something less than a European country, what with one foot in Europe and the other in Asia. Slavs, whose culture was perceived as having yielded few contributions to Western civilization, were not considered "real" Europeans, whose cultures were synonymous with the Renaissance, European liberalism, the European Enlightenment, modernity, and the industrial revolution. As the Cold War began, the Soviet Union (USSR) was seen as militarily powerful but still backward nation. Soon thereafter Europeans and Americans alike would come to see the Soviet Union as one of the world's two superpowers.

A second reason the NSA was drafted was that post–World War II Europe constituted a geopolitical fault line by virtue of proximity to the Soviet Union and by virtue of its philosophical propinquity to the U.S. Between the two emerging superpowers—the U.S. and the USSR—lay an obliterated Europe. Erratic movement along that fault line was likely to result in Western Europe's further demise. World War II already hastened Europe's decline considerably. Europe's placement between the two superpowers put Europe in the unenviable position of being the real estate on which either superpower would likely make its strategic moves to best the other.

Third, the Cold War's commencement meant that the world had become inescapably more complex—certainly from the U.S.'s viewpoint, since it had previously been insulated by its isolationist policies. By the end of the World War II, America's earlier isolationism had been replaced by internationalism or interventionism in which the U.S. no longer perceived itself as linked only to its own hemisphere but linked to global affairs. Congress considered the executive branch ill-equipped to deal with the dangerous new world facing U.S. security and commercial interests. Congress further concluded that Congress's own structure was not amenable to agile policymaking in this new high-stakes environment. For these reasons and others, Congress believed that the presidency needed special assistance. Congress wanted the president to have the requisite tools and institutions necessary to conduct U.S. national security policy in the brave new world policymakers faced. Clearly, much of the impetus behind the 1947 NSA was Congress giving the president additional tools and flexibility in what would become a series of perceived foreign policy crises.[1]

Fourth, policymakers in Congress and the White House fretted over the management style that Roosevelt had left to Truman after the former's death. One excellent book on the NSC explained that President Roosevelt had the unusual habit of telling different people different things, of keeping his own vice president in the dark on critical U.S. national security matters, and of running foreign policy as if it were simply his own personal prerogative rather than the presidency's prerogative (the latter being an institutional prerogative contemplated by the founders).[2]

These were four main reasons that the 1947 National Security Act was drafted. It was signed on July 26th of that year and scheduled to go into effect by year's end. The statute itself was so significant a departure in

U.S. national security policymaking, that we have discussed it repeatedly. Too few Americans understand the critical importance of the 1947 National Security Act and all of the national security institutions, procedures, and processes that it created. We therefore consider it in even greater detail in this chapter as we believe its centrality to America's Cold War foreign policy is nearly impossible to overstate. Additionally, a principal motivation of this book is to compare the creation of the 1947 NSA with its counterpart following 9/11, the Intelligence Reform and Terrorism Prevention Act of December 2004. A comprehensive examination of both statutes is therefore necessary for comparative purposes. Therefore, chapter 4 will serve as a structured examination of the 1947 NSA while chapter 9 will provide the same for the 2004 IRPTA.

The National Security Act of 1947

In Section 101a of Title I, "Coordination for National Security," the 1947 NSA read: "There is hereby established a council to be known as the National Security Council (hereafter in this section referred to as the 'Council')." Rarely in the United States' history have fewer legislative words had more momentous reverberations in terms of how the U.S. would relate to other global actors politically, diplomatically, and economically. The National Security Act's effects in terms of the Cold War alone make it one of America's most important pieces of national security legislation ever committed to paper. What did its originators envisage as its purpose?

> The function of the Council shall be to advise the President with respect to integration of domestic, foreign, and military policies relating to the national security so as to enable the military services and the other departments and agencies of the Government to cooperate more effectively in matters involving the national security. The Council shall have a staff to be headed by a civilian executive secretary who shall be appointed by the President.

The drafters determined that the "President of the United State shall preside over the meetings of the Council: Provided, That [*sic*] in his absence he may designate a member of the Council to preside in his place."[3]

Its statutory "members," apart from the president already designated as presiding over the Council, were enumerated thusly: the secretary of state

(then the preeminent foreign policy arm of the executive branch), the secretary of defense (a newly created position supplanting both the secretary
of war and the navy secretary), and the vice president. Augmenting the
statutory members were statutory advisers.[4] The statutory advisers eventually became the director of central intelligence (DCI), the chairman of
the Joint Chiefs of Staff (CJCS) and, arguably, the "executive secretary."[5]
As will be seen, over time the executive secretary evolved from its original staff-management role to the role of an actual personal adviser to the
president on national security. Once the executive secretary disappeared
entirely, the national security advisor became officially known as the special assistant to the president for national security affairs. By convention
and for our purposes, the statutory members provided the basis for what
became known as the *NSC principals* or *NSC principals committee*. We
will hereafter refer to the national security advisor as the *NSC advisor* to
avoid confusion with other acronyms and initializations.

Additional members have been included in the principals committee,
but those members were selected for particular presidents' idiosyncratic
reasons. That is, different presidents included and excluded members
based on presidents' personal preferences, quite apart from those specified
in the 1947 legislation. Here, the individuals whom a particular president
included in his NSC principals committee, insofar as those members *were
not* specified by statute, are referred to as *ad hoc NSC principals*. The advisory layer of the NSC that was slightly less august than the principals
was comprised of the principals' deputies (and/or undersecretaries) and
was known as the deputies' committee of the NSC.

What is important to understand is that an enormously complex,
labyrinthine set of bureaucracies was created in 1947 and remains largely
intact today (2007). As bureaucracies are wont to do, it has evolved over
time into an ever-larger complex of interacting pieces. Prior to the 1947
NSA, the U.S. of course conducted foreign policy, trade, and diplomacy,
and it certainly conducted war. Thus a rudimentary form of what became
America's behemoth national security bureaucracy obviously predated the
1947 NSA. To cite just a couple of examples, during World War II America had intelligence assets deployed under the aegis of the U.S. Office of
Strategic Services (the OSS), a precursor of sorts to the CIA. (The CIA
was created by the 1947 statute.) The War Department as well as the historically important U.S. Department of the Navy existed prior to the deci-

sions to consolidate them into a unified military structure with the 1947 NSA and its 1949 reorganization bill. Prior to the 1947 NSA and its creation of the NSC, a combined State-War-Navy Coordinating Committee (SWNCC) acted as a prototype of the NSC. The SWNCC, however, was effectively a type of president-cabinet policymaking model. The NSC significantly supplanted that model. Though the original statute did not envision the NSC principals, much less the NSC deputies or staff, as policymakers, the reality is they have evolved over time into policymakers of significance in the world's most powerful nation.

An important point here is that the pre-1947 national security bureaucracy paralleled the United States' 140 years of isolationism. Prior to World War II and the Cold War, the U.S. essentially approached international politics in two ways. The first was in terms of free trade and commercial transactions assumed to be beneficial to all parties. Since America became a republic, most policymakers agreed that commercial intercourse between the United States and the rest of the world (effectively Europe) ought to be done strictly on a basis of economic liberalism. The Founding Fathers' beliefs in the tenets of "Liberalism" held that individuals—having primacy over the collective—ought to be able to trade with individuals in other countries (essentially, Ricardo's theory of comparative advantage). The belief was that trade, overall, benefited all involved and therefore, with very little regulation, the federal government ought not to interfere with private commercial transactions.

The second approach to international politics in the republic's early history was complexly linked to America's experience with war. America's history, fundamentally, was that of fleeing tyranny in order to form a "more perfect union": an experiment with a mythology that persisted and shaped U.S. international relations from the republic's origins. In leaving Europe behind, the new republic also left behind Europe's tendencies toward war for abstract notions of "national interests" that were invariably defined in terms of the sovereign's, rather than the people's, interests. Power politics, or realpolitik, was according to American mythology something America's founders wished to eschew. It was the way Europeans conducted their international behavior and therefore suspect. "Lie down with dogs and you wake up with fleas," claimed an old Spanish proverb. This proverb is not too strong a reflection of the founders' concerns with respect to the new republic's non-commercial interactions with

Europe. By analogy, were America to involve itself in European intrigues and wars, it too might become "infected" with Europeans' diseases.

Thus, according to American mythology and ethos, the more perfect union was fated never to follow the European habit of searching abroad for empire. In chapter 2 we quoted President John Quincy Adams, who told the U.S. Congress on Independence Day (1821) that America's foreign policy favored freedom and independence. "But she goes not abroad in search of monsters to destroy. She is the well-wisher to the freedom and independence of all."[6] America's mythology held that the republic only entered war when forced to do so, resorting to war only as the last resort. Accordingly, when the U.S. was dragged into wars, it was dragged in against its better instincts. World War I, that quintessentially European war fought over European colonial possessions, was something many American found distasteful. Not until the British *Lusitania* was attacked carrying American-made ammunition and war matériel was the U.S. compelled to defend its rights to sell manufactured goods—war matériels— abroad, its rights of navigation, and its honor. Similarly, not until the Japanese bombed Pearl Harbor was America compelled to defend itself and enter World War II on the side of the Allies.

Both of these impulses meshed particularly well with the U.S. view of itself as an isolationist power. President Monroe's doctrine (the 1823 Monroe Doctrine) limited the U.S. to its hemisphere and, importantly, limited Europeans to theirs. Consequently, the U.S. never felt a particular need to create or keep a standing military. Military matters were handled on an ad hoc basis. If some tyrant was perceived by America's policymakers as forcing the U.S. into defending itself, the appropriate military force was created to deal with the particular tyranny. Therefore, the U.S. had little in terms of a modern military-industrial complex prior to World War II. As noted, the war department and the Department of the Navy existed, but they were largely a function of U.S. economic liberalism and the resulting trade that flourished between the U.S. and foreign powers. Navies had traditionally protected such trade and were consistent with the basic isolationist posture that the U.S. evinced until well into the twentieth century.

By the time the United States emerged as a superpower following World War II, the world had grown exceedingly more complex for U.S. policymakers. As the world seemingly closed in on America, it no longer enjoyed the luxury of avoiding far-flung wars. It is also worth noting that preserving and rebuilding Europe was in America's commercial interests too, as there were few alternative markets where American goods and services could be sold. Whether guided by America's mythology, altruism, or naked self-interest, by the beginning of the Cold War, U.S. national security policy had begun a new trajectory. On this new trajectory, America would become increasingly powerful; would guarantee the security of its allies; would no longer await being dragged into war but, rather, would proactively seek to arrange international affairs in ways that suited the needs of America and its allies; and would become one of the world's two superpowers, arrayed against the other superpower, which U.S. policymakers perceived as an expansive world tyranny. The Cold War era had dawned. The attendant changes in terms of national security processes, procedures, institutions, and interbranch governmental relationships were, in retrospect, as understandable as they were remarkable. The U.S. national security state rose as the proverbial phoenix from the ashes of World War II and evolved during the crucible of the Cold War.

Below we consider each Cold War administration and how each formulated and implemented America's national security policy. Rather than looking thematically at each administration in terms of the Cold War, we are interested in how each post-1947 president used his NSC as the primary locus of U.S. national security policymaking. Was each president contented to use the statutory principals created by the 1947 NSA? If so, were each of the statutory members and advisers relatively equal in terms of influence? Or did the president under consideration reshuffle the statutory members and advisers of his NSC creating ad hoc configurations of key policymakers to suit his needs? In examining each administration, we attempt to identify the unique ways in which each president employed the powerful tools given to the executive via the 1947 NSA. Conversely, we also focus on generalizable trends—e.g., the rise of the NSC as the locus of national security policy power—that have characterized U.S. national security policy over the course of the Cold War years and prior to 9/11. The portrait of each Cold War and post–Cold War administration may then be used to provide a baseline from which to compare post-9/11 changes in subsequent chapters. We therefore turn our focus in the remainder of this chapter to developing a comparative baseline of each administration's president-NSC-policymaking model. Following the brief examination of each administration's NSC a graphic representation of its key features is rendered.

THE EVOLUTION O.F THE NSC:
THE PRESIDENT-NSC-POLICYMAKING MODEL FROM
HARRY TRUMAN TO GEORGE W. BUSH

We noted the relatively few scholarly books and papers that have been written specifically about the NSC despite its tremendous import to U.S. national security. It is not our purpose to attempt to recreate what has already been done in exemplary fashion elsewhere. Rather, we intend to document changes in each of those administrations' president-NSC models of policymaking and then compare those models with President George W. Bush's most recent changes. A central thesis of this book is that 9/11 began a significant series of changes to America's national security infrastructure originally created by the 1947 NSA. The changes made after 9/11 were memorialized in the Intelligence Reform and Terrorism Prevention Act of December 2004. So significant were those changes that President Bush's White House characterized them as the "most significant reorganization since the 1947 National Security Act."[7] The mammoth reorganization occurred partly as a result of 9/11's unique features: 9/11 constituted a U.S. foreign policy crisis, a rare event in U.S. national security policymaking. Following 9/11, the Bush administration intervened in Iraq. Between 9/11 and the end of 2004, a post-9/11 consensus formed. The issue of a post-9/11 consensus will be considered in subsequent chapters.

As we noted, 9/11 made possible those changes in U.S. national security policymaking and the vast bureaucracy that implements those policies. Since the trend from Truman to Bush (43) was increasingly that of a president-NSC-policymaking model where the NSC became even more important, it stands to reason that if U.S. national security policymaking changed as a result of 9/11, so too did the president-NSC-policymaking model. In fact, it did. The president-NSC model of policymaking provides a useful level of analysis for comparative purposes. Thus while the current attempt is not a re-examination of the NSC of each administration in detail, we shall nevertheless establish the president-NSC policymaking model for each administration, and to the extent that trends have emerged over the years, identify those trends.

President Truman: The Emergence of the President-NSC-Policymaking Model

The National Security Act of 1947 was signed into law during Truman's tenure on July 26, 1947, with an effective date set for December that year. President Harry S. Truman largely ignored the NSC until the onset of the Korean War. As the war began, President Truman began to employ his NSC as its drafters envisaged. Before the Korean War, Truman met with principal members, chaired some of the meeting, and limited its attendees to the policymakers whom Truman most trusted. After the Korean War began, Truman's use of the president-NSC-policymaking model changed. Before the outbreak of the Korean War, Truman only used the president-NSC policymaking model cautiously and infrequently. Truman's own memoirs made clear that he eyed the NSC with some degree of circumspection. Truman jealously and understandably guarded his constitutional prerogatives. The beginning of the Korean War in June 1950 changed President Truman's relationship with his newly created NSC.[8]

As a result of the Korean War, Truman used the NSC regularly for the remainder of his presidency. President Truman's statutory members included Secretaries of Defense James V. Forrestal (until March 28, 1949), Lewis A. Johnson (until September 19, 1950), George C. Marshall (until September 12, 1951), and finally Robert A. Lovett. Forrestal's death by suicide ended his tenure early, after which Secretary Lewis Johnson and Secretary George C. Marshall were the next two most influential secretaries of defense in the Truman administration. For secretary of state, President Truman chose George C. Marshall, whose service overlapped with the 1947 NSA and lasted until 1949; following Marshall was the important Dean G. Acheson. In addition to statutory members and advisors, Truman also included ad hoc members. In Truman's case, William Averell Harriman and the ubiquitous Clark Clifford constituted ad hoc members. Truman trusted and respected both men tremendously. In employing ad hoc members, Truman set a precedent for each subsequent president to add or subtract from the statutory membership according to the president's pleasure and personality and according to his perception of the national security environment. Truman's other innovations included inclusion of under secretary-level representatives from the Department of Defense, the Department of State, and from the CIA. Truman also used the NSC for covert and psychological warfare against the Soviets. "The objective was to develop and manage the implementation of psychological warfare strategies that were seen to be central to victory in the Cold War."⁹ What Truman once viewed as a legislative encroachment on Truman's constitutional prerogatives became the apex of policymaking following the onset of the Korean War. Truman, therefore, became the first president formally to supplant the historical president-cabinet model of policymaking in favor of a new model based on the 1947 legislation.

The president-NSC-policymaking model permanently replaced the presidential-cabinet model that had existed since America's origins. As the 1947 statute made clear, the NSC would henceforth be a presidential redoubt for policymaking where the president could go to get advice "with respect to integration of domestic, foreign, and military policies relating to the national security so as to enable the military services and the other departments and agencies of the Government to cooperate more effectively in matters involving the national security." Each president constructed his own president-NSC-policymaking model slightly differently. In fact, the legislation foresaw different presidents inviting different participants depending on the issue and the president's view of the stakes. The NSC was composed of what the legislation called the NSC members but what are commonly called the president's NSC principals: the vice president (until recently a nominal member of the NSC principals), the secretaries of state and defense, and what subsequently became the NSC advisor. Arguably, the executive secretary created by the 1947 NSA mutated into today's NSC advisor. Additionally, the president was advised by the statute to include "the Secretaries and Under Secretaries of other executive departments and of the military departments when appointed by the President . . ."¹⁰ therefore encouraging each president to include those whom he thought important for a particular national security issue. This would be repeated by many subsequent administrations.

Each president after Truman has similarly configured the president-NSC-policymaking model with the NSC principals (some presidents excluding one or more) as well as ad hoc members depending upon whom a particular president trusted. The statutory advisers, as noted, were to be the DCI and the Pentagon's Chairman of the Joint Chiefs of Staff; various presidents have included or excluded these advisers according to that president's particular views of how integral the advisers were. Some presidents broadened the membership to include official historians-cum-advisers (Kennedy) while others narrowed its membership to a handful, often excluding even statutory members. Together, the flexibility in the 1947 legislation and the precedents set by Truman led to subsequent presidents configuring their NSC principals, including their statutory members and advisers, according to their particular desires and comfort levels, something that continues to this day.

President Truman debuted the Psychological Strategy Board (PSB), an important innovation that became the template for subsequent covert plans and actions the NSC recommended and managed during Truman's and subsequent administrations. Truman insisted that the membership of the PSB be limited to the statutory members and advisers of the NSC with the addition of three ad hoc principals! Truman included Averell Harriman (arguably the prototype for what later became the NSC advisor); Sidney Souers (later replaced by James Lay); the executive secretary of the NSC; and his treasury secretary, a man named John W. Snyder, as ad hoc principals. Secretary Snyder was a close personal friend of Truman's and served as the treasury secretary for Truman's entire tenure as president. Reportedly, President Truman was proud of the fact that neither he nor his NSC principals recommended policies for which the U.S. Treasury Department could not pay, a pattern later followed by President Eisenhower, among others. Despite Truman's pride at not selecting policies for which the U.S. Treasury could not pay, the process of deficit spending in order to thwart the Soviets was memorialized in an NSC document (NSC 68), which also created a vast array of new national security policy instruments, including an array of covert options.

Following the beginning of the Korean War, Truman's president-NSC-policymaking model was involved in multiple high-profile national security incidents and evolved incrementally even over Truman's relatively short tenure. President Truman's Psychological Strategy Board would subsequently be folded into something Truman's successor, Dwight D. Eisenhower called the Operations Coordinating Board.[11] However, in one form or another, the remnants of Truman's original PSB have become part of the president-NSC-policymaking model, particularly in terms of sub rosa and/or paramilitary operations as well as "psychological" operations from which the United States government might wish to plausibly deny its association. The president-NSC-policymaking model thus became the preeminent policymaking institution of U.S. national security and foreign policy as the Cold War escalated in the 1950s. Thanks largely to President Truman's perception of the Korean War the NSC became integrally involved in what would thereafter become two new tenets of U.S. Cold War policy: deficit spending during times of war and covert and other psychological instruments as normalized tools of U.S. national security policy. Though President Truman only rarely used his NSC prior to the Korean War, a couple of notable exceptions existed: the Berlin Airlift (1948), and Truman's policy vis-à-vis the flight of the Chinese nationalists from their communist brethren on China's mainland in 1949. While the NSC has undergone many iterations and permutations since, it has remained integral to policymaking. Truman's firm hand on the tiller during the stormy days of the early Cold War was, in no small part, the reason the model became the preeminent level of U.S. national security policymaking.

Though the NSC was created in 1947, Truman continued to use the familiar president-cabinet model characteristic of previous twentieth-century presidential administrations. This meant, practically speaking, that Truman and his secretary of state more or less decided on foreign policy, then for-

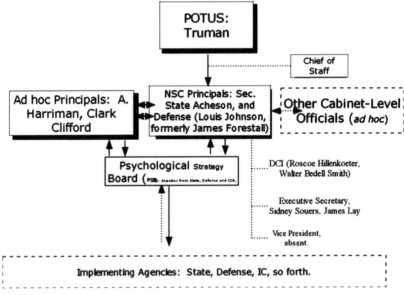

Figure 4.1.   Truman's president-NSC-policymaking model, June 1950 through the reminder of his presidency. Note that even in this model the secretary of state remained the "first among equals." It would be some time before the secretary of defense—just created by the 1947 NSA—became the bureaucratic lodestar that position is today. Also, note that the vice president is absent in the model despite the statutory language making the vice president an NSC member. (Solid lines represent direct policymaking responsibilities; dashed lines indicate indirect policymaking and/or feedback to policymakers.)

warded the decisions to the implementing bureaucracies, as they then were organized. Feedback or evaluation of a particular policy's efficacy was brought back to the president's attention through the same mechanism in reverse. After the Korean War, President Truman found that adopting the recommendations of the 1947 NSA proved useful to the high-stakes policymaking so characteristic of particularly tense periods of the Cold War. The above graphic is representative of Truman's ultimate version and America's first president-NSC-policymaking model, used after June 1950 and for the remainder of Truman's presidency.

President Eisenhower:
The Formalization of the President-NSC Model

Many excellent biographies have been written about President Eisenhower. Among them are Ambrose's excellent histories of "Ike" as the allied commander and as the president.[12] For whatever reason—and there were many—the early characterizations of Eisenhower's presidency were nearly uniformly unflattering. To believe them, one would necessarily believe that the president-NSC-policymaking model magically vanished during the mid to late 1950s. Many early accounts have President Eisenhower more interested in time on the golf course than time with his NSC principals. Later scholarship corrected earlier misperceptions. Above all else, Eisenhower was a leader of people. Most of his early career was dedicated to leading men into war. He became the Supreme Allied Commander— something one does not become without demonstrating talent for leadership. As president, too, he was a leader of people. In this case, President Eisenhower was the leader of the entire executive branch of government. Too many early accounts had President Eisenhower as an underrated policymaker. In fact, the very opposite is closer to the truth.

If Truman prototyped the first president-NSC-policymaking model, Eisenhower refined and formalized it, making the model that every subsequent president has used with only minor modifications since. President Eisenhower made it a routine part of U.S. national security policymaking. Some confusion arose in early scholarship regarding Eisenhower's presidency. It may have arisen from the difference in personalities between Truman and Eisenhower. For Truman, the "buck stops here" was the straightforward, "I'm in charge" mantra of a modern presidency. In fact, Eisenhower was no less involved. However, Eisenhower was used to a more hierarchical management style where responsibilities were delegated. By the time Eisenhower became president of the United States, there was very little he had not accomplished and very little reason to believe he needed to "prove" himself, something Truman may have felt the need to do due to the circumstances under which he became president and his pedestrian private life prior to becoming a public servant.

With complete self-confidence, Eisenhower surrounded himself with excellent staff people. Luminaries such as Robert "Bobby" Cutler, James Lay, and the ever-faithful NSC regular Andrew Goodpaster (who remained in the NSC beyond Eisenhower's tenure) were, figuratively speaking, Eisenhower's sergeants major. Robert Cutler, for example, drafted the memoranda that suggested the creation of what became known as the NSC advisor. Whether the NSC advisor evolved from the executive secretary office that Cutler once filled or evolved from ad hoc members is subject to some debate. It was not that the buck failed to stop with Eisenhower. Rather, it was that the buck had better have been well-staffed, well-considered, and well-examined from every plausible angle before it reached his level of decision making. But once there, the president-NSC-policymaking model engaged every bit as efficiently—arguably more efficiently—than under Truman.

It is also useful to remember that the Cold War intensified and became more complex during Eisenhower's years in office (1953 through January 1961); for instance, the balance of nuclear terror. Consider some of the Cold War confrontations during those years. In 1954, the French were defeated at Dien Bien Phu, at which time the U.S. considered entering Indochina to forestall French defeat to the Viet Minh (the communist Vietnamese). The NSC under Eisenhower's leadership considered using tactical nuclear weapons in Indochina! To Eisenhower's great credit, the president decided that without support from America's allies (notably the British), there existed no reasonable justification for such a momentous act. In 1956, a reelection year for the president, Eisenhower and his NSC faced a three-ring circus. As an editorial cartoonist depicted it that fall, in ring 1 was Eisenhower's reelection; in ring 2, the Suez-Sinai "crisis"; and in ring 3, the Soviets' heavy-handed moves to suppress an uprising in Hungary. Covert operations, effectively organized and managed from the NSC principals, also increased during the Eisenhower years. The U.S. was involved in toppling at least two governments: the government in Iran of Mohammed Mossagdeh, whom the U.S. replaced with the Shah of Iran, and the Arbenz government in Guatemala. There is little doubt that Eisenhower faced extremely important periods of the Cold War between the U.S. and the USSR and did so using the president-NSC-policymaking model to its fullest extent. At least two flare-ups over the Taiwan Straits, between the Nationalist Kuomintang in Taiwan and the Chinese Communist Party in the People's Republic of China, occurred. Importantly, toward the end of Eisenhower's tenure, the Soviets launched Sputnik (1957) resulting in a space race, and the seeds of what would become the Bay of Pigs (implemented under Kennedy) were germinating by Eisenhower's last full year in office.

How did President Eisenhower use the president-NSC-policymaking model compared to President Truman? What innovations did he contribute? How exactly did the model evolve or change under Eisenhower? First, President Eisenhower's NSC principals included Secretary of State John Foster Dulles, who remained in the administration until being incapacitated by cancer in 1959. Following Dulles, Secretary of State Christian Archibald Herter served until President Kennedy's inauguration. Charles E. Wilson served as President Eisenhower's second and last secretary of defense. Secretary of State John F. Dulles' brother, Allen Dulles, served as Eisenhower's director of central intelligence. Second, when Eisenhower campaigned against Truman for the presidency, Eisenhower targeted Truman's NSC structure and management, which Eisenhower believed were ineffectual. As noted, Eisenhower was steeped in the martial traditions of managing soldiers and simply considered the Truman's NSC model a disorganized disaster. Thus very early on—apparently during the transition between presidencies—one of Eisenhower's advisers, Robert Cutler, drafted two memoranda on improving the day-to-day management of the model Eisenhower inherited. Cutler drafted memoranda that implied that the 1947 NSA legislation had been remiss in the composition of the NSC principals. It needed what Cutler called a "Special Assistant to the President for National Security Affairs."[13] The second memo involved what became Eisenhower's Planning Board (PB), an innovation comparable to Truman's Psychological Strategy Board. This was an exclusive group wherein policymaking was to be distinguished from policy implementation. Accordingly, the PB was to collect and present the president with positions on a given challenge as it was viewed by the constituent bureaucracies: state, defense, treasury, and so forth. In short, the Planning Board was the policymaking entity in Eisenhower's president-NSC-policymaking model.

It made good sense to distinguish, for analytic purposes, decision making, which was a function of a relatively exclusive group of persons, from implementation, which involved the vast bureaucratic infrastructure. The NSC itself had been created much more for decision making and policymaking than for implementation. The same 1947 NSA created the necessary bureaucracies to implement important decisions once made. The implementation of policy required, at minimum, scores of people (hundreds of thousands in war). Bureaucratic standard operating procedures and routines and inter- and intraagency coordination guided implementation. Selecting one option from among a handful was a function of an exclusive group and was, therefore, a very different matter. Cutler's idea was to formalize this distinction in reality. This would make management of the president-NSC-policymaking model more efficient, and Cutler was renowned for squeezing efficiencies out of the bureaucracy.

> In effect, the [Planning] Board structured proposals for the National Security Council principals. The council itself was the top . . . of "a pyramid"; others called it "Policy Hill." Here proposals were modified, expanded, often rewritten, distilled, with items that could not be agreed upon passed up to the council. Such disagreements, often called "splits," went to the NSC in the form of alternative language for paragraphs or sentences listed directly in the draft NSC papers.[14]

President Eisenhower's Planning Board was a clear innovation and modification from President Truman's earlier prototype.

A second innovation was the Operations Coordination Board (OCB), in some ways a natural successor to Truman's PSB. The OCB took policies that flowed into it from the PB, staffed the policies for implementation, and followed through to see that implementation was successful. At least two books on the NSC have described Eisenhower's NSC policymaking model as a "policy hill." At the top of the hill was the PB; at the bottom was the OCB. Policy flowed or "rolled" down the hill where the OCB saw to its proper disposition. Though the OCB was created in 1953, President Eisenhower was said to never have been fully satisfied with its operation. Eisenhower apparently saw it, in retrospect, as a place where assistant secretaries of various executive agencies could reargue decisions already made by the NSC principals, thereby keeping a decision alive bureaucratically. He also saw it, retrospectively, as an entity that ultimately exacerbated parochial bureaucratic positions as its members ultimately returned to their respective bureaucratic homes after leaving the OCB.[15]

A third innovation was Eisenhower's penchant for interesting combinations of ad hoc members, many of whom came from outside the government proper. President Eisenhower employed industrialists and accomplished businesspeople as consultants to the NSC. (Eisenhower and Kennedy both used such ad hoc arrangements, which are impractical today due to security clearances and the time it takes to get them.) President Eisenhower also created a professional management structure for the NSC, a staff secretariat. General Pete Carroll served in that role, what Eisenhower called his "sergeant major." Though first in the role, Carroll did not serve long. Instead, Eisenhower's friend, Andrew Jackson Goodpaster, came to the position in 1954 just around the time of one of two Taiwan Straits "crises." A recipient of multiple military distinguished awards, Andrew Goodpaster served President Eisenhower in the role through the remainder of Eisenhower's tenure. Goodpaster turned the job into a liaison between Eisenhower—the office of the presidency—and other NSC principals. Whereas other NSC principals (ad hoc and statutory) were housed in the Old Executive Office Building, Goodpaster was housed in the West Wing of the White House, another precedent.

Though the reader might be tempted to think of Vice President Nixon, who served as vice president for the entirety of the Eisenhower tenure, as an early example of an active and influential vice president in the Eisenhower model, Nixon in fact was not particularly influential. Subsequently, President Nixon became known for his expertise in foreign policy, and after rehabilitation (following Watergate) was generally considered a "wise man" in terms of U.S. foreign policy. In fact, he apparently did not factor into Eisenhower's president-NSC-policymaking model in any significant way. A story frequently retold involved President Eisenhower's assessment of Vice President Nixon while Nixon ran against John Kennedy in the 1960 presidential campaign. When reporters asked President Eisenhower to identify major ideas Nixon had contributed to policy as vice president, Eisenhower answered bluntly: "If you give me a week, I might think of one."[16]

President Eisenhower's version of the president-NSC-policymaking model may be represented graphically as follows. The following graphic represented the model more or less as it appeared over the eight years President Eisenhower served. There were, of course, exceptions and subtle changes over the years as the Cold War tensions waxed and waned.

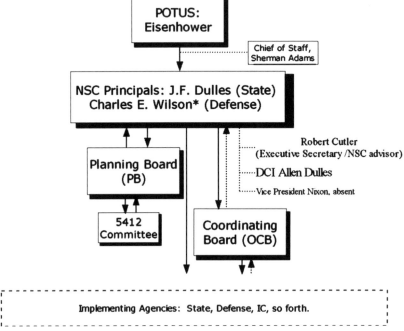

Figure 4.2.   President Eisenhower's president-NSC-policymaking model for his entire eight years. Andrew Goodpaster, though not represented graphically, freelanced
with the president's approval from the NSC principals, to the PB and the OCB. Secretary of State John Foster Dulles became incapacitated by cancer. His effective termination date was April 1959, although he had been ill by that time for a year or
more. Therefore, Dulles's replacement, Christian A. Herter, served during Eisenhower's last nine months in office. Little is written about Mr. Herter's tenure, suggesting he was not very influential in Eisenhower's president-NSC-policymaking
model. Finally, note the 5412 committee, a covert operations entity that has remained more or less part of the NSC ever since.

The secretary of defense was symbolized with an asterisk in the above
graphic. The reasons were twofold. First, General Eisenhower considered
himself his own best adviser with respect to defense. Secondly, during
Eisenhower's presidency three secretaries of defense served him, none of
whose names is particularly familiar even to students of U.S. foreign policy. In chronological order and in order of import they were: Charles E.
Wilson, his best known secretary of defense, who served Eisenhower from
January 28, 1953, through October 8, 1957; Neil H. McElroy, far less
known, who served Eisenhower from October 9, 1957, through December
1, 1959; and Thomas S. Gates, who served President Eisenhower from December 2, 1959, through January 20, 1961, giving Gates the dubious dis-

tinction of being secretary of defense during much of the Bay of Pigs planning. Truman's earlier Psychological Planning Board was folded into the OCB and to a lesser extent the PB. The covert operations that came to typify the Eisenhower administration were largely planned by CIA. Eisenhower's director of central intelligence (DCI) was Allen Dulles, brother of Eisenhower's secretary of state John Foster Dulles. President Eisenhower employed a relatively secret NSC covert-operations committee known as the 5412 Committee. According to David Rothkopf, it was named after the NSC document that created it in 1955, NSC 5412/2.[17]

Under President Eisenhower, the president-NSC-policymaking model found its purpose in U.S. national security policymaking. It became the de facto and permanent locus of high-level policymakers. Under this model, the NSC also conceived of and managed the manifold covert operations that had become used increasingly as instruments of U.S. policy. Covert operations, as originally conceived, were supposed to be plausibly deniable: that is, the president and others could plausibly deny that the United States was involved in some operation, thereby potentially contributing to the confusion of the enemy. As with many such bureaucratic innovations, plausible deniability began with a reasonable premise. Over time, however, presidents and their various advisers came to see plausible deniability as an asset in a different way: for denying something that might prove embarrassing should the American public discover its government's involvement.

President Kennedy: The Personalization of the President-NSC Model

John F. Kennedy's campaign against Eisenhower was that of a young, vibrant, aggressive senator as a candidate against an older—albeit highly respected—man whose glory days had been associated with his military career. President Kennedy's campaign consciously chose to attack Eisenhower's NSC operations as moribund, a characterization that a senate committee, headed by Senator Henry "Scoop" Jackson (D-WA) provided to the Kennedy campaign. The irony, of course, is that Eisenhower had used a similar strategy against Truman. Relative to Eisenhower's storied military career, Kennedy was no Eisenhower but neither was Kennedy a slouch. Kennedy himself had garnered a hero's image for his bravery in the face of danger on a PT boat in the Pacific during World War II. The young senator, who may otherwise have admired Eisenhower, aimed directly at Eisenhower's age. He linked Eisenhower's age and ill health with Eisenhower's version of the president-NSC-policymaking model: the president-NSC-policymaking model was labeled as moribund, and by implication, so too was the man who directed it as chief executive and commander in chief. That Secretary of State John Foster Dulles—in early scholarship seen as the power behind the Eisenhower presidency's policymaking—remained in office while ill may have subliminally helped the Kennedy campaign portray Eisenhower's national security team as tired, aged, and even sick. (In another irony, President Kennedy suffered from a variety of ailments including a reported addiction to prescription drugs.)

Late in Eisenhower's eight years in office Senator "Scoop" Jackson accused Eisenhower of improperly using the president-NSC-policymaking model Congress had given the presidency via the 1947 NSA. Senator Jackson held hearings and prepared a report which provided fodder for candidate Kennedy's campaign salvos. Among other things, the Jackson report made the following observations. "An important question facing the new President . . . is how he will use the [NSC] to suit his own style of decision and action." Jackson suggested that the NSC model had been underutilized in the previous Eisenhower administration—action being the key for a new administration. Senator Jackson characterized the incoming president's choices as twofold:

> *First*, he can use the [NSC] as an intimate forum where he joins with his chief advisers in searching discussions and debate of a limited number of critical problems involving long-term strategic choices or demanding immediate action . . .
>
> *Second*, the President can look upon the [NSC] differently. He can view it as the apex of a highly institutionalized system for generating policy proposals and following through on presidentially approved decisions.

The Jackson report then turned to problems it found under Eisenhower's president-NSC-policymaking model. The meetings were scheduled as routine meetings where participants met once weekly (or whatever the particular schedule was) rather than meeting when the president *needed* the NSC's advice and counsel. It had become too mechanical and did not serve the president well. By implication, Senator Jackson may have been cryptically suggesting that the NSC had met when Eisenhower had the time—that is, when he was not golfing. Additionally, the NSC meetings had grown too large. By implication, again, Jackson may have been playing on the conventional wisdom (wrong as it turned out) that President Eisenhower neglected making his own decisions but rather relied on a large number of statutory and ad hoc principals and deputies as well as staffers to make decisions. "[NSC] meetings should, therefore, be considered gatherings of principals, not staff aides. Staff attendance should be tightly controlled." Finally, Jackson took aim at Eisenhower's Planning Board. "The NSC Planning Board now tends to overshadow in importance, though not prestige, the [NSC] itself. However, some group akin to the present Board, playing a rather different role than it now does, can be of continuing help in the future." The Jackson report also raised an issue of balance in NSC decision making between the historically predominate Department of State and the increasingly important Department of Defense. "The Secretary of State is crucial to the successful operation of the [NSC]. Other officials, particularly the Secretary of Defense, play important parts. But *the President must rely mainly upon the Secretary of State for the initial synthesis of political, military, economic, and other elements that go into the making of a coherent national strategy.*"[18] The creation of the unified defense department by the original 1947 NSA (and 1949 Reorganization Bill) presaged a much more muscular Defense Department in the future of U.S. national security policy. From Secretary Robert S. McNamara (Kennedy's and Johnson's defense secretary) through Donald Rumsfeld (President George W. Bush's first defense secretary) the secretary of defense began to surpass the secretary of state in terms of bureaucratic importance. While secretary of state is arguably still viewed as the most important billet of the U.S. executive agencies, the Department of Defense has become the bureaucratic behemoth. Its budget alone dwarfs the combined budgets of the State Department and the entire intelligence community.

   The Jackson critique became the blueprint for the way President Kennedy would structure and organize his own president-NSC policymaking model upon taking office. The new creation was fitted to the president's image, personality, and decision-making style. Out were the Planning Board and the Operations Coordinating Board. In was an enhanced stature for the NSC advisor (McGeorge Bundy)—which will be recalled was an Eisenhower innovation stemming from one of the two Cutler memoranda—as well as the elevation of military staff into the president's national security staffers. One account refers to them as "servants to the president."[19] Action, not long-range planning, became the hallmark of Kennedy's president-NSC-policymaking model. Unfortunately, as was perhaps inevitable, to the extent that long-range planning was sacrificed for the expediency of short-term, crisis management, the former suffered.

Quite early in his administration, President Kennedy used the model for an operation he inherited from the Eisenhower administration: the use of Cuban Americans and others to launch an uprising in Cuba. Perhaps reflecting the little long-range planning in Kennedy's NSC, his NSC advisers—in a rather large group of ad hoc advisers—considered the Eisenhower plan, made revisions, and disastrously launched the operation in April (fewer than three months into Kennedy's presidency). That "perfect failure" became known as the Bay of Pigs and would haunt the administration for the remainder of its thousand-day tenure. It also caused Kennedy to perform an impromptu reorganization of the president-NSC-policymaking as well as to trim the sails of his inherited DCI and some of his military leaders.

Interestingly, it was in Kennedy's administration that for the first time the president's secretary of defense, Robert S. McNamara, became arguably the most influential NSC principal (statutory or otherwise) at the expense of the secretary of state, Dean Rusk. Indeed, those who have studied the Vietnam War during the Kennedy tenure doubtlessly know that it was called "McNamara's war," not Kennedy's, not Secretary of State Dean Rusk's, and not the war of the highly influential NSC advisor, McGeorge Bundy. Inarguably, Secretary McNamara dramatically increased the influence of the secretary of defense in the president-NSC-policymaking model, jeopardizing the historical "special role" of the secretary of state in foreign affairs.

The neglected long-range planning that resulted in the Bay of Pigs did not result in President Kennedy and his NSC principals lamenting their fate for too long. Some eighteen months later, moreover, the crisis-management focus of Kennedy's president-NSC-policymaking model functioned in the rarified atmosphere of the Cuban Missile Crisis with demonstrably better results. (We should note that scholarship on the Kennedy administration's policymaking brilliance notwithstanding, many of Kennedy's successes during the Cuban Missile Crisis were, as are so many U.S. successes, just plain luck and serendipity.) In October 1962, the Executive Committee of the NSC (known as Excomm) managed the Cuban Missile Crisis much more deftly than had its counterpart during the Bay of Pigs. During the crisis, the Excomm was comprised of Kennedy's NSC principals and additional ad hoc members from state, the Pentagon, and elsewhere, comprising a group of a dozen or more persons at any given time during the roughly two-week event. Importantly, one of Kennedy's ad hoc principals was his attorney general and younger brother, Robert F. Kennedy. The inclusion of the attorney general became another precedent of sorts, as some subsequent administrations have included the attorney general in their NSC principals.

By Kennedy's assassination in November 1963, the president-NSC-policymaking model had undergone noticeable change. Ad hoc NSC committees and configurations surpassed the NSC principals as the preeminent policymaking unit. Said configurations were flexible: depending upon the situation, different experts from different agencies might be invited to attend an ad hoc NSC principals meeting. Kennedy's NSC advisor, McGeorge Bundy, became more the president's personal advisor on national security affairs than an adviser for the presidency. He was intimately involved in the highest levels of policymaking; for instance, he chaired the secretive "303 Committee," which approved covert operations. (The 303 Committee was named after a room in the Old Executive Office Building in which it had once met.) Bundy moved from the OEOB to an office near the Situation Room in the White House, as Andrew Goodpaster had done during Eisenhower's time.

NSC staffers grew in import and influence in terms of hands-on policymaking. The NSC staff had grown slightly over time: in 1963, for example, there were between fifteen and twenty NSC staffers detailed to Kennedy. One scholar of U.S. presidential foreign policy decision making has called Kennedy's model the *collegial model*, suggesting that NSC principals, staffers, and other advisers, had a more or less open door to the president and eschewed the sort of "stovepipes" or formal strictures precluding effective interagency communications that would later become the subject of the 9/11 Commission's final report.[20] On balance, while the action-centered version of the Kennedy president-NSC-policymaking model had its virtues, it had its vices too. Communication may have flowed well between staffers, deputies, principals, and the president, but long-range planning suffered. The Kennedy version of the president-NSC-policymaking model may be represented graphically as follows.

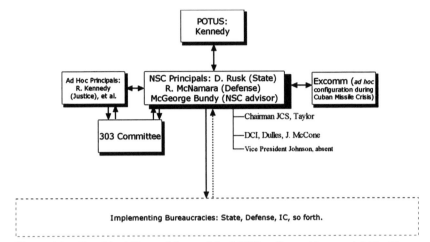

Figure 4.3.   President Kennedy's president-NSC-policymaking model. The Executive Committee of the National Security Council is depicted as an example of the ad hoc configurations characteristic of President Kennedy's president-NSC-policymaking model. Note the 303 committee, a covert-operations and planning committee.

Kennedy's vice president, Lyndon Baines Johnson, would inherit this highly adaptable, highly ad hoc president-NSC-policymaking model when he took the oath of office as Kennedy's death was confirmed. Though Johnson would try to work with it, the assassinated president's model simply did not fit President Johnson's personality and style of policymaking. Perhaps it was inevitable. President Johnson, after all, was not considered or treated as an insider of Kennedy's NSC model. The model he inherited was laden with Kennedy people. Their loyalty to President Johnson therefore may have been suspect. This may have been inevitable for an already suspicious president who became president only because President Kennedy was assassinated at his zenith of power. More NSC changes lay ahead.

President Johnson: Inheritance of the Kennedy Personalized President-NSC-Policymaking Model

Lyndon Baines Johnson became president under extremely trying circumstances. First, he had not been influential in the inner circles of the Kennedy administration's policymaking, despite his statutory membership in the NSC principals. Second, assuming the presidency of an assassinated president who was compellingly popular complicated Johnson's ability to fit into the presidency. Third, Johnson inherited Kennedy's president-NSC-policymaking model, and an array of other advisers from his predecessor, and he was never quite certain of their loyalty. Fourth, he was left with the unenviable task of attempting to pick up the pieces of the disaster known as the Vietnam War, something he was never able to do effectively. Rather, Vietnam became President Johnson's albatross.

A few words about Vietnam are in order. President Kennedy, of course, inherited Indochina from Eisenhower, though the concern then was more about Laos than Vietnam. During Kennedy's tenure the United States deployed upwards of 17,000 U.S. troops in Vietnam, and virtually all of them were sent to Vietnam under the guise of "advisers," "flood workers," or other covers, which allowed Kennedy to violate the Geneva Accords. (North Vietnam also violated the Geneva agreements.) Among the problems that Kennedy left Johnson to deal with was the number of U.S. troops "illegally" deployed in Indochina. President Johnson inherited a number of additional problems. Just weeks before Kennedy was assassinated, President Kennedy's NSC had effectively supported a coup d'état in Saigon. President Ngo Dinh Diem, a holdover in Vietnam from the Eisenhower period, was increasingly dictatorial and aloof, even from his own small constituency (anticommunist Catholics). Diem had become the tail wagging his American patrons' dog.

After a convoluted series of events, including Kennedy and his NSC principals being out of town on a crucial weekend, the United States encouraged military opponents of Diem's in a coup that the Vietnamese had considered hatching earlier. Vice President Johnson was one of the persons in the Kennedy administration whom various authors have characterized as having been against the coup plot.[21] Some scholars have attempted to portray the Kennedy administration as divided neatly between those who supported the coup and those who opposed it. More accurately, all his advisers thought that Diem was more or less hopeless. Their real division came in terms of whether they believed that South Vietnam needed to take demonstrable action first, before the U.S. could realistically commit more resources, and those who believed the U.S. needed to take demonstrable action first and commit more resources in order to demonstrate to Diem that the U.S. was fully behind him. For present purposes, such fine distinctions matter little. What can be said is that Johnson was not a member of the group often described as being eager to find a more pliable client in Vietnam.

The coup began a series of additional coups and Vietnam quickly devolved into a mess of incredible proportions. Ultimately, Johnson would Americanize the war by openly sending U.S. troops in vastly larger numbers, and with Congress's tacit approval (the Tonkin Gulf Resolution). The point is this: from about 1955 through 1975, there was never a good time to inherit another president's Vietnam policy, as Vietnam was a rats' nest of problems. But Johnson suffered from the rare distinction of inheriting Vietnam at one of the worst possible times in that twenty-year period.

Johnson simply was not well-adapted to fit Kennedy's rather freewheeling president-NSC-policymaking model. Whatever one wishes to think about Kennedy, Johnson could not have been much more different in personality. Johnson was smart, but more street-smart than intellectual. He had risen through rough-and-tumble Texas politics to gain a key leadership role in the United States Senate. He could be charming, self-effacing, and occasionally magnanimous. He could as easily be a bully: he took pleasure in humiliating subordinates—and when one is the U.S. president virtually everyone else is a subordinate—simply to demonstrate that he had the power to do so. Legendary stories have Johnson walking one of his cabinet officers or advisers—say McGeorge Bundy—into the water closet, where Johnson would relieve himself, forcing the adviser to continue whatever dialogue was taking place. Johnson was much more comfortable in his former position in the Senate, where deals were brokered and agreements were made through reciprocity, quid pro quo, and the "old boys" network, than as president.

Thus, Kennedy's president-NSC-policymaking model invariably changed under President Johnson, but it changed slowly and incrementally. One change was a diminution of the NSC advisor, McGeorge Bundy, who was later elevated again as Vietnam continued to grow in relevance and consumption of U.S resources. In 1965, Bundy was sent to the Dominican Republic during a fracas in which he basically made U.S. foreign policy in situ by acting as a temporary proconsul (a precedent of sorts). Another change was in the NSC staff, which had grown influential during Kennedy's tenure. The NSC staff's influence became considerably diminished under Johnson. Johnson preferred smaller meetings with fewer advisers. Perhaps he felt he could force consensus in smaller groups. Perhaps he simply did not have the confidence to debate every detail of every issue with the type of NSC staffers Kennedy's administration drew to government work. Whatever the reasons, President Johnson reconfigured the president-NSC-policymaking model over time rather than in one or two major reorganizations. In one of his best-known innovations, President Johnson created an ad hoc group of NSC principals and other advisers (some of whom were not actively serving in U.S. government) in what became known as "Tuesday Lunches." In that sense, Johnson followed the Eisenhower and Kennedy precedents of inviting important "outsiders" into the hallowed halls of policymaking, regularizing a process of ad hoc entities attached to the NSC model—a bit of an oxymoron.

"Tuesday Lunches" for Johnson were semiformal affairs but they were comprised of a small group of individuals orchestrated by the president. One of the principal differences between Kennedy's and Johnson's president-NSC-policymaking models was that the Tuesday Lunches normally *excluded* NSC staffers. There was no systematic way for the attendees to involve staffers in terms of presidential priorities and preferences in a given situation. There were no staffers to take notes memorializing things said or decisions made. The NSC staff therefore withered as the Tuesday Lunches replaced Kennedy's open-door policy with NSC staffers.

Over time, the "best and the brightest," who had sojourned to Washington to work for Kennedy, left the Johnson administration one by one. NSC advisor McGeorge Bundy left the administration in late 1966. It was a most inconvenient time to leave and therefore likely indicated a certain estrangement between Johnson and McGeorge Bundy. Secretary of Defense McNamara left in early 1968, which similarly reflects duress and estrangement. While many of the aforementioned differences between Kennedy and Johnson may plausibly account for the number of former Kennedy inner-circle advisers abandoning the Johnson national security team, Vietnam was clearly a cause of tremendous tension from 1965 until Nixon replaced Johnson in January 1969. President Johnson's version of the president-NSC-policymaking model is represented below graphically. Apart from those changes already noted, it had few major innovations. Rather, it was largely adapted from the Kennedy model President Johnson inherited, then adjusted slightly and incrementally to fit the new president's personality.

By the end of the Johnson administration, of course, the Vietnam War had become fully "Americanized." Some 500,000-plus U.S. troops were fighting in Vietnam and the U.S. was no closer to its goal of forestalling a

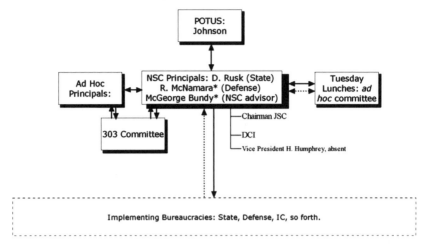

**Figure 4.4. President Johnson's president-NSC-policymaking model. Conceptu-
alize the Johnson model as an incremental adaptation of the Kennedy model in the
previous section. President Johnson used ad hoc configurations that became so
formalized they could scarcely be considered ad hoc after a time. Asterisks next
to Secretary McNamara's and NSC advisor McGeorge Bundy's names are indicative of the changes during Johnson's tenure of just over three years. Specifically,
McGeorge Bundy's deputy Walt Rostow became Bundy's successor. The ubiquitous Clark Clifford (see Truman administration) replaced Secretary of Defense
McNamara in early 1968 following the Tet Offensive.**

communist takeover of South Vietnam than it was when Johnson replaced
Kennedy. Johnson had become tremendously frustrated over the war; consequently he turned with increasing frequency to a smaller group of advisers whose views approximated his own, thereby obviating a main justification for the president-NSC-policymaking model. Clark Clifford, a
trusted Johnson adviser who replaced McNamara as secretary of defense
following the Tet Offensive, also began to turn against the war. By the end
Johnson turned inward and became a caricature of the larger-than-life gre-
garious personality who replaced the assassinated President Kennedy. The
president-NSC-policymaking model perforce became dysfunctional.
Speaking of dysfunctional, President Richard Millhouse Nixon would
soon get his chance to put his distinct imprimatur on the president-NSC-
policymaking model.

President Nixon: An Aberration of the President-NSC Model

Richard Millhouse Nixon was Eisenhower's vice president for eight
years. Similar to Johnson, Nixon had risen to prominence in western pol-

itics, had come to the attention of his party, and eventually paid his dues in state and national office. Few rise to such prominence without sullying themselves at some point along the way. Nixon sullied himself repeatedly. Richard Nixon made a name for himself by attacking his political opponents. In California politics he used a classic Red-baiting strategy to overwhelm his opponents. Jerry Voorhis and Helen Douglas (the "pink lady") were just two who found themselves on the wrong end of a Nixon campaign. By the 1950s, Nixon was a rising star in the Republican Party (at least in one of its wings). His years as Eisenhower's vice president burnished his image as an expert on foreign policy.

It is instructive to consider Nixon's management style (presumably a function of his personality and life experiences) briefly before examining his formulation of the president-NSC-policymaking model. Nixon was raised in California, in a rural part of southern California. He had a sickly brother, a father whose relationship with his sons has been subject to much speculation, and a mother who was a Quaker. A good student in his cohort, Nixon longed for bigger things. Volumes have been written on Nixon's personality, his distaste for personal confrontation (interestingly since he used the politics of confrontation in many campaigns), and his resentment of East Coast establishment types and the products of Ivy League educations. In the early post–World War II period, both the State Department and CIA were staffed by many from those groups. Nixon's disdain towards (coupled with jealousy of) the bureaucrats was evidenced early and often in his career. By the time he became president, it was clear Nixon continued to harbor ill will toward the professional bureaucracy that would implement his policies.[22]

It is no insignificant matter, given Nixon's aversion to Ivy League liberals, that Nixon chose one of the eastern establishment's brightest, Dr. Henry A. Kissinger, to be his NSC advisor. Kissinger had for years careened around the corridors of power between Washington, D.C., Boston, and New York working with Democrats *and* Republicans. He worked briefly in the Kennedy and Johnson administrations. (Though beyond the scope of this book, he has been accused, in effect, of spying for then-candidate Nixon on Johnson's "peace talks" with Hanoi, with the implication that his position once Nixon was elected was a sort of quid pro quo for his duplicity.[23]) Though recognized as a talent, his political career had never amounted to much—though the opposite is true of his academic career. That would change with Nixon's election.

Nixon and Kissinger both believed that the liberal elite had unfairly abandoned Johnson with respect to Vietnam. Nixon's connection to Vietnam, of course, dated to the Eisenhower days, so he had a personal stake in Vietnam's outcome. Further, Nixon was on record as suggesting an Eisenhower-like solution for Vietnam: namely, when Eisenhower inherited Korea from Truman, President Eisenhower let it be known that he would consider using nuclear weapons if necessary to end the conflict. Nixon apparently believed this had caused the North Koreans (and their Chinese allies) to exercise more prudence. Nixon believed a similar feint might be used vis-à-vis North Vietnam. Eventually this suggestion became known as Nixon's "madman" theory, sometimes referred to as the "mad bomber" theory. Upon telling his chief of staff and one of his chief domestic and foreign advisers, H. R. "Bob" Haldeman, about it, he suggested that Hanoi needed simply to be made to believe that Nixon was mad enough to use nuclear weapons to end the war "honorably." "I call it the Madman Theory, Bob. I want the North Vietnamese to believe I've reached the point where I might do anything to stop the war. We'll just slip the word to them that, 'for God's sake, you know Nixon is obsessed about Communism. We can't restrain him when he's angry—and he has his hand on the nuclear button'—and Ho Chi Minh himself will be in Paris in two days begging for peace."[24]

Upon being elected, the president-elect set about putting together his president-NSC-policymaking model with the critical choice of Henry Kissinger as his collaborator, if not coconspirator. "I planned to direct foreign policy from the White House. Therefore, I regarded my choice of National Security Advisor as crucial," wrote Nixon.[25] Nixon selected William Rogers, a personal friend, to be secretary of state. He chose Melvin Laird, a man with some of his own credentials in public service, as secretary of defense. Nixon's vice president, Spiro Agnew, was a firebrand and might, under different circumstances, have become an active member of Nixon's president-NSC-policymaking model. However, Agnew found himself enmeshed in constant controversy and eventually left the administration under suspicion of impropriety. H. R. "Bob" Haldeman's diaries made clear that Nixon never connected with Agnew and that from Nixon's perspective, Agnew never understood the role that was expected of him as vice president, namely, to do the president's bidding and take the flack for it.[26]

During the transition from Johnson to Nixon, Richard Nixon assigned Kissinger to draft a plan for structuring his president-NSC-policymaking model that essentially recreated it as a national security (foreign policy) decision-making duopoly: Nixon and Kissinger. As a personal Nixon friend, Secretary of State Rogers may have thought his friendship with Nixon would protect Rogers's influence. Rogers was known to be easily bored by excessive staff and briefing papers and it is likely the case that Nixon thought Rogers sufficiently disinterested in the process of the state department that Rogers would be no obstacle for the truncated structure Nixon hatched. Whatever Rogers may have thought, Nixon plans were clear. Nixon considered himself a statesman of some import. Rogers's own credentials paled by comparison—and also paled in comparison to Kissinger's credentials. With a weak secretary of state, Nixon therefore "effectively displace[d] the secretary of state from any meaningful role and substitute[d] the national security adviser in his place" under Nixon's tutelage.[27]

Laird turned out to be a tougher nut to crack. In short order, however, even Laird was effectively sidelined leaving Nixon and Kissinger to make national security policy for the United States. Kissinger employed bright people to help him create the aberration that Nixon desired. Morton Halperin, for instance, was one who drafted the plan to ensure the NSC would supplant the state department. Halperin later left the administration in frustration and subsequently sued Kissinger for illegally bugging Halperin's phone. Together, this team of academics and politicians created a president-NSC-policymaking model never contemplated by the drafters of the 1947 NSA. To cite one significant example of how Rogers and Laird were circumvented, just two months following Nixon's inauguration (in March 1969), Nixon and Kissinger essentially bypassed both the state department and much of the defense department, working through various back channels including the U.S. Ambassador to Cambodia (a Rogers subordinate) to bomb Cambodia secretly in what became know as the Menu and Breakfast bombings. To isolate pesky bureaucrats in Defense who had to account for the use of bombs and bombers, Nixon and Kissinger developed a creative and complex accounting process.[28]

The premise of the structure was streamlining: streamline the NSC principals, streamline the interagency ad hoc meetings, and streamline the interaction between Nixon and NSC staffers. Alexander George described

Nixon's presidential-NSC model as highly "formalistic model" with Nixon heading "by far the most centralized and highly structured" president-NSC-policymaking model of any president before him. George further noted that its purpose, beyond preventing personal confrontation and policymaking inertia "was to enhance and protect [Nixon's] personal control over high policy."[29] Streamlined it was. With Nixon at the apex of decision making, Kissinger effectively acted as Nixon's national security vicar. Virtually all national security matters perforce flowed from the top down to the implementing agency, circumventing to a large extent the secretaries of state and defense and the uniformed military. The model was comprised of six special committees: the Vietnam Special Studies Group, the Special Actions Group (for foreign policy crisis management), the Defense Programs and Review Committee, the Verification Panel or Committee (for strategic arms limitation talks or SALT), the 40 Committee (similar to Kennedy's and Johnson's 303 Committee for covert operations), and the Senior Review Group (an umbrella committee for virtually all other national security matters). All significant and important information dealing with U.S. foreign policy was thereby channeled through one of the six committees, all of which Kissinger chaired, and thereafter was channeled directly to the apex of the Nixon-Kissinger duopoly.[30]

The model was simple, clean, avoided bureaucratic policymaking pathologies, and was basically unconstitutional. Nor did it follow the contours of the 1947 NSA. A good description of the way the presidential-NSC model functioned under Nixon was provided by two scholars of presidential decision making, Crabb and Mulcahy.

> The National Security Council Staff, under the direction of Henry Kissinger, emerged as not simply a claimant for presidential attention in foreign policy machinery but as the principal vehicle for the articulation and implementation of the administration's objectives.[31]

By staff, Crabb and Mulcahy do not mean the traditional NSC "staffers." Rather, they are talking about Henry Kissinger's staffers—a nuanced but important distinction. NSC staffers, as we have seen, are professionals whose tenure with the NSC is not necessarily conterminous with a given administrations. Of course, NSC staffers existed in the Nixon presidential-NSC-policymaking model. But Kissinger hired a team of bright academics and policy wonks who essentially came to work for Nixon by way of

Kissinger, a precedent begun under Presidents Kennedy and Eisenhower. These staffers, though professional, were selected by Kissinger and/or sometimes Nixon specifically to fit the president's or Kissinger's views of how the president-NSC-policymaking model should operate in the Nixon aberration of the model.[32] Other authors distinguished the large NSC staff that evolved during the Nixon years in terms of professionals (those whom Kissinger primarily assembled) versus support staffers. "Another instrument for exerting control was the high-powered NSC staff Kissinger had assembled. With some fifty professionals and eighty support personnel, it was the largest staff in the Council's history."[33] President Nixon's version of the president-NSC-policymaking model may be represented graphically as follows.

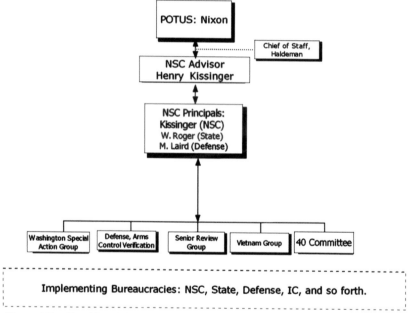

Figure 4.5.   President Nixon's president-NSC-policymaking model. Though Haldeman is represented, as have been previous chiefs of staff, with a dashed line (indicative of no direct NSC connection), in fact, in the Nixon-Kissinger duopoly, Haldeman was a policymaker, both foreign and domestic.

It was, by all accounts, a unique presidential-NSC-policymaking model. According to many, it functioned in exemplary fashion in terms of outcomes, if not always in terms of the U.S. Constitution and/or statutes. It generated reams of National Security Study Memoranda (NSSMs). The memoranda were effective in making the bureaucracy function and think in new ways about old problems, the sorts of long-term planning President Kennedy's model lacked. In addition to having an active role in policy formulation, Kissinger as the NSC advisor (and later as both NSC advisor and secretary of state) became the public face of the behemoth bureaucracy behind him and Nixon. Kissinger became a high-profile NSC advisor, shuttling between the Middle East and various capitals, Moscow and Washington, and eventually Beijing and Washington. Indeed, the term *shuttle diplomacy* was created to describe one of Kissinger's modes of operation. Diplomacy, of course, is the traditional turf of the Department of State. It is therefore instructive that shuttle diplomacy during the Nixon presidency was largely absent the secretary of state—at least until Dr. Kissinger replaced Rogers. In the end, however, Nixon's peculiar personality may have made nearly inevitable the system's demise. Secret policymaking has the clear virtue of avoiding bureaucratic bottlenecks and turf wars. In tiptoeing along lines of legality, however, one is likely to cross them at some point. As is well-known, Nixon eventually resigned (August 9, 1974) and then-Vice President Gerald R. Ford was left to pick up the NSC pieces in Nixon's wake.

President Ford: Restoration of the President-NSC-Policymaking Model

We earlier discussed the situation Johnson inherited when President Kennedy was assassinated. In short, President Johnson inherited a mess that was scarcely of his own making. President Ford inherited a similar mess, though Nixon resigned rather than dying by an assassin's bullet. Sworn into office upon Nixon's resignation, Ford inherited a broken president-NSC-policymaking model as well as a broken country. He inherited Vietnam after the 1973 Paris Accords, the putative peace deal brokered by Kissinger, but before Congress completely turned off the funding spigot. President Gerald R. Ford inherited not just Vietnam but the expanded war in all of Indochina. Nixon's and Kissinger's plan to win peace with honor apparently involved invading two additional countries (Laos and Cambodia) and cutting deals of dubious providence with the North Vietnamese. Though much of the country's Vietnam backlash occurred late in Johnson's administration, the "incursion" into Cambodia during Nixon's tenure (spring 1970) and its aftermath (e.g., Kent State) rent the fabric of American civil society.

All this and more was waiting for the former University of Michigan football player and former congressional leader, Gerald Ford, as Nixon flew back to his San Clemente, California home in disgrace.

In some texts, President Ford's administration doesn't warrant a separate chapter. After all, Ford assumed the presidency upon Nixon's resignation and was never elected to the presidency in his own right. He inherited Nixon's NSC machinery and did little to alter it on paper, though ultimately he put it back together as it existed only in theory under President Nixon. Ford also inherited the end of the Vietnam War, a collective blight on the U.S. policy of containment that included an ignominious withdrawal in spring 1975. Due to his short tenure and the fact that he did so little to alter the president-NSC-policymaking model, many scholars and authors simply append a section for President Ford to their chapters on Nixon. Here, President Ford shall be treated in the same way as his peers.

It is worth spending a few moments considering the procedural alterations President Ford made. President Ford, for many complex reasons, perhaps including the circumstances of his presidency and his relative lack of foreign policy experience, largely deferred to his inherited NSC principals. Former NSC advisor Henry Kissinger became secretary of state by the time President Ford inherited the presidency. Kissinger's former deputy, Brent Scowcroft, became President Ford's NSC advisor. President Ford inherited a relatively influential, certainly strong-willed secretary of defense, James Schlesinger, who replaced Melvin Laird late in the Nixon presidency (July 1973). Secretary of Defense Schlesinger remained as President Ford's secretary of defense until he was replaced by Donald Rumsfeld in late November 1975. Secretary Schlesinger headed the Defense Department under one of the Ford administration's more intense national security tests, the *Mayaguez* incident. Secretary Rumsfeld served President Ford from fall 1975 (after the *Mayaguez* fiasco) through the remainder of Ford's tenure until January 1977. Given the circumstances in which Gerald Ford became president, it was not terribly surprising that President Ford listened carefully to his statutory NSC principals for most national security decisions. In so doing, President Ford importantly reestablished the president-NSC-policymaking model which under Nixon had secretly been abolished.

Another reason for examining the Ford administration was that it evidenced one of this text's secondary theses: overall continuity in the president-NSC-policymaking model yet with idiosyncratic changes that occurred from president to president incrementally and gradually. Obviously, the initial president-NSC-policymaking model under President Ford represented continuity. Secretary of State Kissinger, NSC advisor Brent Scowcroft, and Secretary of Defense Schlesinger were all inherited from President Nixon's model. President Ford chose a young rising star in the Republican Party, Dick Cheney, to be his chief of staff. The reader may be surprised to learn that current Vice President Dick Cheney served as President Ford's chief of staff while George W. Bush's first Secretary of Defense Donald Rumsfeld served as President Ford's secretary of defense. They became close friends, which helps to explain much about the George W. Bush administration. It also demonstrates a truism of both the Republican and Democratic parties: there is tremendous intellectual incest, for lack of a better term, when it comes to America's national security and policymaking gene pool. The same names turn up again and again in Democratic and Republican administrations over time.

President Ford kept Henry Kissinger as his secretary of state, a move that represented continuity and also continued reliance on Kissinger as the architect in chief of U.S. national security. Kissinger, as noted, was initially the NSC advisor under Nixon and, as such, was perhaps the most influential NSC advisor in America's history. At one point, Kissinger was both NSC advisor and secretary of state. Shortly thereafter, however, this perceived imbalance was corrected by limiting Kissinger to the secretary of state's portfolio. Upon Kissinger becoming secretary of state his then-deputy, Brent Scowcroft, replaced him. President Ford therefore inherited a stellar NSC advisor in Brent Scowcroft. Some have argued that Scowcroft was simply Kissinger's alter ego; his subsequent record (below in the George H. W. Bush administration) should disabuse the reader of that oversimplification. Scowcroft provided steady leadership, whether he deferred to Kissinger or not. James Schlesinger, inherited from Nixon, was a strong-willed, influential policymaker in his own right. Schlesinger and Kissinger, unsurprisingly, clashed on a variety of issues. As an influential person in terms of the president-NSC-policymaking model under President Ford, Secretary Schlesinger's days were numbered. There simply was not enough room in the situation room or anywhere the NSC principals met to contain both Kissinger's and Schlesinger's egos. Interestingly, at first William Colby continued as Ford's director of central intelligence, the head of CIA and titular head of all of America's disparate intelligence agencies created in the original 1947 statute. William Colby eventually was sacrificed for political expediency whereupon the then relatively un-known George H. W. Bush became Ford's DCI for about one year. Filling out the principals, Ford's chairman of the Joint Chiefs of Staff was the United States Air Force's, General David Jones and his vice president, though not particularly influential in national security policymaking, was Nelson Rockefeller.[34]

A few important points are worth making when assessing the Ford ad-ministration's president-NSC-policymaking model. First, unlike most pres-idents, Ford did not get the roughly eighty-day transition period during which presidents normally cobbled together their domestic or foreign poli-cymaking teams. Second and similarly, due to the circumstances under which Ford became president, he was denied any "honeymoon" period, a period of less intense criticism that presidents often receive. (As seen below, President George W. Bush also experienced this oddity, for different reasons entirely.) Third, Ford became president under extreme circumstances when the nation was deeply split over Vietnam (and arguably over the projection of American power in the post–Vietnam War world). Fourth, as noted, Ford inherited his presidential-NSC-policymaking team more or less intact from Nixon. Finally, Ford saw his own role in minimal terms. That is, Ford real-ized he came to office with no particular mandate. In his memoirs President Ford noted that "he had no mandate from the people, and [that] the Con-gress" understood this reality as did many Americans.[35]

Recall that Ford had only been Nixon's vice president for some eight months when he was thrust into the presidency by Nixon's resignation. Thus, in addition to inheriting Nixon's cabinet and presidential-NSC-policymaking model, Ford inherited operations begun under Nixon—and those went well beyond Vietnam. One operation begun during Nixon's presidency was a plot to recover a Soviet submarine that had sunk some six years earlier. The question was how. Eventually, Nixon bought into a scheme (partially and somewhat dubiously funded by Howard Hughes) in which a sophisticated spy ship, the *Glomar Explorer*, was disguised as a research vessel, outfitted with the newest technology, and employed to reach the submarine deep in the ocean (some 16,000 feet below the sur-face). On Ford's second morning as president, he was informed in his morning briefing (a function of NSC advisor Brent Scowcroft as well as an official from CIA) of the operation. Apparently, the Soviets were onto the ruse and following the *Explorer* with some interest. As has been seen with many vice presidents, Ford was not included in the inner circles of policymakers when the ruse was launched. President Ford, understandably, deferred to his NSC advisor and the CIA expert on the matter since he had virtually no basis of understanding.

In May 1975, an important event occurred which illustrated the procedural alterations Ford made in Nixon's president-NSC-policymaking model. On May 12, 1975, a merchant ship, the *Mayaguez*, was seized in the Gulf of Thailand not far from Cambodia. (It is important to realize that the U.S. had left Indochina, including Vietnam and Cambodia, just weeks earlier.) The SOS signal sent from the ship was relayed to the U.S. military's national military command center and thence to the Situation Room at the White House where Brent Scowcroft received the news upon his arrival at work that morning. Scowcroft and David Peterson (CIA) prepared a morning brief for President Ford. The same two had briefed the president months earlier on the *Glomar Explorer*.[36] President Ford viewed it as a "very serious matter" particularly as the U.S. had so recently left Indochina under duress. The president believed that the U.S. had been "humiliated" by its retreat from Indochina, magnifying the importance of the current seizure. Around the same time Ford was being briefed by Scowcroft, Secretary Kissinger was briefed through his own apparatus at the State Department. According to one report, Kissinger became "extremely concerned and called the president at once." Kissinger apparently made the quick trip to the White House (a short drive from Foggy Bottom), because he met with Brent Scowcroft for twenty-five minutes just a short while later. Both Kissinger and Scowcroft met with President Ford in the Oval Office at around 0930 (about two hours from the time Scowcroft and Peterson had briefed President Ford). As a result of this initial meeting with Kissinger and Scowcroft, President Ford called what would become the first of four NSC meetings during the affair for around noon.[37] At least one scholar who studied the *Mayaguez* incident noted that it was Kissinger who instructed President Ford to hold the meeting rather than the reverse.[38]

The attendees were President Ford, who chaired the meeting; Vice President Nelson Rockefeller (more a formality than for substantive reasons); Secretary of State Kissinger; Defense Secretary James Schlesinger; DCI William Colby; the chairman (interim) of the Joint Chiefs of Staff, David Jones; and a few other individuals President Ford asked to attend the meeting, including his then-assistant, Donald Rumsfeld. In all, there were eleven attendees.[39] In this first NSC meeting, Secretary Kissinger apparently took the lead. Kissinger "argued strongly" that the stakes were high. This was more than a simple act of piracy! Kissinger argued that America's image, its perception as a world power, and the principles of American will were being severely tested. Kissinger was not the only one who felt more than mere piracy was at stake—as noted, Ford himself considered the matter serious. Others were concerned that the Korean peninsula was ripe for trouble given America's withdrawal from Indochina. References to the seizure of the U.S. spy platform the *USS Pueblo* were made.[40] (The *Pueblo* was a NSA spy platform and vessel that was captured by the North Koreans in 1968 and held for roughly a year.)

Three additional NSC meeting were held over the next two days and nights, in addition to more informal ad hoc meetings—one of these important meetings was held at the White House with Ford meeting with Kissinger and Scowcroft with Secretary Schlesinger participating by phone. The *Mayaguez* incident ended badly and perhaps little could have been done to change the ultimate outcome. The U.S. eventually launched punitive strikes against Cambodia, though there was plausible evidence that it was not the Khmer Rouge in Cambodia (America's former enemy during the Vietnam War) who had ordered the ship seized but, rather, simply a commander (or even a local pirate) acting on his own. The *Mayaguez* incident illustrated how central Kissinger and Brent Scowcroft were to Ford's president-NSC-policymaking model during what the principals considered a relatively high-stakes national security event. That is, it demonstrates how Ford had reestablished and rebalanced the president-NSC-policymaking model. Apparently, efforts were made to include the secretary of defense as well thus returning the NSC process to what its founder intended. Oddly, the person who ultimately raised the possibility of a renegade commander directing the seizure of the ship rather than high Khmer Rouge official was not a Ford NSC or national security advisor at all. Presidential photographer David Hume Kennerly spoke up while shooting pictures of the Ford administration policymaking apparatus in action.[41] Kennerly turned out to be correct.

Clearly, President Ford deferred to Secretary Kissinger. That would seem a natural enough tendency under the circumstances. President Ford realized his own national security experience paled in comparison to Kissinger's. Kissinger controlled the State Department and was at the apogee of his power in government. Ford characterized Kissinger as "superb" in his memoirs and he noted further that he considered Schlesinger brilliant but somewhat suspect in terms of interacting with the administration and, importantly, Congress, which Ford knew full well needed to be assuaged following Vietnam.[42] Eventually Secretaries Kissinger and Schlesinger both entered into internecine, bureaucratic turf battles between their respective departments, very likely serving President Ford poorly. The net result was Secretary Schlesinger replacement by a young presidential assistant, Donald Rumsfeld, who became the youngest secretary of defense to date (November 20, 1975). In any case, President Ford's president-NSC-policymaking model, adopted from Nixon but formally reestablished so that it followed the 1947 statute, may be represented as follows.

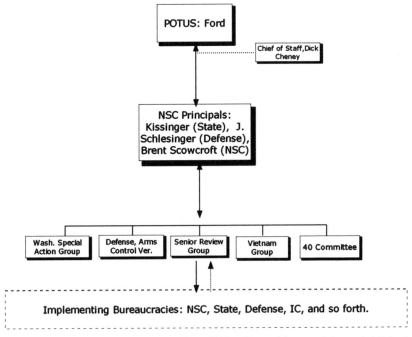

Figure 4.6.   President Ford's president-NSC-policymaking model, reestablished after the Nixon aberration.

It is important to note that President Ford's version actually operated largely as it appeared graphically whereas Nixon's looked one way on paper and functioned entirely differently in reality; the latter was intended to be a sleight of hand by its two practitioners. President Ford restored the NSC process to something the 1947 drafters would have recognized.

President Ford ran for election to the presidency but lost to newcomer Jimmy Carter. Whether Ford would have eventually put his own signature on the president-NSC-policymaking model is impossible to know. We can say that President Ford altered the NSC more or less as his predecessors (Eisenhower and Kennedy) had with minor adaptations for style. President Ford was the commander in chief but was comfortable enough to defer to Secretary of State Henry Kissinger. With Brent Scowcroft as Ford's perspicacious NSC advisor (far more behind the scenes than in front) President Ford returned the president-NSC-policymaking model to the balance and natural stability that it had obtained before President Nixon.

President Carter: A New Equilibrium in the President-NSC-Policymaking Model?

James E. "Jimmy" Carter was a new president with a new way of looking at national security and foreign policy. He had been governor of Georgia, was a former U.S. Navy nuclear engineer, and had cultivated national contacts while coming up through the Georgia state Democratic apparatus. When he broke onto the national stage he was a little-known man with a famous smile, a self-effacing style, and a seemingly earnest desire to return U.S. national security to its democratic roots. President Carter attempted to deemphasize the imperial presidency image that had developed during the Nixon administration. Moreover, he campaigned for and in fact acted to change the equilibrium of the president-NSC-policymaking model: for Carter, the Nixon-Kissinger duopoly was to blame for much of what had gone wrong in Vietnam and elsewhere. President Carter aimed to correct the disequilibrium he perceived by bringing the Department of State, the Department of Defense, the CIA, and the NSCl advisor formally back into a more balanced alignment.

President Carter had cultivated contacts in the policymaking and academic communities by way of the Trilateral Commission, a group of "wise" men and women who focused on North-South relations. The Trilateral Commission was similar to the Council on Foreign Relations, an older and broader version that represented U.S. national security orthodoxy and bipartisan consensus. Zbigniew Brzezinski was Governor Carter's entrée to the Trilateral Commission. Apparently both men consciously cultivated the other, which ultimately served them both well. It was therefore unsurprising when Carter eventually chose Brzezinski to be his NSC advisor. What may have been surprising is that Carter apparently believed that Brzezinski could be fitted into a lower-profile conceptualization of the NSC advisor. Carter believed Kissinger and Nixon had acted more like "Lone Rangers" than particularly good stewards of America's national security. Alas, Carter would learn that Brzezinski could not be fitted into the balanced, behind-the-scenes version of the president-NSC-policymaking model that Carter, at least initially, hoped to recreate. It simply was not in Brzezinski's style. For his secretary of state, President Carter chose the mild-mannered "lawyerly" Cyrus Vance. President Carter selected a former Pentagon "whiz kid" and intellectual, Harold Brown, to be his secretary of defense. Filling out the main ranks of President Carter's president-NSC-policymaking model were Carter's vice president, Walter "Fritz" Mondale and the somewhat unlikely Stansfield Turner (retired admiral) as his director of central intelligence (DCI). In selecting Admiral Turner, President Carter selected a fellow navy peer who was a member of the Christian Science faith.

President Carter made explicit his foreign policy aims upon inauguration. In Presidential Directive (PD)/NSC 2—known, previously, as National Security Action Memoranda (NSAMs) and National Security Decision Memoranda (NSDMs)—Carter identified those whom the president would expect to attend the NSC principals meetings as follows: the president, *the vice president*, the secretaries of state and defense, the chairman of the Joint Chiefs of Staff, and the DCI (that is, the so-called statutory principals); as well as the secretary of the treasury, the attorney general (the justice department), the U.S. ambassador to the United Nations, and eight additional cabinet secretaries. To quote PD/NSC 2, under the subject heading of "The National Security Council System," President Carter intended the aforementioned to "assist [Carter] in carrying out [his] responsibilities for the conduct of national security affairs." Further, President Carter thereby directed "the reorganization of the National Security Council system. The reorganization [was] intended to place more responsibility in the departments and agencies while insuring [*sic*] that the NSC, with [Carter's] Assistant for National Security Affairs, continued to integrate and facilitate foreign and defense policy decisions." How much reorganization PD/NSC 2 actually constituted was subject to debate. Nevertheless, in the president's view it constituted a significant reorganization.

Importantly, the same PD directed that two principals' committees would exist henceforth. The first was the "NSC Policy Review Committee" (or PRC as it has been called in other analyses[43]) "to develop national security policy for Presidential decisions in those cases where the basic responsibilities" fell "primarily within a given department but where the subject also ha[d] important implications for other departments and agencies." The chairman of the NSC Policy Review Committee would be designated by President Carter depending on the nature of the matter brought before the committee and its propinquity to a given department's or agency's mission. For instance, a "primarily" military matter would be brought before the PRC and presumably chaired by the secretary of defense.[44] Given the ad hoc determination of who was the chair in a given situation, it is reasonable to assume that an aggressive and ambitious NSC advisor might have viewed the PRC as less than an ideal venue in which to exert his particular influence. Since Brzezinski was not going to be the chair of the PRC on a consistent basis, he may reasonably have looked elsewhere to exercise his influence. Further, given Carter's intellect, it is reasonable to believe Carter too intended the PRC as such: neither his NSC advisor nor anybody else was likely to dominate the PRC with a frequently rotating chair.

The second principals' committee contemplated by President Carter in PD/NSC 2 was the Special Coordination Committee (SCC). The SCC was intended "to deal with specific cross-cutting issues requiring coordination in the development of options and implementation of Presidential Decisions." (One may reasonably ask whether that was not the role of the NSC as contemplated by the drafters of the 1947 NSA in the first place.) Accordingly, the SCC would deal with "oversight of sensitive intelligence activities, such as covert operations," and "arms control evaluation" and, importantly, "crisis management." Carter designated the NSC advisor as the chair of the SCC.[45] The SCC clearly dealt with both policy selection and policy implementation. Structured as such, the SCC permitted its members and especially its chair, Brzezinski, to wield power over both policy process and implementation—to be sure, an important guarantee of Brzezinski's influence overall in policymaking and specifically in the president-NSC-policymaking model. It also gave an incentive—at least from Brzezinski's viewpoint—to ensure that matters often were seen in terms of crisis management rather than more broadly! Finally, it suggested a dearth of long-range planning similar to that which had characterized President Kennedy's model discussed above.

Importantly, as far as we can determine Carter was the first modern president to actually rely on his vice president, Walter Mondale, for policy advice. Mondale was said to have had incredible access to Carter and the president-NSC-policymaking model. Perhaps presaging Vice President Cheney in Bush (43), Mondale was apparently integral to policymaking. "What at the time was a welcomed upgrade for . . . Mondale" was subsequently considered by Walter Mondale as having "produced" what he termed "the 'metastasizing' of the idea with the Cheney vice presidency."[46] Whether or not the Bush presidency was affected (or infected) by the Carter president-NSC-policymaking model, President Carter created a precedent in the use of his vice president, Walter Mondale, which eventually led to the increasing influence of the vice president among the NSC principals. Former Vice President Mondale viewed the subsequent Cheney metamorphoses as aberrant. Ironically, Mondale's own influence during President Carter's NSC model presaged Cheney's incredible influence later.

Since President Carter served only one term and those four years became dominated by the overthrow of the Shah of Iran relatively few case studies exist for scholars of U.S. national security policy to make comparisons to other administrations. It is worth noting, however, that the Cuban Brigade (*Brigada*) "crisis" and the crisis-management mode into which the Carter administration propelled itself over the hostage seizure following the Shah's overthrow, provided circumstantial evidence to support our suggestion that incentives existed for NSC advisor Brzezinski to move policy into a crisis-management mode. One NSC scholar noted, "To enhance the functioning of this [NSC] structure at Carter's first cabinet meeting he informed his team that he was elevating the national security advisor to cabinet status. It was a first and sent an unmistakable message."[47] The message was that the NSC advisor would be on an equal footing with secretaries of state and defense. While NSC advisor Henry Kissinger had, effectively, already been elevated to de facto cabinet status, he was not recognized as such formally. Therefore, notwithstanding President Carter's rhetoric about rebalancing the president-NSC-policymaking model away from the Nixon-Kissinger duopoly, from the beginning President Carter empowered his NSC advisor, which may have made clashes between the secretary of state and the NSC advisor nearly inevitable.

Whatever Carter's intentions, and there is some reason to believe his intentions were good, the chemistry was not conducive to stability. Rather, Brzezinski and Vance clashed early and often. Secretary Vance ultimately resigned in protest to Carter's policies (particularly the failed hostage rescue attempt), but much ill will had built up by the time Vance tendered his resignation. Predictably, Brzezinski accrued power and the power accrued necessarily came at someone's expense (that of the secretaries of state and/or defense). Perhaps unexpectedly, neither Secretary of Defense Harold Brown nor DCI Stansfield Turner, nor anybody else, stepped in to increase their influence in Carter's president-NSC-policymaking model to offset NSC advisor Brzezinski's.

Some might argue Carter was simply the victim of bad luck. For instance, the second great oil shock for the U.S. occurred on his watch in 1979. The overthrow of the shah was something that was nearly inevitable once the world and Iranians discovered that the CIA had installed the shah and Carter, by this same reasoning, had the misfortune of inheriting a mess begun much earlier under President Eisenhower. However, too many other presidents have inherited bad situations from which they recovered. Nixon was faced with the 1973 oil shock and a still-smoldering mess in Vietnam at the same time and his president-NSC-policymaking model did not find itself paralyzed. Further, President Carter and members of his NSC model simply made matters worse in many cases. That Carter was a product of bad timing therefore is a plausible though not a very compelling argument. Still, as one author has noted, Carter was faced with an "arc of crises" in the 1979–1980 period and never successfully recovered from events that were not entirely in his control.[48]

Nor was the Carter administration without successes. The Camp David Accords and the Panama Canal Treaty can both be viewed as policymaking successes. Moreover, though excoriated for it by conservatives at the time and for years thereafter, President Carter foresaw the unhealthy dependency of the U.S. on Middle East oil and the implications of that dependency. President Carter attempted, albeit unsuccessfully, to move the huge U.S. national security and domestic policy machinery to face the reality of its oil dependency. Also, it is today taken for granted that U.S. foreign policy seeks to promote human rights. Prior to President Carter's tenure, however, human rights were seen as "low politics" and practitioners of realpolitik in United States' policymaking and academic circles often considered the notion of human rights as little more than a quaint value or preference. Carter deserves credit for making human rights part of U.S. national security priorities. Recently, President George W. Bush made the promotion of human rights and democracy part of his administration's national security goals.

Moreover, President George W. Bush recently told Americans that they had become "addicted" to oil, which he admitted hamstrung U.S. national security. In some sense, President Carter may have been a president before his time. President Carter's president-NSC-policymaking model may be represented graphically as follows.

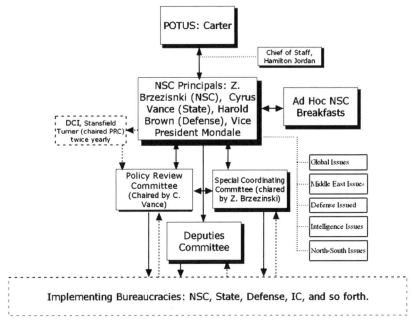

Figure 4.7. *President Jimmy Carter's president-NSC-policymaking model. The NSC was organized by committees with regional and/or functional specialties. Note the elevation of North-South issues, illustrative of President Carter and NSC advisor Brzezinski's Trilateral Commission affiliation. Note, further, that Carter's president-NSC-policymaking model included the vice president as a member in reality.*

For analytic purposes, the Carter administration may be divided into two distinct phases: Carter I, which corresponded to the period from President Carter's inauguration in January 1977 through 1978. During Carter I, President Carter was considered by at least some analysts as somewhat naive with respect to United States' national security threats. Carter and his NSC advisers understandably underwent some growing pains—the very growing pains one might expect when such an outsider assumed the presidency in Vietnam's wake, and while the Soviets sought to take advantage of the U.S. following the Vietnam debacle. Carter II corresponded to the period from 1979 through the end of President Carter's presidency (effectively

January 1981). During Carter II, many of the wrinkles were worked out of the system. President Carter changed and became more realistic about the type of threats that existed. National security policymaking correspondingly matured.[49] By the end of Carter's presidency, it is safe to conclude that Carter had grown into his "reorganized" president-NSC-policymaking model. Carter had come to rely on Brzezinski, despite his campaign promise not to mirror the Nixon administration. Additionally, the last two years of Carter's presidency featured the realpolitik he sought to avoid when he criticized Nixon and Kissinger for their similar power politics bereft of U.S. values.

Candidate Ronald Reagan made a great deal of the "Carter debacles" in Iran and, as he saw it, with respect to the Soviet Union. The president-NSC-policymaking model was again ripe for a shake up. President Reagan provided the shake up in more ways, one must presume, than he had intended in his campaign against President Jimmy Carter.

President Reagan: The Presidentless-NSC-Policymaking Model

Put simply, Ronald Reagan was an affable guy. There is just no getting around it. People just plain liked Ronald Reagan, a former Democrat, former union leader, former B-movie actor, and, by the 1970s, spokesman for many conservative causes. Beyond the positive message he carried on the campaign trail, candidate Reagan campaigned on fixing a poorly managed NSC, a recurring theme of this chapter. Part of President Reagan's prescription for fixing it was bringing back the old cabinet model of policymaking that existed before the 1947 NSA or at least a version that was similar to earlier versions of the president-NSC-policymaking model. Many have written, mistakenly, that President Reagan sought to emphasize the U.S. Department of State at the necessary expense of the NSC advisor. In fact, he sought to emphasize multiple cabinet secretaries at the inevitable expense of the NSC advisor and the president-NSC-policymaking model, including the NSC staff. Before President Reagan turned over the reins of power to his vice president of eight years, the NSC staff would prove a force in and of itself that the drafters of the 1947 NSA could not possibly have imagined and would never have countenanced.

President Reagan selected Alexander Haig as his secretary of state. Apparently, Reagan actually chose George Shultz (who would subsequently become his second secretary of state) for the position originally. A phone call between Reagan and Shultz somehow went awry leaving both men misunderstanding the other. Consequently, his backup selection, Alexander Haig, became his first secretary of state.[50] It is clear that Reagan and his brain trust intended to devalue the position of NSC advisor. Reagan selected the relatively young, relatively inexperienced, and far-from-Reagan-insider Richard Allen as his first NSC advisor. Together with some campaign rhetoric about the importance of the secretary of state, these actions led many to conclude that Reagan intended to raise the secretary of state with the result necessarily being a diminution of the NSC advisor in the zero-sum formulation. What appears more likely is that Reagan and his "Californians" intended to run U.S. foreign policy from inside the White House using Reagan's trusted confidantes as proxies for the secretary of state, the secretary of defense, *and* the NSC advisor.

In Reagan's case, it is almost superfluous to enumerate his NSC principals and other key advisers. Rather, the Californians and other proven Reagan loyalists were intended to hold policymaking authority from the beginning. There was at least one and possibly two White House troikas. By all accounts, the insiders included Reagan political adviser and friend Michael Deaver (called Reagan's personal "imagemeister"[51]). Filling out one "troika" were President Reagan's friend Edwin Meese (eventually Reagan's attorney general) and James Baker (chief of staff and nearly Reagan's third NSC advisor). James Baker had the distinction of being included in what some have identified as both domestic and foreign policy-making "troikas." It is interesting that James Baker—sometimes cited as a member of the White House troika, sometimes as a member of Reagan's national security troika—*was not* one of the Californians and yet apparently held considerable sway. The second troika noted as influential in President Reagan's tenure was the so-called national security or foreign policy troika. It reportedly consisted primarily of the old spymaster William Casey who became Reagan's CIA director or DCI (and who had multiple unsavory connections to the Iran-Contra affair that later embroiled the administration) as well as Secretary of Defense Weinberg and Secretary of State Shultz,[52] and sometimes including James Baker.

However many troikas comprised the Reagan national security and domestic policymaking team(s), it is clear that during the bulk of the Reagan presidency (two terms in office) power was held in the hands of relatively few persons. To the extent that a president-NSC-policymaking model emerged, a couple of features became apparent. First, Reagan's personality and management style, even according to Reagan's friends, was aloof. He preferred to delegate. The president delegated power to White House insiders and a select few others who made President Eisenhower's putative aloofness look hyperactive. The NSC advisor was not a completely meaningless position. But until the last couple of years of the administration—following the Iran-Contra scandal and the Tower Report it produced—the NSC advisor was not a policymaker per se. That is, he was not formally a part of the policymaking team. This did not stop a few of Reagan's six NSC advisors, as it turned out, from freelancing or being policy entrepreneurs.

Nor was Reagan's vice president an especially influential player in national security policymaking. Vice President Bush did get appointed to oversee the so-called Special Situations Group, an NSC committee that Vice President Bush chaired. The Special Situations Group was not an entirely meaningless committee and may, in fact, belie Vice President George H. W. Bush's subsequent claims that he was "out of the loop" during the Iran-Contra scandal. But neither was it an especially important position as the White House troika was a bottleneck through which all policy initiatives necessarily passed. It is therefore entirely possible that Vice President George H. W. Bush directed an important NSC entity and yet was not au courant in terms of the shenanigans that some of Reagan's NSC staffers (and two NSC advisors) were running.

One example illustrative of the operations and procedures of the Reagan president-NSC-policymaking model is worth brief consideration. As noted, Richard Allen was selected to be NSC advisor because the NSC advisor was not intended to be a policymaking position and Allen was assumed to be comfortable with that arrangement. David Rothkopf noted that Richard Allen was correctly assumed to be a weak NSC advisor who would cause no problems for the White House policymaking troika. Rothkopf also noted that Secretary of State Haig, apparently suffering from the mistaken impression that campaign rhetoric was meaningful, thought that there was a place in the Reagan president-NSC-policymaking model for a strong secretary of state. The opposite was more accurate. In fact, the White House insiders were going to make foreign policy—of course they would get Reagan's signature when necessary. To Secretary Haig's dismay, there was simply no place in such a model for a secretary of state—strong or otherwise—or frankly in most circumstances for the Department of State. Unfortunately and embarrassingly for Haig, he either missed the briefing, did not get the memo, or both. The delusional Haig wrote a memorandum effectively attempting to memorialize Reagan's campaign rhetoric. "He [Haig] gave the memo to Meese. It disappeared into his inbox." David Rothkopf noted that the "troika ran the White House, and for Allen to see the president . . . or to get virtually anything of substance done required that Baker, Deaver, and [Allen's] immediate superior Meese, sign off."[53]

Edwin Meese was the *de facto* NSC advisor and the *de facto* secretary of state until Judge William Webster, another Reagan California friend, became Reagan's second NSC advisor. "In the second month of the administration Edwin Meese, all but ignoring Haig's suggested structure [his aforementioned memo] and Allen's very existence, created three coordinating committees"—one for defense, another for intelligence, and a third for foreign policy.[54] Thus, the president-NSC-policymaking model under the Reagan administration was a presidentless, NSC-less model. Instead, one or more White House troikas operated and orchestrated NSC operations through one of the coordinating committees, thereby circumventing the NSC model almost entirely. In Reagan's first year (the summer of 1981) the troika realized a crisis-response group was necessary and created one. The group in the Reagan administration "evolved into the National Security Planning Group" for crises and terrorism problems as they arose.[55] It became critical to the United States' early responses to terrorism in the 1980s and may be considered an innovation during the Reagan two-term tenure. Interestingly, one of the motive forces behind the crisis center that evolved from this early impetus was John Poindexter, a bookish navy man who was on the NSC staff. (Poindexter, of course, would become Reagan's fourth NSC advisor, following Allen, William Webster, and Robert McFarlane.)

Reagan's presidentless, NSC-less policymaking model endured through most of his two terms in office. It was a system destined to fail as it relied on Reagan's personal friends creating a phalanx of protection for the president's aloof management style. And fail it did. Without a strong NSC advisor; with Secretaries of State and Defense, George Shultz and Caspar Weinberger respectively, effectively canceling each other out; and with the old spymaster, William Casey (DCI), who managed to move into the Old Executive Office Building, the model was bereft of institutional checks and balances and a significant void was created. Into the void charged members of the NSC staff. It took, of course, certain types of

NSC advisors (Robert "Bud" McFarlane and John Poindexter); that is, ultimately, it took those who believed in Reagan's worldview to create an environment in which NSC staffers could become policy entrepreneurs. Once that began, however, the Iran-Contra scandal was waiting to happen.[56] That it did should surprise nobody. President Reagan's president-NSC-policymaking model may be represented as follows.

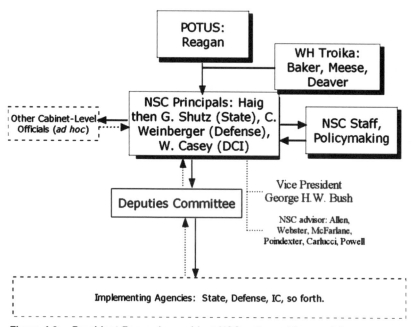

Figure 4.8.   President Reagan's president-NSC-policymaking model.

Following the Iran-Contra scandal, the Tower Commission was formed and issued a report in which the commissioners pointed out the predictable flaws in the system. The most glaring flaw was that when the president-NSC-policymaking model existed without a president to direct its actions, power diffused outward and away from the apex of statutory policymakers. In such a vacuum, it was unsurprising that Reagan insiders and even the NSC staff filled it. What was more significant was that George H. W. Bush, an out-of-the-loop vice president in such a system, would, upon becoming the next president, restore the president-NSC-policymaking system to something approaching the original Truman, Eisenhower, and Kennedy models.

President Bush (41): The Second Restoration of the President-NSC-Policymaking Model

President George H. W. Bush was one of the most experienced presidents in America's history. His was a family who had served in public office extensively. He was appointed to be the America's representative to the People's Republic of China. He served as chair of the GOP National Committee. He served briefly in the Ford administration as the director of central intelligence (DCI). And as seen, he served for eight years as the vice president during the Reagan administration. George H. W. Bush was nearly peerless in terms of national security experience.

President Bush (41) represented a return to the traditional president-NSC-policymaking model, pioneered by Truman, refined by eight years of Eisenhower's tenure, and only incrementally changed during Kennedy's tenure. Notably, during the four Bush (41) years, the president became the nation's chief national security decision maker and resumed that office's constitutional role as commander in chief. President Bush selected for his secretary of state journeyman insider James Baker, not only a close friend but a person who had served in government in a host of positions. Secretary Baker returned the U.S. Department of State to its traditional role of America's diplomatic bureaucracy and strengthened the Washington, D.C., connection to multiple U.S. embassies spread around the world. President Bush selected another well-traveled politician-cum-policymaker, Dick Cheney, as his secretary of defense. President Bush first nominated the late Senator John Tower (R-TX) as his secretary of defense in one of the Bush administration's early and rare missteps. At the time President George H. W. Bush selected Cheney, Cheney had served as President Ford's chief of staff, as well as in leadership positions in the U.S. House of Representatives. The chairman of the Joint Chiefs of Staff (originally created by the 1947 NSA) was restored to a position of prominence during the Bush tenure. The 1947 statute envisaged the CJCS as a statutory adviser rather than member of the NSC. Over time, however, both statutory advisers mentioned in the 1947 NSA had atrophied. Each president had been given wide berth in terms of whom the president wished to include or exclude in his principals and/or deputies committees. That had resulted in the CJCS and the DCI rising and falling in importance over time. George H. W. Bush selected a high-profile CJSC, General Colin Powell (the sixth and last NSC advisor in Reagan's two terms), someone certain to restore the CJCS adviser's prominence. For his national security advisor, President Bush chose Brent Scowcroft (former deputy NSC advisor to Henry Kissinger during Nixon's presidency and NSC advisor during Ford's), an incredibly important and competent choice. In short, Bush's own impressive foreign policy résumé inclined him to select others with impressive résumés—Bush was unlikely to be awestruck by those who comprised his NSC principals. A well-run, well-organized president-NSC-policymaking model resulted from the balance President George H. W. Bush struck in the NSC principals setting.

The exception from the norm found in the Bush president-NSC-policymaking model's balance was the conscious demotion of the director of central intelligence (DCI) who, as statutory adviser, had frequently served as an NSC principal. DCI William Webster was not an integral part of the Bush administration's president-NSC-policymaking model. Webster remained on with President Bush from the transition between Presidents Reagan and Bush. There appeared to be two reasons that President Bush did not seek a high-profile policymaker for his DCI. One, President Bush, as seen previously, served briefly as DCI during the Ford administration and was therefore less enamored with the position of DCI than many other presidents might otherwise be. That is not to say that President Bush considered the DCI an unimportant part of his national security policymaking team. He did not. Reportedly, Bush told his son, Bush (43) that one of the most important parts of his day—at least in terms of national security—would be the younger Bush's CIA briefing. The presidential daily briefing (PDB) historically included the NSC advisor as well as a relatively high-ranking CIA professional. But it was not unheard of to have the DCI himself brief a president when an important national security matter was on a president's agenda.

The second reason Bush retained a relatively low-profile DCI is that he personally believed that the DCI should only rarely serve in a policymaking capacity. In his memoirs (coauthored with Brent Scowcroft) George H. W. Bush wrote the following. As President Ford's DCI George H. W. Bush "learned the proper role for the director [DCI] in the national security structure." The former president concluded that the DCI was not "and should not be, a policy-maker or implementer, and should remain above politics, dealing solely in intelligence." He wrote, further, the "only exception to that role," was when it "concerned covert action as part of a specific policy decision. I never asked to be accorded cabinet rank and I felt strongly that the DCI should not even attend" most NSC meetings.[57] In order for the DCI to retain the semblance of objectivity, President George H. W. Bush believed the DCI should remain outside the inner circle.

The Bush administration approached national security policy in textbook fashion. President George H. W. Bush was a strong foreign policy president surrounded by a strong group of national security experts. His short time in office (one term) resulted in relatively few foreign policy case studies. Nevertheless, one must remember that the Bush (41) administration was the first administration to be in office when the Cold War ended. The transition from a Cold War, bipolar-structured system was a momentous time in world history and probably proceeded as smoothly as it did due to the complement of expertise assembled in President Bush's NSC principals. Additionally, two other important events, the first Gulf War and the Panama invasion, occurred under George H. W. Bush's stewardship.

President Bush (41), oversaw the U.S. post–Cold War transition at a critical time in world politics. During his tenure the Soviet Union, America's national security and foreign policy raison d'être, ceased to exist. Earlier, President Bush and his president-NSC-policymaking model expanded U.S. national security policy to include new concepts of national security (e.g., world drug trade). As was well-documented in Bob Woodward's *The Commanders*, the Bush administration went after and captured Manuel Noriega near the end of the Cold War. When the Bush administration removed Noriega from power, the administration also restored procedural democracy in Panama, arguably an important accomplishment and oddly presaging the subsequent Bush (43) administration's interest in regime change and democratization. Following the Cold War, academics and policymakers alike began considering all sorts of novel definitions of what constituted U.S. national security policy—again causing President Bush's time in office to parallel interesting times. The other well-documented case study was President Bush's decision to send U.S. troops into the Persian Gulf to forestall Iraq's invasion of Saudi Arabia once Saddam's troops had successfully sacked Kuwait. Much has been written and argued about both events. To be sure, President Bush's decision to snatch Mr. Noriega in 1989 was not well-executed. Beyond its execution, many have criticized the invasion of Panama as America throwing its power around unnecessarily. That will be left for others to debate.

With respect to the first Gulf War (1991), many have criticized President Bush for not finishing the job; that is, in hindsight critics have

charged that President George H. W. Bush and the broad coalition he assembled should have continued to Baghdad where, presumably, the U.S.
would have toppled Saddam Hussein in 1991. Had President Bush decided to do so, he would have exceeded the mandate of the U.N. and the
coalition the Bush team had so tirelessly assembled. Moreover, it is our
contention that President Bush made the correct decision at the time in
stopping short of Baghdad. Those who remember the situation on the
ground at the time may also recall that prior to President Bush's suspension of hostilities, U.S. and coalition troops were routing the Iraqis as the
latter fled back toward Baghdad. So overwhelming was military defeat of
Iraqi's once-vaunted military that pictures shown on CNN were disturbing. Miles of carnage resulted in the final throes of the war as Iraq's troops
scrambled to avoid U.S. and coalition forces. It is difficult to see how
President Bush made anything other than the correct decision at the time.
Had U.S. and coalition troops continued on to Baghdad, they may well

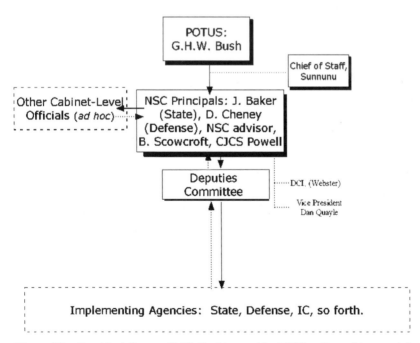

*Figure 4.9. President George H. W. Bush's president-NSC-policymaking model.
Balance was the key to President George H. W. Bush's successful iteration of this
model. President Bush was a strong and experienced national security policymaker. Both secretaries of state and defense too were powerful and experienced
policymakers. The sometime underrated NSC advisor Brent Scowcroft played an
inestimable part in the model's smooth operations.*

have finished Saddam Hussein then and there—something that may have been a good thing for the world—but they would have perforce employed such gratuitous violence that they would have lost the moral high ground that they held at the time.

President Bush's restoration of a model that largely approximated earlier versions under Eisenhower and Kennedy may be represented as shown above. It is worth noting that strong secretaries of state and defense were critical to the restoration. Furthermore, NSC Brent Scowcroft restored the appropriate role of the NSC advisor. Scowcroft was much more behind the scenes than his predecessors since Eisenhower. Moreover, he was effective and influential without the accoutrements of power that had come to festoon the NSC advisor since Kissinger.

President Clinton: The President-NSC-Policymaking Model and Its Growing Pains in a New Century

President Clinton was both the first fully post–Cold War president as well as the first "Vietnam-generation" president. As is well-known, William Jefferson Clinton went to some lengths to avoid serving in Vietnam, and much was made of it during his tenure.[58] Another distinguishing characteristic of the post–Cold War Clinton administration was that it came to office amid the post–Cold War turmoil that quickly began to manifest itself in the absence of the Cold War's predictable effects. The Gulf War—the first war of the post–Cold War era—was successfully concluded by Clinton's first inauguration. Saddam's generals signed instruments of surrender that normally would have proscribed further Iraqi menace in the region. However, nationalism (i.e., separatism and irredentism) was rearing its head across the former Soviet Union again after years of being mostly latent. Whatever else one might wish to say about the Cold War, it had the predictable effect of keeping nationalism suppressed by dint of force. The former Yugoslavia dogged the Clinton administration virtually its entire eight years in office.

Thus a new kind of president entered the White House just as a new world disorder manifested itself. Clinton's early years were also characterized by new academic thinking about the post–Cold War years. As Rothkopf noted in his coverage of the Clinton administration, writers such as Francis Fukuyama and Samuel Huntington published their treatises on America's appropriate role in the world.[59] Fukuyama wrote that the Soviets' demise represented the "end of history" and that the U.S. and other liberal, capitalist, secular democracies were the victors. The future seemed bright as capitalism and democratic governance appeared the rule. Huntington, by contrast, envisaged a future in which geostrategic fault lines between "civilizations" were likely to lead to future wars in a "clash of civilizations." In short, the times were changing and a new Vietnam-era president entered office during the post–Cold War tumult.

President Clinton believed that national security policy was an extension of U.S. domestic policy and that domestic policy was about economics. "It's the economy, stupid," was the mantra of Governor Clinton as he campaigned for the presidency. Accordingly, when Clinton approached national security—and by necessity how to assemble his president-NSC-policymaking model—he determined that the NSC needed some reorganization. Not that he changed the basics of the NSC (viz., the principals and deputies committees), for he actually borrowed heavily from the Bush administration's president-NSC-policymaking model. Instead, he simply grafted what he believed a commonsensical approach to the globalization of the international political economy: the national economic council was created as a parallel entity to the NSC. One of Clinton's chief advisers was the influential Robert E. Rubin from Wall Street. As Rothkopf noted, Rubin, Clinton, and other colleagues collaborated on an idea to create a "White House economic council modeled on the NSC." Rothkopf also suggested that the hubris of the Clinton administration was revealed in some of its early thinking about economics-cum-international politics.[60] (Of course, as seen repeatedly, hubris underlay several Cold War presidents' foreign policy and international politics.)

On the day of Clinton's inauguration, January 20, 1993, the new president signed Presidential Decision Directive 2 (PDD-2), which created the parallel NSC-NEC structure. Bureaucracies are resistant to change by nature and some of the old-school politicos of Washington initially resisted the National Economic Council (NEC).[61] As seen, virtually every new president has felt compelled to reinvent the basic nomenclature of the NSC's work product. Consequently, former President Bush's national security directives (NSDs) became presidential decision directives (PDDs) and national security reviews (NSRs) became presidential review directives (PRDs).[62]

Clinton's cabinet included political journeyman Warren Christopher, the former deputy secretary of state during Carter's presidency, as Clinton's first secretary of state (until 1997). It is anybody's guess what caused Clinton to reach out to Mr. Christopher. That is not to suggest that Secretary Christopher was anything less than a seasoned bureaucrat and diplomat; still his exceptionally cautious, lawyerly demeanor seemed at odds with the young Clintonites. Clinton's first secretary of defense was the well-respected Leslie "Les" Aspin, a bright and ambitious former U.S. Representative from Wisconsin. Les Aspin held a Ph.D. in economics from MIT. Secretary of Defense Aspin had previously chaired multiple important national security committees in the U.S. House during his years in Congress, so it was understandable when President Clinton reached out to him. He was well-respected by both Republicans and Democrats as a known quantity in terms of his military and national security experience. Still, and similar to Secretary Christopher, Secretary Aspin belied the youthful infusion that otherwise characterized Clinton's NSC apparatus. Indeed, Les Aspin experienced heart problems in February 1993, a month after Clinton's inauguration. Neither Secretary Aspin nor Secretary Christopher would last for the full two terms of the Clinton administration. Clinton's NSC staff, predictably and understandably, contained many holdovers from George H. W. Bush's NSC staff.

Clinton's first NSC advisor was Anthony Lake, the bookish, bright former academic and former aide to Henry Kissinger when the latter was NSC advisor. Lake in many ways was far more similar to George W. Bush's second NSC advisor, Stephen Hadely, than to Henry Kissinger, McGeorge Bundy, or Brent Scowcroft. Anthony Lake, Les Aspin, and Warren Christopher did not last the entire eight years of the Clinton administration but they comprised Clinton's statutory NSC principals initially, with the addition of the NEC and Robert Rubin. Aspin was first to go. Following America's first "humanitarian" intervention in Somalia, which was actually begun during the former Bush administration, Aspin was roundly criticized for "mission creep" and the debacle that became known as Black Hawk Down. Whether the blame belonged singly to Secretary of Defense Aspin is another matter. However, he also was a victim of his own indiscretions, using military aircraft to fly him and companions to conferences around the world, using a summit or important meeting as a pretext for a junket. Secretary Aspin lasted just over a year (like Alexander Haig during President Reagan's first term). Secretary Aspin was eventually replaced by Secretary of Defense William J. Perry, one of the most respected cabinet officials (and NSC principals) of the Clinton administration years. Secretary Perry, a bright man with a Ph.D. in mathematics from Stanford, lasted until January 23, 1997. Secretary Perry was then replaced by a former Republican Senator, William Cohen (R-ME), who served on military and national-security-related committees during his Senate career. Secretary of State Warren Christopher actually lasted beyond Clinton's first term, though much of his tenure lacked positive national security highlights. He was eventually replaced by America's first female secretary of state, Madeleine Korbel Albright, on January 23, 1997. She remained throughout the rest of Clinton's tenure. Anthony Lake also lasted until 1997, in his case March 1997, by which time Clinton's old college friend and deputy NSC advisor, Samuel "Sandy" Berger, became Clinton's second and last NSC advisor.[63] Like President George H. W. Bush, President Clinton did not believe that the director of central intelligence (head of CIA) ought to be a policymaker or even conceived of as a cabinet member. Thus his relationship with DCI James Woolsey was far from ideal and the two never formed a good working relationship. Certainly, former DCI James Woolsey has been critical of the former Clinton administration on a number of occasions.[64]

Perhaps the most noteworthy global change inherited by the Clinton administration was not the demise of the Soviet Union, though this clearly was an historical global change of manifold consequence. The reemergence of nationalism in former Yugoslavia and elsewhere, however, did affect Clinton's NSC. President William Jefferson Clinton inherited one of the byproducts of the Cold War's end. Importantly, Clinton and his NSC constituted the first post–Cold War administration that was compelled to deal with the new international phenomenon of transnationalism, the global jihadi hydra, attacking the U.S. David Rothkopf's description of the Clinton administration from an insider's perspective noted as much. "This process would be the hallmark of the Clinton NSC/NEC approach to emerging security threats worldwide, although as new transnational threats emerged, fueled in part by the information age and globalization, a new mix of players would be central to achieving America's next generation foreign policy goals."[65]

Transnationalism is the proliferation of new global actors who are not attached to particular nation-states, and it is therefore in some sense the antithesis of nationalism. Multinational corporations and nongovernmental international organizations (NGOs) are both transnational organizations; so too are global jihadis. Historically, and certainly during the Cold

War, nation-states or the system of them was the unit of analysis for academics and policymakers. During the Cold War, international politics was dominated by theories about the nation-state system and the systemic balance of power that characterized it. Thus, theories, analogies, and lessons learned generally came from the system of nation-states that came into existence shortly following the Treaty of Westphalia in the seventeenth century, which ended the Thirty Years' War between religious qua tribal groups that rampaged around Europe during the period. That was the system into which a nascent America entered in 1776. That was not the system into which Clinton's national security bureaucracies entered in 1993, as the nation and the president would shortly come to know.

Though not a suicide attack, America awoke to an omen of 9/11 on February 26, 1993, at eighteen minutes after noon, when a rented moving truck parked below the World Trade Center detonated. A hole in the underground parking garage created by the detonation reached seven stories in height. It resulted in the killing of six persons and the wounding of some 1,000 but not, to the chagrin of the jihadis who planned it, the toppling of the World Trade Center. President Clinton ordered his NSC principals to coordinate America's response to its first post–Cold War experience with terrorism inside America's territory. America's nascent Counterterrorism Center, located in the CIA, immediately launched a global investigation while its domestic counterpart, the FBI, also sprang into action. All of America's vast intelligence assets were immediately used to gather information. At the time, virtually no American had ever heard of Osama bin Laden or al Qaeda. America's general ignorance of global jihadis coupled with America's focus on emerging issues from the fall of the Soviet Union may have caused Americans and their policymakers to miss the symbolic importance of what had just occurred. America had just received the first salvo in which America's enemy was an amorphous, poorly understood set of Sunni jihadis associated not with a single nation-state but with scores of them. Put differently, the global jihadis who first struck America in 1993 were associated with no specific nation state; indeed their plans included substituting the nation-state system with the historic Caliphate system. Neither was the new war about nationalism. It was an ideology that was grounded in theology—albeit a misappropriated one—at its core. An existential war had begun early in President Clinton's watch and most Americans, including many in the government, had no idea.

Clinton's NSC, working with America's vast national security bureaucracy, successfully tracked down, captured, and prosecuted some of the co-conspirators in the February 1993 Twin Tower attack, including the so-called "Blind Sheik," Sheikh Omar Abdel Rahman, and discovered another even more dramatic plot while doing so. However, the Clinton administration, its president-NSC-policymaking model, and the vast bureaucracy whose job was to implement the president's decisions, all neglected to appreciate the full importance of the February 1993 attack on the U.S. That the Clinton team discovered additional plots, nevertheless, warrants some credit. It began a long unraveling of global jihadis that still continues today. And though the 9/11 hijackers got past the defenses erected during the Clinton administration, a number of innovations and successes were also implemented during President Clinton's two terms in office. One might consider the administration's successes even more positively given the manifold distractions President Clinton brought on himself in his final years. Whatever indiscretions President Clinton committed cannot reasonably be blamed on his president-NSC-policymaking model nor on his NSC principals. His NSC principals were nonetheless tainted by association and presumably distracted by the various investigations into the Clinton administration which culminated in his second term.

Eventually, what began as the CIA and the FBI working more or less independently following the first Twin Towers attack resulted in some major successes for Clinton's president-NSC-policymaking model. First, Clinton's national security staffers helped thwart Project Bojinka before it was hatched, albeit after serendipitous discovery by Filipino investigators. The plot was discovered when Manila firemen and police personnel stumbled onto evidence of the plot while putting out a fire in a Manila building. The plot consisted of placing bombs on a dozen transpacific flights crossing either direction. The bombs would simultaneously (or nearly simultaneously) explode killing untold numbers, destroying a dozen or so jumbo jets, and stunning the world in unimaginable ways. (In fact, had it been successful, Bojinka might have affected U.S. national security policy as 9/11 eventually did.) One connection between the 1993 Trade Center attack and the 1995 Bojinka plot was an angry young Sunni Muslim named Ramzi Yousef, who was captured in Manila in 1995 before he could carry out the Bojinka plot. Another was Khalid Sheikh Mohammed, Yousef's uncle and a person whom the U.S. would actively hunt and capture after 9/11. Khalid Sheikh Mohammed (known variously as "the brain" and as KSM by the U.S. government) was the mastermind working at al Qaeda's behest who planned and prepared the 9/11 attacks years later.[66] Since 9/11, America's national security consensus has held that global jihadis and other transnational threats must be treated in a more rigorous, proactive way. The Clinton administration's reliance on traditional law enforcement mechanisms to thwart global jihadis has, partially, been criticized as insufficient. Still, the Clinton NSC team began to unravel the jihadi puzzle well before 9/11 occurred.

In summary, President Clinton largely adopted the president-NSC-policymaking model that his predecessor, President George H. W. Bush restored to its rightful place. Apparently, President Clinton recognized a good thing when he saw it and chose not to change the model fundamen-

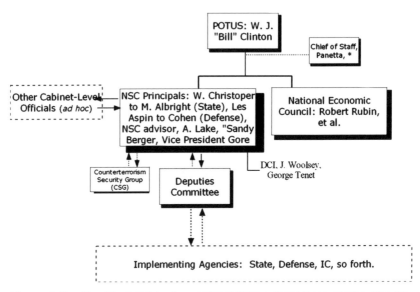

Figure 4.10. President Clinton's president-NSC-policymaking model. The National Economic Council was an innovation, albeit an incremental adjustment, given the globalized nature of the international political economy that America found itself a part of when President Clinton was inaugurated. Though only briefly mentioned above, part of Clinton's attempt to reorient the government, including the president-NSC-policymaking model, was the counterterrorism security group, which came to be headed by Richard Clarke. So influential did Clarke become that he became an ad hoc principals in Clinton's NSC principals meetings. Clarke's group was quite successful in the so-called Millennium plots and other emphases on jihadi groups. It was still operating when 9/11 occurred but was unable to cobble together the disparate pieces of evidence to thwart the plot. Richard Clarke had actually left the group by then and become somewhat disenchanted with the Bush administration.

tally from the way it worked under Bush (41). Over his two terms in office, there were of course adjustments. The NSC began to reorient the government's focus on transnational phenomena, though well short of what would eventually be needed. Also, as noted, Clinton elevated the national economic council as a parallel entity to the NSC, a needed addition given the globalization of the international political economy. Doing so constituted one of Clinton's president-NSC-policymaking model innovations. President Clinton's version of the president-NSC-policymaking model may be represented as the above figure indicates.

While President Clinton's NSC principals and other foreign and national security advisers may be credited with thwarting some early global jihadi plots against the United States, it is also the case that they did not sufficiently prepare for 9/11. Perhaps no administration could have prepared the American public for such a radical attack that so few anticipated. That horrific attack would come during the next administration's first year in office. We will turn to the George W. Bush administration in a separate chapter.

Summary of President-NSC-Policymaking Model:
President Harry S. Truman to William Jefferson Clinton

The previous pages demonstrated several important points about America's premier national security and foreign policy decision-making locus, the president-NSC-policymaking model. First, we demonstrated that the model clearly and unambiguously supplanted America's historical president-cabinet model—associated with America's isolationist period. Second, each president between 1947 and 2000 took advantage of the 1947 NSA's flexibility regarding those whom he made part of his "inner circle," the NSC principals. Third, the statutory principals were frequently seen to be different from the ad hoc principals a particular president chose. Thus, what we called the ad hoc principals were frequently demonstrated as a level of comparison between one administration and another. We have demonstrated how surprisingly agile the model itself proved as the model created by the 1947 NSA accommodated various presidential personalities over time. Fourth, the president-NSC-policymaking model changed incrementally from 1950 through 2000: that is, it evolved and adjusted slightly over the Cold War and post–Cold War years. No president dramatically changed the president-NSC-policymaking model, at least not in ways that survived that particular president's tenure in office. (Presidents Nixon and Reagan came closest to radical changes but both attempts to supplant the president-NSC-policymaking model ended badly, leaving the pieces to be reestablished under each president's successor.) Fifth, a lack of new talent in the gene pool characterized (and continues to characterize) the course of the president-NSC-policymaking model's history. From the ranks of both the Republican and the Democratic parties came the same foreign policy experts and elites who were routinely recycled as one party replaced another in the White House. Sixth, the president-NSC-policymaking model typically functioned in a way that reflected America's values in the national security policies most of the administrations enacted. And finally, though less substantively, new presidents tend to replace their predecessors' NSC nomenclature, as if changing the name of the NSC's work product changes the NSC.

AMENDMENTS TO THE 1947 NATIONAL SECURITY ACT, THE PRESIDENT-NSC-POLICYMAKING MODEL, AND THE INTELLIGENCE COMMUNITY

In the following pages we examine some additional institutions that, along with president-NSC-policymaking model, determined and implemented U.S. national security policy during the same timeframe during which the president-NSC-policymaking model became predominant. Since its passage in July 1947, the 1947 National Security Act (1947 NSA) has been amended multiple times. Congress, as part of its Article I constitutional oversight responsibilities, amended the act as circumstances dictated and as the original act was perceived as inadequate. Most of the amendments, however, have been relatively minor. Presidents amended the 1947 NSA, in effect, through the presidential tool of executive orders, some of which subsequently became codified in United States law. In other instances, executive orders have not been codified in U.S. law, in which case they typically remained in place until some subsequent president reversed them or replaced them with new orders. By both executive order and codification in law, an elaborate set of national security institutions, procedures, and processes has evolved over the two generations since the 1947 NSA. Though mostly incremental, changes were intended to tweak the president-NSC-policymaking model as the Cold War dictated that minor adjustments were needed.

The 1949 Reorganization Bill:
Amending the 1947 National Security Act

In 1949 Clark Clifford and William Averell Harriman (both ad hoc NSC principals under Truman) worked with NSC principal James Forestall (the former secretary of the U.S. Navy) and key Truman cabinet members who helped draft the original 1947 NSA. Clark Clifford and Ferdinand Eberstadt, in particular, were instrumental in the original 1947 legislation. These men as well as others worked on the 1949 amendment as well; many of the same men were the principal architects of America's *containment* policy against the Soviet Union. Clifford and Forrestal proposed "new points for subsequent legislation" which formed the 1949 amendment, or the so-called Reorganization Bill of 1949. According to Rothkopf, Clifford and Forestall proposed eleven new points of reorganization to the original act, despite its original hard-fought negotiations, because they believed that the original National Security Act proved too weak in some rather important ways. Included in their proposals was "a real Department of Defense with more authority," "reforms to the Joint Chiefs," and "a deputy secretary of defense." (In fact, the deputy secretary of defense has become an extremely powerful position in certain administrations, particularly George W. Bush's.) The Reorganization Bill also reduced the original number of "statutory members" to the NSC principals and relocated the NSC and its staff from its original and temporary home to the White House's Old Executive Office Building (OEOB),[67] where the NSC has been housed ever since. The 1949 Reorganization Bill has sometimes been a point of confusion as some scholars argued that the defense department was created by the 1949 Reorganization Act as opposed to the original NSA of 1947. The 1949 Reorganization Act housed the U.S. Defense Department and its secretary of defense in the executive office of the president; the department's creation was clearly stated in the original 1947 NSA.

President Truman, of course, presided over the Reorganization Bill of 1949. Documents on the 1949 Reorganization Bill in particular may be found in Truman's library among calendars and agenda notes. On May 9, 1949, according to the Truman Library chronology for 1949, President Truman sent "to Congress a special message asking it to act on the several measures before Congress concerning the reorganization of the Executive Branch. These measures included legislation to *improve the organization of national security and foreign affairs* activities of the government," as well as other matters. For August 10, 1949, the Truman Library chronology noted that Truman signed "the National Security Act Amendments of 1949." The amendments noted the Department of Defense—already "created in the 1947 National Security Act but apparently insufficiently recognized as such" also "strengthened greatly the office of Secretary of Defense, and gave statutory recognition to the position of Chairman of the Joint Chiefs of Staff."[68] The 1949 Reorganization Bill actually *recreated* the department of defense by placing it under the president's executive control. It did not, however, make the chairman of the Joint Chiefs a member of the NSC principals; rather, his status remained as it had initially been devised by the 1947 NSA; namely, a "statutory adviser." Additional reorganization occurred over the years.

Below, a particularly interesting amendment to the U.S. military's interactions with the president-NSC-policymaking model is briefly analyzed. The law, known as the Goldwater-Nichols Act, affected the president-NSC-policymaking model indirectly rather than directly. Otherwise, until 2004, no significant or substantive structural changes were effected to the president-NSC-policymaking model. The model remained largely as created in 1947 and slightly altered in 1949 with only incremental change until the post-9/11 environment. Following 9/11 and three years of postmortems and/or commissions to determine "what went wrong" dramatic change occurred. Consequently, the Intelligence Reform and Terrorism Prevention Act (December 2004) which we will discuss in detail in chapter 9, was passed.

The Goldwater-Nichols Act (GNA)

As America emerged as one of the world's two superpowers and its main policymakers perceived Western conceptions of democratic governance and capitalism as gravely imperiled, the president and the Congress both agreed that a new model of foreign policymaking was imperative. In addition to the creation of the NSC, a unified defense department was created. Prior to the creation of the defense department, the Department of State typically dominated U.S. foreign and national security policy. Naturally, some bureaucratic resistance to a unified defense department was predictable and indeed occurred. In fact, the defense department since its creation in 1947 and recreation in the 1949 Reorganization Bill slowly but ineluctably began to surpass the Department of State in its "special role" as the first among equals in a president's cabinet agencies vis-à-vis U.S. national security policy. The Department of Defense's budget alone made it a formidable bureaucracy. Defense's budget became many times larger than that of the state department's and the Department of Defense increasingly came to hold sway bureaucratically. Bureaucratically, the Department of Defense was therefore fated to become more powerful than other national security institutions. And more powerful it became, though predictably not without bruising bureaucratic battles along the way. Over time, the defense department clashed with and eventually dominated the Department of State's previously preeminent role. There is little question that in the first term of George W. Bush, the Department of Defense was a bureaucratic giant compared to the Department of State and other institutions created by the 1947 NSA.

The Defense Department and the Pentagon are two slightly different entities, albeit overlapping ones, working for the same secretary and, of course, the same president and nation. The defense department is the civilian bureaucracy that ensures that the Pentagon and the nation's uniformed forces are always under civilian control. Additionally, the *service chiefs*, the chiefs of the respective branches of the U.S. military, each answer to their own civilian secretary who in turn answers to the secretary of defense. The service chiefs also have a relationship with the chairman of the Joint Chiefs who, by law, is the president's personal military adviser as well as the military adviser to the NSC. Therefore, the chairman of the Joint Chiefs is the military adviser to the president-NSC-policymaking model. We have seen how the 1947 NSA created the chairman of the Joint Chiefs of Staff (CJCS) and made that military position a statutory adviser to the president and the NSC principals. In the 1980s, the Goldwater-Nichols Act entered the bureaucratic fray as it attempted to integrate the various military services to better serve the nation, the president, and the president's NSC principals.

The Goldwater-Nichols Act (GNA) was created in order to unify the disparate and hitherto distinct elements of the uniformed military services. Prior to the GNA, each service operated separately and according to its own parochial interests within the larger national security context. Accordingly, when the president of the U.S. and/or his NSC principals recognized a threat to U.S. national security, the various service chiefs would have been expected to offer their particular service as the ultimate solution to whatever national security threat arose, a basic law of bureaucratic survival. Consider the Cuban Missile Crisis. It occurred during the fall of 1962. During the crisis, President Kennedy convened what he called the "executive committee" (Excomm) of the NSC to determine options to thwart the Soviets' intentions to install offensive nuclear missiles some 90 miles from America's territory. During the myriad meetings convened to plot a solution to the Soviet threat, President Kennedy and his NSC principals (the Excomm effectively became Kennedy's NSC principals during the crisis) met repeatedly to discuss options.

Now consider the sort of solutions President Kennedy's service chiefs might have offered during the event, in our hypothetical case. The reader need not know the actual substance of the various Excomm meetings to imagine the sorts of solutions the service chiefs might have offered to their NSC counterparts. It was determined that installations were being erected on the island of Cuba to house offensive nuclear weapons. That determination was made principally by the director of central intelligence (DCI), who was privy to information from U-2 spy planes and other intelligence sources (DIA). Thus began the crisis. The members of the Excomm believed that the offensive missiles had not yet arrived at their final destination, Cuba, a crucial misperception. It is now well-known that offensive nuclear missiles had already arrived, though they were short-range tactical missiles. The Excomm members did not know this fact and instead deliberated on the basis that the missiles had yet to arrive in Cuba. In fact, that the Excomm believed they had days in which to respond before the missiles reached Cuba, after which their deliberations would necessarily change. That is, the president and his advisers believed, erroneously, that they had several days before the missiles arrived and were installed, after which time the options available to policymakers would decrease. Once the missiles were installed, Excomm members believed, virtually every option considered incurred substantially different risks.

Under our hypothetical conditions, what would the various military chiefs likely have recommended to the president and the Excomm of the NSC? In all likelihood, the U.S. Air Force chief would have suggested a "surgical strike" with U.S. Air Force assets that could have targeted and bombed the installations. Without installations, once the missiles arrived neither the Cubans nor the Soviets would have been able to deploy them against America. At the very least, the president and his NSC would have gained valuable time (perhaps months) to discuss the situation with the

Soviets and convince them that it was contrary to their own security interests to proceed with the installation of missiles. By contrast, the Commandant of the Marine Corps would likely have recommended an amphibious assault on the island whereby U.S. Marines would secure the installments, doubtless in a very bloody battle, rendering them unserviceable to the Soviet missiles thought to be somewhere in the Atlantic Ocean on their way to Cuba. The U.S. Navy chief may have sided with the Marines. Perhaps the U.S. Navy chief might have suggested a naval blockade of Cuba, thereby preventing Soviet ships from delivering their deadly cargo and preventing the missiles from ever reaching their destination, in which case the benefits of the solution might have accrued solely to the Navy. In short, each of the military chiefs, all believing their solutions were the best solutions for America's national security, would hypothetically have recommended parochial solutions that would have involved their own branch of the military at the expense of others. Their various parochial recommendations would have derived from the branch with which each was associated and that branch's mission. Since each service ultimately competed for finite budget dollars, it behooved each chief to recommend a military solution that also helped secure more scarce budget dollars for that chief's branch of the military, provided the solutions proved successful. In fact, it is well-known that each of these recommendations were made as well as others and the crisis was eventually averted via a naval blockade which was renamed a naval "quarantine," so that it might plausibly be argued as not an act of war and hence not a violation of international law.

Senator Barry M. Goldwater (R-AZ) and Representative Bill Nichols (D-AL) sought to change the parochial nature of America's military establishment by creating a unified command and simplifying the chain of command, in effect, forcing the various branches of the military to be happy in their work and be happy in the "jointness" of it. Since the Pentagon already housed elements of each branch, the GNA took for granted what existed: that there existed "in the Department of Defense the Joint Chiefs of Staff, headed by the Chairman of the Joint Chiefs of Staff. The Joint Chiefs of Staff consist[ed] of the following:" the chairman of the Joint Chiefs of Staff, the vice chairman, the chief of staff of the Army, the chief of Naval Operations, the chief of staff of the Air Force, and the commandant of the Marine Corps. Under the title of "Function as Military Advisers," the GNA directed that the chairman of the Joint Chiefs of Staff existed as the principal military adviser to the president, the National Security Council, and the secretary of defense. Thereafter, the other members of the Joint Chiefs of Staff were also specified as *"military advisers* to the President, the *National Security Council*, and the Secretary of Defense" themselves. In short, it created a direct advisory role for each service chief to the president, the NSC principals, and their civilian boss (the secretary of defense) apart from the CJCS as the filter of the potentially different advice that the various chiefs might give the president or NSC. The CJCS had important authorities that none of the other chiefs had, but the chiefs were given, in theory, unfettered access to the president of the United States and his NSC principals. That alone would do little if anything to change the parochial nature of the military's advice.

However, the CJCS had what the GNA specified as somewhat ambiguous authority over the other chiefs: under the heading "Consultation by the Chairman," the GNA noted "in presenting advice with respect to any matter to the President, the National Security Council, or the Secretary of Defense," the Chairman, "as he considers appropriate," would thereafter inform "the President, the National Security Council, or the Secretary of Defense, as the case may be, of the range of military advice and opinion with respect to that matter."[69] Under the heading of "Advice and Opinions of Members Other Than the Chairman," GNA said the following: any member of the Joint Chiefs "other than the Chairman" had the authority and/or responsibility to "submit to the Chairman advice or an opinion in disagreement with, or advice or an opinion in addition to, the advice presented by the Chairman to the President, the National Security Council, or the Secretary of Defense." That is, if any uniformed service chief, other than the chairman, had an opinion he wished the president and/or the NSC to hear, the chairman was compelled by the GNA to "present the advice or opinion of such member at the same time" he presented "his own advice to the President, the National Security Council, or the Secretary of Defense, as the case may be."[70] The clause "as he considers appropriate" resulted in some ambiguity as it was arguably incongruent with the directions to "present" the military chief's "advice and opinions" when the CJCS presented his own advice.

Additionally, the GNA empowered the creation of the regional commanders in chief (known in typical military style as CINCs, pronounced "sinks.") The CINCs were the jointness of GNA as it created unified combatant commanders for each of the defense department's regional commands. The unified combatant commanders have intermilitary forces under their control, thereby creating incentives for the CINCs to use the forces that make most sense rather than using a particular service's forces for parochial reasons. The *Washington Post*'s excellent national security and military reporter, Dana Priest, neatly summarized the essence of the GNA as well as the parochial resistance that attended its creation.

> The Goldwater-Nichols Act gave the [CINCs] the power they have today. The law elevated the chairman of the Joint Chiefs to the role of principal military adviser to the president [and NSC]. It gave [CINCs] the power to direct and "unify" all weapons use, training, and tactics in their theaters. The "unified combatant commands" it established would be the military's "war-fighting" headquarters. Each [CINC] had oversight of a geographical region of the world. Each had generals and admirals from all four services reporting directly to him. Inter-service rivalry linger[ed], however.[71]

According to Priest, despite the best intentions of Goldwater and Nicols, parochialism continued after the Goldwater-Nichols Act became law. Parochialism will always exist—though diminished at particular times such as during a foreign policy crisis—so long as distinct organizations, whether military or civilian, have distinct missions and they are forced to compete for finite, limited budget dollars. Prior to the GNA the only commander in chief was the president as provided by Article II of the U.S. Constitution. Following the GNA, the CINCs were formed as commanders in chief of the military's geographical regions. The Pentagon divides the world into regional commands: Pacific, Southern, European, Central, and Northern. Since 9/11, the Northern Command has been fortified considerably. After the GNA, a CINC, who had the ability to cull troops and materiel from across the military branches for his particular uses in joint missions, existed for each of the regions.

The Goldwater-Nichols Act of 1986 "also simplified the chain of command. The four-star service chiefs who headed the Army, Navy, Air Force, and Marine Corps" thereafter answered to a civilian service secretary appointed by the president. Among other things, presumably this was intended to ensure and reemphasize termination of the chain of command in the civilian rather than military realm! However, a CINC's line of authority ran "directly to the defense secretary and the president—even the Chairman of the Joint Chiefs was explicitly removed from the [CINC's] chain of command." The CINCs have become a force unto themselves and have evolved into, as Priest so aptly demonstrated in her book, "proconsuls to the empire;"[72] that is, proconsuls of the American national security state or *Pax Americana*.

Evolution of the Intelligence Community during the Cold War and How It Affected the President-NSC-Policymaking Model

The president-NSC-policymaking model has always relied on intelligence. In fact, any model of decision making must rely on intelligence. The president-NSC-policymaking model has relied on intelligence "to collect and convey essential information needed by the President and other members of the U.S. policymaking, law enforcement, and military communities for the performance of their duties and responsibilities." "Intelligence," according to the Robb-Silberman WMD report, included "collecting and assessing information concerning international terrorist and narcotic activities; other hostile activities by foreign powers, organizations, persons, and their agents; and foreign intelligence activities directed against the United States."[73] In short, intelligence comprises the eyes and ears of the president-NSC-policymaking model. Intelligence forms the information the president-NSC-policymaking model must have about a threat or opportunity to ensure America's national security in a complex global environment with manifold state and nonstate actors who may seek to harm the United States of America.

The Central Intelligence Agency (CIA), created by the 1947 NSA, replaced World War II's Office of Strategic Service (OSS). Clearly the framers of the 1947 NSA wished to create a permanent intelligence entity that would counter Soviet intelligence and espionage as well as the Soviet's competent use of propaganda and diplomacy to achieve Soviet foreign policy objectives. The framers of the 1947 NSA decided that the U.S., in its monumental battle with the Soviet Union, should have a professional corps of intelligence officers. Thus was born the Central Intelligence Agency. Prior to World War II, some policymakers viewed espionage and spying as something only "others" did. Americans, so the thinking went, had no need for such perfidy. In a famous quote, former Secretary of State Henry S. Stimson said: "Gentlemen do not read other gentlemen's mail."[74] The Cold War consensus understood that gentlemen or not, governments did in fact read other governments' mail and electronic signals, and just about any other source of intelligence or information they could get. Once the CIA was born, the proliferation of additional intelligence agencies was only a matter of time. As different types of intelligence needs developed over time, the number of disparate agencies to provide it multiplied. In sum, those different agencies became known as the intelligence community.

As a result of the Cold War consensus about the Soviet threat, the CIA evolved over time to meet it. The CIA's directorate of operations (DO) was responsible for espionage and covert actions. Covert actions were seen by many as a distinct instrument of U.S. foreign policy. Covert action made its operators policymakers on the ground, albeit in limited fashion. The directorate of operations became the National Clandestine Service, recommended by the 9/11 Commission and created after 9/11. The directorate of intelligence evolved into the analytic arm of CIA. Data collected by CIA or other agencies of the intelligence community were passed along to the directorate of intelligence for analysis and thence up the chain of command to the NSC where policymakers grappled with the implications from the analysis. Other branches of CIA evolved as well. For instance, the CIA intended to reinvest by way of research and development. Thus, a directorate of science and technology evolved. Over time the directorate of science and technology conducted research and development for future intelligence needs. Other divisions developed but for our purposes are unimportant.

Apart from the CIA the U.S. developed other intelligence collection and analysis branches. During President Kennedy's shortened tenure, the defense intelligence agency (DIA) was created apart from the various services' intelligence branches. The DIA "became operational on October 1, 1961, as the nation's primary producer of foreign *military intelligence*. The DIA filled a critically important need for a central intelligence manager for the Department of Defense to support the requirements of the secretary of defense, the Joint Chiefs of Staff, and the "warfighter."[75] Its creation in 1961 suggests the DIA was created as a result of Kennedy's Bay of Pigs fiasco in Cuba in April 1961 and other occurrences that summer: Kennedy's meeting with Premier Khrushchev in Geneva where the latter reportedly browbeat the former and, two months later, the building of the Berlin Wall, which sealed off the Soviet-controlled sectors of Berlin from the other sectors. The DIA was created explicitly as a "combat support agency." Therefore, in contrast to the CIA whose work product is "strategic," the DIA's work product evolved as "tactical" intelligence. The DIA was and is housed bureaucratically under the Department of Defense.[76] Among America's myriad intelligence-collection and intelligence-analysis institutions and agencies, the CIA alone was left unsubordinated to a larger executive agency of the executive. In its history, this unique position has proved both an asset and a bane.

Prior to World War II the branches of the military—as they were prior to the 1947 NSA—developed their own intelligence agencies. This trend continued following the 1947 NSA. Therefore, intelligence agencies were created over time for the branches of the U.S. military. Branches for Army, Air Force, and Marine battlefield intelligence evolved over time. Naval intelligence predated the 1947 NSA. Coast Guard intelligence also eventually evolved. Historically, all these defense department intelligence agencies were funded and tasked through the Department of Defense's structure. In theory, the 1947 NSA made each accountable, more or less, to the director of central intelligence (DCI) but the DCI, perhaps understandably, never attempted to exert his influence over defense department agencies. This was less than surprising as the defense bureaucracy's budget was at least an order of magnitude greater than the collective intelligence community budget and the DCI, therefore, wisely understood his chances of controlling defense department-related intelligence collectors and analysts were poor at best.

Other intelligence-collection and intelligence-analysis agencies evolved as well. The Department of Energy created its own intelligence entity to monitor nuclear-related issues. The U.S. Treasury Department created its own intelligence branch. Treasury's intelligence included specialized functions for such issues as counterfeiting of U.S. currency and so forth. The Department of State developed its own intelligence agency as well, presumably for the unique needs of America's diplomats and for policymakers from the Department of State, who were also represented in the NSC by virtue of the secretary of state's role as an NSC principal. The U.S. Department of State's Bureau of Intelligence and Research (known as INR) was created for those needs. State's INR gained a reputation for good analytic products.[77]

As they developed, intelligence agencies such as the drug enforcement agency (DEA) were also included in the intelligence community. Finally, highly specialized intelligence agencies were created for highly technical areas of satellite and signals intelligence. These agencies developed as the National Security Agency (NSA) whose mission is signals intelligence, known as SIGINT; the National Reconnaissance Office (NRO), which operated and collected intelligence from America's spy satellites; and the National Geospatial-Intelligence Agency (NGA) whose particular mission, perhaps, is best described by their own mission statement:

> The National Geospatial-Intelligence Agency (NGA) provides timely, relevant, and accurate geospatial intelligence in support of national security objectives. Geospatial intelligence is the exploitation and analysis of imagery and geospatial information to describe, assess, and visually depict physical features and geographically referenced activities on the Earth.[78]

In short, the intelligence community that evolved during the Cold War was diverse and highly specialized. It was also, clearly, full of redundancies. Once policymakers determined to keep a standing military of some size on a permanent basis they spread it out across the country to give national legislators and the American people a stake in its continuation; similarly, the intelligence community was spread out across the country to take advantage of particular comparative advantages as well as for reason of pork-barrel politics. As individual states came to rely on military or intelligence agencies operating in their districts, federal monies followed the work. Thus, senators and U.S. representatives of states blessed with federal largesse tended to fight for such institutional continuation in perpetuity.

Unfortunately, prior to 9/11 many of these agencies failed to work well together. The 9/11 Commission's final report repeatedly referred to "stove pipes" erected from the community to the policymaking level that precluded the essential sharing of intelligence that might have made 9/11 *less* possible. That stove pipes were erected was hardly surprising: bureaucracies are the sine qua non of modern nation-states and are also a modern nation-state's specialized and functional area of expertise. Bureaucracies also may become a bane when strong oversight of their specialized functions is lacking and the specialized parts of the bureaucracy instead work at cross purposes. That was the state of the intelligence community on September 11, 2001.

The President's Foreign Intelligence Advisory Board,
The National Intelligence Council, and Congressional Oversight

Beyond the intelligence community proper, various entities were created over time to advise the president and/or the NSC with respect to intelligence, national intelligence estimates (NIEs), and other accessories useful to America's foreign policy and national security policymakers. Perhaps one of the most important but least understood of these was created in 1956 under President Eisenhower. President Eisenhower enjoyed including outside experts in policymaking circles on occasion to attenuate the tunnel vision and parochialism that developed within bureaucracies. President Eisenhower occasionally invited accomplished businessmen, industrialists, and others to the White House. Given his penchant for seeking outsiders, President Eisenhower created the the President's Board of Consultants on Foreign Intelligence Activities. Subsequently, and following the Jackson Committee Report that criticized President Eisenhower's NSC policymaking as being moribund, President Kennedy transformed Eisenhower's Board of Consultants into the President's Foreign-Intelligence Advisory Board (PFIAB) early in his tenure. The PFIAB has remained ever since.

By law the PFIAB is comprised of persons who serve "at the pleasure of the President," and who were "appointed by the President from among trustworthy and distinguished citizens outside the Government who . . . qualified on the basis of achievement, experience and independence." The law directed the president to designate a "chairman and vice chairman" who with the professional staff also created by the legislation, were to act as a "full-time staff and consultants as authorized by the President." Further, the PFIAB staff were designated as subordinates to the executive director of the PFIAB, appointed by the President." The PFIAB was expected to ensure "the quality, quantity, and adequacy of intelligence collection, of analysis and estimates, and of counterintelligence and other intelligence activities." It was given the further broad responsibility "to review continually the performance of *all agencies* of the Federal Government that are engaged in the collection, evaluation, or production of intelligence or the execution of intelligence policy" as well as a general supervisory role over "management."[79] The PFIAB was additionally given, in theory, unfettered access to the president to "report directly to the President and advise him concerning the objectives, conduct, management and coordination of the various activities of the agencies of the Intelligence Community."[80] The same legislation created an Intelligence Oversight Board (IOB) whose members (four or fewer, all of whom were appointed by the president from the membership of the PFIAB) prepared "for the President reports of intelligence activities that the IOB" believed "may be unlawful or contrary to Executive order or Presidential directive"; forwarded "to the Attorney General reports received concerning intelligence activities that the IOB" believed "may be unlawful or contrary to Executive order or Presidential directive"; reviewed "the internal guidelines of each agency within the Intelligence Community" that concerned "the lawfulness of intelligence activities" as well as "the practices and procedures of the Inspectors General and General Counsel of the Intelligence Community for discovering and reporting intelligence activities that may [have been] unlawful or contrary to Executive order or Presidential directive"; and who were empowered to "conduct such investigations as the IOB" deemed "necessary to carry out its functions under this order."[81]

The PFIAB "acted as a nonpartisan body offering the President objective, expert advice on the conduct of U.S. foreign intelligence." The PFIAB historically offered "advice to the President concerning the quality and adequacy of intelligence collection, of analysis and estimates, of counterintelligence, and of other intelligence activities." Through its Intelligence Oversight Board, the PFIAB has advised "the President on the legality of foreign intelligence activities," during the Cold War and after. Finally, part of the PFIAB's unique role included being "tasked with providing the President with an independent source of advice on the effectiveness with which the intelligence community [was] meeting the nation's intelligence needs and the vigor and insight with which the community plan[ed] for the future."[82]

Another relatively specialized part of the intelligence community that evolved was the National Intelligence Council (NIC). The NIC was created as the "center of strategic thinking within the US Government."[83] Prior to the changes wrought by 9/11 and its aftermath, the NIC reported to the director of central intelligence (DCI). Through the DCI, the NIC provided the president and "senior policymakers with analyses of foreign policy issues that have been reviewed and coordinated throughout the Intelligence Community." The NIC created the national intelligence estimates (NIEs) used by presidents and their NSC principals as the basis for policymaking vis-à-vis particular threats or opportunities. For instance, the NIC created a National Intelligence Estimate (NIE) in late October 2002 that became President Bush's and his "war cabinet's" (that is, is NSC principals') basis for going to war in Iraq.[84] Congress looked into intelligence failures related to 9/11 and found that even as it interviewed FBI Director Robert S. Mueller's III, on October 17, 2002, the NIC had still failed to produce an NIE on the jihadi threats to the U.S.[85] The NIC, housed at CIA's Langley headquarters before 9/11, was comprised of the National Intelligence Officers of the CIA, their staff, and an analytic group. Together, the intelligence community's intelligence officers and staff supported the DCI as the primary producers of national intelligence estimates as well as additional interagency intelligence assessments that formed the basis of the DCI's advice to the president and the NSC.

Following the 9/11 attacks and the various postmortems analyzed in subsequent chapters, the NIC was moved (organizationally) to the office of the director of national intelligence (ODNI) where it continues to produce NIEs. It produced, for instance, the NIE on Iran's capabilities with respect to nuclear weapons that was released in 2004.[86] Part of another NIE leaked to the media several weeks before the 2006 midterm election demonstrated that the intelligence community considered the Iraq War a cause célèbre for terrorists. This NIE was controversial because it was leaked so close to the midterm elections and because it belied what the Bush administration had said about the Iraq War.[87] Though the NIC's organizational placement is not rendered in the organizational charts of the president-NSC-policymaking model produced elsewhere in this manuscript, it is important for the reader to understand that it has been part of the larger foreign and national security policymaking bureaucracy since the late 1950s.[88]

SUMMARY

This chapter's main objectives included the following. First, we intended to define the president-NSC-policymaking model as our unit of analysis and comparison. Second, we used the construct to compare each post–World War II president's particular use of the model. In doing so, we sought to look for innovations and change from administration to administration, something we contended happened only slowly and incrementally. We also sought to identify generalizable trends over the course of the Cold War and following the demise of the Soviet Union. One clear generalizable trend was the increased prominence of the president-NSC-policymaking construct as the highest locus of U.S. foreign policy and national security policy decision making. As a few recent books have looked in great detail at the NSC's role in U.S. foreign policy decision making, we constructed our own conceptual model, the president-NSC-policymaking model, for comparative purposes. We briefly examined each administration using that construct. Third, we represented the president-NSC-policymaking model graphically. Those renderings were presented to make it easy to compare differences and continuity over time.

Additionally we considered amendments to the original 1947 National Security Act, the legislation that created America's national security infrastructure for thwarting Soviet communism and expansionism. Two amendments in particular—the 1949 Reorganization Bill and the Goldwater-Nichols Act (1986)—were examined. Doing so allowed us to demonstrate how the president-NSC-policymaking model has evolved incrementally over most of its history. Both amendments were incremental changes codified in law slightly altering the way the model was intended to function. That so little amending occurred demonstrated how prescient the drafters of the 1947 NSA were. They were clearly remarkable Americans who deserve their country's thanks. Additionally, we examined two important appendages to the intelligence community: the National Intelligence Center (whose work product, the National Intelligence Estimates, informs policymakers) and the President's Foreign Intelligence Advisory Board. While both may seem esoteric to many Americans, they have become central to America's national security.

We then undertook a brief analysis of the evolution of the intelligence community over the course of the Cold War. Some intelligence assets existed prior to the 1947 NSA. However, this historic legislation created the Central Intelligence Agency and what became known as the director of central intelligence (DCI). Further, as the Cold War demanded innovations, the intelligence community also evolved over time. We therefore considered what is euphemistically called the intelligence community—clearly it evolved as multiple empires or fiefdoms. Instead of a single intelligence community functioning seamlessly to keep America's national security policymakers fully informed, multiple disparate agencies with multiple lines of funding (military and other) competed and eventually worked at cross purposes. While each may have perceived itself as invaluable to

America's national security policymakers, competition and finite budget dollars led to parochialism and worse. Nevertheless, that was the state of the intelligence community when America first experienced Sunni jihadi terror in 1993, during President Clinton's first term, and subsequently. It was essentially in the same state when America experienced its traumatic assault from Sunni jihadis on 9/11 when President George W. Bush had only been in office some nine months.

In subsequent chapters we will compare changes since 9/11, the Iraq War, and the Intelligence Reform and Terrorism Prevention Act (IRTPA) to the model that existed before 9/11 and served U.S. national security relatively well over some nearly sixty years. We will specifically seek to compare the 1947 NSA with the 2004 IRTPA. The IRTPA was the first major, demonstrable reorganization of the entire president-NSC-policymaking model, including the intelligence community and other attendant parts, since 1947. As a result, U.S. national security and foreign policy have changed to meet the needs of a new century and new transnational threats. At least, that was supposed to be the result of the seminal reorganization of U.S. national security and foreign policy; we will therefore also be keenly interested in how well the reorganization has succeeded to date. The reorganization, as such, will be central to scholars and analysts as they seek to understand U.S. national security and foreign policy in the future. For professors, understanding the reorganizations begun and hastened in 2004 will be imperative for teaching today's students and potentially tomorrow's policymakers what they need to understand about America's national security and foreign policy. Before we turn to those comparisons, however, we need to look closely at the George W. Bush administration and its president-NSC-policymaking model. Since the Bush (43) administration is in its second term, we will briefly examine the changes made between the model as it existed when the 9/11 attacks occurred as well as how it has since changed. Personnel changes were made following the first term; additionally, structural changes recommended by multiple blue-ribbon panels have changed the model over time. We turn to that examination next.

NOTES

1. As discussed in chapter 3, the beginning of the Cold War and most of its contests did not fit the criteria of a foreign policy crisis. Nevertheless, policymakers repeatedly framed confrontations with the Soviets as crises and seemed to believe they were.

2. David J. Rothkopf, *Running the World: The Inside Story of the National Security Council and the Architects of American Power* (New York: Public Affairs, 2005), 5. Other important scholarship on the NSC exists though relatively little on the NSC per se. See Karl Inderfurth and Loch Johnson, eds., *Fateful Decisions: Inside the National Security Council* (Oxford: Oxford University Press, 2004), another exemplary examination of the NSC. Additionally, John Prados', *Keepers of the Keys: A History of the National Security Council from Truman to Bush* (New York: William Morrow and Company, 1991), was a good book on the NSC for its day (mid-1990s). Unfortunately, the latter was written some 15 years ago making it less comprehensive. Another excellent examination of the CIA, as well as the Joint Chiefs of Staff and NSC, was published late in Clinton's tenure: Amy B. Zegart, *Flawed by Design: The Evolution of the CIA, JCS, and NSC* (Palo Alto, CA: Stanford University, 1999).

3. *The National Security Act of 1947*, Public Law 253, 80th Cong., 2d sess. (July 26, 1947), Section 101 (c).

4. Karl Inderfurth and Loch Johnson, eds., *Fateful Decisions*, xiv.

5. Some scholars have noted that Robert "Bobby" Cutler drafted the memoranda for President Eisenhower during the presidential transition period from Truman to Eisenhower and became President Eisenhower's first NSC advisor. David Rothkopf made this point in his excellent book on the NSC's evolution during the Cold War and through 9/11. Rothkopf also argued, however, that "Clark Clifford continued to perform as a quasi-national security advisor by retaining his role as aide closest to the president in the White House with a national security and foreign policy brief [under Truman]. Later, when Averell Harriman became an assistant to the president he played a similar role and Truman subsequently made Harriman a member of the council—the first time such an *advisor* was also actually on the group." See David Rothkopf, *Running the World*, 57. Another researcher of the National Security Council, John Prados, argued in the early 1990s that Averell Harriman effectively became the first de facto NSC advisor. See John Prados, *Keeper of the Keys: A History of the National Security Council from Truman to Bush* (New York: William Morrow and Company, 1991), pp. 46–47, 50. (Note: in this text "advisor" is used intentionally rather than "adviser"—two words with precisely the same definition in the *Oxford English Dictionary*—to help distinguish the NSC advisor from other national security advisers to the president.)

6. John Quincy Adams, speech before Congress in celebration of Independence Day (Washington DC, July 4, 1821), http://www.bartleby.com/73/613.html (retrieved on December 22, 2005) (my emphasis).

7. White House, *National Security Strategy of the United States, March 2006*, White House, http://www.whitehouse.gov/nsc/2006/nss206.pdf, 43 (Acrobat Reader pagination, 48).

8. Harry S. Truman, *Years of Trial and Hope* (New York: Double Day and Company, 1956), 359–381.

9. David Rothkopf, *Running the World*, 60.

10. Two versions of the 1947 National Security Act were used in this book. The most accessible was found at the United States Intelligence Community's Web site, entitled simply "National Security Act of 1947," (July 26, 1947), http://www.intelligence.gov/

0-natsecact_1947.shtml (accessed December 4, 2005). As researchers of U.S government documents may appreciate, often a hard copy is preferable to a copy that has been tweaked for the Internet. Therefore, the second copy used here was the Government Printing Office's 1973 copy, the only hardcopy we discovered that contained the entire original 1947 NSA language and subsequent amendments. *National Security Act of 1947, as amended through September 30, 1973*, Public Law 253, 80th Congress, 1st sess., (July 26, 1947), Section 101. [U.S.C. 402] (a)7. (Washington, DC: Government Printing Office, 1973).

11. Rothkopf, *Running the World*, pp. 60, 69–70; Inderfurth and Johnson, *Fateful Decisions*, 29–30; and Prados, *Keeper of the Keys*, 64.

12. See Stephen E. Ambrose, *Eisenhower, Volume I: Soldier, General of the Army, President-Elect* (New York: Simon and Schuster, 1983), and *Eisenhower, Volume II: The President* (New York: Simon and Schuster, 1984).

13. John Prados, *Keepers of the Keys*, 61–62; Rothkopf, *Running the World*, 65.

14. John Prados, *Keepers of the Keys*, 63.

15. Inderfurth and Johnson, *Fateful Decisions*, 29–30; John Prados, *Keepers of the Keys*, 64–65.

16. John Prados, *Keepers of the Keys*, 68; David Rothkopf, *Running the World*, 111.

17. Rothkopf, *Running the World*, 75.

18. Karl Inderfurth and Loch Johnson, editors, *Fateful Decisions*, 57–61. (My emphasis.)

19. Prados, *Keeper of the Keys*, 99–109.

20. See Alexander George, *Presidential Decision Making in Foreign Policy* (Boulder, CO: Westview Press, 1980). "Stovepipes" as a metaphor began circulating in Washington, D.C., during the 9/11 Commission's work in early 2004. The metaphor is repeatedly used in the final report, sometimes nearly synonymously and incorrectly with Irving Janis' "groupthink" phenomenon, which is usually applied to small, exclusive groups. For instance, see the National Commission on Terrorist Attacks Upon the United States, *The 9/11 Commission Report*, created by Public Law 107–306, November 27, 2002, and published online in Acrobat format on July 24, 2004, 403 (Acrobat Reader pagination p. 420), where it is even used as a verb as in "stove-piped," and 418 (Acrobat Reader pagination, 435), http://www.9-11commission.gov/report/911 Report.pdf (accessed July 24, 2004).

21. See Arthur Schlesinger, Jr., *Bitter Heritage: Vietnam and American Democracy, 1941–1966* (NY: Houghton Mifflin Co, 1967); and Stanley Karnow, *Vietnam: A History* (New York: Penguin Books, 1983); also see Robert S. McNamara and Brian VanDeMark, *In Retrospect: the Tragedies and Lessons of Vietnam* (New York: Vintage,1996). Each book makes the same basic distinction of some being pro-coup and others being anti-coup.

22. Stephen E. Ambrose, introduction to *The Haldeman Diaries: Inside the Nixon White House*, by H. Robert Haldeman (New York: G.P. Putnam & Sons, 1994), 5–6, and *ad passim*. See also Alexander George, *Presidential Decision Making in Foreign Policy* 154–156; Cecil V. Crabb and Kevin Mulcahy, *Presidents and Foreign Policy Making: From FDR to Reagan* (Baton Rouge, LA: Louisiana State University Press, 1986), 251–253.

23. An example is Seymour M. Hersh, *The Price of Power: Kissinger in the Nixon White House* (New York: Summit Books, 1983).

24. Joan Hoff, *Nixon Reconsidered* (New York: Basic Books, 1994), 176 and 177–78.

25. Richard M. Nixon, *The Memoirs of Richard Nixon* (New York: Grosset and Dunlap, 1978).

26. Haldeman's *Diaries* is replete with almost clinical observational comments about the vice president failing to fit the role as conceived by President Nixon and Haldeman himself. See, for example, H. R. Halderman, *The Haldeman Diaries*, 27.

27. Cecil V. Crabb and Kevin Mulcahy, *Presidents and Foreign Policymaking* 237; M. Kent Bolton, "How Decision Time and Degree of Anticipation Affect the Decision Making Process as U.S. Decision Makers Confront Various Foreign Policy Challenges" (PhD dissertation, The Ohio State University, 1992), 94.

28. William Shawcross, *Sideshow: Kissinger, Nixon, and the Destruction of Cambodia* (New York: Simon and Schuster, 1979).

29. Alexander L. George, *Presidential Decision Making in Foreign Policy*, 155.

30. Alexander L. George, *Presidential Decision Making in Foreign Policy*, 155; Seymour M. Hersh, *The Price of Power* (New York: Summit Books, 1983), 29; M. Kent Bolton, "How Decision Time and Degree of Anticipation Affect the Decision Making Process as U.S. Decision Makers Confront Various Foreign Policy Challenges," 94 and 96–97.

31. Cecil V. Crabb and Kevin Mulcahy, *Presidents and Foreign Policy Making*, 260–261.

32. David Rothkopf, *Running the World*, 14–21.

33. Inderfurth and Johnson, eds., *Fateful Decisions*, 69.

34. Gerald R. Ford, *A Time to Heal: The Autobiography of Gerald R. Ford* (New York: Harper and Row Publishers, 1979). Other information on the Ford administration came from Richard G. Head, Frisco W. Short, and Robert C. MacFarlane, *Crisis Resolution: Presidential Decision Making in the Mayaguez and Korean Confrontations* (Boulder, CO: Westview Press, 1978); and Christopher Jon Lamb, *Belief Systems and Decision Making in the Mayaguez Crisis* (Gainesville, FL: University of Florida Press, 1989).

35. Gerald R. Ford, *A Time to Heal*, 126.

36. Richard G. Head, Francisco W. Short, and Robert McFarlane, *Crisis Resolution: Presidential Decision Making in the Mayaguez and Korean Confrontations*; M. Kent Bolton, "How Decision Time and Degree of Anticipation Affect the Decision-Making Process as U.S. Decision Makers Confront Various Foreign Policy Challenges," 156–166.

37. Head, Short, and McFarlane, *Crisis Resolution*, 107.

38. Christopher Jon Lamb, *Belief Systems and Decision Making in the Mayaguez Crisis*, 80.

39. Head, Short, and McFarlane, *Crisis Resolution*, 109.

40. Head, Short, and McFarlane, *Crisis Resolution*, 108; Christopher Jon Lamb, *Belief Systems and Decision Making in the Mayaguez Crisis*, 81.

41. Gerald Ford, *Time to Heal*, 279–280.

42. Gerald Ford, *Time to Heal*, 132.

43. Prados, *Keepers of the Keys*, 387–389; and Rothkopf, *Running the World*, 167.

44. Inderfurth and Johnson, eds., *Fateful Decisions*, 94–95.

45. Inderfuth and Loch Johnson, eds., *Fateful Decisions*, 95.

46. Rothkopf, *Running the World*, 170.

47. Rothkopf, *Running the World*, 174.

48. Richard A. Melanson, *American Foreign Policy since the Vietnam War: The Search for Consensus from Nixon to Clinton* (New York: M.E. Sharpe, 1996), 110–117.

49. Melanson, *U.S. Foreign Policy since the Vietnam War*, ad passim.

50. Rothkopf, *Running the World*, 228.

51. Rothkopf, *Running the World*, 215.

52. Melanson, *American Foreign Policy since the Vietnam War*, 142 and 144.

53. Rothkopf, *Running the World*, 217.

54. Rothkopf, *Running the World*, 218.

55. Rothkopf, *Running the World*, 218.

56. It is beyond our scope to attempt to explain the Iran-Contra scandal (or as one periodical called it, Iran-Amok). Many excellent books have been written on it and the reader would do well to investigate them. The reader may find the so-called Tower Commission report for starters. It was a postmortem of the fiasco conducted by a blue-ribbon panel, including Brent Scowcroft and then-Senator John Tower (R-TX). Inasmuch as we too examine postmortems of 9/11, both policymaking and intelligence failures, we believe the Tower Commission report is an excellent place to begin. Briefly, two separate and distinct initiatives, one dealing with Iran during its war with Iraq and the other dealing with the Nicaraguan *Contras*, became intermingled with money from one appearing as money in the other. The persons behind the initiatives were William Casey (DCI), Robert McFarlane, John Poindexter, Oliver North, and other NSC staffers. It was a debacle of tremendous proportions.

57. George H. W. Bush and Brent Scowcroft, *A World Transformed* (New York: Alfred A. Knopf, 1989), 21.

58. In fairness to Clinton, it should be noted that many of the neoconservatives who so opposed Clinton and who are discussed later in detail also found ways to avoid Vietnam. Indeed one of Clinton's most ardent foes, current Vice President Dick Cheney, received five deferments allowing him to avoid Vietnam and instead to attend college and raise his family. Dick Cheney of course served as secretary of defense in George H. W. Bush's administration. Further, while President George W. Bush served in the guard during the Vietnam War, it has been well established that he and his similarly privileged Texas-elite peers (both Democratic and Republican) likely knew that serving in the guard's "Champagne" unit would almost certainly ensure they never would see action in Vietnam.

59. White House, "Clinton Administration, 1993–1997," National Security Council, http://www.whitehouse.gov/nsc/history.html#clinton (accessed March 17, 2006); see also Rothkopf, *Running the World*, 304–305.

60. Rothkopf, *Running the World*, 304.

61. Rothkopf, *Running the World*, 308–310.

62. White House, "Clinton Administration, 1993–1997," National Security Council, http://www.whitehouse.gov/nsc/history.html#clinton.

63. Most of the information cited comes from the official biographies of secretaries of state, secretaries of defense, and NSC advisors. See http://www.defenselink.mil/specials/secdef_histories/bios/aspin.htm for a biography of Secretary Les Aspin and (http://www.defenselink.mil/specials/secdef_histories/bios/) for the biographies of former secretaries of defense, as portrayed by the Defense Department. See http://www.state.gov/secretary/

former/ for the "official" biographical information on former secretaries of state; see http://www.whitehouse.gov/nsc/history.html for biographical and historical information on previous NSCs.

64. Rothkopf, *Running the World*, 323–327; Daniel Benjamin and Steven Simon, *Age of Sacred Terror* (NY: Random House, 2002), 239.

65. Rothkopf, *Running the World*, 363.

66. The National Commission on the Terrorist Attacks on the United States [known as the 9/11 Commission], *The Final Public Report*, http://www.9-11commission.gov/report/index.htm, ch. 3 "Counterterrorism Approach Evolves," subsection "From the Old Terrorism to the New,", 71–73 (Acrobat Reader pagination, 88–90) and, 147 (Acrobat Reader pagination, 164).

67. Rothkopf, *Running the World*, 56–57.

68. Truman Museum and Library, "Chronology 1949," http://www.trumanlibrary.org/chron/49chrono.htm and http://www.trumanlibrary.org/chron/49chron2.htm #government, entries from May 9 and August 10 (accessed March 16, 2006). One other source of limited information on the NSC negotiations and reorganizations that occurred during Truman's presidency may be found among Ferdinand Eberstadt's papers. Eberstadt was a close collaborator of Secretary Forestall's during the period. Forestall soon thereafter took his own life and some believe the stress of wrestling with the bureaucracy over the change from a state-war-Navy-cabinet model to the Defense Department and the president-NSC policymaking model took its toll on Forrestal, perhaps resulting in his untimely demise. The papers may be found at Princeton University, *Ferdinand Eberstadt Paper*,: http://infoshare1.princeton.edu/libraries/fires-tone/rbsc/finding_aids/eberst/eberstlist1b.html (accessed November 12, 2005).

69. *Goldwater-Nichols Act, U.S. Code* (1986), Title 10, Subtitle A, Part I, Chapter 5, § 151, a, b, and c, http://www.jcs.mil/goldwater_nichol_act1986.html (accessed March 19, 2006) (my emphasis).

70. *Goldwater-Nichols Act, U.S. Code* (1986), Title 10, Subtitle A, Part I, Chapter 5, § 151, d(1).

71. Dana Priest, *The Mission: Waging War and Keeping Peace with America's Military,* (New York: W.W. Norton and Company, 2004), 95. The reader should remember this language as we subsequently examine the Intelligence Reform and Terrorism Prevention Act, particularly the power the law gave to the director of national intelligence it created!

72. Priest, *The Mission,* 95–96.

73. The Commission on the Intelligence Capabilities of the United States Regarding Weapons of Mass Destruction, *Report to the President of the United States* (Robb-Silberman WMD Report), Appendix C: "An Intelligence Community Primer," 579 (Acrobat Reader pagination, 595).

74. Maurice R. Greenberg and Richard N. Haas, eds., *Making Intelligence Smarter: The Future of U.S. Intelligence* (New York: Council on Foreign Relations, 1995) found on the Federation of American Scientists Web site at http://www.fas.org/irp/cfr.html (accessed March 17, 2006).

75. Defense Intelligence Agency, "History," http://www.dia.mil/history/index.htm (accessed March 17, 2006).

76. Defense Intelligence Agency, "Introduction to the DIA," http://www.dia.mil/thisisdia/intro/index.htm (accessed March 18, 2006).

77. The Office of the Inspector General, "Inspection of the Bureau of Intelligence and Research," (November 28, 2005), http://oig.state.gov/documents/organization/58019.pdf (accessed on March 18, 2006).

78. National Geospatial-Intelligence Agency, "Fact Sheet," http://www.nga.mil/portal/site/nga01/index.jsp? epicontent=GENERIC&itemID=31486591e1b3af00VgnVCMServer 23727a95RCRD&beanID =1629630080&viewID=Article (accessed March 18, 2006).

79. Executive Order no. 12,863, *Federal Register,* title 3, sec. 1.2 (1993), http://www.archives.gov/federal-register/executive-orders/pdf/12863.pdf.

80. Executive Order no. 12,863, *Federal Register,* title 3, sec. 1.3 (1993).

81. See "Notes" to Title 50, chapter 15, § 401 Executive Order 12863. President's Foreign Intelligence Advisory Board, Executive Order 12863, Sept. 13, 1993, 58 F.R. 48441, as amended by Executive Order 13070, Dec. 15, 1997, 62 F.R. 66493, Part II, "Oversight and Intelligence Activities," sec, 2.2, parts a–e. Cornell University Law Collection, http://www.law.cornell.edu/uscode/html/uscode50/usc_sec_50_00000401 — —000-notes.html

82. White House, *The President's Foreign Intelligence Advisory Board,* http://www.whitehouse.gov/pfiab/ ,"The Introduction," "History of the Board," and "The Role of the Board," respectively (accessed in August 2005, revisited on March 18, 2006).

83. National Intelligence Council, "Welcome," http://www.cia.gov/nic/NIC_home.html (accessed March 21, 2006).

84. The Federation of American Scientists is intensely interested in U.S. foreign policy among other things. Its website hosts many government documents that have been declassified. The October 2002 National Intelligence Estimate on Iraq may be found at http://www.fas.org/irp/cia/product/iraq-wmd.pdf (accessed July 2005).

85. House Permanent Select Committee on Intelligence and the Senate Select Committee on Intelligence, *Report of the Joint Inquiry into the Terrorist Attacks of September 11, 2001,*107th Cong,, 2d sess. (December 2002), 238 (Acrobat Reader pagination, 290). This document is known as the Joint Inquiry. The Joint Inquiry is examined in detail in chapter 8.

86. Dana Linzer, "Iran Is Judged 10 Years From Nuclear Bomb: U.S. Intelligence Review Contrasts With Administration Statements," *Washington Post,* August 2, 2005, http://www.washingtonpost.com/wp-dyn/content/article/2005/08/01/AR2005080101453.html.

87. Office of the Director of National Intelligence, "Declassified Key Judgments of the National Intelligence Estimate 'Trends in Global Terrorism: Implications for the United States Dated April 2006,'" September 26, 2006, http://dni.gov/press_releases/Declassified_NIE_Key_Judgments.pdf.

88. *Intelligence Reform and Terrorism Prevention Act, December 2004,* Title I, "Reform of the Intelligence Community," § 1011. The IRPTA shall be examined in detail in chapter 8.

CHAPTER 5

The Transition Between the Clinton and Bush Administrations

The duties of our day are different. But the values of our nation do not change. Let us reject the blinders of isolationism, just as we refuse the crown of empire. Let us not dominate others with our power—or betray them with our indifference. And let us have an American foreign policy that reflects American character. The modesty of true strength. The humility of real greatness.

—Governor George W. Bush,
"A Distinctly American Internationalism," speech presented at the
Ronald Reagan Library, Simi, California, November 19, 1999

AMERICA'S INTRODUCTION TO THE GLOBAL JIHADI HYDRA: THE TRANSITION BETWEEN PRESIDENTS WILLIAM J. CLINTON AND GEORGE W. BUSH

The U.S. experienced "terrorism" from jihadi extremists well in advance of 9/11 and well in advance of the presidency of George W. Bush. During the Reagan administration, U.S. troops were stationed in Lebanon as part of a coalition intervention effort to forestall Lebanon's continued destruction. Apparently, the U.S. and the French were seen by some of the disputants as taking sides in Lebanon's complex domestic politics, in which Islam and Christianity have historically mixed. Sadly, in the fall of 1983, U.S. and French troops were specifically targeted in coordinated car-bomb attacks by "martyrs" who attempted to punish the U.S. and France for taking sides, as they perceived it, against Islam.

Most Americans, of course, were horrified that U.S. troops were targeted in a battle in which America perceived itself as a neutral arbiter. That the attacks in Lebanon were against "combatants" or soldiers may have made the event seem less urgent to most Americans, including policymakers. Among the results of the Lebanon attacks was authorization from the U.S. Congress for the FBI to conduct investigations of terrorist attacks that occurred outside the U.S., an important new authority for the FBI. In fact, by 1987, Congress authorized the FBI to make arrests outside U.S. sovereign territory (that is, abroad) without the consent of the host government. This authorization, controversial at the time, proved invaluable as jihadis began targeting the U.S. directly following the end of the Cold War. Indeed, "extraordinary renditions" continued to be controversial during both the Clinton and Bush (43) administrations. Joint CIA-FBI staffing of a counterterrorism center soon followed. (The counterterrorism center was begun under the Reagan administration, housed in the CIA. The FBI seconded staff to work with the center and liaison with the FBI.) This collaboration proved its value in December 1988 after it ultimately broke the case of Pan Am Flight 103, which exploded over Lockerbie, Scotland. The collaboration ultimately detected Libya's involvement.

"Despite sharpened focus in the years before September 11, terrorism remained only one concern of many and counterterrorism efforts had to compete with other priorities," wrote the authors of the Joint Inquiry (the House Permanent Select Committee on Intelligence and the Senate Select Intelligence Committee). Furthermore, the "process for setting intelligence priorities [remained] vague and confusing, and neither the Clinton nor the Bush Administration developed an integrated counterterrorism strategy that drew on all elements of national power before September 11." Though terrorism was briefly on the intelligence community's radar screen in the 1980s, during President George H. W. Bush's term in office, U.S national security focus returned to the Cold War and the Soviet Union. Old habits proved resistant to change. As America's national security institutions returned to Cold War thinking, the vast bureaucracy below the policymaking level found few incentives for thinking anew about looming transnational threats, including global jihadis. According to an important participant at the time, even following the end of the Cold War, jihadi attacks on the U.S. were the furthest thing from the Clinton administration's mind. That apparently changed when, shortly following Clinton's first inauguration, Mir Amal Kansi—who subsequently fled to Pakistan—murdered two CIA employees just outside CIA headquarters in Langley, Virginia. The CIA murders together with Saddam Hussein's plot to assassinate former President George H. W. Bush in 1993, made counterterrorism a top foreign policy priority[1] for the first time.

As the priority increased, the bureaucracy and the Clinton administration gradually responded. In 1995, the Clinton administration's National Security Council produced presidential decision directive (PDD) 35. PDD 35 formally established terrorism as a top intelligence priority. Later that year PDD 39 was promulgated by Clinton's NSC and signed by the president, becoming the first such NSC document on terrorism since the Reagan administration. PDD 39 mandated more robust efforts to capture terrorists abroad and made the detection and thwarting of weapons of mass destruction (WMDs) a foreign policy objective. Instruments and authorities such as "extraordinary renditions" began to gain currency as necessary tools to defend America's interests against global jihadis. In 1998, President Clinton's NSC released PDDs 62 and 63. These directives established counterintelligence as national security instrument and established a procedure for responding to terrorist attacks on the U.S. According to the Joint Inquiry's interview with former NSC staffer Richard Clarke, known as the counterterrorism tsar, PDDs 62 and 63 established an interagency coordination process which included counterterrorism as a formal national security policy. (Richard Clarke directed the NSC's counterterrorism group in the second Clinton term and became an ad hoc NSC principal in the Clinton model.) The Joint Inquiry reported that following al Qaeda's attacks on the embassies in Africa in 1998, al Qaeda and Osama bin Laden specifically "dominated" U.S. counterterrorism efforts. The report quoted former Clinton NSC advisor, Samuel "Sandy" Berger as having indicated that al Qaeda attacks were clearly on the NSC's radar screen and, therefore, the larger bureaucracy's radar screen, by 1998.[2] While policymakers began to formulate national security objectives to thwart nonstate transnational threats, President Clinton's tenure in office was nearing its end and apparently lost its focus at a critical time: just as the global jihadi hydra was preparing to strike the American homeland.

THE GEORGE W. BUSH ADMINISTRATION'S NATIONAL SECURITY PRIORITIES

The first inauguration of George W. Bush as the 43rd president of the United States of America and its commander in chief occurred on January 20, 2001.[3] For Republicans and roughly half of the voting public, it was a happy occasion. Two terms of President William Jefferson Clinton must have been frustrating for Republicans, not just because it kept them out of office but because Clinton remained immensely popular even after the Lewinsky episode. President George W. Bush intended to be a different kind of president than Bill Clinton. From the beginning, Bush sought to bring "accountability" and "responsible government" to Washington. Whether objectively true or not, Bush and his team perceived their Clinton counterparts as unwieldy and not fully cognizant of their responsibilities to the American people and the world. Whereas Clinton was perpetually running behind schedule and held meetings that devolved into amorphous, floating "graduate-school seminars," Bush planned to be punctual. He intended to tame the vast bureaucracy at his disposal in order to help him make good decisions, and then to implement his decisions once they were made. President George W. Bush saw himself as a uniter rather than a divider. Bush also saw himself as a man of big ideas.

The official White House biography (c. 2006) characterized the Bush administration as one that was shaped largely by 9/11, some four-plus years after the trauma. It read:

> On the morning of September 11, 2001, terrorists attacked our Nation. Since then, President Bush has taken unprecedented steps to protect our homeland and create a world free from terror. He is grateful for the service and sacrifice of our brave men and women in uniform and their families. The President is confident that by helping build free and prosperous societies, our Nation and our friends and allies will succeed in making America more secure and the world more peaceful.[4]

In January 2001, President Bush could not have known how big a role 9/11 would play in his time in office. Whatever had once been President George W. Bush administration's raison d'être, by year's end 9/11 and the resulting war on global terrorism (including the Iraq War) would come to dominate his two terms in office.

In its first nine months President George W. Bush's administration was relatively similar to President Clinton's, despite the rhetoric that accompanied the campaign of 2000. Moreover, President Clinton's NSC was largely based on the template created by his predecessor, President George H. W. Bush, demonstrating one of our recurring themes: continuity in U.S. national security policy. While Clinton changed the nomenclature of the former Bush administration's NSC work product, he wisely kept important staffers who had formerly worked in his predecessors' president-NSC-policymaking machinery. That is not to say that Clinton's president-NSC-policymaking model was identical to that of George H. W. Bush. Clearly, there were differences, particularly in terms of process. President George W. Bush inherited a template adjusted for a post–Cold War globalized economy that was nevertheless similar to his father's model at the end of the Cold War.

Our objective in this chapter is twofold. First, we consider broadly the first months of the administration and its national security policymaking from January 21, 2001, through September 11, 2001. What, if anything, did the new Bush administration do to prepare for what became 9/11? What information, if any, could reasonably be expected to have motivated the administration to have done more to bend the bureaucracy to the administration's will? The "system" had, in fact, anticipated some type of attack. George Tenet, director of central intelligence (DCI) in 2001, told the 9/11 commissioners that from his perspective during summer 2001, "the system was blinking red." Is it fair to expect President Bush to have done more to shake up the bureaucracy? Was a terrorist attack on the United States homeland on the president's radar screen? Or was it simply so far down in terms of presidential priorities that the risk-averse bureaucracy he headed was unlikely to have begun to prepare for an attack on America?

Second, the George W. Bush president-NSC-policymaking structure and processes and its innovations are examined; that is, we examine the model as we did with previous post–World War II presidents in chapter 4. Included in our examination is how the president-NSC-policymaking model changed following 9/11. We also begin an examination of changes to the president-NSC policymaking model during the president's second term.

GEORGE W. BUSH: A "HUMBLE" BUT "STRONG" NATION

George W. Bush spoke philosophically of a "humble" U.S. foreign policy during the 2000 campaign. Candidate Bush and Vice President Gore debated each other during the 2000 campaign. During one debate, Governor Bush said, "If we're an arrogant nation, they'll resent us; if we're a humble nation, but strong, they'll welcome us. And our nation stands alone right now in the world in terms of power, and that's why we've got to be humble, and yet project strength in a way that promotes freedom." Mr. Gore apparently agreed with Mr. Bush. Gore responded: "So I think that the idea of humility is an important one."[5]

Prior to becoming president, Governor George W. Bush was noticeably lacking in foreign policy experience. He had rarely traveled abroad. He lacked intellectual curiosity regarding how peoples in other parts of the world lived and interacted or even how they eked out their daily existence. But that did not prevent Mr. Bush from forming strong convictions and preferences about foreign affairs. While campaigning for the presidency, Mr. Bush articulated some reasonably coherent foreign policy priorities. In the order in which he articulated them during his "Citadel speech," Bush said that his first priority, if elected president, was to "work with our strong democratic allies in Europe and Asia to extend the peace." Second, candidate Bush said he would seek to "promote a fully democratic Western hemisphere, bound together by free trade." Third, the governor said, if elected, he planned to "defend America's interests in the Persian Gulf and advance peace in the Middle East, based upon a secure Israel." Governor Bush noted that as president he would necessarily "check the contagious spread of weapons of mass destruction," including various modalities of delivering those weapons. Finally, Governor Bush said if elected he would provide leadership to "lead toward a world that trades in freedom," and that he "would pursue all these goals with focus, patience, and strength."[6]

However, priorities are not necessarily goals or strategic objectives, and Bush enumerated very few measurable strategic objectives. Nor would one necessarily expect him to have mentioned specific objectives in a campaign speech. In the debate cited above, Vice President Gore baited candidate Bush on Bush's position on Serbia and former Yugoslavia. Bush was apparently on record (or so Gore thought) as saying the Clinton administration intervention in former Yugoslavia could not be justified on the ethnic-cleansing criterion alone. Bush responded, "If I think it's in our nation's strategic interest, I'll commit troops. I thought it was in our strategic interests to keep Milosevic in check because of our relations in NATO, and that's why I took the position I took. I think it's important for NATO to be strong and confident. I felt like an unchecked Milosevic would harm NATO. And so it depends on the situation, Mr. Vice President."[7]

If Bush's record as governor of Texas reveals little of how a Bush administration's foreign policy might be distinct, Dr. Condoleezza Rice, his first NSC advisor—and his second-term secretary of state—provided some early indications well before Bush's election of the emerging Bush administration's thinking on foreign policy. Roughly a year before entering office, Dr. Rice published a piece in *Foreign Affairs* entitled "Life after The Cold War." In it, Rice acknowledged how difficult it was for the United States to find a common purpose or a proper role for the U.S. in the world, absent the tyranny of Soviet Communism. Among other things, she noted how economics and other transnational forces transcended national boundaries. "In such an environment," Rice wrote, "American policies must help further . . . favorable trends by maintaining a disciplined and consistent foreign policy that separate[d] the important from the trivial." According to Rice, the Clinton administration failed on that score. "The Clinton administration has assiduously avoided implementing such an agenda. Instead, every issue ha[d] been taken on its own terms—crisis by crisis, day by day." Dr. Rice suggested that the Clinton administration had not set "priorities." She noted that this lack of priorities had the advantage of being difficult to criticize but was less than beneficial for U.S. interests.

Under "Alternatives," Dr. Rice identified several goals a new Republican administration would have. Among them, the first was "to ensure that America's military" could "deter war, project power, and fight in defense of its interests *if deterrence fail[ed]*"; second, "to promote economic growth and political openness by extending free trade and a stable international monetary system to all committed to these principles . . ."; third, "to renew strong and intimate relationships with allies" whom she considered as sharing "American values" and who could therefore "share the burden of promoting peace, prosperity, and freedom"; fourth, "to focus U.S. energies on comprehensive relationships with the big powers, particularly Russia and China, that [could] and [would] mold the character of the international political system;" and fifth, "to deal decisively with the threat of rogue regimes and hostile powers," which she argued were "increasingly taking the forms of the potential for terrorism and the development of weapons of mass destruction (WMDs)."[8]

In light of 9/11 and the failure of deterrence, Dr. Rice's first priority was particularly interesting. Clearly, U.S. military power was insufficient to deter al Qaeda from striking the U.S. on 9/11. Priority three, to renew strong ties with allies who shared America's values, was also quite interesting in light of President Bush's post-9/11 explicit and unapologetic promotion of democracy as a remedy to the world's many problems. Dr. Rice's fourth priority was to focus America's energies on its relationships with Russia and China, something the former Bush and Clinton administrations had done. In April 2001, an incident occurred while an American spy plane cruised over international waters near China's Hainan Island. A U.S. Navy EP-3 intelligence platform was forced to land on Chinese territory, where Chinese forces held U.S. military personnel, resulting in a multiweek standoff between U.S. and Chinese forces that was eventually handled principally by Secretary of State Powell and the state department.[9]

Dr. Rice's fifth and final priority, perhaps, was most intriguing. She suggested that U.S. foreign policy must deal decisively with the threat of rogue regimes—presumably Libya, Iraq, Iran, Syria, North Korea, and the like—in anticipation of a nexus between such regimes, "terrorism," and weapons of mass destruction (WMDs). That al Qaeda openly discussed attacking the U.S. homeland was not a new issue, though neither was it exactly featured by either the Bush or Gore campaigns. Presumably, the Bush administration was aware of essentially the same information Vice President Gore had the opportunity to know. Later, "Bush and his principal advisers had all received briefings on terrorism, including bin Laden. In early September 2000, Acting Deputy Director of Central Intelligence John McLaughlin led a team to Bush's ranch in Crawford, Texas, and gave him a wide-ranging four-hour review of sensitive information." One of the four hours of the briefing was "to deal with terrorism." In fact, to "highlight the danger of terrorists obtaining chemical, biological, radiological, or nuclear weapons," a CIA expert on such weapons briefed the president. Apparently, then-DCI George Tenet, his deputy James Pavitt, and others set up an "office in Crawford to pass intelligence to Bush and some of his key advisers."[10] Though the normal transition between the outgoing Clinton and Bush administrations was half its usual length due to the election fiasco, the Bush administration was, seemingly, well-prepared for taking over foreign policy.[11]

Sometime in early January 2001, Richard Clarke—national counterterrorism coordinator for the NSC and holdover from both the Clinton and Bush (41) administrations—met with NSC advisor Condoleezza Rice. In the same period, Clarke also briefed Vice President Dick Cheney and Rice's deputy Stephen Hadley. The briefs emphasized Clarke's view of the al Qaeda menace including a comment (apparently a line on one of the

Power Point slides) that al Qaeda had "sleeper cells" in some 40 countries including the United States. Former NSC advisor to President Clinton, Samuel "Sandy" Berger, dropped in on the briefing intentionally to stress the importance of the al Qaeda threat. Later that day Berger briefed Rice personally and reportedly told NSC advisor Rice that "the Bush administration would spend more time on terrorism in general and al Qaeda in particular than on anything else." In the Blair House briefing, Clarke reportedly confronted the new administration with a dramatic conclusion: the new administration had a lot to do to get up to speed with respect to al Qaeda and the jihadi threat.[12] (Blair House is the government's residence across the street from the White House in which the president-elect and his staff are often housed during transitions.)

Richard Clarke had risen to a position of trust and responsibility in the Clinton administration. Though not a statutory NSC principal, he rose to the level of an ad hoc principal in the Clinton administration. Understandably, Clarke's star rose following the successful thwarting of the Millennium Attacks as 1999 came to a close. Thus, under the Clinton configuration of the president-NSC policymaking model, Clarke's counterterrorism security group (CSG) was represented in the NSC principals setting. The Bush administration had no particular obligation to put Clarke in a similarly critical position upon assuming power in January 2001. In fact, as was often the case with holdovers, the Bush administration may have viewed Clarke and his advice somewhat askance. In the Bush administration, Clarke was repositioned to report to the NSC principals through the NSC deputies. In retrospect, Clarke's former role in the NSC principals setting might have helped the Bush administration to focus earlier on al Qaeda. Nevertheless, the administration soon learned that al Qaeda was an important transnational threat in the post–Cold War era. In fact, the 9/11 Commission concluded that "significant continuity in counterterrorism policy" existed between the Clinton and Bush administrations over the transition.[13]

On the other hand the 9/11 Commission indicated that "between the January inauguration of the new administration and early September, no NSC principals' meeting was held on al Qaeda or to discuss al Qaeda." Clarke wrote a memorandum to NSC advisor Rice on January 25, 2001, just after the inauguration. In it, Mr. Clarke told Dr. Rice that al Qaeda was not merely a minor irritant about which the new administration could make decisions in some broader geopolitical or regional discussion.

Rather, according to Clarke, al Qaeda comprised a serious national security threat the new administration needed to meet as quickly as possible, since the Bush team needed to make some immediate decisions on how they were going to counter the al Qaeda threat. Clarke worried that toward the end of the Clinton administration decisions had been deferred since a new team was scheduled to take over. Now those decisions were pressing and Clarke attempted to make that point with Rice and others. Of course there is no telling whether a meeting or two during this period would have changed anything with respect to 9/11. In retrospect, however, the Bush administration would likely do it differently given the chance. But Dr. Rice did not respond directly to Clarke nor did the NSC principals meet to consider al Qaeda until September 4, 2001.[14] The Bush administration's president-NSC-policymaking model held its first principals meeting on al Qaeda just one week before the 9/11 attacks!

In early March, the Bush administration decided to postpone a decision on increased aid to the Northern Alliance in Afghanistan. (The Northern Alliance was the multiethnic coalition of anti-Taliban fighters and *mujahideen* in Afghanistan. It had been funded by the Clinton administration at various times.) Rather, Dr. Rice determined that a wide-ranging review of policy vis-à-vis Afghanistan was needed and she put that review in motion in March 2001. Importantly, Stephen Hadley (then deputy NSC advisor or Rice's number two person) held a NSC deputies' meeting on March 7, 2001, to review Clarke's suggestions of how to respond to the Taliban in Afghanistan, what to do about the fact that Afghanistan apparently harbored al Qaeda, and whether or not to use the Unmanned Ariel Vehicle (UAV or drone) called the Predator in Afghanistan. From this meeting Hadley concluded that a NSC directive on terrorism needed to be promulgated. Such a directive would instruct the bureaucracy as to the new administration's strategic objectives. The Bush administration memorialized such instructions via national security policy directives (NSPDs). The deputy level of the NSC discussed what to do about al Qaeda on April 30, 2001.[15] Had Dr. Rice not demoted Richard Clarke to report through the deputies committee to the principals committee, perhaps the NSC principals would have held a meeting on al Qaeda months earlier than their September 4, 2001, meeting.

Though more or less demoted to a position subordinate to the deputies, the Clarke counterterrorism security group (CSG) continued to grind away at the al Qaeda threat. During the spring of 2001, there was a spike in the number of intelligence reports on al Qaeda coming into the NSC—specifically Clarke's CSG. The 9/11 Commission's final report included an excellent chapter on the increased "chatter" during summer 2001 and its implications, "The System Was Blinking Red." (The quote came from an interview the 9/11 commissioners conducted with then-DCI George Tenet.) In May, the White House announced that Vice President Dick Cheney would lead a group to examine worst-case scenarios with respect to weapons of mass destruction and attacks on the U.S. The 9/11 Commission reported that Dick Cheney's task force on WMDs had just begun its work when 9/11 happened.[16] That Vice President Cheney was entrusted with such an important function in the new Bush administration may have signaled two important points. First, the vice president was truly an NSC principal, arguably more influential than *any* previous vice president. Second, it may have signaled that President Bush was willing to defer to the vice president on important matters of national security as Bush himself had relatively little national security experience. As a former secretary of defense in George H. W. Bush's administration, Vice President Cheney had ample national security experience. By temperament, Vice President Dick Cheney seemed to come from central casting for the important, sobering task of examining America's worst-case scenarios involving WMD attacks.

Meanwhile, in the bureaucracy, if not at the president-NSC-policymaking level, concerns over al Qaeda continued. DCI Gorge Tenet had declared "war" on al Qaeda in 1998. "On December 4, 1998, DCI Tenet issued a directive to several CIA officials and his deputy for community management, stating: 'We are at war. I want no resources or people spared in this effort, either inside CIA or the Community.'" However, the 9/11 Commission concluded that the "memorandum had little overall effect on mobilizing the CIA or the intelligence community."[17] On May 29 2001, DCI Tenet requested a meeting with NSC advisor Rice to discuss al Qaeda. The meeting was held and attended by Tenet, his chief of CIA's Counterterrorism Center (CTC) Cofer Black, NSC advisor Rice, counterterrorism chief Richard Clarke, and another CIA specialist on Bin Laden. Dr. Rice asked Tenet about taking the offensive against al Qaeda. Clarke and Black argued that the CIA was *already* taking the offensive. The meeting turned to an overall discussion of al Qaeda and what was being done. Tenet used the discussion to refer to the CIA's "ambitious plans" for covert action designed to break al Qaeda's back, which were created during the Clinton administration. According to the 9/11 Commission, which interviewed all the attendees, the CIA specialist told the Commission that Condoleezza Rice "got it," meaning she understood the gravity of the threat and understood what the CIA was attempting to accomplish. The report noted that the CIA specialist said Dr. Rice "agreed with his conclusions about what needed to be done, although he complained to [the 9/11 commissioners] that the policy process did not follow through quickly enough."[18] Apparently, one result of this meeting was that NSC advisor Rice asked Richard Clarke to draft a document for approval by the NSC for an NSPD "to eliminate" al Qaeda as a threat to the U.S. and its allies. The draft NSPD called for:

> a multiyear effort involving diplomacy, covert action, economic measures, law enforcement, public diplomacy [propaganda], and if necessary military efforts. The State Department was to work with other governments to end all al Qaeda sanctuaries, and also to work with the Treasury Department to disrupt terrorist financing. The CIA was to develop an expanded covert action program including significant additional funding and aid to anti-Taliban groups. The draft also tasked [The Office of Management and Budget] with ensuring that sufficient funds to support this program were found in U.S. budgets from fiscal years 2002 to 2006.

Rice's deputy, Stephen Hadley, circulated the draft on June 7, 2001.[19] The 9/11 Commission noted that Rice viewed the draft NSPD as "as the embodiment of a comprehensive new strategy employing all instruments of national power to eliminate the al Qaeda threat. Clarke, however, regarded the new draft as essentially similar to the proposal he had developed in December 2000 and put forward to the new administration in January 2001," the so-called Delenda Plan. Unfortunately, just as NSC advisor Rice appeared to be "getting it," Richard Clarke's frustrations with the new administration, his demotion to the deputy level, and bureaucratic inertia converged. Around the same time Richard Clarke asked to be reassigned to cyber-security issues for the NSC. Clarke told the 9/11 Commission "that he was frustrated with his role and with an administration that he considered . . . not 'serious about al Qaeda.' If Clarke was frustrated, he never expressed it to her," Rice told the 9/11 Commission.[20] Clearly, Clarke believed the new administration was not moving with sufficient alacrity on al Qaeda. Clarke had for some time been predicting al Qaeda attacks on U.S. assets abroad and potentially even on the U.S.

homeland. For his effort, the new administration had demoted him to deputy-level status in the president-NSC-policymaking model. After serving as an ad hoc principal under Clinton, that must have rankled Clarke.

Over the next two months, the new Bush administration turned toward the larger issue of Afghanistan and the Taliban regime there. It was well-known that the Taliban harbored al Qaeda, and the Clinton administration had essentially signed off on the *assassination* of bin Laden under particular circumstances before leaving office, something known as a presidential finding.[21] Multiple bureaucratic reasons complicated implementation of Clinton's finding. Many of the same kind of complicating bureaucratic factors were soon to be experienced by the new Bush administration; sadly, the history of presidential transitions has too often been the history of a new NSC team learning lessons the previous NSC team had already learned on its watch. For instance, if the U.S. continued or increased aid to the Northern Alliance, it risked upsetting Afghanistan's Pashtun majority, whom the U.S. ultimately hoped to co-opt against al Qaeda. It risked, furthermore, upsetting the Pakistanis who largely created the Taliban and whom the U.S. now needed in the larger war on jihadi extremism. Ironically, the deputies committee of the NSC and the bureaucracy were just beginning to come to agreement on these larger issues and how they affected U.S. national security on *September 10, 2001*,[22] a day before the attacks were launched on the United States.

The new administration's NSC principals committee held its first meeting on al Qaeda on September 4, 2001.[23] A week later, on 9/11, nineteen hijackers implemented their plan to attack America using jet airliners. One may only speculate as to whether a more timely handling of the threats might have stopped 9/11 or parts of the attack. What can be said is that the administration was aware of the increased threat reporting. While the president vacationed in August at Crawford, Texas, he continued to receive reports from the intelligence community. On August 6, 2001, for instance, the president received a briefing entitled "Bin Laden Determined to Strike in U.S." The presidential daily briefing (PDB) informed the president that, among other things, the FBI was then conducting some seventy "full field investigations throughout the U.S. that it [the FBI] consider[ed] Bin Laden-related." Additionally, the briefing instructed the president that both the FBI and CIA were investigating a report from May (2001) that came through America's embassy in the United Arab Emirates. The report that the FBI was investigating was that *al Qaeda was in the United States* "planning attacks with explosives." Apparently, a so-called walk-in appeared at the U.S. embassy in the UAE with the information.[24] Technically, the Bush administration was forewarned of 9/11 in May 2001.

"No CSG [Counterterrorism Security Group] or other NSC meeting was held to discuss the possible threat of a strike in the United States as a result of" the August 6 PDB. Indeed, the 9/11 Commission's final report concluded that there was no indication of further discussion before 9/11. Former DCI George Tenet told the Commission that Tenet visited the president at the ranch in Crawford on August 17 and subsequently participated in other presidential daily briefings between August 31 and September 10, 2001. But Tenet did "not recall any discussion with the President of the domestic threat during this period."[25] In the NSC principals committee, the looming attacks did not result in particular policies or activities. Given another month or more, President Bush's president-NSC-policymaking team might have acted on the al Qaeda threat. But the new administration, in retrospect, did not have an additional month or more. Was this normal or routine behavior for that level of the bureaucracy?

To answer that question it is necessary to look at other national security policymaking routines during the administration's early months. During the same period, the NSC principals "routinely" talked on the phone daily and met periodically on a variety of foreign policy topics. Thus the following question must be posed: Why was no meeting held on the chatter that predicted a large, substantial attack perhaps in the United States itself? The answer appears to be that there was no particular protocol for holding such a meeting other than what was then already being done. Unlike, say, missile defense, an issue that the administration held as a priority, thwarting al Qaeda had no champion in the new administration once Clarke opted out. Nor was there within the bureaucracy a domestic national security agency tasked with protecting the U.S. homeland. The FBI nominally had authority, but prior to 9/11 was far more focused on what the FBI normally did: fighting crime, perfecting and prosecuting cases, and so on. The 9/11 Commission noted in its final report, "Numerous actions were taken overseas to disrupt possible attacks—in part, surely, because to the extent that specifics did exist, they pertained to threats overseas." Put simply, apart from Clarke and his CSG, no entity existed in the U.S. bureaucracy to protect America's own territory from al Qaeda. And Clarke had recently abandoned the CSG due to his frustrations with the new administration and, in fairness to the Bush administration, his frustrations with the larger bureaucracy in general. As stunningly simple as it appears, nobody considered other things that they might do under normal operating procedures that may have forestalled the 9/11 attacks.

That does not mean that the larger bureaucracy was inactive or insulated, however. Indeed, the contrary appeared nearer the truth. The bureaucracy continued disrupting and attacking al Qaeda within the parameters of previous actions. "Most of the intelligence community recognized in the summer of 2001 that the number and severity of threat reports were unprecedented." Many intelligence community officials told the 9/11 Commission that they knew something terrible was planned, and they were desperate to stop it."[26] For the most part, however, various parts of U.S. national security policymaking apparatus continued to function per normal routines.

> The September 11 attacks fell into the void between the foreign and domestic threats. The foreign intelligence agencies were watching overseas, alert to foreign threats to U.S. interests there. The domestic agencies were waiting for evidence of a domestic threat from sleeper cells within the United States. No one was looking for a foreign threat to domestic targets. The threat that was coming was not from sleeper cells. It was foreign—but from foreigners who had infiltrated into the United States.[27]

Alas, it took the 9/11 attacks themselves to change the bureaucratic inertia that had accumulated over multiple presidential administrations. Only the shock of 9/11 ultimately demanded that U.S. policymakers protect the U.S. homeland from the threat that had been building for years. As the 9/11 Commission concluded, disparate parts of the investigation continued doing what they were supposed to do but with little overall effect. Indeed, they saw "little evidence that the progress of the plot was disturbed by any government action. The U.S. government was unable to capitalize on mistakes made by al Qaeda. Eventually, time ran out."[28]

GEORGE W. BUSH'S PRESIDENT-NSC-POLICYMAKING MODEL

With the above chronology of the early Bush administration's procedures and processes outlined, a basic evaluation of the pre-9/11 Bush model may be made. In his first nine months, President George W. Bush's president-NSC-policymaking model looked very similar to that of his two predecessors: President George H. W. Bush and Bill Clinton. It was based on Bush's (41) template adopted largely by Clinton and tweaked to account for the increasingly important post–Cold War complex global economy. It also, at least on paper, appeared to adopt the Clinton administration's realization that transnational phenomenon would require increasing NSC attention. Further, even before 9/11, Vice President Dick Cheney was the most important vice president in NSC history, which demonstrated a departure from all of the president-NSC-policymaking models examined in chapter 4. Put differently, one unique feature that distinguished George W. Bush's NSC model from either Bush's (41) or Clinton's was the elevation of the vice president (already a statutory principal) to an actual statutory principal; not only was he an actual NSC principal but Vice President Cheney's lieutenants constituted ad hoc principals on a wide range of issues. Vice President Cheney, by all accounts, insisted on his own national security staff, some of whom (notably, I. Lewis "Scooter" Libby) attended principals meetings. Additionally, in the defense department, Douglas Feith was another member of the Cheney "brain trust."

> [Douglas Feith was] seen much the way enemies of the Clinton administration saw Hillary Clinton. Others associated with the Bush administration who [were] seen this way include[d] the consultant Richard Perle; Lewis "Scooter" Libby, the chief of staff for Vice President Dick Cheney; and the vice president himself. What these officials ha[d] in common [was] their presumably great private influence and—even in the case of the vice president—their limited public visibility and accountability."[29]

Vice President Cheney and his allies in the ranks of the civilian leadership in the defense department formed a true center of power inside the NSC principals.[30] Though Douglas Feith was in the Department of Defense he was seen, at least by Secretary of State Colin Powell, as little more than a lackey in Cheney's chain of command, marching in lock step to Cheney's and other neoconservatives' ideological orders. "Powell thought that Cheney had the fever. The vice president and Wolfowitz kept looking for the connection between Hussein and Sept. 11." Powell considered Douglas Feith's policy shop inside the Department of Defense an aberration; it was not the Department's turf in the first place. "It was a separate little government that was out there—Wolfowitz, Libby, Undersecretary of Defense Douglas J. Feith, and Feith's 'Gestapo office,' as Powell privately called it."[31]

Conversely, while Colin Powell was an influential person with tremendous *gravitas* in his own right prior to joining the Bush administration, except for the China spy plane incident in spring 2001 he was largely circumvented by Cheney and Rumsfeld who clearly attempted to supplant the Department of State. The secretary of state, a statutory principal, attended NSC principals meetings throughout his tenure but apparently was seldom consulted in reality. Rather, Rumsfeld and Cheney were President Bush's principal NSC advisers; they became even more so following 9/11. By definition, President Bush's "war cabinet" (his post-9/11 NSC principals) was not particularly amenable to diplomacy, the Department of State's traditional turf. As far as can be determined, NSC advisor Dr. Condoleezza Rice acted as a sort of liaison between the Cheney-Rumsfeld nexus, the president, and Secretary of State Powell.[32] That left Powell outside the traditional realm of the secretary of state's importance to the president-NSC-policymaking model dating back to the original 1947 NSA.

On Vice President Cheney, Bob Woodward wrote:

> Cheney, the 61-year-old conservative hard liner, had already carved out a special position in the administration and held great sway with the president . . . He served [as Halliburton CEO] until Bush picked him to be his running mate in the summer of 2000 with these words: "If times are good, I'm going to need your advice, but not nearly as much as if times are bad."[33]

Elsewhere, Woodward unearthed interesting tidbits regarding Deputy Secretary of Defense Paul Wolfowitz and Vice President Cheney's alter ego, I. Lewis "Scooter" Libby. First, Woodward noted that Scooter Libby wore three hats simultaneously, unusual in itself. First, he was Cheney's chief of staff. Second, he was Cheney's national security adviser. And third, Libby was organizationally an assistant to the president, not just the vice president. Woodward also noted Libby's close relationship with Wolfowitz: the latter was the teacher and mentor of the former at Yale when Dr. Wolfowitz was a young professor there. Finally, in "his current role, Libby was one of only two people who were not principals to attend the National Security Council meetings with the president *and* the separate principals meetings chaired by Rice. (The other was Rice's deputy, Stephen Hadley.)"[34] In particular, Woodward focused in one chapter on

Libby's extraordinary role in the NSC setting and in national security generally. Writing about the escalation to the Iraq War following the success in Afghanistan, Woodward related Libby's views on whether Iraq should be next. "Libby felt that keeping the focus on Afghanistan initially was wise, and now with Afghanistan going well, he believed if the war on terrorism was properly and broadly defined that Iraq had to be dealt with. It was impossible, in his view, to deal definitively with terrorism, as he put it privately, 'without facing up to the issue of Iraq.'"[35] In short, Deputy Secretary of Defense Wolfowitz, presidential adviser and Cheney *aide de camp* Scooter Libby, and Stephen Hadley, a much mellower version of Libby, all comprised ad hoc NSC principals in the Bush administration's president-NSC-policymaking model and their influence grew at Powell's expense, especially after 9/11.

Scholars and journalists who published accounts of the first George W. Bush administration may have unwittingly downplayed the actual power and influence Vice President Dick Cheney wielded in the first Bush term. That is not to say Vice President Cheney's influence went unnoticed. Rather, many acknowledged that he was exceptionally influential and that he stayed behind at specific NSC principals' meetings where he had the opportunity to influence President Bush even more. However, prior to the Iraq War, Secretary Rumsfeld's influence was discussed much more in contemporaneous media accounts. Consequently, Secretary Rumsfeld's influence, perhaps wrongly, was made to appear even more influential than Vice President Cheney's.[36]

Woodward's *Plan of Attack* disabused many of that misapprehension. Woodward further provided additional information that confirmed that the Cheney-neoconservative nexus was arrayed against Colin Powell. For instance Woodward noted: Rarely "had there been such deep division within a national security team as between Cheney and Powell. Each had a fundamentally different definition of what was possible, and what was necessary."[37] Elsewhere Woodward noted that Prince Bandar of Saudi Arabia was told about Bush's decision to invade Iraq a full day prior to Secretary of State Colin Powell—an extraordinary breach of protocol. Furthermore, the setting in which Prince Bandar was informed had the vice president, then-Secretary of Defense Rumsfeld, then-chairman of the JSC General Richard Myers, and Prince Bandar jocularly discussing America's "top secret" war plans. All of this occurred before the president called Powell in to inform Powell of the president's decision.[38] Finally, Woodward described a conversation that took place at a dinner hosted by the Cheneys with notable neoconservatives in attendance (one flew back early from a vacation in Europe to attend). This conversation eventually ended up focusing quite negatively on Secretary Powell. Powell was neither popular with Vice President Cheney nor with the neoconservatives Cheney headed. Secretary Powell was described as follows.

It was a pretty amazing accomplishment [what the president had done with his decision to invade Iraq], they all agreed, particularly given the opposition to war. Here was [Brent] Scowcroft [NSC advisor for Bush (41)], the pillar of establishment foreign policy, vocally on the other side, widely seen as a surrogate for the president's father. There had been James A. Baker III, the former secretary of state, insisting on a larger coalition of nations. And Lawrence Eagleburger, Baker's successor in the last half year of the first Bush administration, on television all the time saying war was justified only if there was evidence that Hussein was about to attack us. Eagleburger had accused Cheney of "chest thumping."

They turned to the current secretary of state, Colin L. Powell, and there were chuckles around the table.

Cheney and Wolfowitz remarked that Powell was someone who followed his poll ratings and bragged about his popularity. Several weeks earlier in a National Public Radio interview, Powell had said, "If you would consult any recent Gallup poll, the American people seem to be quite satisfied with the job I'm doing as secretary of state."

He sure likes to be popular, Cheney said.

Wolfowitz said that Powell did bring credibility and that his presentation to the United Nations on weapons of mass destruction intelligence had been important. As soon as Powell had understood what the president wanted, Wolfowitz said, he became a good, loyal member of the team.

Cheney shook his head, no. Powell was a problem. "Colin always had major reservations about what *we were trying to do*."[39]

The purpose in recounting Woodward's account, which was written well after most of the events and therefore is subject to "revisionism," is not to illustrate how petty even high-level bureaucrats may be. Rather, it was to illustrate just how important the Cheney-Rumsfeld-neoconservative nexus was from 9/11 through at least the invasion of Iraq. Using the zero-sum game formulation common in politics (that power and influence necessarily come at someone else's expense), Cheney's and Rumsfeld's influence within the NSC principals benefited at Colin Powell's expense.

Not long thereafter, Paul Wolfowitz left the Department of Defense to head the World Bank. In fall 2005, Scooter Libby was indicted for lying and obstructing justice with respect to a leaked case concerning a CIA officer. Given the high-level departure of some of the neoconservative luminaries, one might think that their influence would wane in the administration's second term. To date, however, Vice President Cheney apparently remains highly influential. Graphically and for comparative purposes, we present the following rendering of the president-NSC-policymaking model as it has thus far emerged in President George W. Bush's second term. Clearly, names on organizational charts tell only one part of the reality. Nevertheless, they may in fact presage specific procedures and processes that subsequently emerged.

Following the midterm elections on November 7, 2006, Secretary Rumsfeld was forced to resign.[40] Robert M. Gates (another Republican moderate and internationalist, ironically from the Brent Scowcroft wing of the party) replaced Rumsfeld in December 2006. Secretary Rumsfeld's resignation, along with the other defections noted, makes the neoconservatives' experiment in governance an open question. Vice President Cheney, of course, remains. Speculation is rampant in Washington about Cheney's ultimate shelf life. The James Baker–Lee Hamilton Iraqi Study Group released its findings on December 6, 2006.[41] James Baker worked

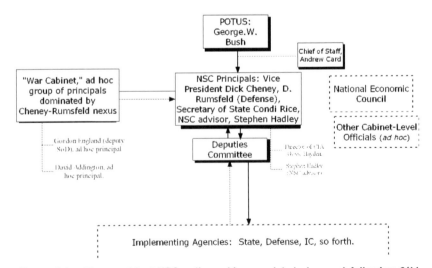

Figure 5.1.   The president-NSC-policymaking model during and following 9/11 through the present.

as secretary of state for George H. W. Bush and some have suggested the elder Bush had once again sent in the "velvet hammer" to remove President George W. Bush's chestnuts from the Iraq War fire. Perhaps the neoconservatives reached their apogee in influence in 2003–2005 and are now on their way out, but we would not count them out so soon.[42] Many defections were made public in late 2006, including even prominent neoconservatives who once supported the Bush administration's war in Iraq.[43] Time will tell. Any neoconservative gambits the president may wish to enact will have to be done prior to January 2009, after which a new president will occupy the White House.

SUMMARY

What can be said is that following 9/11, Bush increasingly became comfortable in his role as commander in chief. The 9/11 attacks proved a crucible in which strong relations were forged and "forward leaning" was rewarded over cautious political realism. During foreign policy crises, in contrast to more routine times, individual policymakers may exert an unusual degree of influence. By definition, the bureaucracy is circumvented for a short while thereby permitting already influential policymakers to become even more so, thrusting them into high relief. Vice President Cheney and Secretary of Defense Rumsfeld were the NSC principals to whom Bush turned insofar as 9/11 required a military response. Vice President Dick Cheney remains peerless in terms of vice presidents in the NSC principals setting. Cheney also became an advocate and close confidante of the president's. The president's own penchant for accomplishing "big things" and never shrinking from challenge probably led him to favor elevating Rumsfeld and Cheney at Powell's expense. After all, though diplomacy was part of America's 9/11 response, it was secondary if not tertiary. Powell therefore was under the circumstances nearly inevitably fated to the bureaucratic oblivion he eventually met.

Further, since Rumsfeld and Cheney were elevated in the president-NSC-policymaking model at Powell's expense after 9/11, it stands to reason that their respective deputies and lieutenants—Wolfowitz, Libby, and Feith in that order—were also elevated over Powell's deputy, Richard Armitage. Clearly, that happened.[44] Finally, Rumsfeld, Cheney, Wolfowitz, Libby, and a group of mostly academic neoconservatives were already on record well in advance of 9/11 as signatories of the neoconservative manifesto, the statement of principles of the Project for the New American Century. In 1997, this manifesto argued that American foreign and defense policy was "adrift." Not only had the Clinton administration, accordingly, failed to advance "a strategic vision of America's role in the world," but so too had Republican traditionalist internationalists. What were those strategic objectives these Republican interventionists wished to project for America's national security? Included were reversing the "[c]uts in foreign affairs and defense spending," as well as correcting "inattention to the tools of statecraft, and inconstant leadership" which were making it "difficult to sustain American influence around the world." As they perceived it, Clinton's penchant for "short-term commercial benefits" threatened "to override strategic considerations. As a consequence, [Clintonites and traditional conservative internationalists were] jeopardizing the nation's ability to meet present threats and to deal with potentially greater challenges that lay ahead." They lamented Clinton but also other conservatives who "seem to have forgotten the essential elements of the Reagan administration's success: a military that is strong and ready to meet both present and future challenges, a foreign policy that boldly and purposefully promotes American principles abroad, and national leadership that accepts the United States' global responsibilities."[45]

Following 9/11, U.S. national security policy increasingly and markedly reflected those principles and strategic objectives. The Bush administration began by responding to Afghanistan and the Taliban's facilitation of al Qaeda's training camps. Al Qaeda declared jihad on America in 1996 and 1998. The attacks on 9/11 personalized al Qaeda's jihad. Republicans and Democrats alike joined hands in supporting President Bush in his response, but Afghanistan was just the opening salvo. "Drain the swamp" was the mantra of the Bush-Cheney-Rumsfeld neoconservatives. Draining the swamp meant taking the battle to Iraq as soon a possible. Indeed, sufficient evidence exists to assume that the neoconservatives planned to revisit the issue of Iraq, a residual of their unfinished business from Bush (41) days, with or without the attacks on 9/11. The attacks, however, galvanized Americans and hastened the neoconservative plans to end tyranny and replace it with democratic governance. The attacks on 9/11, in short, allowed a few in the higher ranks of the Bush administration to substitute their strategic objectives for America's traditional international objectives, to test their ideas against empirical results, and to end once and for all America's foreign policy drift.

We may generalize somewhat about the president-NSC-policymaking model that has emerged and evolved since 9/11 and since the president's reelection in 2004. As has been seen, President Bush perceived himself as having changed following 9/11. He has stated so explicitly in multiple speeches. Presumably, his own change is related to his much more proactive, "forward leaning" (to use one of the administration's own characterizations) approach to U.S. national security. After 9/11, President Bush took a personal interest in U.S. national security as it related to the war against global jihadis. He certainly became one of the hands on the tiller if not the principal one. Next to Bush (figuratively and literally at times) has been Vice President Cheney, an unabashed neoconservative who believes one of his jobs is to protect the presidency and increase the presidency's power at the expense of the Congress (the so-called unitary theory of the presidency's war-power prerogatives).[46] Since President Bush changed the trajectory of U.S. national security policy away from decades of containment toward five years and counting of preventive strikes against transnational and national threats, Cheney's job has been to backstop President Bush. Nuclear deterrence, of course, continues to be America's defensive posture against state actors but *not* against nonstate transnational actors. The Bush administration argued—in both the December 2002 version and the March 2006 version of the *National Security Strategy of the United States*—that deterrence was virtually useless against global jihadis. Who or what of value might the U.S. government hold hostage to superior force in order to deter a transnational threat such as al Qaeda, President Bush might reasonably ask.

The Bush White House published its updated version of *The National Security Strategy of the United States* in spring 2006. The document detailed the positions just noted and more. Regarding the lack of efficacy for deterrence against such threats the document's NSC authors wrote:

> Defeating terrorism requires a long-term strategy and a break with old patterns. We are fighting a new enemy with global reach. The United States can no longer simply rely on deterrence to keep the terrorists at bay or defensive measures to thwart them at the last moment. The fight must be taken to the enemy, to keep them on the run.

We must join with others to deny the terrorists what they need to survive: safe haven, financial support, and the support and protection that certain nation-states historically have given them."[47]

In fundamental ways, this national security strategy was typical of what has been seen in earlier chapters with respect to classic American ethos. It divided the world into two parts: the democratic world where freedoms and individual choices are maximized by definition; and tyranny, the opposite of political freedom defined in a classic American way. For instance, it read: "In today's world, no tyrant's rule can survive without the support or at least the tolerance of other nations. To end tyranny we must summon the collective outrage of the free world against the oppression, abuse, and impoverishment that tyrannical regimes inflict on their people—and summon their collective action against the dangers tyrants pose to the security of the world."[48]

Once former NSC advisor Condoleezza Rice moved to the Department of State, she also apparently increased her influence but decreased her proximity to the president. Part of her increased influence likely came from Dr. Rice no longer needing to divide her time between her NSC duties on the one hand and her duties as the liaison between the Departments of State and Defense and the vice president's office on the other. Despite former Secretary of State Colin Powell's impressive résumé, the evidence supports the conclusion that he was an ineffectual secretary of state; in retrospect, it would appear he never had a chance. From the time Vice President Cheney established Cheney's national security staff and Secretary of Defense Donald Rumsfeld his counterparts in the Pentagon, Secretary of State Powell's influence decreased and, in fact, his days were numbered.

Obviously, names have changed on the organization chart of the president's NSC-policymaking-model. As noted, Donald Rumsfeld, Paul Wolfowitz, and Lewis "Scooter" Libby are now absent. It should be noted that beyond their absence, there is no evidence that their successors have become ad hoc principals. That is, we found no indication from media reports or White House reports that Deputy Secretary of Defense Gordon England had become the influential ad hoc principal that Wolfowitz, England's predecessor, was. Mr. England is a former corporate executive from a large U.S.-based defense contractor, General Dynamics. Secretary England has managed to stay out of the news for the most part and seems a fairly pedestrian deputy secretary compared to former Deputy Secretary Wolfowitz.

Little has been written about David Addington's replacement of "Scooter" Libby as the vice president's roving commando. In fact, the White House announcement that Addington had replaced Libby noted that Addington would serve only as Vice President Cheney's chief of staff; that is, unlike "Scooter" Libby, Addington had been given only one portfolio. Yet a third person was named, John P. Hannah, who replaced Lewis Libby as the assistant to the vice president for national security affairs.[49] It would appear that the White House decided that Libby's and Wolfowitz's replacements would not transcend the heights of power that their predecessors did in President Bush's president-NSC-policymaking model.

Other name changes were also prominent. After nearly besting Sherman Adams, a truly influential adviser and Eisenhower's trusted chief of staff, as longest-serving presidential chief of staff, Andrew Card tendered his resignation in late March 2006. "Mr. Card was approaching the record of the longest serving White House chief of staff, with a tenure close to that of Sherman Adams, the chief of staff to President Eisenhower." Card's replacement, Joshua Bolten, was the former director of the White House Office of Management and Budget (OMB), another long-time Bush adviser but one who was predicted to shake things up a bit more than was Card's habit.[50] Finally, two other former aids resigned in spring 2006. First, White House Press Secretary Scott McClellan resigned shortly after Joshua Bolten took over from Card. Apparently, Karl Rove, cited elsewhere as President Bush's brain, may have been demoted as well. However, there is some evidence that the demotion was in name only; moreover, while Karl Rove most certainly has functioned as an ad hoc principal from time to time, he has not done so consistently and was therefore not discussed as influential in terms of Bush's president-NSC-policymaking model. The other recent resignation was from the reportedly long-suffering Director of Central Intelligence, Porter Goss. The implications of the Goss resignation are unclear at this writing, though his resignation was reported as "abrupt." One pieced noted of Goss resignation that the "unexpected resignation was the latest in an administration shakeup during Bush's second term."[51]

Presently there is no reason to believe that Vice President Cheney is any less influential than previously. During spring 2006 a series of negative stories about Cheney appeared in the media that built on 2005's charges of an inner circle or cabal of Cheney, Rumsfeld, and their respective aides. In early May 2006, Vice President Cheney was traveling to Europe on his way to the pre-G8 meeting being hosted by Russia's Vladimir Putin. Cheney made pointed comments about Russia's backsliding vis-à-vis democracy that were "vetted" by the White House.[52] Finally, on December 6, 2006, the Iraqi Study Group (the bipartisan group of "wise" men and woman reflecting the Bush [41]–James Baker–Brent Scowcroft traditional internationalists) published its long-awaited bipartisan report for extricating America from its Iraq morass. While President Bush hailed the group's work publicly, as did Secretary of State Condoleezza Rice, newspapers noted that neoconservatives and "others" inside the vice president's office and the NSC argued that "the risks" of accepting the 79 recommendations were "too high."[53] It appeared that he was influential as ever.

A clear demarcation exists between the president-NSC-policymaking model seen in the first nine months of the George W. Bush administration and after 9/11. Some of the changes occurred nearly instantaneously after the trauma of 9/11. Others evolved over the course of two or three years' time. Still others occurred only after the various blue-ribbon panels and official postmortems were conducted. We have intentionally stayed agnostic in terms of whether or not a cabal took over the president-NSC-policymaking model. Important persons with unique insights into the administration's inner workings have made that charge. We do quarrel with their assessments. However, for present purposes the focus has been on the president-NSC-policymaking structure and the procedures that derive from it. It is inarguable that Vice President Cheney and former Secretary of Defense Donald Rumsfeld worked in tandem for essentially the same objectives: assertion of the president's war-power prerogatives; invigoration of what they saw as an insufficiently muscular foreign policy; and reduction of the historic influence and import of the U.S. State Department. Each objective has been accomplished. It will be up to Secretary of State Condoleezza Rice to rebalance the State Department's influence in George W. Bush's president-NSC-policymaking model in the future.

NOTES

1. House Permanent Select Committee on Intelligence and the Senate Select Committee on Intelligence, *Report of the Joint Inquiry into the Terrorist Attacks of September 11, 2001*, 107th Cong, 2d sess. (December 2002), 227–228 (hereafter cited as the Joint Inquiry, with page number). Note: the Joint Inquiry, published in Acrobat format, included pagination intended to be consistent with the Government Printing Office's hard copy. Thus, the page numbers used here match the hard copy's pagination.

2. *Joint Inquiry*, 228.

3. George W. Bush was of course reelected on November 2, 2004. His second inauguration was on January 21, 2005.

4. White House, "Biography of George W. Bush," http://www.whitehouse.gov/president/.gwbbio.html (accessed on February 12, 2006).

5. George W. Bush, presidential debate between Vice President Albert Gore and Governor George W. Bush, *Online NewsHour*, PBS, October 11, 2000, http://www.pbs.org/newshour/bb/politics/july-dec00/for-policy_10-12.html (accessed February 23, 2006).

6. George W. Bush, "A Distinctly American Internationalism," speech presented at the Ronald Reagan Library, Simi, California, November 19, 1999, http://www.mtholyoke.edu/acad/intrel/bush/wspeech.htm (accessed February 23, 2006)(my emphasis).

7. George W. Bush, presidential debate between Vice President Albert Gore and Governor George W. Bush, *Online NewsHour*, PBS, October 11, 2000, http://www.pbs.org/newshour/bb/politics/july-dec00/for-policy_10-12.html (accessed February 23, 2006).

8. Condoleezza Rice, "Life after the Cold War," *Foreign Affairs*, 79, no. 1 (January/February 2000), http://www.foreignpolicy2000.org/library/issuebriefs/readingnotes/fa_rice.html (accessed September 2002).

9. CNN Cable Network, "The Big Story: High Stakes in Standoff," April 6, 2001, http://archives.cnn.com/2001/WORLD/asiapcf/east/04/06/china.big.picture/ (accessed February 12, 2006).

10. The National Commission on Terrorist Attack upon the United States, "The 9/11 Commission Report," 196. (Hereafter referred to as the 9/11 Commission final report.)

11. The 9/11 Commission final report, 199.

12. The 9/11 Commission final report, 199. Also see Bob Woodward, *Bush at War* (New York: Simon and Schuster, 2003), 34–35.

13. The 9/11 Commission final report, 200.

14. The 9/11 Commission final report, 201.

15. The 9/11 Commission final report, 203. An earlier chapter discussed the nomenclature and designation that new administrations have so commonly changed upon entering office. Under Clinton, the NSC produced Presidential Decision Directives (PDDs). The George W. Bush administration called similar documents National Security Presidential Directives or NSPDs.

16. The 9/11 Commission final report, 204.

17. The 9/11 Commission final report, 357.

18. The 9/11 Commission final report, 204.

19. The 9/11 Commission final report, 204–205.

20. The 9/11 Commission final report, 205; see also 120 where *Delenda* is first discussed in the 9/11 Commission's final report. *Delenda* is a Latin word that defies simple translation, but means substantially something that needs to be deleted or destroyed.

21. The 9/11 Commission final report, 187–190, section titled "Afghan Eyes."

22. The 9/11 Commission final report, 206.

23. The 9/11 Commission final report, 212.

24. See the 9/11 Commission's Ninth Public Hearing, Testimony of Condoleezza Rice, April 8, 2004, http://www.9-11commission.gov/archive/hearing9/9-11Commission_ Hearing_2004-04-08.pdf. See also The 9/11 Commission final report, 261–262.

25. The 9/11 Commission final report, 262.

26. The 9/11 Commission final report, *Ibid.*

27. The 9/11 Commission final report, 263.

28. The 9/11 Commission final report, 277.

29. James Fallows, "Blind into Baghdad," *Atlantic Monthly*, January–February, 2004, http://www.the atlantic.com/issues/2004/01/fallows.htm (accessed May 6, 2004).

30. Daniel Benjamin, "President Cheney: His Office Really Does Run National Security," *Slate.com*, November 7, 2005, http://www.slate.com/id/2129686/ (accessed December 24, 2005).

31. Bob Woodward, *Plan of Attack*, 281.

32. M. Kent Bolton, *U.S. Foreign Policy and International Politics: George W. Bush, 9/11, and the Global-Terrorist Hydra* (NY: Prentice Hall, 2005). Bob Woodward, *Bush at War* (NY: Simon and Schuster, 2003).

33. Bob Woodward, *Plan of Attack* (NY: Simon and Schuster, 2004), 27–28.

34. Bob Woodward, *Plan of Attack*, 48, and 48–49 respectively (my emphasis).

35. Bob Woodward, *Plan of Attack*, 50.

36. M. Kent Bolton, *U.S. Foreign Policy and International Politics,* especially chapters 4 ("Governmental Inputs") and 6 ("Process").

37. Bob Woodward, *Plan of Attack*, 155.

38. Bob Woodward, *Plan of Attack*, 263–66.

39. Bob Woodward, *Plan of Attack*, "deep divisions" quote, 155, others from 409–415 (my emphasis).

40. Sheryl Gay Stolberg and Jim Rutenberg, "Rumsfeld Resigns as Defense Secretary After Big Election Gains for Democrats," *New York Times*, November 8, 2006, http:// www.nytimes.com/2006/11/08/us /politics/09BUSHCND.html;William Branigin, "Rumsfeld to Step Down as Defense Secretary," *Washington Post*, November 8, 2006, http:// www.washingtonpost.com/wp-dyn/content/article/2006/11/08/AR 2006110801180.html.

41. The Baker-Hamilton report was found on the *New York Times* website. *The Iraq Study Group Report*, *New York Times*, December 6, 2006: http://graphics8.nytimes.com/ packages/pdf/international/20061206_btext.pdf.

42. For speculation about Cheney and Rumsfeld's fate as well as the Bush (43) administration's fingerprints on the Iraqi Study Group, see Maureen Dowd, "A Come-to-Daddy Moment," *New York Times,* November 9, 2006, http://select.nytimes.com/2006/11/09/ opinion/09dowd.html; Walter Pincus, "Gates May Rein In Pentagon Activities," *Washington Post*, November 14, 2006, http://www.washingtonpost.com/wp-dyn/content/article/ 2006/11/13/AR2006111301135.html; Robin Wright, "Bush Initiates Iraq Policy Review Separate From Baker Groups" *Washington Post*, November 15, 2006; http://www .washington-post.com/wp-dyn/content/article/2006/11/14/AR2006111401095.html; Michael Abramowitz and Spencer S. Hsu, "Cheney Rejects Idea Of Iraq Withdrawal," *Washington Post*, November 18, 2006, http://www.washingtonpost.com/wp-dyn/ content/article/2006/11/17/AR2006111701638.html.

43. Peter Spiegel, "Perle Says He Should Not Have Backed Iraq War," *Los Angeles Times*, November 4, 2006, http://www.latimes.com/news/nationworld/nation/la-na-neocons 4nov04,1,1461704.story?coll=la-headlines-nation.

44. Daniel Benjamin, "President Cheney: His Office Really Does Run National Security," *Slate.com*, November 7, 2005, http://www.slate.com/id/2129686/ (accessed December 24, 2005); Bob Woodward, *Plan of Attack*, 281; Lawrence B. Wilkerson, "The White House Cabal," *Los Angeles Times*, October 25, 2005, http://www.latimes.com/news/opinion/commentary/la-oe-wilkerson25oct25,0,7455395.story?coll=la-news-comment-opinions; Dan Froomkin, "Insider Lashes Out," *Washington Post*, October 20, 2005, http://www.washingtonpost.com/wp-dyn/content/blog/2005/10/20/BL2005102001131.html.

45. Project for A New American Century, "Statement of Principles," dated June 3, 1997, http://www.newamericancentury.org/statementofprinciples.htm (accessed July 25, 2005).

46. The debate was recently framed in an op-ed piece by a history professor from the University of Missouri as between administration intellectuals, Republicans, and "Federalists." The author argued that each group, the "Federalists and modern Republicans alike have often indicated their belief, expressed with varying degrees of regret, that the methods of democratic, accountable, transparent government are not strong enough to meet these challenges. Jeffersonian Republicans and modern Democrats, in turn, have tended to respond that they are." He further noted, presumably facetiously, "This recurring argument has often turned on the question of whether the norms and procedures of democracy and republicanism are adequate to national survival in a dangerous world of Terrorists, Commies, and Frenchmen." Jeffrey L. Pasley, "An Old Debate on Presidential Power," *New York Times*, April 2, 2006, http://www.nytimes.com/2006/04/02/weekinreview/02read2.html.

47. White House, *National Security Strategy of the United States, March 2006*, White House, http://www.whitehouse.gov/nsc/2006/nss206.pdf, Acrobat Reader pagination, 13.

48. White House, *National Security Strategy of the United States, March 2006*, White House, http://www.whitehouse.gov/nsc/2006/nss206.pdf, Acrobat Reader pagination, 9.

49. White House, "Personnel Announcement," October 31, 2005, http://www.whitehouse.gov/news/releases/2005/10/print/20051031-2.html (accessed May 5, 2006).

50. David Sanger and John O'Neil, "In First Major Shift of Second Term, Bush Looks to Inner Circle," *New York Times*, March 28, 2006, http://www.nytimes.com/2006/03/28/politics/28cnd-bush.html.

51. For McClelland resignation and analysis see Dan Balz, "White House Shifts Into Survival Mode," *Washington Post*, April 28, 2006, http://www.washingtonpost.com/wp-dyn/content/article/2006/04/19/AR2006041902517.html; Elisabeth Bumiller, "Rove Is Giving Up Daily Policy Post to Focus on Vote," *New York Times*, April 20, 2006, http://www.nytimes.com/2006/04/20/ washington/20bush.html. For DCI Goss's resignation see William Branigin, "CIA Director Porter Goss Resigns ," *Washington Post*, May 5, 2006, http://www.washingtonpost.com/wp-dyn/content/article /2006/05/05/AR200605050 0937.html; David Stout, "C.I.A. Director Porter Goss Resigns," *New York Times*, May 5, 2006, http://www.nytimes.com/2006/05/05/washington/05cnd-cia.html.

52. Paul Richter and David Holley, "Cheney Has Harsh Words for Moscow," *Los Angeles Times*, May 5, 2006, http://www.latimes.com/news/nationworld/world/la-fg-cheney5may05,1,41783.story?coll=la-headlines-world; Steven Lee Meyers, "Strong Rebuke for the Kremlin From Cheney," *New York Times*, May 5, 2006, http://www.nytimes.com/2006/05/05/world/05cheney.html.

53. Jim Rutenberg and David Sanger, "Bush Aides Seek Alternatives to Iraq Study Group's Proposals, Calling Them Impractical," *New York Times*, December 10, 2006, http://www.nytimes.com/2006/12/10/world/middleeast/10prexy.html; Michael Abramowitz and Glenn Kessler, "Hawks Bolster Skeptical President," *Washington Post*, December 10, 2006, http://www.washingtonpost.com/wp-dyn/content/article/2006/12/09/AR2006120900443.html.

CHAPTER 6

9/11, a Foreign Policy Crisis, the Iraq War, and U.S. National Security Policymaking

Thus far we have examined U.S. national security and foreign policymaking from America's origins to its emergence after World War II as one of the world's two superpowers. We have also examined U.S. national security during the Cold War as well as the Cold War consensus we argued was a requisite for America's pivot from an isolationist nation with regional ambitions to America's national security state or *Pax Americana*. As America emerged from the ashes of World War II, insightful policymakers understood that the brave new world into which they perceived themselves as being thrust—an existential contest with the Soviet Union as the world's other superpower—caused those policymakers to depart from the "script" that the U.S. Constitution dictated. Consequently, and in light of the Cold War consensus that quickly formed, policymakers who were "present at the creation" drafted important legislation to guide U.S. national security policymaking during tumultuous times. As we have seen, the 1947 National Security Act (1947 NSA) created a new set of executive branch tools and protocols that formed the new script for U.S. national security during the Cold War.

Among the creations was the president-NSC-policymaking model. Additionally, a unified Department of Defense and a permanent standing military were born of that critical legislation. For America to prevail against the Soviets, policymakers understood that the president-NSC-policymaking model required a permanent intelligence community to feed timely and accurate intelligence to policymakers. The 1947 NSA therefore created the central intelligence agency (CIA) and cobbled it to the relatively anemic intelligence infrastructure that predated the 1947 NSA. Over time, the president-NSC-policymaking model became the preeminent locus of national security policymaking. We therefore examined innovations and generalizable trends in the NSC as it supplanted the old president-cabinet policymaking model that existed until World War II. We noted that the intelligence community evolved ever more complex and disparate agencies and functions. Together, the president-NSC-policymaking model, the unified Department of Defense, and the intelligence community became the template used by policymakers of both Democratic and Republican administrations to conduct their continuous multigenerational contest against what they perceived as Soviet tyranny.

The institutions created by the 1947 NSA were resilient and effective. From roughly 1950 through 1991, these institutions collectively implemented the strategy of containment of the Soviet Union and communism— both seen as antithetical to America's interests, democracy, and laissez-faire economics. Since horrible weapons were available and, if employed beyond World War II, would have destroyed both superpowers, nuclear deterrence grew out of the stalemate of both superpowers being able to destroy the other. America became an interventionist nation for arguably the first time in its history as it orchestrated its Cold War strategies.

Following the demise of the Soviet Union, America might have returned to its isolationist past. Clearly, however, that was not what happened. Rather, the machinery that had been created at dawn of the Cold War and which evolved over the Cold War's length persevered well through the 1990s. Bureaucratic inertia ensured that the machinery could not be quickly disassembled. Thus, though the Cold War ended, *Pax Americana* continued to do what it did best: search for an appropriate role for America in the world, seek to identify the next tyranny for the U.S. to contain, and seek to create a stable international environment that was amenable to America's interests. As the Cold War ended, the first salvo in what would become a new battle against a new enemy was fired. In February 1993, Sunni jihadis attempted to topple New York's Twin Towers. Had the perpetrators been successful, it is likely that U.S. national security policy would have pivoted then to adjust to nontraditional, transnational groups who intended to harm America. So resistant to change were America's national security institutions that the policymakers in charge (both Democrat and Republican) dismissed global jihadis. After all, these jihadis seemed amateurish by comparison with traditional state threats. In fact, they were not amateurish; rather, they had yet to build a critical mass and probably launched the first Twin Tower attacks years ahead of when they might have had more effect.

Soon, nationalism (something that had plagued the international system for centuries) reappeared in former Yugoslavia and elsewhere. *Pax Americana* focused on the disintegration of the former Soviet Union as its next national security challenge. The disintegration of former Yugoslavia alone occupied most of the Clinton administration's time in office. Meanwhile, the global jihadi hydra spread. It was agile. It was adaptable. It was not confined to a particular nation-state; it consciously transcended national borders. It had begun near the end of the Cold War when the Soviets invaded Afghanistan and unleashed the *mujahideen*. Islamists from around the world but predominately the Middle East poured into Afghanistan to take on the godless communists. In what can only be described as acts of short-term expediency, multiple presidential administrations aided and abetted the jihadi movement. Little did U.S. policymakers realize that they were helping to create an agent that ultimately sought America's destruction; these same jihadis would ultimately launch the deadly attacks of 9/11.

In the following three chapters, we consider the inputs that would cause yet another pivot in U.S. national security policymaking, the first major change of direction and reorganization since the early Cold War. The first category of inputs—external-systemic—are considered here in chapter 6. External inputs are those stimuli that occur outside U.S. borders to which U.S. policymakers react and respond. We first consider 9/11 as a foreign policy crisis and consider the implications of that crisis. The main implication was that as a result of 9/11 being a crisis, President Bush and his administration were permitted considerable leeway to begin a change of direction for U.S. national security. However, 9/11 was a discrete event whose effects diminished over time. Moreover, the Bush administration used 9/11 as cudgel to revisit business some of the Bush administration's policymakers considered unfinished: namely, Iraq. Following brief examination of 9/11 as a crisis we therefore consider the Iraq War as an external source of U.S. national security policy since 9/11. We introduced Graham Allison's *Essence of Decision* in Chapter 2. In Allison's terms, external-systemic causes are model I (rational choice) inputs. In the traditional jargon of political realism, external-systemic inputs may be conceptualized as simple stimulus-response cues to which policymakers respond by assessing the nature of the threat or opportunity. Policymakers then weigh alternative solutions using a formal or informal cost-benefit analysis to maximize national security interests.

In chapter 7, we consider an array of societal sources of U.S. national security policy. Societal causes are domestic sources. They are inputs or stimuli that occur within U.S. borders that reverberate throughout American society thence to America's policymakers and cause the latter to respond. They include the media and how it shapes what Americans think about with respect to U.S. national security policy. Other societal inputs are special-interest groups who lobby for specific policies. In chapter 7, we consider a philosophical debate that occurred in U.S. policymaking circles over the future of U.S. national security during the critical time of change and reorganization largely afforded by 9/11 and its aftermath. As Republicans have been in power since 9/11, the philosophical debate was mainly a debate over the way Republicans would conduct national security as opposed to their Democratic counterparts. But it was also a debate within the Republican Party for the heart and soul of that party vis-à-vis national security. Political realism traditionally has little use for domestic sources of U.S. national security policy. In terms of theories, therefore, those societal sources that hastened America's national security changes are beholden to neoliberalism.

In chapter 8, we consider another set of domestic sources of national security change and reorganization, governmental causes or inputs. The sheer size of the national security bureaucracy and the standard operating procedures and routines needed for its vast and disparate parts to communicate, coordinate, and interact to implement policy once made are the main focus of chapter 8. Following 9/11 and the debacle in Iraq, inevitable postmortems followed with respect to U.S. national security policymaking, how the intelligence community interacted with policymakers, and how America's national security institutions failed. Postmortems were conducted to consider policymaking and intelligence failures surrounding 9/11 as well as failures related to the Iraq War. These governmental inputs have also been a source of changes to U.S. national security and foreign policymaking. In terms of international relations theories, these governmental sources are also beholden to neoliberalism.

9/11 AS A FOREIGN POLICY CRISIS AND THE IRAQ WAR AS AN EXTERNAL STIMULUS

The Attacks of 9/11: A Foreign Policy Crisis and Its Effects

If it has not already, in time 9/11 will be classified as one of those events during which virtually every American of a certain age—and many worldwide—remembers where (s)he was and what (s)he was doing. As were Pearl Harbor Day and perhaps President Kennedy's assassination for other generations, 9/11 became a new generation's day of infamy. Why? Was it simply the horror of the events? The brutal killing of some 3,000 American noncombatants clearly made 9/11 one of the most horrific attacks in modern U.S. history. But Americans have experienced other horrific events even where noncombatants were involved. Pearl Harbor, as noted, was such a day for many. Perhaps, however, something more profound about 9/11 made the day so important. It was one of the rare times *after which U.S. foreign policy demonstrably and substantively changed its trajectory.* The 9/11 attacks constituted a genuine foreign policy crisis which made the memories all the more searing and the consequences all the more important to analyze. President Bush certainly felt the weight of 9/11 when he made the subsequent decision to invade Iraq and topple Saddam Hussein, as we will demonstrate presently.

Before considering the implications of 9/11 as a foreign policy crisis it is useful to recount how the attacks specifically fitted the criteria developed by Charles F. Hermann more than a generation ago. Foreign policy crises are rare events characterized by grave threat that surprise policymakers and for which they perceive themselves as having only a short time in which to respond before the event potentially worsens.[1] The arguments that the 9/11 attacks constituted a U.S. foreign policy crisis are relatively straightforward and have been made elsewhere.[2] First, did 9/11 constitute a high threat to U.S. policymaking and/or America's existence? Clearly, the answer is yes. While fewer than 3,000 persons ultimately perished in the 9/11 attacks, policymakers (as well as most Americans) clearly perceived 9/11 as an existential threat to America. Indeed, the attacks were designed to make Americans and their policymakers feel as though they were under siege by hitherto unknown or poorly understood forces. Recall, for example, how the attacks unfolded. with the first plane hitting one of the Twin Towers, the second plane hitting the other Tower, and a third plane striking the Pentagon a short time later. Within a short period of time one then the other of the Twin Towers collapsed and, finally, there were rumors throughout the day while those traumas were unfolding that additional planes were headed for various targets in the U.S. America was under attack and the crashing of jumbo jets into America's symbols of power was perceived initially as existential. Only attacks involving WMDs might have been perceived by policymakers as a graver threat.

Did policymakers perceive the 9/11 attacks as presenting them with a short time in which to respond before things potentially worsened? That the attacks were perceived as requiring immediate attention is similarly straightforward, though some have made much of President Bush's seeming paralysis for fewer than ten minutes at the Florida primary school. Clearly, President Bush was stunned by the events as told to him that day by aides while he read to elementary school students. The issue, however, is not whether President Bush stayed too long at the Florida elementary school (say, eight minutes versus two). Rather, the issue is whether President Bush and his NSC principals believed the attacks required nearly instantaneous responses. They did. In Washington, the White House staff including the vice president, the NSC staff, and the NSC advisers were instantly evacuated and sequestered to where command and control could be reestablished for immediate reactions. America's policymakers feared the White House would come under attack at any minute. President Bush and Vice President Cheney both established contact and convened an electronically-transmitted NSC principals meeting with those principals who were available almost immediately. Decisions were demanded at every level of policymaking but most critically from the president and his NSC principals. The president-NSC-policymaking model may not have been constituted as such, but the NSC principals available were immediately gathered to communicate with President Bush. Recall that the Secret Service spirited the president around in Air Force One to keep him out of harm's way and in communication with those NSC principals who were in Washington. The vice president was taken to an underground bunker for communications and continuity in policymaking in case the president was somehow harmed in the attacks; that is, policymakers also believed Air Force One might come under attack at any moment. Similarly, other key decision makers were protected and put in contact with the president throughout the day so they could implement the decisions the president and others were improvising.

Did the 9/11 attacks surprise America's NSC policymakers? That 9/11 surprised U.S. foreign policymakers is inarguable. Whether or not they should have known the attacks were coming is a different issue and ultimately a value judgment. Much has been made of the fact that the president and his top NSC principals should have known more. In chapter 5 we examined evidence of the forthcoming 9/11 attacks that was available had Bush administration NSC policymakers wished to know it. Nevertheless, there is no credible evidence that President Bush or his top NSC decision makers did know of the 9/11 attacks a priori. On the contrary, not only were the key policymakers shocked and surprised, virtually every American was as well. Many of us who had predicted attacks on America from al Qaeda were also surprised by the 9/11 attacks. The 9/11 attacks have been described as movie-like: so unreal or surreal that people had difficulty processing the attacks even after seeing them with their own eyes. Contingency plans existed (they were perhaps not adequate to the task, but they existed nevertheless) for chemical and biological attacks from global jihadis. But no such contingency plans existed for passenger jets being used as missiles to destroy America's economic, political, and military infrastructure. As demonstrated previously, the intelligence community and others were furiously working to unravel what al Qaeda planned to do to the United States that fall morning but no one anticipated what al Qaeda did. Clearly, the 9/11 attacks surprised America's top policymakers.

Having established that the 9/11 attacks constituted a foreign policy crisis, what were the practical consequences in terms of national security policymaking? During a foreign policy crisis, decision makers are necessarily forced to improvise and live with the consequences of those improvised decisions. In the first few hours following the attacks, the president made the decision to punish those responsible for and/or who aided al Qaeda's attacks. President Bush decided to punish the perpetrators of 9/11 and he decided it early that day, before he returned to Washington DC on 9/11. It is difficult to conceive of any president who would have decided anything less. Nevertheless, President Bush made the decision and announced it to his key NSC principals upon returning to the White House later that evening. President Bush's NSC principals subsequently became known as President Bush's "war cabinet." Implementers of the president's decisions began planning their responses that very day. The president decided on 9/11 that for the foreseeable future U.S. national security would be dominated by a war against "evil," "evil-doers," and jihadis who wished to reestablish the Islamic Caliphate system. In short, President Bush made the decision that launched the U.S. on a long-term existential battle between the West (with the United States leading it) and a nebulous transnational, non-state actor called al Qaeda and its state sponsor the Taliban regime in Afghanistan. Notwithstanding understandable discontent over the Iraq War, the president made clear to Americans that the trajectory on which he launched U.S. national security following the attacks would be long-term, and he repeated it many times to the American people. It is important to remember, now that the Iraq War has become unpopular, that the president's decision so soon after the trauma of 9/11 was incredibly popular with the American people at the time. Even his subsequent decision to invade Iraq was relatively popular through 2003 and popular enough that he was reelected in 2004.

The consequences were profound. It did not guarantee that the U.S. would invade Iraq in 2003 but it certainly made military action in Iraq—already ongoing in enforcing the UN-mandated no-fly zones—much more likely. The consequences included a roughly 40 percent increase in defense spending in the U.S. over a short time and the consequences of the steep increases were manifold.[3] The human toll was profound as well. Well more than 3,000 additional Americans—U.S. military troops—have lost their lives and thousands more have been wounded in a host of life-altering ways since the Iraq War began in March 2003. That many Americans who once supported or at least acquiesced to President Bush's decision to invade Iraq subsequently soured on the war is hardly surprising. Many of the strategies developed for Iraq—and it should be clear that the decision to invade Iraq was not a crisis, in contrast to the immediate post-9/11 context—have proved ineffective.

What we can say with certainty is that the Bush administration, on behalf of the American people, launched America on a new national security and foreign policy trajectory following 9/11. The Iraq War has become an external source of U.S. national security policymaking with important consequences of its own. One consequence of the Iraq War has been that America's image internationally has been affected negatively. Polling data have demonstrated a deteriorating image of America internationally. Multiple opinion polls since have reflected growing international unease with America's war in Iraq and even its war against global extremism, insofar as people distinguished between the two. For instance, a poll released in spring 2006 noted the following: "Public opinion against the war [in Iraq] also is growing because of what many Europeans see as dubious U.S. tactics in the broader fight against terrorism, including the use of secret prisons and abusive interrogations."[4] Americans' opinions of their policymakers as well the world's opinion of American and its behavior in world politics decreased.

Later we will discuss the interactions between exogenous variables as policymaking process. External events affect public opinion as well as the opinion of an administration's top NSC policymakers. Once NSC policy-makers' opinions were affected by 9/11, their subsequent actions—by virtue of the checks and balances of the U.S. Constitution—affected congressional leaders. Congressional leaders responded. They appointed commissions and drafted legislation. A critical piece of legislation was drafted, the Intelligence Reform and Terrorism Prevention Act, which amended large portions of the 1947 NSA and which we examine subsequently. In the remainder of this chapter we examine how external stimuli (viz., the Iraq War and other events) helped continue what 9/11 began and how both have changed the direction of U.S. national security policy and ultimately hastened the reorganization of U.S. national security institutions, including the president-NSC policymaking model and the intelligence community.

THE IRAQ WAR AND ITS AFTERMATH AS SOURCES
OF CHANGE IN U.S. NATIONAL SECURITY POLICYMAKING

It's important for people to understand the context in which I made a decision [to invade Iraq] here in the Oval Office. I'm dealing with a world in which we have gotten struck by terrorists with airplanes, and we get intelligence saying that there is, you know, [Iraq wanted] to harm America. And the worst nightmare scenario for any president is to realize that these kind of terrorist networks had the capacity to arm up with some of these deadly weapons, and then strike us.

And the President of the United States' most solemn responsibility is to keep this country secure. And [Saddam Hussein] was a threat, and we dealt with him, and we dealt with him because we cannot hope for the best. We can't say, "Let's don't deal with Saddam Hussein. Let's hope he changes his stripes, or let's trust in the goodwill of Saddam Hussein. Let's let us, kind of, try to contain him." Containment doesn't work with a man who is a madman. (President George W. Bush, Interview with Tim Russert for NBC's "Meet the Press," aired February 14, 2004.)

On Wednesday night, March 19, 2003, the United States military (with coalition forces) launched the Iraq War. President George W. Bush gave the order to Secretary Rumsfeld, Chairman of the Joint Chiefs of Staff General Richard Myers, and the military chain of command to remove the regime. The campaign began with the "shock and awe" of air strikes on the outskirts of Baghdad where intelligence suggested Saddam Hussein, possibly his two sons, and Baathist politicos and military commanders were sequestered in anticipation of America's attacks. Those air strikes were followed by many others on the command and control infrastructure of Hussein's regime. Combinations of U.S. Air Force sorties and a variety of missiles pounded Baghdad and surrounding environs throughout the first and several subsequent nights. Soon after the initial air strikes, ground forces began what turned out to be a remarkable blitzkrieg toward Baghdad. Though Saddam avoided capture for some months, March 19, 2003, comprised the beginning of the end of Saddam Hussein and his regime.[5]

The Decision to Invade Iraq: The Effects of 9/11

According to preliminary reports, just prior to the final decision for war, President Bush met with his "war cabinet" and queried each member in turn as he went around the table seeking affirmation of a decision the president had already made.

> One more time, he polled each adviser. He reviewed for the last time an unexpected eleventh-hour intelligence bonanza regarding the whereabouts of senior Iraqi leaders, possibly including Saddam Hussein.
> Then Bush gave the order
> "Let's go," the president said.
> Thus the war against Iraq began.[6]

So orderly a process in which rational actors weighed the costs against benefits only after which the president gave the go order was subsequently belied by Bob Woodward's *Plan of Attack* and even more by Woodward's *State of Denial*. The precise process and language matters little for our purposes. That the Bush administration fully committed to toppling the Hussein regime at some date is what is crucial. (The range of views of when President Bush precisely made the decision to invade Iraq vary from early in his administration, to shortly after 9/11, to somewhere during the summer of 2002, and finally to February 2003.) Whatever its precise date, clearly such a commitment was made.

From that decision onward, Iraq became a constant external source of U.S. national security policy. The decision to invade Iraq was not made in a political vacuum. Rather, other external stimuli concomitant or nearly so with the invasion of Iraq provided a backdrop for the decision. The week-end following the invasion, the *Washington Post* noted that "Al Qaeda leaders, long known to covet biological and chemical weapons," had "reached at least the threshold of production and may already have manufactured some [WMD], according to a newly obtained cache of documentary evidence and interrogations recently conducted by the U.S. government." The evidence for the *Post*'s assertion was the capture of Khalid Sheik Mohammed (KSM) in Pakistan on March 1, 2003. Accordingly, "people with access to written reports said the emerging picture" depicted "the al Qaeda biochemical weapons program as considerably more advanced than U.S. analysts knew." Reportedly the evidence from KSM's computer demonstrated "completed plans" and that al Qaeda had "obtained the materials required to manufacture two biological toxins—botulinum and salmonella—and the chemical poison cyanide."[7]

Around the same time on the Korean peninsula, while "American forces fought for real in Iraq, the U.S. and South Korean armies staged one of their biggest mock battles for training just 14 miles from the Demilitarized Zone, the border with North Korean forces." Clearly, the U.S. and its ally the Republic of Korea (ROK) were signaling North Korea's Kim Jong Il as to America's new "forward leaning" policy. (President Bush identified Iraq, North Korea, and Iran as the axis of evil in a famous State of the Union address earlier that year.)[8] The result of America's warning clearly registered with the North Korean regime as just a week later North Korea commenced some signaling of its own. North Korea's regime replied to America's signal on the last day of the month (March) by firing an anti-ship missile off North Korea's *west* coast. President Kim Jong Il apparently thought better of firing a missile off North Korea's east coast where U.S. ally Japan had recently sent "spy" satellites into orbit.[9] When in 1998, North Korea tested a two-stage rocket whose trajectory took it over Japan, it caused a serious and tense standoff between the U.S. and Japan on the one hand and North Korea on the other. (It should be noted that during the editing of this manuscript, Kim Jong Il's regime fired seven missiles just as America celebrated its independence on July 4, 2006. The regime detonated an atomic weapon on October 9, 2006. In both instances, the UN Security Council unanimously denounced the regime.)

Additionally, Arabs and Muslims around the world who, arguably, empathized with the U.S. immediately following 9/11, reacted to the U.S.

invasion of Iraq in ways that critics of Bush's decision had predicted in the months of run-up to the war. "The U.S.-led invasion of Iraq has blurred the lines between mainstream, liberal, and radical politics in the world of Islam and has dissipated much of the empathy felt by Arabs toward the U.S. in the aftermath of the 9/11 attacks." Moreover, "U.S. policy toward Iraq has alienated many of the important moderate voices, both secular and religious, which until then had been unwilling to join with militant anti-American forces." From a Muslim "ladies' tea" in Saudi Arabia to the Muslim Brotherhood in Egypt to Hezbollah leader Sheik Hassan Nasrallah, the U.S. invasion of Iraq created widespread anger among many of the world's Muslims despite Saddam Hussein's tyrannical rule.[10] The initial anger produced by America's invasion of Iraq has simmered and boiled over many times since the original invasion. In early 2006, a Danish newspaper republished drawings of the prophet Mohamed that set off a chain reaction of Arab and Muslim anger that was eventually pointed at the U.S. despite the fact that it was not a U.S. newspaper who had "defamed" Islam's prophet.[11] Similarly, when Israel responded to Hezbollah killing Israeli soldiers and kidnapping two, then went after Hezbollah in Lebanon (mid July 2006), eventually the U.S. was denounced widely in the "Arab street."[12]

Even among some of America's strongest allies, President Bush's decision to topple Saddam Hussein caused transatlantic consternation. As soon as U.S. troops arrived in Baghdad, reports of a rift between allies appeared prominently in U.S. papers. "The battle of Iraq is over. The battle of Europe has begun." Or at least that was how it appeared "in France and Germany, where the contest over war in the Middle East now" transitioned "to the future of Europe." The recent discovery of bugging devices in the offices of the European Union—and the near-universal suspicion that they were planted by the U.S.—only heighten[ed] the suspicion and tension between the Cold War allies." Nor did it affect only European Union allies. Turkey, another NATO ally and a Muslim country, differed with the U.S. over its campaign and decided against allowing the U.S. to use Turkey's territory (including America's military bases in Turkey) to launch a northern front into Iraq.[13]

As American and coalition troops rapidly moved toward Baghdad, Iraqis evidently had mixed emotions. Recall news clips of Iraqis celebrating the coalition's advancement. Others took up weapons and fought coalition forces. There was a good deal of confusion over which Iraqis welcomed the invasion and overthrow of the Hussein regime versus which ones fought on the regime's behalf. What became clear fairly early was that the long-suffering Shiite majority, who had been persecuted under Saddam's Baathist and mostly Sunni-minority government, tended to welcome the coalition's successes initially. One of Iraq's most revered Shiite clerics, under house arrest while Saddam controlled the government, issued an edict (fatwa) instructing his followers *not* to resist the coalition troops. On the other hand, Saddam's so-called *Fedayeen*, Republican Guards, and various Sunni factions (and/or foreign fighters) continued to fight the coalition and in some cases put up a formidable resistance.[14]

Clearly, controversy surrounded the Bush administration's decision to invade and occupy Iraq as well as the postinvasion planning. Critics of the administration have asserted since early in the war that the administration failed to plan comprehensively. One early critic was James Fallows, writing for *The Atlantic Monthly*. In an exposé entitled "Blind into Baghdad," Fallows made several important points with respect to war planning, or lack thereof. The first was what Fallows viewed as the actual reason the Bush administration used to justify war. Forget the administration's charges that Saddam Hussein reconstituted his weapons of mass destruction programs and that Saddam maintained connections to al Qaeda and other jihadi groups. Fallows's piece focused on then–Deputy Secretary of Defense Paul Wolfowitz and Undersecretary of Defense for Policy, Douglas Feith, among other neoconservatives in the administration, and argued that their justification for war was an ideological one. Put simply, Fallows argued that these and other high administration officials wished to topple Saddam Hussein, plain and simple, and considered it more or less leftover business from their earlier government tenures. The long-held neoconservative belief that America needed to project its power aggressively for regime change was the thinking that occupied several of the administration's top policymakers and intellectuals.[15] And many of the same persons who served in George W. Bush's NSC had served in similar positions with George H. W. Bush. Some of them, the neoconservatives (so-called Vulcans), believed the first Gulf War was unfinished business needing redress.

Fallows interviewed Douglas Feith (then undersecretary of defense for policy) in order to understand what sort of contingency plans for quick victory were in place before the war began. In an extraordinarily telling response, Undersecretary Feith admitted that no such plans were prepared.

The reason apparently was the policymaking dynamic in the Pentagon's civilian leadership. Specifically, Feith noted that said planning smacked of predictions and Secretary of Defense Rumsfeld detested predictions. Therefore, his top policymaking and intellectual cadre avoided making predictions in discussions with Rumsfeld, including discussions of the war's aftermath. Secretary Rumsfeld's practice was to be ready for the unexpected and consequently avoid trying to prepare for a specific scenario to unfold. According to Feith, strategic uncertainty was Rumsfeld's modus operandi.

> [T]his meant being ready for whatever proved to be the situation in postwar Iraq. "You will not find a single piece of paper . . . If anybody ever went through all of our records—and someday some people will, presumably—nobody will find a single piece of paper that says, 'Mr. Secretary or Mr. President, let us tell you what postwar Iraq is going to look like, and here is what we need plans for.' If you tried that, you would get thrown out of Rumsfeld's office so fast—if you ever went in there and said, 'Let me tell you what something's going to look like in the future,' you wouldn't get to your next sentence!"[16]

Having top policymakers who neglected to plan for worst-case scenarios, however, did not mean the larger bureaucracy neglected to run extensive contingency planning prior to the intervention in Iraq. On the contrary, Fallows found reams (literally) of contingency plans that various bureaucracies—some of which were under Secretary Rumsfeld's purview—completed ahead of the Iraqi invasion. "Almost everything, good and bad, that has happened in Iraq since the fall of Saddam Hussein's regime was the subject of extensive prewar discussion and analysis." Fallows identified the bureaucracies involved in a tour de force of bureaucratic contingency planning. Included were the central intelligence agency (CIA), the state department, the U.S. Army and Marine Corps, the United States Agency for International Development, and any number of lesser-known agencies and bureaucracies. By itself, "the State Department's Future of Iraq project produced thousands of pages of findings," that were left virtually unread by those who actually decided that war was unavoidable.[17] Certainly President Bush did not read them, perhaps understandable as presidents often rely on others' counsel rather than digest the lengthy analyses from the bureaucracy. Less understandable is that other top policymakers failed to brief the president on the findings. It appeared that nobody at the highest levels wished to discuss such hypothetical contingencies.

To cite one specific example in Fallows's article, consider early to mid 2002 following the rapid success that U.S. and coalition forces experienced in Afghanistan. Apparently, as success progressed in Afghanistan, the CIA began considering similar scenarios for Iraq, believing it reasonable to think that such exercises might be needed eventually. In late May 2002 the CIA implemented a series of war game exercises intended to consider the best- and worst-case scenarios for Iraq, should President Bush decide that Saddam was to be overthrown. "According to a person familiar with the process, one recurring theme in the exercises was the *risk of civil disorder after the fall of Baghdad*." The CIA also considered "whether a new Iraqi government could be put together through a process like the Bonn conference" as had happened with Afghanistan. Fallows noted that Pentagon representatives participated in the exercises. Stunningly, however, "[w]hen their Pentagon superiors at the Office of the Secretary of Defense (OSD) found out about this, in early summer, the representatives were reprimanded and told not to participate further." Fallows identified who the Pentagon superiors were: "Rumsfeld, Wolfowitz, Feith, and one of Feith's deputies, William Luti."[18]

Such thinking was verboten among the administration's war planners. They had already decided whom they wished to head the Iraqi government once Saddam Hussein was toppled. Accordingly, Ahmed Chalabi,[19] an exiled Iraqi who maintained strong relations with the Pentagon and whose integrity the U.S. government had reason to suspect, furnished the Pentagon with a stream of intelligence separate from the U.S. intelligence community; Chalabi's intelligence included the infamous "Curveball" informant. Once U.S. and coalition forces moved into Iraq, the Bush administration's hoped-for government-in-waiting hunkered down in Kuwait. In Kuwait, Chalabi and his entourage waited for the fiercest fighting to expire. In a somewhat odd twist of U.S. foreign policy the Pentagon, rather than the Department of State, groomed various Iraqi expatriates. "Paul D. Wolfowitz, the undersecretary of defense," dispatched "some of his protégés . . . to prepare key Baghdad ministries for American management" following the fall of Saddam. Wolfowitz was second only to Secretary Rumsfeld in the Department of Defense. Among the Iraqi émigré community, some of whom Rumsfeld's office had coddled and paid handsomely to form an Iraqi government-in-waiting, Wolfowitz was known as "Wolfowitz of Arabia."

Extraordinarily, "State Department officials" said that "the Pentagon deemed the most senior State Department appointees as unsuitable for the enterprise." Ahmed Chalabi, the leader of the "Iraqi National Congress," was being touted by Wolfowitz and Rumsfeld despite the fact that the state department reportedly resisted, as the state department believed Chalabi's character was dubious at best.

Proving prescient, the *Washington Post* reported early on that as the coalition and U.S. troops began to secure Baghdad for what the Bush administration initially thought would be a relatively short occupation, rumors that would later embarrass the administration began to circulate presaging the lack of evidence for weapons of mass destruction (WMDs). "U.S. forces in Iraq yesterday [April 4, 2003] found sites and substances they described as suspected components of a forbidden Iraqi weapons program. But the discoveries that U.S. troops displayed, and the manner in which they were described at a Central Command briefing, struck experts in and out of government as ambiguous at best." Iraq's continued concealment of WMDs was "at the core of the Bush administration's case for war." As U.S. inspectors and what became the Iraqi Survey Group (ISG) got their first chance at unencumbered searches in Iraq, "experienced investigators" told reporters that the U.S. inspectors faced "a long road to an uncertain result." Additionally, "U.S. officials overseeing the weapons hunt" told reporters they did not expect to find Saddam's WMDs "at sites previously identified as suspicious, noting that Iraq's documented history of concealment relied on constant movement."[20] In a burst of unbridled certitude, one of the Pentagon's neoconservatives, Douglas Feith, "spun" the lack of evidence. "There's lots we don't know about current whereabouts," Douglas J. Feith, undersecretary of defense for policy, said in an interview. "That's going to be true until we have full control of the country, and even a time thereafter," he continued.[21]

The results were not so uncertain after all; rather, the ISG determined no such weapons existed in Iraq during the period that had been claimed by the administration in its run-up to the Iraq War. During the same timeframe Judith Miller, a *New York Times* reporter who was an "expert" on WMDs, as well as others, published reports on WMDs in Iraq and connections between Saddam's regime and WMDs as well as potential connections with jihadi groups. It may be, in retrospect, that one or more reporters were being "spun" by administration officials who, presumably, truly believed the weapons existed.[22]

In a more recent twist to the story of WMDs, the *Washington Post* published an exposé in April 2006. In it, an investigative journalist for the paper wrote that in late May 2003—that is, after most of the major combat for Baghdad and after President Bush officially declared "mission accomplished"—the intelligence community (the Defense Intelligence Agency or DIA) produced a definitive report on one aspect of the administration's charge that Saddam Hussein reconstituted weapons of mass destruction. The DIA relayed a "field report" to the president's NSC. The report concluded that the "mobile labs" that the intelligence community had been arguing about for months and which Secretary Powell made public in his famous February UN speech, in fact could not be used to make biological weapons! President Bush asserted in a speech just two days later that the mobile labs had been discovered, which proved that Saddam's regime in fact had weapons of mass destruction.[23] It is quite plausible that President Bush had yet to hear directly and/or definitively of the DIA's conclusion in the two days between its release and his speech. Subsequently, however, Vice President Cheney made multiple assertions of the same evidence in speeches he gave during the summer and fall of 2003. In other words, Vice President Cheney continued to insist that the biological labs existed well after the DIA's field report was vetted within the NSC principals setting. It is virtually inconceivable that Cheney had not heard of the DIA's determination when he made the same charge yet again in September of 2003.

In another problematic issue for the Bush administration, al Qaeda–associated terrorists who were alleged to control parts of Iraq from their mountain redoubts in the northeastern part of the country, turned out to be less than the global jihadis the administration asserted. Recall that another pretext for intervening in Iraq was the president's assertion—repeated by Vice President Cheney—that Saddam harbored al Qaeda and other Islamists who sought to do the U.S. and its allies harm. The administration made the suggestion that fighting them in Iraq would be far wiser than fighting them in the streets of Washington DC and New York—doubtless true and an equation that resonated with many Americans. As Kurdish fighters, who clearly welcomed the U.S. intervention, seized the terrorists (from Ansar al-Islam) they appeared little more than young, bewildered wannabes. "Some are boys. Others said they had never fired at an enemy." The pre-invasion description of Ansar al-Islam was of battle-hardened warriors who had trained in use of chemical weapons. In fact, intelligence suggested "Ansar had an estimated 120 hard-core Arab fighters from Yemen, Morocco, Israel, Tunisia and other countries," and many of them "reportedly trained in al Qaeda's camps in Afghanistan." Of the many who surrendered, Kurdish leaders described them as being considerably "different from Osama bin Laden and al Qaeda." The Kurdish commander who took their surrender characterized most of them as "brainwashed youths," whom the Kurdish leaders believed had likely "been cheated and deceived" by the jihadi propaganda.[24]

The weeks surrounding the fall of Baghdad were replete with evidence (albeit much of it outside of Iraq) of a global jihadi network, making the administration's assertions of an al Qaeda–Iraq connection at least seem plausible. Plots and/or would-be attacks were discovered, hatched, or thwarted from North Africa (Algeria) to Europe (Italy, Germany, the U.K.) to South Asia (Pakistan) to Central Asia (Afghanistan and former Soviet Tajikistan) to Southeast Asia (Indonesia and the Philippines). On April 10, stories of Algerian jihadis kidnapping German tourists were reported. On April 17 and 18 respectively, reports of Hezbollah vowing to launch attacks on Americans to avenge America's killing of Muslims in Iraq and a hint of an al Qaeda attack in Saudi Arabia were reported. (Hezbollah, of course, was a Shiite jihadi group whose apocalyptic view of Islam was mutually exclusive to al Qaeda's. However, Shiites and Sunnis were believed to cooperate from time to time for short-term expediency.) During the same month, Jemaah Islamiah, an al Qaeda–associated network in Southeast Asia, and associated militants in Indonesia were discovered during a shootout between jihadis and authorities in the Philippines. In Indonesia, a bomb was detonated at a Jakarta airport. In Europe, Italian authorities reported discovery of a plot for al Qaeda to set up training camps in Iraq, putatively the same Ansar al-Islam camps just noted. Similarly, disaffected jihadis in Britain were reported to be preparing to flock to Iraq to take up Jihad against the infidel coalition members. A Moroccan in Italy (apparently with German papers) was reported to have links to the original 9/11 plot in the U.S. From Central Asia and the former Soviet Union, during the same period, bombing plots were carried out in Afghanistan against Western troops and new outbreaks of violence (al Qaeda and/or Taliban fighters sniping at Western troops) were seen. In the former Soviet Union both Chechnya and Tajikistan saw jihadi plots thwarted. Finally, attacks and thwarted attacks occurred in Pakistan, a hotbed of jihadi activity and anti-U.S. and anti-Western hatred. And these were all in a month's time during the same timeframe as the DIA's field report on Iraq's biological labs.[25] It doubtlessly seemed to the Bush's NSC principals that plot after plot discovered in so short a time equaled a global network of jihadis ready to launch more 9/11-like attacks against the U.S. and West.

By mid April the major thrust of the Iraq invasion had succeeded and only pockets of resistance remained. These were heady days for the Bush administration and the neoconservatives. U.S. and coalition troops had accomplished their initial goals: Baghdad was under U.S. control, Basra under British control, and signs of normalcy were seen.[26] Unfortunately, ominous signs that problems lay ahead also soon appeared. The search for WMDs, as noted, proved futile and information for the Iraqi Survey Group dripped out slowly month after month. The problem was largely a symbolic one. Every few days a story appeared that seemed to confirm the administration's assertions that evidence of WMDs had been discovered; invariably, however, such stories were followed days or weeks later by another set of articles that falsified the previous claims.

Another problem though, this one a substantive problem that loomed large, was the beginnings of the insurgency. "Thousands of anti-American demonstrators marched through Baghdad [April 18, 2003] to protest the U.S. occupation of Iraq, while another leading advisor to Saddam Hussein was captured in the northern city of Mosul." It was true that some Iraqis greeted U.S. and coalition troops happily if not quite with flowers and candy, but the sentiment was far from universal. For every Kurd or Shiite who initially welcomed the invasion, multiple Sunnis, Shiites, and even Kurds cautioned the U.S. against staying now that Saddam was toppled. Furthermore, many Iraqis were distressed, to put it charitably, that the Bush administration and the U.S. military had neglected to provide basic security. Recall that looting and chaotic behavior followed Saddam's toppling and made the "occupation," as many Iraqis saw it, seem even worse.

Tens of thousands of people poured through the streets as they carried Korans and waved banners, some that read "Leave our country, we want peace" and "No Bush, No Saddam," according to Reuters. The demonstrations—the largest so far since Hussein lost control last week—met with no opposition from U.S. forces.

In what must have ultimately proved embarrassing for the Bush administration,

> A few hours after the demonstrations, prominent Iraqi opposition leader Ahmad Chalabi made his first public appearance in Baghdad since he returned to the country in the wake of Hussein's fall from power. Chalabi . . . said an Iraqi authority would be ready "in a matter of weeks" to assume control of major government operations from the U.S. military.

Chalabi was ferried into Iraq from Kuwait by the Pentagon following the worst of the fighting. To describe the conflicting evidence as incongruent would be generous. In Baghdad, a "cleric"—the article failed to note whether he was Shiite or Sunni—made a prophetic statement that the administration may have simply ignored as bluster. "Demonstrators poured out of the Abu Haneefa al-Nu'man Mosque after Ahmed al-Kubeisy, a leading Baghdad cleric, criticized the American 'occupation' during his sermon, 'You are the masters today,' al-Kubeisy told worshippers according to Reuters. '*But I warn you against thinking of staying. Get out before we force you out.*'"[27] In fact, at least one reporter noted that the "thousands of protesters" who "poured" into the streets of Baghdad, included "Shiite and Sunni Muslims alike,"[28] in retrospect a clear omen of what was to come. For whatever reason, the administration chose to ignore the omen.

The administration found itself looking at the beginning of an insurgency it had not, as incredible as it sounds, considered. By early May 2003, indications of an emerging insurgency were clear to all but the most obtuse administration boosters. The administration had announced that major combat was over in early May 2003. What they neglected to mention (or apparently failed to fathom) was that a new phase of combat had commenced in earnest. U.S. troops overreacted to protestors in Falluja[29] and killed civilians. Iraqis began demanding revenge while continuing to warn the U.S. to leave Iraq. "Today's attack in Falluja came only hours after soldiers in the compound and in a passing Army convoy opened fire on anti-American demonstrators . . . Hospital officials in Falluja, about 30 miles west of Baghdad, said two Iraqis were killed and 18 were wounded." The *Washington Post* republished a London daily's comments on both Bush's pronouncement of the end to major military operations and the hostilities recently aimed at the occupation of Iraq.

The Independent, a London daily, says Bush's speech, delivered "far out at sea—aboard the aircraft carrier Abraham Lincoln, which is heading back from the Gulf—will not convince many Iraqis."
  "For the people of Falluja . . . the war with the American and British occupiers seems to be just beginning. *Hatred is taking hold here, and throughout Iraq.*"[30]

By mid to late May, clerics and regular Iraqis began openly calling for resistance. "Sheik Jamal Shaker Mahmoud roused the faithful at the Great Mosque" in Iraq "with a simple message: Resist the Americans." Coming from a Sunni cleric in Falluja, perhaps the call was not surprising. However, reports suggested it was widespread: "similar messages blared from loudspeakers outside mosques across central Iraq during services Friday, the day that the U.S. civil authority formally disbanded Iraq's armed forces." And in Shiite neighborhoods of Baghdad, the same calls were heard. "Even in Sadr City, a predominantly Shiite slum that was neglected and occasionally punished by Saddam Hussein's Sunni-dominated regime, many residents" remained "uneasy toward the United States." According to reports, the sources of frustration were manifold. Some believed that the Bush administration's decision to rehire some former Baathists in order to help expedite the rebuilding effort was duplicitous. Others were simply frustrated with the slow pace of reconstruction. Yet others blamed Ambassador Bremer for one of his first decisions since he replaced Mr. Jay Garner:

> [The previous day] L. Paul Bremer III, the American civilian administrator overseeing the reconstruction of Iraq, disbanded the country's armed forces, two key ministries and several security bodies. Together, the entities had formed the military backbone of the regime, and their dissolution [was] a symbolic milestone in the coalition's effort to purge members of Hussein's Baath Party in postwar Iraq and rebuild the nation's institutions under an allied administration.[31]

In a sort of catch-22, the more discontent manifested itself in violence against U.S. troops, the slower reconstruction progressed. The slower reconstruction progressed, the more discontent increased and manifested itself.[32]

  More positively, the U.S. uniformed military leadership appeared to appreciate that the insurgency was comprised of a witches' brew of disparate

elements. Chairman of the Joint Chiefs of Staff General Richard B. Myers pointed out "that despite the continuing attacks in Iraq, anti-coalition
resistance was far from 'monolithic,' coming from at least five distinct
groups operating in a relatively restricted central area." At this early stage
of the insurgency fewer than 70 U.S. troops had lost their lives. It would
appear, however, that General Myers was aware that a long slog lay ahead.
In suggesting the insurgency was not monolithic, Myers believed that the
heart of the insurgency was in the so-called Sunni triangle. "The problem,
[Myers added], was in Sunni-dominated central areas, and particularly in
a triangle formed by Baghdad; Ramadi, to the west, where a bomb explosion on Saturday killed seven United States–trained Iraqi police recruits
marching from their graduation ceremony; and Tikrit, to the northwest, a
stronghold of Mr. Hussein." It is less clear whether the civilian leadership
in the Pentagon and members of President Bush's NSC principals understood the dimensions of the growing problem.[33] They showed no indication that they did.

As noted, the Iraq–al Qaeda connection was proving an embarrassment
for the administration. Nonetheless, the earliest signs that al Qaeda and
other jihadis (what the administration eventually came to call "foreign
fighters") were flocking to Iraq for Jihad against the West appeared in
mid 2003. Before most Americans heard of Abu Asab al-Zarqawi, tapes
surfaced—mostly on Arab media—of something calling itself al Qaeda of
Iraq. "A group calling itself a wing of al Qaeda claimed responsibility
Sunday for attacks on American troops in Iraq, as U.S. forces killed five
Iraqis in raids aimed at preventing such violence during two Iraqi holidays
this week." [34]

In roughly the same time period the coalition scored a major victory.
From the beginning, the U.S. and its partners had taken the surrender of
many of Saddam Hussein's top officials. In the nearly three months since
Bush declared and end to major hostilities, notable former regime members came under coalition control: Tariq Aziz, (a spokesman in the West
for Saddam since the first Gulf War), various high-level Baathist Party
members, and even top scientists thought to have pertinent information on
Iraq's putative WMD program. In late July, both of Saddam's sons, each
notorious in his own right, were cornered in Mosul, a northern city bor-
dering the Kurdish region. Both were legendary for their cruelty and wan-
ton abuse of Iraqis. Qusay Hussein and his younger brother Uday Hussein
died in a firefight at a house in Mosul, boosting the morale of U.S. troops

and relieving many common Iraqis. In addition to taking out two feared relatives of Saddam who might shelter ambitions of returning to power in Iraq, the entire episode suggested that intelligence of the U.S. and the coalition was improving. "The two sons of former Iraqi president Saddam Hussein were killed . . . during a lengthy and intense gun battle with U.S. soldiers who raided an opulent stone mansion after receiving a tip from an informant." Many believed that with the two sons dead, a greater number of Iraqi informants would lead to Saddam's capture.[35] Saddam, however, managed to resist detection for several more months.

By August 2003, what had once seemed a resistance mainly by remnants of Saddam's former regime members morphed into an outright insurgency. The outbreak of the insurgency was covered by the media in spades. In the southern Iraqi city of Basra, a city controlled principally by Shiites, protests erupted against the U.K. Basra was controlled by the British, America's principal coalition allies. Since the fall of Baghdad, discontent had been on a slow boil in Baghdad and in Basra. It boiled over in August. "On Sunday [August 10, 2003], residents protested in Basra for a second day, with small crowds rioting in some areas over gasoline shortages and power blackouts caused by infrastructure problems, sabotage and smuggling. By Monday, electricity supplies had improved, and gasoline stations had worked all night to deliver fuel." Another report was even gloomier about emerging trends in Iraq.

> An uneasy calm returned to Basra today after two days of unrest—some of the worst in Iraq since U.S.-led forces overthrew the government of Saddam Hussein on April 9. But no one in this weary southern city—neither the British officials blamed for its plight, nor residents whose mounting frustration mirror[ed] the spiraling temperatures—seemed to think that the worst was behind them.

Another report noted the growing discontent over the U.S. occupation, this time in Baghdad.

> Although major combat operations may be over in Iraq, the Kawaz family's experience illustrate[d] anew the danger civilians face[ed] under the U.S.-led military occupation. With resistance forces attacking troops daily—another U.S. soldier died Sunday in a blast in Baqubah—soldiers are on high alert. In this tense and broiling-hot capital patrolled by some 36,000 U.S. troops, trigger fingers are at the ready.

What Secretary Rumsfeld and others had earlier termed "dead enders" were now being seen as a growing problem: a much more generalizable resistance across the country.[36] Beyond the ranks of the growing insurgency, evidence of foreign jihadis flocking to Iraq appeared as well. It was particularly ironic as President Bush used the alleged presence of al Qaeda and other jihadis in Iraq as a justification for the invasion in the first place. Once investigated, this justification was found lacking in evidence. Nonetheless, as the insurgency grew, so too did the attraction for outsiders to head to Iraq to wage Jihad against the West.[37]

Another very worrisome trend appeared by the end of August: sectarian violence, which subsequently came to characterize the insurgency. Attacks aimed at Shiite holy sites in Shiite cities such as Najaf occurred throughout the month. Still relatively unknown, Abu Musab al-Zarqawi turned up in reports again. Zarqawi, who infamously went on to lead al Qaeda of Iraq, sometimes know as al Qaeda of Mesopotamia, was known in counterterrorism circles in the West. He was also known to Osama bin Laden and, in fact, some analysts saw him as a competitor of bin Laden's. By 2005, Zarqawi and bin Laden evidently made peace and began to cooperate in Iraq. The precise relationship between Abu Musab Zarqawi and al Qaeda remained a mystery even after Zarqawi's death—Zarqawi was killed by the U.S. military on June 7, 2006. What is known is that Zarqawi pledged fealty to bin Laden—a notable precondition, apparently for al Qaeda's blessing—and continued to be one of America's most-wanted foreign fighters in Iraq until his death.[38] The character of what began as a resistance and tit-for-tat reactions to the heavy-handed tactics of coalition troops soon turned into a high-power insurgency. The Sunni insurgency continued to grow after President Bush announced an end to major hostilities on the USS *Abraham Lincoln* in May 2003. Similarly, the Shiite insurgency began to wreak havoc in late 2003. Moreover, with Zarqawi joining the fray in behalf of Sunni jihadis, increased attacks and counterattacks between Sunnis and Shiites appeared as well and escalated from 2004 through 2006. Hence, in addition to a full-fledged insurgency, early signs of the sectarian violence that became so prominent in 2005 and 2006 appeared in 2003.

By year's end it was fairly clear that Iraq's WMD program had largely been destroyed by UN inspectors during the years of sanctions and from widely erratic leadership in Iraq over developing said capacity. In December, former chief UN weapons inspector Hans Blix said "that it was becoming 'increasingly clear' that Saddam Hussein's regime in Iraq did not have any weapons of mass destruction." "Blix said he believed that most of Iraq's banned weapons were destroyed in 1991." Blix suggested his guess was that no weapons of mass destruction were left after the inspections; even those who had once believed Saddam's WMDs justified the war were left with nothing to counter Blix's statements. Interrogation of high-level Iraqis who should have known whether the regime had WMDs discovered nothing. "Hussein concluded, these prisoners explained, that Saudi Arabia, Kuwait, the United Arab Emirates, and other countries paid him deference because they feared he had weapons of mass destruction. Hussein was unwilling to reveal that his cupboard was essentially bare, these detainees said."[39] Hence, Saddam's deception that he had WMDs had ironically served as a deterrent even as it led to his eventual demise.

More positively, U.S. troops captured Saddam Hussein in December. His capture, and its particularly humiliating circumstances, boosted the morale of U.S., other Westerners, and even Iraq's indigenous forces fighting the insurgency. His imprisonment, further, removed the fear of many that he might one day return to power to settle scores. The effects included better intelligence from Iraqis. Furthermore, unlike Osama bin Laden who has managed to elude capture, Saddam was no longer a factor politically. Even his promoters in Iraq moved beyond the unrealistic belief that they might one day return to their privileged positions—as witnessed by the fact that large numbers of Sunnis participated in the December 2005 elections. Whatever one thinks of Saddam's defiance of U.S. presidents and Western influences in the Middle East, that Saddam had been rendered essentially obsolete clearly accrued as a positive development. That is, bringing Saddam to justice for the tens if not hundreds of thousands of people he and his regime callously murdered was far better than not bringing him to justice.

Unfortunately, his capture had no demonstrable dilutory effect on the insurgency. On the contrary, between the weeks before his capture in mid December and the end of 2003, the insurgency proved increasingly lethal. In fairness, many, including many within the U.S. government predicted that simply putting Saddam in shackles would likely do little to lessen the insurgency. That proved accurate. To cite just a few of the most atrocious of insurgent attacks during the period, in late November, a dozen or more rockets were fired at the Palestine and Sheraton hotels inside the U.S.-controlled green zone. Multiple and seemingly coordinated attacks struck a commercial airplane at the Baghdad airport while suicide bombers attacked two police stations, killing over a dozen and wounding scores. Shiite firebrand and gadfly (from the coalition's perspective) Moktader al-Sadr became a new face of the insurgency representing Shiite passions after years of oppression and the growing sectarian nature of the insurgency. November proved to be the deadliest month in Iraq since the March invasion.[40]

December represented little or no improvement over November. A huge battle between coalition troops and insurgents (apparently Sunnis) occurred in Samarra (in the infamous Sunni Triangle) in which coalition troops learned that insurgents were studying the coalition's tactics and adapting. (Samarra was the same city in which insurgents nearly destroyed a sacred golden-domed mosque on February 22, 2006, an event that arguably changed the insurgency yet again, from complex insurgency to civil war.) Insurgents struck a U.S. base in northern Iraq killing some 40 troops followed by an even larger attack on U.S. troops the following day. U.S troops tangled with insurgents in Falluja again in what would become a recurring flare-up with Sunnis in that troubled city. And the night of the long knives finally appeared for many of Iraq's former Baathist regime members.[41]

Iraq in 2004: The Insurgency Grows, Becomes Bifurcated into a Sunni vs. Shiite Incipient Civil War, and Stability Decreases

During 2004, Iraq demonstrated increasing instability. It was a year of increased sectarian divides between Shiite and Sunni, a year in which Abu Musab al-Zarqawi infamously became a well-known name in the U.S. and the West (for kidnappings and beheadings, among other atrocities), and a year in which the Sunni Triangle (Falluja perhaps most prominently) and a few key cities in the Shiite south, mostly linked to Moktada al-Sadr and his followers, exploded in violence time and again. The year 2004 was also a year in which some, if not spectacular, "progress" was made in Iraq. In June, "sovereignty" was returned to Iraqis from the coalition that toppled Saddam's regime and thereafter occupied Iraq. By year's end, elections were scheduled for the beginning of 2005, and though Sunnis largely boycotted those elections, the elections may be seen, in retrospect, to have been a turning point of sorts for all involved. Sunnis discovered that boycotting the political process left them few political options. Upon learning this lesson, Sunnis would subsequently register and vote in large numbers in the elections held on December 15, 2005. In short, 2004 proved a formidable year for the U.S. and coalition presence in Iraq. By the end of 2004, however, the political situation in Iraq was seemingly headed in a slightly more positive direction. Indeed, the late 2004 through 2005 period proved a relatively stable period in Iraq—for a period of months, during which elections were held, there seemed a respite of relative security. Alas, on February 22, 2006, a Shiite-revered golden-domed shrine along the banks of the Tigris River in Samarra was attacked, setting off a new round of sectarian violence that plagues Iraq to date.

Interestingly, an issue from 2003, namely the composition of the Iraqi Advisory Council, remained a thorny issue throughout the spring of 2004. It will be recalled that the UN presence in Iraq was affected by insurgents targeting the UN offices there in 2003, killing Sergio Vieira de Mello, a high UN official. Given the UN's negative experience, Kofi Annan (then general secretary of the UN) remained reluctant to re-involve the UN in Iraq. In the spring of 2004, however, the UN ultimately reengaged. The UN eventually appointed a new special envoy, Lakhdar Brahimi. Mr. Brahimi, a taciturn UN professional known for his discretion and good work in Afghanistan over the previous two years, was appointed by Kofi Annan in mid January. Reports held that President Bush wanted the "United Nations to provide support and legitimacy" to an agreement crafted between the coalition and the Iraqis the previous November 15 that called "for the establishment of regional caucuses in Iraq to appoint [a] provisional government" by June 30.[42] Kofi Annan's appointment of Brahimi greatly hastened that process. American officials were said to be "struggling" with Brahimi and the UN "to cobble together an electoral process that [would] favor Iraqi moderates in the transfer of sovereignty" scheduled just six months later in June 2004, and Brahimi proved helpful to the administration.[43]

Opposing points of view were arrayed against the U.S., UN, and coalition efforts. The lines of demarcation between those views became clearer in 2004. On the one hand was Grand Ayatollah Ali al-Sistani, perhaps the most revered Shiite cleric in Iraq. Sistani continued to insist on direct elections; since Iraq's population was estimated to have been comprised by a majority of Shiites (some 60 percent or more), Sistani's position was understandable. Shiites were oppressed under Iraq's Sunni minority during Saddam Hussein's reign and even prior to Hussein. If Sistani's position held sway, when the U.S. turned over sovereignty to Iraq on June 30,

2004, it would be handing it over to a Shiite majority, something the Bush administration was loath to do. The Iraqi Governing Council labored to create an entity with which to accept Iraqi sovereignty with representation from Shiites, Kurds, Sunnis, and others. Kurds, who lived in an essentially separate Kurdish portion of Iraq during the previous years of no-fly zones, wished to memorialize what they in fact already had: special status in Iraq with an autonomous or semiautonomous government. After all, Kurds and Shiites more than any other groups supported the toppling of Saddam's regime. Sunnis, of course, lost their position of advantage by virtue of the invasion and Saddam's capture. U.S. officials were counting on Brahimi, who had worked with similarly difficult issues in Afghanistan, to smooth things over between the principals in order to find a mechanism for creating an interim government and constitution that would represent each of these groups and others while protecting minorities.[44] Furthermore, the Bush administration wished to effect all these changes in a relatively short time frame.

Despite the U.S. desires, Iraqis Shiites were feeling the pull of independence and democracy and appeared to be in less than a generous mood concerning decisions on Iraq's future. For the first time in a long time, Iraqi Shiites could make their demands known without fear of recriminations or brutal suppression. And make them known they did. "Tens of thousands of Shiite Muslims marched through Baghdad on Monday in the largest protest since the occupation of Iraq began 10 months ago, demanding that U.S. authorities organize direct elections to choose a new government," read one piece. Reports suggested that the demonstrations sent an unmistakable message: "that the demands of Iraq's emboldened Shiite majority could not be ignored by U.S. and Iraqi officials . . . in the troubled plan to transfer power to Iraqis" later that summer. Iraq's Shiite Muslims, it was noted, held the key to stability and they predictably and "steadily escalated demands for power commensurate with their rights as a majority." For the time being, at least, the U.S. attempted to "paper over" differences, ultimately hoping to hold the entire Iraq gamble together. Militant Shiite cleric, Moktada al-Sadr, was increasing his demands and, while he was arguably less revered than Sistani, his followers comprised a growing group of Shiites whose concerns had to be considered. Sistani appeared to be temporizing. "At the same time, Shiite political parties, such as the Supreme Council for the Islamic Revolution in Iraq [SCIRI], preached patience with the U.S. administration and took part in the American-appointed Governing Council. For much of 2003, despite criticism by some followers, Sistani delivered important edicts but remained largely in the background, content with a spiritual role."[45]

While these political and sectarian negotiations occurred in earnest, Abu Musab al-Zarqawi (the Sunni jihadi) made the news again, unfortunately presaging a recurring problem the U.S. and the coalition experienced throughout 2004. U.S. forces captured what were described as "aides" to the Jordanian jihadi, who continued to wreak terror in Iraq until his death on June 7, 2006. As one report explained, U.S. and coalition forces chased and disrupted Zarqawi and his forces during 2003. However, U.S. officials were concerned that Zarqawi's group and others were regrouping and reconstituting themselves in anticipation of attacking again in 2004 in order to disrupt planned transitions such as the return of sovereignty. "If confirmed, the capture of an al Qaeda operative, especially in the tinderbox of [Falluja], would be a significant development. U.S. officials have long said that foreign fighters were among those attacking the U.S.-led occupation force."[46]

While Falluja appeared a tinderbox again, a largely Kurdish city, Kirkuk, was threatening to explode in violence. Kirkuk was home to some 40 percent of Iraq's oil reserves. Kurds saw the city as an important Kurdish cultural symbol. While Saddam Hussein was under UN sanctions for some 14 years, Kurds were protected from Saddam's direct wrath by no-fly zones. Saddam nevertheless moved Arabs into the Kurdish city during those same years in a conscious effort to "Arabize" a traditionally Kurdish area. The backlash from those policies was building in post-Saddam Iraq. "More than 100,000 Kurds forced from the city and replaced with Arabs during Saddam Hussein's rule" planned "to reclaim what was taken from them. Hundreds of Kurds [were] living in tents at the city's ragged rim, resembling an army of the dispossessed."[47]

On top of these political troubles, the U.S. military reported that al Qaeda was attempting to gain a foothold in Iraq in January 2004.[48] On the one hand were Iraqis positioning for power in the post-Saddam era in Iraq. On the other hand, reportedly, were insurgents and global jihadis seeking to establish a base in Iraq similar to the one they had in Afghanistan prior to 9/11. A letter sent to Osama bin Laden seeking al Qaeda's help was intercepted by coalition troops in Iraq. Reportedly, the jihadis ultimately sought to incite a sectarian war in Iraq. Though it was unclear at the time of the reports, these persons apparently included Zarqawi, who believed that Sunnis must ultimately kill all heretics; that is, Iraqi Shiites.[49]

The on-again off-again insurgency in Falluja was on again in February 2004. Falluja had become a potent flash point in 2003. If it was a flash point in 2003, in 2004 it became an all-out explosion. Noting that the U.S. planned to transfer sovereignty to the Iraqis during the summer of 2004, one report held that "a variety of underground groups" in Falluja were "making a push to grab power through violence." Though even more violent than 2003, the apparent justification for Sunnis and others in Falluja and its environs in the Sunni Triangle was reportedly political. Hence, it was assumed that the explosions of intense violence in spring, again in summer, and again in the fall were an attempt to sway the ultimate balance of power in Iraq's governance once occupation forces were gone. What was becoming clear, as some Iraqis noted, was that at least some of the insurgents were "turning their attention away from battling the occupation and instead trying to influence the situation that [would] emerge after [the occupation] formally" ended. Not everyone agreed with the assessment of political posturing and maneuvering for post-occupation Iraq. Still the conventional wisdom seemed to be that what compelled the violence was the approaching June 30 deadline for transferring sovereignty.[50]

In March, it appeared briefly that a corner was turned in Iraq. "Iraq's Governing Council reached agreement [reported on March 1, 2004] on an interim constitution that would provide a legal basis for running the country once sovereignty [was] restored" later that summer, according to U.S. and Iraqi sources. In a victory for the U.S. and its coalition partners as well as the UN, Shiites, Kurds, and Sunnis agreed on a deal. A "senior coalition official" said "that the document set out a multiperson presidency, with a prime minister who is to lead a cabinet." Further, the agreement addressed "such matters as the separation of powers and include[d] a bill of rights that the coalition official said was 'quite clear on protecting all individual rights'" that we in the West took for granted, "including speech, assembly, and religion."[51] Unfortunately and apparently timed to coincide with the agreement, scores of people were killed and hundreds wounded in attacks launched the following days. One result was that Shiites renewed an earlier call to constitute or reconstitute their own militias. While an understandable response to what was seen as Sunni insurgents and jihadis, it was an ominous development for stability. Indeed, so horrific was the spasm of violence that Shiite leaders actually postponed sign-ing the interim agreement for a time.[52]

Elsewhere, on March 11, 2004 (known as 3/11), jihadis attacked Madrid, Spain in a coordinated explosion of multiple bombs on Spain's commuter train system. Hundreds of persons were killed and many hun-dreds more wounded. Spain awoke to its own 9/11 and the attacks had widespread repercussions. First, the fact that Europe too was the target of jihadis overshadowed events in Iraq for some weeks. Second, Europe be-gan an incremental change toward a more aggressive posture against global jihadis. Third, Spain's domestic politics were turned on their head, a result apparently intended by the jihadis. A strong Bush ally in Spain, then–Prime Minster Anzar was bested in an election just days after the 3/11 attacks. The newly-elected leader, Mr. Jose Luis Rodriguez Zapatero, a Socialist, was less amenable to U.S. interests. In fact, Zapatero cam-paigned on, among other things, pulling Spain's troops out of Iraq ,which he subsequently did. Clearly, while the U.S. had become somewhat teth-ered to Iraq—as opposed to a wider war on the global jihadis—al Qaeda and other jihadis continued to function, with manifold political effects worldwide.

March also ushered in the one-year anniversary of the U.S. and coali-tion intervention in Iraq. As the anniversary approached some notable de-velopments occurred. First, apparently coordinated insurgent attacks were launched around Iraq, spanning northern, central, and southern Iraq. "In-surgents launched more deadly attacks in Iraq . . . in advance of the first anniversary of the U.S. invasion of the country." One such attack which killed some ten Iraqis was near Baqubah in a Sunni area. "A hotel in the southern city of Basra," under British control and a Shiite area, "was hit by a car bomb that claimed five lives."[53] Iraq's Governing Council, under intense pressure from the U.S. and others, requested the UN to help them form a new government to whom sovereignty could be handed at the end of June. "Members of the Iraqi Governing Council said they sent a letter to the United Nations after a tense meeting with L. Paul Bremer III, the chief American administrator, who reportedly gave the Iraqi leaders an ul-timatum," according to one report. This was good news from the Bush ad-ministration's perspective as the decision ended "a diplomatic deadlock that threatened to frustrate the desire of Iraqi leaders to have a revamped leadership in place by June 30," the date set by the Coalition Authority and the U.S. for transferring sovereignty to the Iraqi people. Transferring sovereignty was a necessary but nevertheless insufficient step before elections could be held at year's end.[54]

Near the end of March 2004 long-simmering Falluja boiled over yet again. This time accumulated tensions and anger exacted its vengeance on private contractors, who were pulled from vehicles, beaten and killed, and then either hanged or hung from a bridgelike structure. In a scene reminiscent of Somalia and Black Hawk Down, a "mob of angry Iraqis attacked two vehicles carrying U.S. civilian security workers . . . killing the four contractors, mutilating their remains, and hanging two of the charred corpses from a bridge over the Euphrates River." The attacks "culminated one of the bloodiest months since President Bush declared an end to the major combat phase of the war on May 1 [2003] and came as occupation officials hurried to prepare to hand over sovereignty to a new Iraqi interim government June 30."[55] More violence in Falluja, regrettably still lay ahead. By early to mid April, conventional wisdom was that the insurgency had demonstrably strengthened and increasingly threatened U.S. and coalition interests.[56]

Despite all the turmoil, an interim Iraqi government was put together with the help of the UN and UN envoy Brahimi. This was the sovereign Iraqi government to whom the U.S. transferred sovereignty on June 30, 2004, as promised. The new government—dubbed the caretaker government—rendered the Iraqi Governing Council obsolete. It also theoretically eliminated the need for the U.S. and coalition creation, the Coalition Provisional Authority (CPA). Elimination of the CPA in turn left the Iraqis on their own, in theory, as the transfer of sovereignty occurred.[57] Also in theory, if not quite in practice, the new interim government was empowered to negotiate in behalf of Iraqis. It quickly entered into an agreement with most of Iraq's militias to disband them.[58] A new UN Security Council resolution was passed in which the Bush administration yielded some ground to its French and German allies, both of whom endorsed the new Iraqi interim government.[59] Despite another wave of violence in June—apparently timed to disrupt the transfer of sovereignty—the U.S. transferred sovereignty to the Iraqi government with backing from the UN and its reluctant allies "in a surprise move two days ahead of schedule," on June 28, 2004. Quietly and without ceremony that might have obscured the importance of the transfer, coalition provisional authority administrator L. Paul Bremer slipped out of Iraq before the June 30 deadline.[60] Doubtless, Bremer's return to the U.S. was one of the happiest days of his life. Newly nominated and approved U.S. Ambassador to Iraq John Negroponte presented his credentials and restored diplomatic relations between the U.S. and Iraq for the first time in well over a decade.[61] (Ambassador Negroponte subsequently became America's first director of national intelligence [DNI], one of the important structural changes in U.S. foreign policymaking and national security policymaking since 9/11.)

Though undoubtedly important symbolically and, in fairness to the Bush administration, substantively important, little changed materially over the next several months. The Iraqi government became responsible for decisions in Iraq for the Iraqi people. But U.S. troops remained (indeed increased for the December 15, 2005, parliamentary elections) as did many other coalition troops. Violence continued to rage across Iraq. Falluja and the southern cities of Shiite influence continued to experience increasingly violent spasms. The insurgency continued largely unabated, though slow if uneven progress was also made by coalition military forces over the 2004–2005 period. Foreign fighters continued to be drawn to Iraq. Ironically, one of the rationales the Bush administration used to justify the war became a self-fulfilling prophecy. Additionally, Iraqis continued to suffer the deprivations that war and years of sanctions wrought.

By the end of 2004, with President George W. Bush reelected to a second term, Iraq was prepared to hold its own democratic elections. Large segments of the Sunni population announced they would boycott the vote.[62] Iraq continued to be a magnet for foreign jihadis, reportedly resulting in scores of European Muslims, dispossessed in Europe and angry that the West humiliated their religion, flocking to Iraq. "Hundreds of young militant Muslim men have left Europe to fight in Iraq, according to senior counterterrorism officials in four European countries. They have been recruited through mosques, Muslim centers, and militant websites by several groups" including Abu Musab al-Zarqawi's group. Zarqawi became one of the persons most wanted by the U.S. government, perhaps second in the world only to Osama bin Laden, to whom Zarqawi increasingly linked his actions.[63] Defeating terrorism and standing up a democratic Iraq (presumably in that order) continued to be the primary national security objectives for the Bush administration. In late December the Asia tsunami stuck South Asia, Southeast Asia, and Africa, killing literally hundreds of thousands of persons. *The Guardian* newspaper summed it all up in an editorial at year's end.

News of violence in Iraq has a grimly repetitive feel to it, especially when the world is—understandably—transfixed by the scale of the huge natural disaster of the Indian Ocean tsunami. Yet every day brings new horrors in the run-up to the country's elections at the end of January. This may no longer be surprising but it is deeply worrying. Tuesday's killing of 29 policemen in an ambush in Baghdad was further grisly evidence of the fact that the insurgency is alive, well-coordinated, and successful—and can no longer be dismissed as the work of foreign terrorists and former Baathists. Recent photographs of unmasked men coolly executing election workers in the street in broad daylight attest to the brazen confidence of the rebels.[64]

According to Pentagon statistics as reported in the news, some 1320 U.S. troops were dead by the end of 2004, roughly one thousand of whom were killed following President Bush's end of hostilities speech in May 2003 on the U.S.S. *Abraham Lincoln*. Many more would die in the following years.[65]

Since late 2004, of course, the occupation of Iraq has gone from bad to worse. By year's end the Intelligence Reform and Terrorism Prevention Act was signed into law. Whatever effects the Iraq War may have had on that legislation as an external source of U.S. policymaking therefore ended after its passage in December 2004. Clearly, Iraq has continued to be an external source of U.S. foreign policy even at this writing in early 2007. One of our primary interests here is how the Intelligence Reform and Terrorism Prevention Act changed U.S. national security policymaking and institutions. Therefore, further analysis of Iraq's import as an external source of U.S. foreign policy must await another venue.

While we are less interested in what happened in Iraq in 2005 and 2006, it should be noted that a vote on a referendum was held in Iraq in 2005. True to their word, the Sunnis boycotted participation. On the other hand, large numbers of Sunnis did participate in the national elections on December 15, 2005; the election selected the basis of what became a proportionally representative parliament. By at least one measure, then, the situation in Iraq improved in an empirically demonstrable way. Nevertheless, sweeping "statistics on insurgent violence in Iraq that were declassified for a Senate hearing" appeared "to portray a rebellion whose ability to mount attacks has steadily grown in the . . . years since the invasion."[66]

In 2006, the insurgency persisted. But seemingly some reason for optimism existed. Though the insurgency was unquestionably still active, its lethality appeared to decrease early in 2006 when compared to 2005 and especially 2004. Elections occurred in late 2005 and the Sunnis, in addition to other important groups, the Shiites and Kurds, participated. However, in February jihadis attacked a sacred golden-domed mosque in the city of Samarra. The attack took place on February 22, 2006. What became clear was that following the February 22 attack on the revered Shiite site, tit-for-tat retaliations engulfed Iraq. While the Bush White House had been somewhat reluctant to call it a civil war, others have been less reticent. Former NSC advisor for Bush (41) Brent Scowcroft characterized what was happening in Iraq in spring 2005 as possibly an "incipient civil war." In June 2005, President Bush noted explicitly in a speech that the enemies of freedom had failed to incite civil war in Iraq.[67] The state department's annual report on human rights interestingly came closer to Scowcroft's position than the president's. While it did not quite report that civil war was ongoing, it did note that the Department of State and its various programs worked with appropriate Iraqi counterparts "to mitigate" civil conflict across sectarian and other divides.[68]

The Samarra attack and the violence that followed it might not constitute a trend per se but is nonetheless worth noting. Over the course of just two days in the attack's aftermath, scores of Iraqis (and upwards of a dozen U.S. troops) were killed in what was characterized as a conscious attempt to foment sectarian civil war across the whole of Iraq. "Rarely since the U.S.-led invasion have Iraq's politicians appeared so insignificant and its religious leaders loomed so large as in the 48 hours since the bombing of the Golden Mosque in Samarra," reported the *Los Angeles Times*. In what may become a trend, the "dominance of clerics from both sects on the political scene mark[ed] a dramatic reversal of 85 years of secular rule in Iraq." A *New York Times* piece was similarly alarming. "The threat of full-scale civil war loomed over the country as Sunni politicians lashed out at Shiite leaders . . . accusing them of igniting anti-Sunni reprisals, and at the American military, charging it with standing idly by as the violence erupted." It appeared at least plausible that the attack was a calculated attempt to unleash full-fledged civil war between Iraq's sects. The response was a serious of escalating retaliations, including insurgents or jihadis stopping a bus full of Iraqis and executing nearly 50 persons returning from a protest against the sectarian violence in Iraq.[69] Clearly, despite the elections and Sunni participation, Iraq remains an extremely unstable state—indeed, if recent events presage a trend, Iraq may be described as a failed state, short of some drastic turnaround. To be sure, Iraq's importance to U.S. foreign policy will continue for the foreseeable future. Thus, as an external stimulus or input, Iraq will continue to shape U.S. foreign policy for years to come.

SUMMARY

In this chapter we demonstrated how external inputs, the 9/11 attacks as a foreign policy crisis that created a wide berth for President Bush and his NSC principals to initiate change in U.S. foreign policy and, then, the three years of the Iraq War affected U.S. foreign policy and thereby hastened the change and reorganization in national security policymaking. We are particularly interested in the important legislation, the Intelligence Reform and Terrorism Prevention Act, and will address that in due course. In the following chapters we consider two domestic sources of U.S. national security change and reorganization: societal inputs and governmental inputs. They too affected national security policy (and the institutions that ultimately created and implemented change).

NOTES

1. Hermann first developed many of the hypotheses vis-à-vis foreign policy crises that we have used here and elsewhere. See Charles F. Hermann, *Crises in Foreign Policy* (Indianapolis, IN: Bobbs Merrill, 1969).

2. M. Kent Bolton, *U.S. Foreign Policy and International Politics: George W. Bush, 9/11, and the Global-Terrorist Hydra* (Englewood Cliffs, NJ: Prentice Hall, 2005), especially chapter 6: Process. Charles F. Hermann was among the comparative foreign policy analysis research program considered in chapter 2. In addition to the conceptual framework employed in these pages, the present research owes an intellectual debt to the scholars of that research program generally and to Charles Hermann specifically.

3. In a recent *New York Times* piece about the principal deputy under secretary of defense for policy at the Pentagon, Mr. Ryan Henry, who recently met defense contractors to warn of looming budget cuts, the author noted that the U.S. defense budget had "increased 41 percent since 9/11." See Leslie Wayne, "Contractors Are Warned: Cuts Coming for Weapons," *New York Times*, December 27, 2005, http://www.nytimes.com/2005/12/27/business/27weapons.html. In a recent editorial on the war on terror generally and in Iraq specifically stated, "The war has had a fearsome economic cost as well; the Pentagon is reportedly looking for a boost in military spending next year that would push the costs of the Iraq and Afghanistan wars to nearly half a trillion dollars." See Editorial, "One step at a time in Iraq," *Los Angeles Times*, December 15, 2005, http://www.latimes.com/news/opinion/editorials/la-ediraq15dec15,0,7559925.story?coll

=la-news-comment-editorials. See also chapter 3 of this text, in the section subtitled "Empirical Indicators."

4. John Ward Anderson, "EU Leaders and Public Differ on Pullout in Iraq," *Washington Post*, December 9, 2005, http://www.washingtonpost.com/wp-dyn/content/article/2005/12/08/AR2005120801914.html. For a brief sampling see the following pieces. Claudia Deane, "Opinions Mixed on Next Four Years," *Washington Post*, January 22, 2005, http://www.washingtonpost.com/wp-dyn/articles/A27538-2005Jan21.html; Max Boot "Our Extreme Makeover," *Los Angeles Times*, June 27, 2005, http://www.latimes.com/news/opinion/commentary/la-oe-boot27jul27,0,1437541.column?coll=la-news-comment-opinions (Boot interestingly was pro-Iraq War and argued that the administration has been incompetent in its implementation); Shibley Telhami, "Arabs See Danger, Not Hope, in Iraq," *Los Angeles Times*, March 14, 2004, http://www.latimes. com/news/opinion/commentary/la-op-telehami14mar14,1,293521.story?coll=la-news-comment-opinions; Associated Press, "Bush's Iraq and Overall Job Ratings at New Lows," *Los Angeles Times*, April 6, 2004, http://www.latimes.com/news/nationworld/world/la-fg-poll6apr06,1,7885369.story?coll=la-headlines-world; Arthur Schlesinger, Jr., "Good Foreign Policy a Casualty of War," *Los Angeles Times*, March 23, 2003, http://www.latimes.com/news/opinion/commentary/la-war-opschlesinger23mar23,1,7925658.story?coll=la%2Dnews%2Dcomment%2Dopinions.

5. A sample of the newspaper articles produced by "embedded journalists" who followed U.S. troops as they moved ever closer to Baghdad: James Gerstenzang, "New Air Strikes Hit Targets in Baghdad," *Los Angeles Times*, March 20, 2003, http://www.latimes.com/news/nationworld/iraq/battle/la-032003bombing_lat,1,31327.story?coll=la%2Dhome%2Dheadlines; Rajiv Chandrasekaran and Susan B. Glasser, "Ground War Starts, Airstrikes Continue As U.S. Keeps Focus on Iraq's Leaders," *Washington Post*, March 21, 2003; Walter Pincus, Bob Woodward, and Dana Priest, "U.S. Thinks Hussein, Sons Were In Bunker," *Washington Post*, March 21, 2003; and Edwin Chen, "A Hands-Off President Jumps In," *Los Angeles Times*, March 21, 2003, http://www.latimes.com/news/nationworld/iraq/battle/la-war-bushday21mar21,1,3216193.story?coll=la%2Dhome%2Dheadlines.

6. Edwin Chen, "A Hands-Off President Jumps In."

7. Barton Gellman, "Al Qaeda Near Biological, Chemical Arms Production," *Washington Post*, March 23, 2003.

8. Barton Gellman, "Al Qaeda Near Biological, Chemical Arms Production"; Doug Struck, "Korean Peninsula on Edge as U.S. and S. Korea Stage War Games," *Washington Post*, March 23, 2003, http://www.washingtonpost.com/ac2/wp-dyn/A13984-2003Mar23.html. For Bush's "axis of evil" comment see George W. Bush, "The President's State of the Union Address," January 29, 2002, http://www.whitehouse.gov/news/ releases/2002/01/20020129-11.html.

9. Associated Press, "Officials: N. Korea Test-Fires Missile," *USA Today*, April 1, 2003, http://www. usatoday.com/news/world/2003-04-01-nkorea-japan_x.htm.

10. Fawaz A. Gerges, "Muslims Called to Jihad," *Los Angeles Times*, March 26, 2003, http://www.latimes.com/news/opinion/commentary/la-war-oegerges26mar26,1,6066432.story?coll=la%2Dnews%2Dcomment%2Dopinions; Kim Murphy, "Ladies' Tea Boils Over as Saudis Rail at U.S.," *Los Angeles Times,* March 27, 2003, http://www.latimes

.com/news/nationworld/world/la-war-saudi27mar27002426,1,614041.story?coll=la%2D headlines%2Dworld%2Dmanual.

11. Megan K. Stack, "Beirut Rioters Attack Church," *Los Angeles Times*, February 6, 2006, http://www. latimes.com/news/nationworld/world/la-fg-muslims6feb06,0,4694855 .story?coll=la-home-headlines; Mary Jordan, "Britons Urge Arrest of Protesters Advocating Violence," *Washington Post*, February 7, 2006, http://www.washingtonpost.com/ wp-dyn/content/article/2006/02/06/AR2006020601571.html, and Associated Press, "Protesters Rampage in 2 Pakistani Cities," *New York Times*, February 14, 2006, http://www .nytimes.com/aponline/international/AP-Prophet-Drawings.html.

12. Hassan M. Fattah, "As News Spreads of Deaths in South, Anger Boils Over Into Demonstrations in Beirut," *New York Times*, July 31, 2006, http://www.nytimes.com/ 2006/07/31/world/middleeast/31beirut.html.

13. Walter Russell Mead, "Battlefield Europe: Fight for EU's future is on, with U.S.-German relations at the middle," *Los Angeles Times*, March 30, 2003, http://www.latimes .com/news/opinion/commentary/la-war-opmead30mar30,1,4767155.story?coll=la%2D news%2Dcomment%2Dopinions; Glenn Kessler and Philip P. Pan, "Missteps With Turkey Prove Costly," *Washington Post*, March 28, 2003.

14. Reuters, "Muslim Cleric Urges Iraqis Not to Resist," *New York Times*, April 3, 2003, http://www.ny-times.com/reuters/international/international-iraq-fatwa.html. With respect to the formidable fight Iraqis presented coalition and U.S. troops, it did not result from Hussein's leadership but, rather, despite it. See Kevin M. Woods, Michael R. Pease, Mark E. Stout, et al., *The Iraqi Perspective Project: A View of Operation Iraqi Freedom from Saddam's Senior Leadership* (Joint Forces Command, Joint Center for Operational Analysis, May 2006), http://www.jfcom.mil/newslink/storyarchive/2006/ipp.pdf (accessed March 25, 2006), especially chapter III, "Military Effectiveness."

15. James Fallows, "Blind into Baghdad," *Atlantic Monthly*, January–February, 2004, http://www.theatlantic.com/issues/2004/01/fallows.htm (originally accessed on May 6, 2004 and revisited in February 2006).

16. James Fallows, "Blind into Baghdad," *Atlantic Monthly*, January–February, 2004.

17. James Fallows, "Blind into Baghdad," *Atlantic Monthly*, January–February, 2004.

18. James Fallows, "Blind into Baghdad," *Atlantic Monthly*, January–February, 2004 (my emphasis).

19. Mr. Ahmed Chalabi's name is transliterated as both Ahmed and Ahmad.

20. Barton Gellman, "Banned Iraqi Weapons Might Be Hard to Find," *Washington Post*, April 5, 2003. Also see David Johnston and James Risen, "New Signs of Terror Not Evident," *New York Times*, April 6, 2003, http://www.nytimes.com/2003/04/06/international/ worldspecial/06SECU.html.

21. Barton Gellman, "Banned Iraqi Weapons Might Be Hard to Find."

22. For example, see Judith Miller, "Illicit Arms Kept Till Eve of War, an Iraqi Scientist Is Said to Assert," *New York Times*, April 21, 2003, http://www.nytimes.com/2003/ 04/21/international/worldspecial/ 21CHEM.html. By contrast see Barton Gellman, "Hunt for Iraqi Arms Erodes Assumptions," *Washington Post*, April 22, 2003; David Kelly, "Regime's Priority Was Blueprints, Not Arsenal, Defector Told UN," *Los Angeles Times*, April 26, 2003, http://www.latimes.com/news/nation-world/world/la-war-kamel26apr26,1,4372842.story ?coll=la%2Dheadlines%2Dworld.

23. Joby Warrick, "Lacking Biolabs, Trailers Carried Case for War: Administration Pushed Notion of Banned Iraqi Weapons," *Washington Post*, April 12, 2006, http://www.washingtonpost.com/wp-dyn/content/article/ 2006/04/11/AR2006041101888.html.

24. Jeffrey Fleishman, "Ansar Fighters Surrender to Kurds: Denied Refuge in Iran, Hundreds Have Agreed to Turn Themselves in, A Commander Says," *Los Angeles Times*, April 7, 2003, http://www.latimes.com /news/nationworld/iraq/battle/la-war-ansar7apr07 ,1,4955785.story?coll=la%2Diraq%2Dbattle.

25. Reuters, "29 Tourists Are Missing in Algeria," *Los Angeles Times*, April 8, 2003, http://www.latimes.com/news/nationworld/world/la-fg-missing8apr08,1,7766978.story ?coll= la%2Dheadlines %2Dworld; Josh Meyer, "Hezbollah Vows Anew to Target Americans," *Los Angeles Times*, April 17, 2003, http://www.latimes.com/news/nationworld/ iraq/world/ la-warhezbollah17apr17,1,4681007.story?coll=la% 2Dhome%2Dheadlines; Kim Murphy, "Saudis Tighten Oil Security," *Los Angeles Times*, April 18, 2003, http:// www.latimes.com/news/nationworld/world/la-war-oil18apr18003423,1,7852868 .story?coll=l a%2Dheadlines%2Dworld%2Dmanual; for Southeast Asia see Richard C. Paddock, "Muslim Terrorists Tied to 2 Blasts," *Los Angeles Times,* April 8, 2003; Richard C. Paddock, "Violence Surges Again in Indonesian Province," *Los Angeles Times,* April 8, 2003, http://www.latimes.com/news/nationworld/world/la-fg-phil8apr08002429, 1, 3716068.story?coll=la %2Dheadlines%2Dworld; Raymond Bonner, "Indonesia Accuses Muslim Cleric of Plot to Oust Government," *New York Times*, April 14, 2003, http:// www.nytimes.com/2003/04/14/international/asia/14CND-INDO.html; The Guardian, "Muslim Cleric's Treason Trial Begins," *The Guardian*, April 23, 2003, http:// www.guardian.co.uk/indonesia/Story/0,2763,941986,00.html. For jihadi activities in Europe during the period see Sebastian Rotella, "Terror Suspect Linked to Hamburg Cell," *Los Angeles Times*, April 11, 2003, http://www. latimes.com/news/nationworld/world/ la-fg-terror11apr11,1,7321973.story?coll=la%2Dhead-lines%2Dworld; Alan Cowell, "British Muslims Are Seen Moving Into Mideast Terrorism," *New York Times*, May 1, 2003, http://www.nytimes.com/2003/05/01/international/europe/01CND-BOMB.html. For activities in Afghanistan, Chechnya, and Tajikistan see Carlotta Gall, "2 Afghan Soldiers Slain in Heavy New Outbreak of Clashes," *New York Times*, April 24, 2003, http://www.nytimes.com/2003/04/24/international/middleeast /25 AFGHAN.html; Sharon LaFraniere, "How Jihad Made Its Way to Chechnya," *Washington Post*, April 26, 2003; and David "Russia to Beef Up Tajikistan Presence," *Los Angeles Times*, April 28, 2003, http://www.latimes.com/news/nationworld/world/la-fg-tajik28apr28,1,6602189.story ?coll=la %2Dheadlines%2Dworld.

26. John Daniszewski, "Time of Recovery for Baghdad," *Los Angeles Times*, April 14, 2003, http://www.latimes.com/news/nationworld/world/la-war-baghdad14apr14004417,1 ,3097500.story?coll= la%2 Dheadlines%2Dworld.

27. Alissa J. Rubin and Jesus Sanchez, "Thousands in Baghdad Protest Occupation," *Los Angeles Times*, April 18, 2003, http://www.latimes.com/news/nationworld/iraq/inside/ la-iraq-041803iraq_lat,1,3180485.story?coll=la%2Dhome%2Dheadlines (my emphasis). Also see Thomas W. Lippman, "Iraqi Muslims Protest Against Foreign Troops," *Washington Post*, April 18, 2003, http://www.washington-post.com/ac2/wp-dyn/A50762-2003Apr18 .html; Reuters, "Baghdad Residents Protest U.S. Troops," *New York Times*, April 18, 2003, http://www.nytimes.com/reuters/international/ international-iraq-demonstration.html.

28. Alissa J. Rubin, "Iraqis Protest U.S., Demand Islamic State," *Los Angeles Times*, April 19, 2003, http://www.latimes.com/la-war-iraq19apr19,1,3329182.story?coll=la-headlines-world.

29. As with other Arabic transliterations, Falluja is spelled multiple ways: Falluja, Fallujah, and Fallouja.

30. See Edmund L. Andrews and Terence Neilan, "Attack Injures 7 U.S. Soldiers in Angry Iraqi City," *New York Times*, May 1, 2003, http://www.nytimes.com/2003/05/01/international/worldspecial/01CND-IRAQ.html; Jefferson Morely, "The Fallout from Falluja," *Washington Post*, May 1, 2003, http://www.washingtonpost.com/wp-dyn/articles/A64971-2003May1.html; Dexter Filkins and Ian Fisher, "U.S. Is Now in Battle for Peace after Winning the War in Iraq," *New York Times*, May 3, 2003, http://www.nytimes.com/2003/05/03/international/worldspecial/03IRAQ.html.

31. John Hendren and Azadeh Moaveni, "Anti-U.S. Sentiment Festers as Order and Calm Prove Elusive," *Los Angeles Times*, May 24, 2003, http://www.latimes.com/news/nationworld/world/la-fg-ambush24may24,1,3136853.story?coll=la%2Dheadlines%2Dworld. Also see John Daniszewski and Tyler Marshall, "Disarray in Iraq Threatens U.S. Goals," *Los Angeles Times*, May 25, 2003, http://www.latimes.com/ news/nationworld/world/la-fg-rebuild25may25235423,1,743970.story?coll=la%2Dheadlines%2Dworld.

32. Tyler Marshall and Edmund Sanders, "Iraqi Advisors Are Left Cooling Their Heels," *Los Angeles Times*, May 27, 2003, http://www.latimes.com/news/nationworld/world/la-fg-expats27may27234427,1,5796003.story?coll=la%2Dheadlines%2Dworld; Anthony Shadid, "Unfulfilled Promises Leave Iraqis Bewildered," *Washington Post*, May 27, 2003.

33. Brian Knowlton, "Top General Says Iraqi Resistance Is Far From 'Monolithic'," *International Herald Tribune*, published in the *New York Times*, July 6, 2003, http://www.nytimes.com/2003/07/06/ international/worldspecial/06CND-POLI.html.

34. John Hendren, "Tape Claims Al Qaeda Is at Work in Iraq," *Los Angeles Times*, July 14, 2003, http://www.latimes.com/news/nationworld/world/la-fg-raids14jul14,1,6143435.story?coll=la-headlines-world.

35. Kevin Sullivan and Rajiv Chandrasekaran, "Hussein's Two Sons Killed In Firefight With U.S. Troops," *Washington Post*, July 23, 2003; Eric Shmitt, "Iraqi Informants' Tips Grow After Brothers' Deaths," *New York Times*, July 26, 2003, http://college3.nytimes.com/guests/articles/2003/07/26/1103045.xml.

36. Robyn Dixon, "Basra Could Boil Over Again," *Los Angeles Times*, August 12, 2003, http://www.latimes.com/news/nationworld/world/la-fg-basra12aug12,1,249768.story?coll=la-headlines-world; Anthony Shadid, "In Basra, Worst May Be Ahead," *Washington Post*, August 12, 2003; and Chris Kraul, "U.S. Soldiers Fire on Iraqi Family," *Los Angeles Times*, August 12, 2003, http://www.latimes.com/news/nationworld/world/la-fg-shoot12aug12,1,2595297.story?coll=la-headlines-world.

37. Neil MacFarquhar, "Rising Tide of Islamic Militants See Iraq as Ultimate Battlefield," *New York Times*, August 13, 2003, http://www.nytimes.com/2003/08/13/international/worldspecial/13ISLA.html. It should also be noted that the UN mission in Iraq was attacked in mid August killing several including Sergio Vieira de Mello and resulting in the UN withdrawing from Iraq for many months.

38. Neil MacFarquhar and Kirk Semple, "Blast in Iraq Kills a Leading Shiite Cleric," *New York Times*, August 29, 2003, http://www.nytimes.com/2003/08/29/international/worldspecial/29CND-IRAQ.html; Anthony Shadid and Daniel Williams, "Blast Kills at Least 95 at Iraqi Shrine," *Washington Post*, August 30, 2003. On Zarqawi in Iraq see John Hendren and Josh Meyer, "A Suspected Operative of al Qaeda Is Held in Iraq," *Los Angeles Times*, August 30, 2003, http://www.latimes.com/news/nationworld/world/la-fgqaeda30aug 30,1,2023828.story?coll=la-headlines-world; Peter Finn and Susan Schmidt, "Al Qaeda Is Trying to Open Iraq Front," *Washington Post*, September 7, 2003. Finally, on Zarqawi's death, see John F. Burns, "US Strike Hits Insurgent at Safe House," *New York Times*, June 8, 2006, http://www.nytimes.com /2006/06/08/world/middleeast/08cnd-iraq.html; Ellen Knickmeyer and Jonathan Finer, "Insurgent Leader Al-Zarqawi Killed in Iraq," *Washington Post*, June 8, 2006, http://www.washingtonpost.com/wp-dyn/content/article/2006/06/08/AR2006060800114.html.

39. Associated Press, "Blix Doesn't Expect Capture to Yield Banned Weapons," *Los Angeles Times*, December 17, 2003, http://www.latimes.com/news/nationworld/world/la-fg-blix17dec17,1,5294922.story?coll=la-headlines-world; Steve Coll, "Hussein Was Sure of Own Survival," *Washington Post*, November 10, 2003.

40. John Burns, "Insurgents Use Rockets on Donkey Carts to Hit Sites in Iraqi Capital," *New York Times*, November 21, 2003, http://www.nytimes.com/2003/11/22/international/middleeast/22IRAQ.html; Rajiv Chandrasekaran and Anthony Shadid, "Ministry, Hotels in Baghdad Attacked," *Washington Post*, November 22, 2003; Ian Fisher and Dexter Filkins, "Bombers Kill 14 in Iraq; Missile Hits Civilian Plane," *New York Times*, November 23, 2003, http://www.nytimes.com/2003/11/23/international/middleeast/23IRAQ.html; John Daniszewski, "Shiite Cleric Could Make or Break Transition," *Los Angeles Times*, November 24, 2003, http://www.latimes.com/news/nationworld/world/la-fg-sadr24nov24,1,5093743.story?coll=la-headlines-world; Bradley Graham, "November Deadliest Month in Iraq," *Washington Post*, November 29, 2003.

41. John Daniszewski, "Troops Tell of Street Fight With Dogged Foe," *Los Angeles Times*, December 2, 2003, http://www.latimes.com/news/nationworld/world/la-fg-samarra2dec02,1,7960049.story?coll=la-headlines-world; Anthony Shadid, "Battle Reveals New Iraqi Tactics," *Washington Post*, December 2, 2003; Carol J. Williams and Patrick J. McDonnell, "31 U.S. Soldiers Hurt in Iraq Blast," *Los Angeles Times*, December 9, 2003, http://www.latimes.com/news/nationworld/world/la-fg-blast9dec09,1,5477784.story?coll=la-headlines-world; Associated Press, "Car Bomb Wounds 41 U.S. Troops in Iraq," *New York Times*, December 9, 2003, http://www.nytimes.com/aponline/international/AP-Iraq.html; Carol J. Williams, "62 U.S. Troops Injured in Iraq" *Los Angeles Times*, December 10, 2003, http://www.latimes.com/news/nationworld/world/la-fg-iraq10dec10,1,2673466.story?coll=la-headlines-world; Alan Sipress, "Bomber Wounds 58 Troops in Iraq," *Washington Post*, December 10, 2003; Ian Fisher, "Suicide Bombers Strike at 2 U.S. Bases, Wounding Dozens of G.I.'s," *New York Times*, December 10, 2003, http://www.nytimes.com/2003/12/10/international/middleeast/10IRAQ.html; Tracy Wilkinson, "U.S. Troops Clash With Insurgents, Kill 18 Iraqis," *Los Angeles Times*, December 17, 2003, http://www.latimes.com/news/nationworld/world/la-fg-iraq17dec17,1,5884744.story?coll=la-headlines-world; Alan Sipress, "Iraqis Exact Revenge on Baathists," *Washington Post*, December 20, 2003.

42. Colum Lynch, "Brahimi to Be UN Adviser on Iraq," *Washington Post*, January 12, 2003.

43. Edward Wong. "U.S. Tries to Give Moderates an Edge in Iraqi Elections," *New York Times*, January 18, 2004, http://www.nytimes.com/2004/01/18/international/middleeast/18BAGH.html.

44. Edward Wong. "U.S. Tries to Give Moderates an Edge in Iraqi Elections."

45. Anthony Shadid, "Shiites March for Elections in Iraq," *Washington Post*, January 20, 2004. Also see the excellent analysis by Sonni Efron and Alissa J. Rubin, "U.S. Asks UN to Go to Iraq, Assess Feasibility of Vote," *Los Angeles Times*, January 20, 2004, http://www.latimes.com/news/nationworld/world/la-fg-uniraq20jan20,1,6457296.story?coll=la-headlines-world. Finally, Robin Wright, "UN to Consider Request to Study Earlier Elections in Iraq," *Washington Post*, January 20, 2004.

46. Josh Meyer and Patrick J. McDonnell, "U.S. Says It Has Captured Suspected Terrorist Leader's Aides in Iraq," *Los Angeles Times*, January 24, 2004, http://www.latimes.com/news/nationworld/world/la-fg-terror24jan24,1,7632365.story?coll=la-headlines-world; Walter Pincus "Al Qaeda Figure Captured," *Washington Post*, January 24, 2004; Reuters, "U.S. Seizes Terror Suspect," *New York Times*, January 24, 2004, http://www.nytimes.com/2004/01/24/politics/24ANSA.html.

47. Jeffrey Fleishman, "Iraqi Melting Pot Nears Boiling Point," *Los Angeles Times*, January 26, 2004, http://www.latimes.com/news/nationworld/world/la-fg-kirkuk26jan26,1,7309277.story?coll=la-headlines-world.

48. Jeffrey Fleishman, "Iraqi Melting Pot Nears Boiling Point," *Los Angeles Times*, January 26, 2004; Daniel Williams, "Kurds Press for Independence," *Washington Post*, January 30, 2004; Daniel Williams, "As Kurds Mourn, Resolve Hardens," *Washington Post*, February 3, 2004. On al Qaeda see Associated Press, "U.S. Commander Says Qaeda Working in Iraq," *New York Times*, January 29, 2004, http://www.nytimes.com/aponline/international/AP-Iraq.html; Megan K. Stack, "U.S. General Sees Al Qaeda Evidence in Iraq," *Los Angeles Times*, January 30, 2004, http://www.latimes.com/news/nationworld/world/la-fg-iraq30jan30,1,6933323.story?coll=la-headlines-world.

49. William Branigin, "Al Qaeda Trying to Spark a 'Civil War' in Iraq, U.S. Says," *Washington Post*, February 9, 2004, http://www.washingtonpost.com/wp-dyn/articles/A25736-2004Feb9.html; Dexter Filkins, "U.S. Says Files Seek Qaeda Aid in Iraq Conflict," *New York Times*, February 9, 2004, http://www.nytimes.com/2004/02/09/international/middleeast/09INTE.html.

50. Daniel Williams, "Falluja Insurgents Find a New Focus," *Washington Post*, February 8, 2004.

51. Patrick J. McDonnell, "Iraqi Leaders Agree on Draft of an Interim Constitution," *Los Angeles Times*, March 1, 2004 http://www.latimes.com/news/nationworld/world/la-fg-iraq1mar01,1,7300123.story?coll=la-headlines-world; Rajiv Chandrasekaran, "Iraqi Council Agrees on Terms of Interim Constitution," *Washington Post*, March 1, 2004, A1, and Dexter Filkins, "Iraqi Leadership Gains Agreement on Constitution," *New York Times*, March 1, 2004, http://nytimes.com/ 2004/03/01/international/middleeast/01IRAQ.html. Also see Sebastian Rotella, "Iraq Takes a Step Toward Democracy," *Los Angeles Times*, March 2, 2004, http://www.latimes.com/news/nationworld/world/la-fg-iraq2mar02,1,

7758877.story?coll=la-headlines-world; Rajiv Chandrasekaran, "Iraqis Hail Compromise On Interim Constitution," *Washington Post*, March 2, 2004; Dexter Filkins, "Iraqis Receive U.S. Approval of Constitution," *New York Times*, March 2, 2004, http://www .nytimes.com/2004/03/02/inter-national/middleeast/02IRAQ.html.

52. Rajiv Chandrasekaran, "Iraq's Shiites Renew Call For Militias," *Washington Post*, March 4, 2004. On postponement of signing see Associated Press, "Iraq Interim Constitution Signing Delayed," *Los Angeles Times*, March 5, 2004, http://www.latimes.com/ news/nationworld/iraq/la-030504iraq_wr,1,6798742. story?coll=la-home-headlines; Dexter Filkins, "Signing of Iraqi Charter Is Delayed by Shiite Objections," *New York Times*, March 5, 2004, http://www.nytimes.com/2004/03/05/international/middleeast/ 05CND-IRAQ.html.

53. Karl Vick and Fred Barbash, "More Violence in Iraq as Invasion Anniversary Nears," *Washington Post*, March 18, 2004, http://www.washingtonpost.com/ac2/ wp-dyn/A3893-2004Mar18.html. See also Mark Magnier, "Attacks Continue as Invasion Anniversary Nears," *Los Angeles Times*, March 19, 2004, http://www.latimes.com/news/ nationworld/world/la-fg-iraq19mar19,1,3651943.story?coll=la-headlines-world.

54. Dexter Filkins, "Iraq Council, Shifting Stance, Invites the UN to Aid Transfer," *New York Times*, March 18, 2004, http://www.nytimes.com/2004/03/18/international/ middleeast/18COUN.html.

55. Edmund Sanders, "Iraqi Mob Kills 4 Americans," *Los Angeles Times*, April 1, 2004, http://www.latimes. com/news/nationworld/world/la-fg-iraq1apr01,1,7300126 .story?coll=la-headlines-world. Also, Sewell Chan, "U.S. Civilians Mutilated in Iraq Attack," *Washington Post*, April 1, 2004; Jeffrey Gettleman, "U.S. Officials in Iraq Vow to Avenge Killings in Falluja," *New York Times*, April 1, 2004, http://www.ny-times .com/2004/04/01/international/middleeast/01CND-IRAQ.html.

56. Tony Perry, "Fallouja Neighborhood Suddenly Turns Fierce," *Los Angeles Times*, April 7, 2004, http://www.latimes.com/news/nationworld/iraq/la-fg-fallouja7apr07,1, 6602210.story?coll=la-home-headlines; Alissa J. Rubin, "12 Marines Are Killed as Violence Spreads in Iraq," *Los Angeles Times*, April 7, 2004, http://www.latimes.com/ news/nationworld/world/la-fg-iraq7apr07,1,2052657.story?coll=la-headlines-world; Karl Vick, "Muslim Rivals Unite In Baghdad Uprising," *Washington Post*, April 7, 2004; Jeffrey Gettleman and Douglas Jehl, "Fierce Fighting With Sunnis and Shiites Spreads to 6 Iraqi Cities," *New York Times*, April 7, 2004, http://www.nytimes.com/2004/04/07/ international/middleeast/ 07CND-IRAQ.html; John Hendren, "Uprising Could Signal a Second War for Iraq," *Los Angeles Times*, April 8, 2004, http://www.latimes.com/news/ nationworld/iraq/la-fg-turn8apr08,1,7881902.story ?coll=la-home-headlines; Rajiv Chandrasekaran, "Anti-U.S. Uprising Widens in Iraq; Marines Push Deeper Into Falluja," *Washington Post*, April 8, 2004; Jeffrey Fleishman and Edmund Sanders, "Clashes Go On as Radical Shiite Hints at Accord," *Los Angeles Times*, April 14, 2004, http://www. latimes.com/news/nationworld/world/la-fg-iraq14apr14,1,1358176.story?coll=la-headlines-world; Sewell Chan and Thomas E. Ricks, "Army Girds to Confront Radical Cleric," *Washington Post*, April 14, 2004; Edmund Sanders, "Cleric's Militia Has Surprised American Forces," *Los Angeles Times*, April 18, 2004, http://www.latimes.com/ news/nationworld/world/la-fg-najaf18apr18,1,6880460.story?coll=la-headlines-world;

John F. Burns and Christine Hauser, "Bremer Is Increasing Pressure for a Quick End to Iraqi Uprisings," *New York Times*, April 19, 2004, http://www.nytimes.com/2004/04/18/international/ middleeast/18CND-IRAQ.html.

57. Daryl Strickland, "Iraq Council Disbands," *Los Angeles Times*, June 1, 2004, http://www.latimes.com/news/nationworld/iraq/la-060104iraq_lat,1,4465904.story?coll =la-home-headlines; Dexter Filkins, "New Government Is Formed in Iraq as Attacks Go On," *New York Times*, June 2, 2004, http://nytimes.com/2004/06/02/international/middleeast/02IRAQ.html.

58. Dexter Filkins and Kirk Semple, "9 Militias to Disband in Iraq, but Not Rebel Cleric's Force," *New York Times*, June 7, 2004, http://www.nytimes.com/2004/06/07/international/middleeast/07CND-IRAQ.html; Robin Wright, "U.S., Iraq Reach Security Accord," *Washington Post*, June 7, 2004; also see Peter Y. Hong, "Iraqi Militias to Disband, Join Official Forces," *Los Angeles Times*, June 8, 2004, http://www.latimes.com/news/nationworld/world/la-fg-militias8jun08,1,736213.story?coll=la-headlines-world.

59. Maggie Farley, "UN Endorses Iraq's Interim Government," *Los Angeles Times*, June 9, 2004, http://www.latimes.com/news/nationworld/iraq/la-fg-un9jun09,1,563648 .story?coll=la-home-headlines.

60. Alissa J. Rubin and Carol J. Williams, "U.S. Transfers Sovereignty to Iraq," *Los Angeles Times*, June 28, 2004, http://www.latimes.com/news/nationworld/iraq/ la-062804iraq_lat,1,3085056.story?coll=la-home-headlines; Rajiv Chandrasekaran, Mike Allen, and Doug Struck, "U.S. Transfers Political Authority in Iraq," *Washington Post*, June 28, 2004, http://www.washingtonpost.com/wp-dyn/articles/A10917-2004Jun28 .html; Edward Wong and Ian Fisher, "Wary Iraqis Welcome the Handover but Ask, Now What?" *New York Times*, June 28, 2004, http://nytimes.com/2004/06/28/international/middleeast/28CND-REAC.html.

61. Carol J. Williams, "U.S. Ambassador Takes His Post," *Los Angeles Times*, June 30, 2004, http://www.latimes.com/news/nationworld/world/la-fg-iraq30jun30,1,4176230 .story?coll=la-headlines-world. As shall be seen later, Ambassador Negroponte became the first director of national intelligence following the passage of the IRTPA in December 2004.

62. Ashraf Khalil, "Top Sunni Party Quits Election," *Los Angeles Times*, December 28, 2004, http://www. latimes.com/news/nationworld/world/la-fg-iraq28dec28,1,6933324 .story?coll=la-headlines-world. On the wave of violence at year's end see Associated Press, "Insurgents Lure Police to House, Kill Dozens," *Los Angeles Times*, December 29, 2004, http://www.latimes.com/news/nationworld/iraq/la-122904iraq_ wr,0,1262650.story?coll= la-home-headlines; Jackie Spinner and Khalid Saffar, "At Least 28 People Killed by Explosion in Iraq," *Washington Post*, December 29, 2004, http://www.washingtonpost.com/ wp-dyn/articles/A32855-2004Dec29.html; Edmund Sanders, "28 Die in Wave of Insurgent Attacks in Iraq," *Los Angeles Times*, December 29, 2004, http://www.latimes.com/news/ nationworld/world/la-fg-iraq29dec29,1,7392078.story?coll=la-headlines-world; Jackie Spinner, "26 Die in String of Attacks on Iraqi Forces," *Washington Post*, December 29, 2004, http://www.washingtonpost.com/wp-dyn/articles/A30605-2004Dec28.html; Richard A. Oppel, Jr., and Khalid al-Ansary, "Iraqi Rebels Set Trap for Police, Killing at Least 32," *New York Times*, December 29, 2004, http://nytimes.com/2004/12/29/international/middleeast/

29cnd-iraq.html; Josh White, "Calm Is Broken in Hussein's Home Town," *Washington Post*, December 29, 2004; Richard A. Oppel Jr. and Khalid al-Ansary, "25 Insurgents Are Killed Trying to Overrun U.S. Outpost in Mosul," *New York Times*, December 30, 2004, http://nytimes.com/2004/12/30/international/middleeast/30iraq.html.

63. Craig S. Smith and Don Van Natta, Jr., "Officials Fear Iraq's Lure for Muslims in Europe," *New York Times*, October 23, 2004, http://www.nytimes.com/2004/10/23/international/europe/23france.html. Also see Edward Wong, "Iraq Is a Hub for Terrorism, However You Define It," *New York Times*, June 20, 2004, http://nytimes.com/2004/06/20/weekinreview/20wong.html.

64. Editorial, "No Good Choices," *The Guardian*, December 30, 2004, http://www.guardian.co.uk/ leaders/story/0,3604,1380690,00.html.

65. Reuters, "Iraq Blast Kills U.S. Soldier," *Los Angeles Times*, December 28, 2004, http://www.latimes.com/news/nationworld/world/la-fg-deaths28dec28,1,2206638.story ?coll=la-headlines-world. As of August 2006, the Defense Department reported nearly 2600 killed in action. See "Names of the Dead," *New York Times*, August 12, 2006, http://www.nytimes.com/2006/08/12/us/12list.html.

66. James Glanz, "Report Says Number of Attacks by Insurgents in Iraq Increases," *New York Times*, February 9, 2006, http://www.nytimes.com/2006/02/09/international/middleeast/09attacks.html.

67. David E. Sanger and Eric Schmitt, "Hot Topic: How U.S. Might Disengage in Iraq," *New York Times*, January 10, 2005, http://nytimes.com/2005/01/10/politics/10policy .html; White House, "President Addresses Nation, Discusses Iraq, War on Terror," June 28, 2005, http://www.whitehouse.gov/news/releases/2005/06/20050628-7.html.

68. U.S. Department of State, *Supporting Human Rights and Democracy: The U.S. Record 2004–2005*, March 28, 2005, http://www.state.gov/g/drl/rls/shrd/2004/ (accessed March 29, 2005), 190 ("Middle East and North Africa" Acrobat Reader pagination, 17).

69. Borzou Daragahi, "Clerics Take Lead After Iraq Bombing," *Los Angeles Times*, February 24, 2006, http://www.latimes.com/news/nationworld/world/la-fg-clerics24feb 24,0,405063.story?coll=la-home-headlines; Edward Wong, "More Clashes Shake Iraq; Political Talks Are in Ruins," *New York Times*, February 24, 2006, http://www .nytimes.com/2006/02/24/international/middleeast/24iraq.html. Also see Megan K. Stack, "Sectarian Violence Sweeps Iraq," *Los Angeles Times*, February 24, 2006, http://www.latimes.com/news/nationworld/world/la-fg-iraq24feb24,0,7711680.story?coll= la-home-headlines; Jonathan Finer and Bassam Sebti, "Sectarian Violence Kills Over 100 in Iraq," *Washington Post*, February 24, 2006, http://www.washingtonpost.com/wp-dyn/content/article/2006/02/23/ AR2006022300216.html; Edward Wong, "As Violence Ebbs, U.S. Envoy Warns of Danger to Iraq's Future," *New York Times*, February 24, 2006, http://nytimes.com/2006/02/24/international/middleeast/24cnd-iraq.html;, Bradley Graham, "U.S. Looks to Baghdad to Deal With Violence," *Washington Post*, February 24, 2006, http://www.washingtonpost.com/wp-dyn/content/article/2006/02/23/AR2006022302193 . html.

CHAPTER 7

The Rise of the Vulcans and Special-Interest Groups in U.S. National Security Policymaking

The United States is in the early years of a long struggle, similar to what our country faced in the early years of the Cold War. The twentieth century witnessed the triumph of freedom over the threats of fascism and communism. Yet a new totalitarian ideology now threatens, an ideology grounded not in secular philosophy but in the perversion of a proud religion. Its content may be different from the ideologies of the last century, but its means are similar: intolerance, murder, terror, enslavement, and repression.

> —*The National Security Strategy of the United States*,
> *March 2006*

There is a debate, and I think it's a debate that's healthy. This is obviously a really big change in American foreign policy, to put the promotion of democracy at the center of it. And people take very seriously what this president is doing and intends to do.

> —Secretary of State Condoleezza Rice, March 17, 2006,
> as Secretary Rice Traveled to South America, *New York Times*

Given President Bush's "political capital" and his continuing popularity in the polls for confronting al Qaeda, it is reasonable for one to wonder how the president was re-elected with a mandate to change the government institutions which he controlled as chief executive when those institutions apparently failed. Changes in intelligence gathering and analysis, changes in how the president interacted with the behemoth intelligence community, changes in how America constituted its very national security (and what became known as homeland security), and changes in national security policymaking were demanded broadly by the American public by the time of 2004's presidential campaign. Indeed, changes in the fundamental way the president-NSC-policymaking model functioned were demanded. In this chapter we ask what societal factors caused the federal government to reorganize and reorient America's national security bureaucracy for the foreseeable future to fight the global jihadis. We also consider what caused President Bush's reelection, once nearly a foregone conclusion, to be a difficult election-year slog. A multiplicity of societal influences proved critical.

In the previous chapter, an analysis of external sources of U.S. foreign policy identified as external-systemic sources or external inputs was undertaken. In the following chapter domestic sources identified as "governmental sources" are identified as hastening the changes in America's National Security Council and how it will interact with America's other national security institutions in the future. However, in this chapter we examine domestic sources. Societal sources played an important part in what eventually became the Intelligence Reform and Terrorism Prevention Act of December 2004.

THE PHILOSOPHICAL DEBATE FOR BUSH'S BRAIN

One important societal factor was a philosophical-ideological debate that raged inside and outside the administration before and during President George W. Bush's first term in office, that is, before and after 9/11. Only after one faction's ideology won outright did the rise of the neoconservatives (the "Vulcans") in the Bush administration become widely and publicly known. As Americans and others discovered who represented whom on which ideological side of the debate, and only as the winning side became increasingly associated with the war in Iraq, did President Bush's 9/11 popularity demonstrably begin to wane. As President Bush's popularity waned, the post-9/11 consensus that formed shortly after 9/11 also began to deteriorate.

To be clear, punishing al Qaeda in Afghanistan and toppling the Taliban regime proved widely popular among Americans and even internationally. The administration won plaudits for quickly scattering al Qaeda in late

2001 and seemed willing to press the attack globally until the job was finished. There was virtually no initial controversy surrounding U.S. action in Afghanistan, and therefore little reason to debate it politically either in the U.S. generally or inside the corridors of power in Washington D.C. specifically. In the State of the Union speech in early 2003, President Bush told Americans that in Afghanistan his administration had "helped liberate an oppressed people." He argued, moreover, that his administration would "continue helping [Afghanis] secure their country, rebuild their society, and educate all their children—boys and girls." "In the Middle East," said President Bush, "we will continue to seek peace between a secure Israel and a democratic Palestine."[1] Undeniably, finishing the work in Afghanistan and helping to bring peace to the Middle East were popular with most Americans, including members of both major political parties in Congress.

But a larger philosophical debate about the use of American power was being waged inside the Bush White House in late 2001, even while the U.S. military continued to destroy al Qaeda camps and al Qaeda's Taliban sponsors in Afghanistan. The debate continued throughout most of the first four years of George W. Bush's presidency. The "battle royal" as a former state department official characterized it[2] over the Bush administration's decision to topple Saddam Hussein's regime reflected the two main camps in the debate. One result of the battle royal was the political consequences: winners and losers. While Americans generally supported defeating al Qaeda, they were less than unified when it came to toppling the Hussein government.

Ideological battles are far from uncommon in presidential administrations, both in domestic terms and foreign policy terms. That such a battle royal would appear in George W. Bush's administration, then, is hardly surprising. In this case, the philosophical rift was a residual of the George H. W. Bush administration. It had bureaucratic (rather than ideological, though at times it became difficult to discern the differences) aspects to it as well. But the philosophical debate was a larger debate about America's role in the world and the principles on which U.S. national security policy rested. It was a debate about ideas, the means of achieving those ideas, and the philosophical underpinnings of both. In short, the battle royal created potent societal sources of national security policy. Those societal sources ultimately led to demonstrable changes in U.S. national security policy, the president-NSC-policymaking model, the entire intelligence community, and the way the former interacted with the latter.

THE RISE OF THE VULCANS DURING THE LATE 1980s

A group of former governmental officials (both from the Reagan and George H.W. Bush administrations) were openly critical of the Clinton administration and its efforts vis-à-vis the Middle East; indeed, they were critical of the Clinton administration's foreign policy generally during the 1990s. They believed that as the century neared its end, the U.S. stood as the "world's preeminent power." Having gained said preeminence at such a high cost (viz., trillions of dollars and tens of thousands of lives in the Cold War's proxy battles), these neoconservative ideologues[3] believed that America now faced historic opportunities and challenges. Moreover, they firmly believed that the Clinton administration had lacked the vision to build upon the achievements of past presidencies (notably the Reagan presidency). "Does the United States have the resolve to shape a new century favorable to American principles and interests?" asked the neoconservatives in the late 1990s.[4]

Paul Wolfowitz was then a leading intellectual among the neoconservatives who criticized the Clinton administration, particularly its national security policy. Wolfowitz had served in the Pentagon during Bush (41) and returned as the number two person (the deputy secretary of defense) in the George W. Bush administration's Pentagon—making him both a statutory member of the NSC deputies committee and an ad hoc member of the NSC principals committee. During the Clinton administration, Wolfowitz criticized U.S. national security from academia. As dean of the Johns Hopkins School for Advanced International Studies (1994–2001), Wolfowitz maintained an important policy-influencing perch "inside the beltway" but outside the government from which he could launch neoconservative salvos at the Clintonites. As a founding member of the Project for the New American Century (PNAC), he and other neoconservatives argued for a more muscular U.S. national security policy and military transformation to accomplish it. PNAC emerged as arguably the most influential "conservative" national security policy interest group since the Committee on the Present Danger (c. late 1970s), which argued for a similarly aggressive policy against the Soviet Union. Once back inside government as the Pentagon's second most powerful person Wolfowitz openly espoused his neoconservative solutions. Anyone who has ever listened to Dr. Paul Wolfowitz give a speech would likely be surprised at his ideological fervor; his speeches are those of a mild-mannered academic. However, he is anything but mild-mannered when it comes to righting U.S. national security policy when he thinks it is headed in the wrong direction.

PNAC was created in the late 1990s as an inside Washington special interest group. Its principles, enumerated in 1997, were set in high relief against the "drift" of the Clinton administration's national security policies cited by PNAC. PNAC and the neoconservatives also felt compelled to set themselves apart from traditional conservatives whom the neoconservatives believed had failed to advance a coherent strategic vision of America's role in the world. For neoconservatives, America's role in the world was the key. In contrast to the Clintonites and/or traditional conservatives, both of whom were mostly realist-internationalists, the neoconservatives of PNAC saw themselves as setting a clear case for "American leadership" in the world. They singled out the Clinton administration for its military cuts, somewhat ironically: as noted in chapter 3, the decreases in military spending had begun under the former Bush administration, an administration in which many of them served. They openly harkened back to the Reagan administration, or at least its mythology. While admitting that America must exercise its power prudently, they nonetheless stated that the United States could not "safely avoid the responsibilities of global leadership or the costs that are associated with its exercise. America [had] a vital role in maintaining peace and security in Europe, Asia, and the Middle East." If U.S. policymakers continued to "shirk" their responsibilities, the neoconservatives argued, they would invite challenges to America's "fundamental interests." Furthermore, they argued that the "history of the twentieth century should have taught" the U.S. that it was important "to shape circumstances before crises" emerged, and "to meet threats before they" became dire. "The history of [the twentieth] century should have taught [the U.S.] to embrace the cause of American leadership."[5] As seen elsewhere in these pages, the question of America's proper role in the world has been a recurring theme since America's origins; PNAC members joined that search as they filled the ranks of the George W. Bush administration.

The neoconservatives increasingly saw the historical purviews of a powerful Department of State (in both Democratic and Republican administrations) as work for the Department of Defense. In the zero-sum game of politics, that meant that the state department's power would atrophy insofar as the Department of Defense's power increased. That the ideological battle had carried over from academia and the private sector into the Bush (43) administration became clear shortly after 9/11. The *Washington Post*'s Alan Sipress described the neoconservative ideologues at the Pentagon. Secretary Rumsfeld and "his key lieutenants, notably Deputy Defense Secretary Paul D. Wolfowitz and Undersecretary of Defense Douglas J. Feith, figure[d] prominently" in interagency discussion on the Middle East that occurred in spring 2002. Israel and the Middle East figured prominently for the neoconservatives, but their bailiwick covered far more than the Middle East. Secretary of Defense Rumsfeld included himself among the signatories to the statement of principles.[6]

Secretary of State Powell, whom one might normally expect to be engaged in a major philosophical debate on the Middle East, was instead said to be frustrated and exasperated. Powell apparently was unwilling to go public with his complaints, but it was clear that fissures existed. The same *Washington Post* piece noted that the "rift in President Bush's inner circle, some State Department officials said, has left the administration's [Middle East] policy 'dead in the water.'" Further, these "officials used words like 'despondent' and 'disheartened' to describe the mood in Foggy Bottom [the State Department], saying they cannot remember a time in recent years when they have felt so badly beaten up." In the reporter's scoop on the ideological battle between traditionalists and neoconservatives, he also noted where the vice president's office fitted. "Vice President Cheney and his staff largely share the Pentagon's perspective, though Cheney has increasingly expressed concern about how the conflict is affecting other administration priorities in the Middle East."[7]

In late 2001 and early 2002, the president evidently had yet to convert fully to the neoconservative ideology. It is not surprising, therefore, that a battle raged between traditionalists at the Department of State (Colin Powell, Richard Armitage, Lawrence Wilkerson) and from outside government (Brent Scowcroft, Lawrence Eagleburger, and even former President George H. W. Bush by proxy). The president's attachment to either cause was still in play, as it were. What was clear was the identity of the key neoconservatives were in the administration, who worked tirelessly to get President Bush to adopt their agenda. Of those who signed the PNAC Statement of Principles, a number of recognizable names from the Bush administration were included. We list them here alphabetically—the order of this list is in no way intended to connote any particular certitude in the neoconservative pantheon of founding members. First was Elliot Abrams, a former Reagan administration official (made somewhat infamous in the Iran-Contra scandal), who subsequently was made special assistant to the president and senior director for Near East and North African affairs in the NSC staff. Next was Vice President Dick Cheney, the vice president during George W. Bush's two terms and former secretary of defense for Bush (41), as well as chief of staff in the Ford administration when he first teamed up with Donald Rumsfeld. Following Cheney came Paula Dobriansky, undersecretary for global affairs (State Department) and Aaron Friedberg, an aide to the vice president (May 2003–2005), both former academics. Fred C. Ikle, a one-time undersecretary of defense in the Pentagon, followed Friedberg on the signatories' list and following Ikle was Ambassador Zalmay Khalilzad, current ambassador to the UN, formerly ambassador to Iraq and Afghanistan. Following Khalilzad's signature was the influential I. Lewis "Scooter" Libby. (Libby was the vice president's NSC advisor and his chief of staff and was also a special assistant to President Bush on national security until he was indicted in late 2005 for his alleged role in the cover-up of Valerie Plame leak investigation.) Secretary of Defense Rumsfeld and his then-deputy Paul Wolfowitz provided the penultimate and ultimate names on the PNAC statement of principles.[8] As is obvious at a glance, PNAC is a veritable who's who of prominent Republican neoconservative policymakers. With so many of them serving in the Bush (43) administration and virtually all of them with more national security experience than the president, perhaps Bush's ultimate conversion was inevitable.

Arrayed against the neoconservatives inside the administration, however, were the well-respected Republican traditionalists. They constituted the older Republican guard, many of whom had served with distinction in Bush (41). They represented the moderate-internationalist Republican tradition that existed through much of the Cold War years and was largely shared by moderate Democrats. Indeed, they and their Democratic fellow travelers formed the basis of the Cold War consensus discussed in chapter 3. Prominent among them were former President George H. W. Bush and his former NSC advisor, Brent Scowcroft. Another prominent Republican traditionalist was Laurence Eagleburger, a former secretary of state. Inside the new Bush administration were Colin Powell and his deputy, Richard Armitage (the number two person in the state department and therefore state's counterpart to Defense's Wolfowitz). Less visible but a traditionalist nonetheless was Lawrence Wilkerson, Secretary Powell's chief of staff. Prior to 9/11, the traditionalists held sway in Bush's policymaking circles. For example, one of the early "crises" in Bush's first year occurred when an American spy plane was forced to land on China's territory. Powell and the Department of State took the lead in ending the diplomatic row. Though fewer in number, these traditionalists were exceedingly confident policymakers who had been involved in important decision making roles in previous administrations; additionally, they knew their way around bureaucratic elbows. Indeed, one would be hard-pressed to find a shrinking violet among either the neoconservatives or the traditionalists. Now they found themselves back in policymaking positions in George W. Bush's administration following the fallow years of two Clinton terms. It was therefore virtually inevitable that these two groups with differing ideological leanings would thrash things out sometime during Bush's presidency. The 9/11 attacks provided the catalyst.

Manifold indicators of the philosophical battle were evident from the earliest days of the Bush administration in 2001. But it was after 9/11 that the neoconservatives were able to gain a toehold against the moderate traditionalists. Why? First, 9/11 demanded dramatic and demonstrable changes in order for U.S. national security policy—historically built on the threats from nation-states—to face the transnational global jihadi hydra. Putatively, the neoconservatives offered an agenda for the new threats. Second, President Bush was inclined to do what he considered "big things."[9] If nothing else, the neoconservatives were calling for big things. Whatever one wishes to think of the neoconservative agenda, projecting America's power well into the twenty-first century and continuing America's world leadership while China and India and the EU continued to make gains was easily characterized as a big idea. Third, while the record demonstrated that the neoconservatives attempted to broaden the 9/11 response to include Iraq from the beginning, they failed to convince the president until sometime later, in 2002, when they found President Bush's mind fertile ground in which to sow their ideological seeds. President Bush, as may be recalled, said on innumerable occasions that for him the world changed following 9/11; the neoconservatives simply took advantage of the change. Fourth, prior to 9/11 President Bush had yet to gain the self-confidence he eventually gained, something that would prove necessary to move U.S. national security policy in a new direction. Fifth, the "traditionalist Republican internationalists" were a formidable force in the Republican Party prior to President Bush's soaring popularity following 9/11, having guided the U.S. through a successful war in the Persian Gulf against Saddam Hussein; therefore, the Republican international-traditionalists were still the Party's main intellectual source of national security thinking. Simple inertia made the traditionalists powerful before 9/11. And sixth, during Bush's first term, re-election to a second Bush term was an imperative. President Bush wished not to repeat his father's failure to be re-elected. Karl Rove (called "Bush's brain") and his ilk likely contributed to the influence of the traditional conservatives insofar as moderation worked to Bush's reelection benefit. The 9/11 attacks surely mitigated Rove's moderating effects to the extent that such effects existed.

Precise reasons aside, an early skirmish over the lessons of Afghanistan and public diplomacy (i.e., propaganda) loomed publicly in early 2002. For neoconservatives, a clear lesson from Afghanistan was that public diplomacy was an important instrument of U.S. national security policy, one that had been underused hitherto. While discussions were at a "preliminary stage, officials said there was general agreement in the administration that the intense shaping of information and coordination of messages that occurred during the fighting in Afghanistan should become a permanent feature of national security policy" read one *New York Times* piece. Neither hawks and doves nor traditionalists and neoconservatives were mentioned, but it was clear that the discussed debate between the two camps on public diplomacy was ongoing. The *Times* piece even used language reminiscent of the Vietnam-era debate over public diplomacy: winning hearts and minds.[10]

The ideological fault lines ran between the Departments of State and Defense. (Though parts of the NSC and vice president's office were also arrayed with the neoconservatives, and the CIA often lined up on the side of the traditionalists.) Following the administration's success in Afghanistan, the battle between the traditionalists and neoconservatives evidenced itself over the discussion of peace in the Middle East. Diplomacy in America's long-term effort to bring peace to the Middle East and the Israeli-Palestinian negotiations in particular were clearly in the state department's portfolio. Powell, having performed loyally during and after 9/11, was attempting to get the president to use his (the president's) ample political capital to influence Israel's Ariel Sharon in order to move forward peace between the Palestinians (then still represented by the Palestinian Authority leader, Yasser Arafat) and the Israelis.[11] Powell visited the Middle East, a move somewhat reminiscent of Kissinger during the Nixon years. Powell may or may not have realized he was sticking out his neck in attempting to pressure Sharon; he would soon learn. The neoconservatives responded and attempted to chop Powell's extended neck off once and for all. "State Department officials say Secretary of State Colin L. Powell has been repeatedly *undercut* by other senior policymakers in his effort to break the Middle East deadlock, warning this has left U.S. diplomacy paralyzed at an especially volatile moment." Many in the state department cited resistance to their diplomatic efforts coming from "Defense Secretary Donald H. Rumsfeld, who has more of a voice in shaping Middle East policy than his predecessors."

> The opinions of Rumsfeld and his key lieutenants, notably Deputy Defense Secretary Paul D. Wolfowitz and Undersecretary of Defense Douglas J. Feith, [figured] prominently because the Pentagon [had] been given a seat at interagency discussions over the Middle East conflict. In recent years, the peace process was largely the purview of the State Department and the White House.

Rumsfeld and his advisers had "advocated giving Sharon wide latitude to press his military operations, viewing the Israeli campaign as a legitimate war on terrorism. At the same time, they [saw] little value in trying to engage Palestinian leader Yasser Arafat in renewed negotiations."[12] Officials in the Department of State were quoted to the effect that they perceived neoconservatives in defense and elsewhere as undermining the state department's efforts in the Middle East, so much so as to leave the administration's policy "dead in the water." These were the same officials quoted above who characterized the mood in the state department as despondent and disheartened, and they were the same officials who could not remember a time when the morale at the state department was so low.[13]

Evidence of a rift in the defense department between its civilian leadership and the Pentagon brass had also been evident from the early days of President Bush's first term. Newspaper articles and even books had documented it. (Bob Woodward's *Bush at War* and *Plan of Attack* both noted it.) In early 2003, a *New York Times* piece raised the issue anew. The piece detailed how, in a White House meeting (apparently an NSC principals or "war cabinet" meeting), Bush asked his then–chairman of the Joint Chiefs of Staff (CJCS) General Richard Myers how long a war in Iraq would last, whereupon Rumsfeld interrupted General Myers before the general could answer. The Goldwater-Nichols Act examined in chapter 4 gave the CJCS the prerogative of giving his best advice to the president and the NSC; Secretary Rumsfeld's behavior, therefore, was a serious breach of protocol. The same authors cited the "Pentagon brain trust of about two dozen that Mr. Rumsfeld" convened "each workday morning to review war planning for Iraq and other global hot spots." Furthermore, the piece noted that if President Bush ordered "the nation to war in the hours ahead, decisions reached by Mr. Rumsfeld and his brain trust after months of fierce debate [would] be weighed and tested on the battlefields of Iraq."

Who comprised the brain trust? The piece named several: "Deputy Defense Secretary Paul D. Wolfowitz, the administration's chief hawk on Iraq; but also more anonymous but influential aides like Stephen A. Cambone, the undersecretary for intelligence, who as Mr. Rumsfeld's roving bureaucratic commando, is in his third senior Pentagon post in two years." (As will be seen in chapter 10, Stephen A. Cambone remained a roving commando who attempted to marginalize the director of national intelligence throughout 2006.) In other words, Rumsfeld's roving commandos prepared at the Pentagon before meeting the president at the White House for NSC meetings where the traditionalists were on hand to counter the neoconservatives' influence. "From these meetings [meetings at the Pentagon], Mr. Rumsfeld and General Myers take their war brief to the White House for near-daily gatherings with Mr. Bush and his top advisers, including Vice President Dick Cheney, Secretary of State Colin L. Powell and the national security advisor, Condoleezza Rice."[14]

The piece also raised a companion issue: the relationship between Secretary Rumsfeld and his commandos and Vice President Cheney's own neoconservative-laden staff.

> But perhaps Mr. Rumsfeld's closest relationship outside the Pentagon war council is with his former protégé, Mr. Cheney. The two have known each other for more than 30 years, dating to the Nixon administration—when Mr.

Rumsfeld hired Mr. Cheney—and they have both served before as White House chief of staff and as defense secretary.

"They're very, very close friends, and they trust each other's judgments," said one senior Defense Department official.

Mr. Cheney's experience leading the Pentagon during the 1991 Gulf War gives him an unusual insight into the challenges Mr. Rumsfeld faces.[15]

Though most Americans probably had never heard of I. Lewis "Scooter" Libby until he was indicted in 2005, Libby attended NSC principals meetings. Thus, the neoconservatives were able to get more than one bite at the apple, as it were. They "had a bite" while plotting at the Pentagon, then again in NSC principals meetings where they were counterbalanced by the traditionalists (Powell, et al.), and then again when Vice President Cheney, who would often stay after NSC meetings, would meet one-on-one with Bush. In Bob Woodward's *Plan of Attack*, the author noted the following of Libby: "In his current role, Libby was one of only two people who were not [statutory] principals to attend the National Security Council meetings with the president and the separate principals meetings chaired by Rice. (The other was Rice's deputy, Stephen Hadley.)" Woodward further noted that Libby was a former student of Professor Paul Wolfowitz when Wolfowitz was a professor at Yale.[16] Cheney's influence as vice president was well-chronicled in Woodward's book, but the following passage is illustrative.

Cheney, the 61-year-old conservative hard liner, had already carved out a special position in the administration and held great sway with the president. He was a résumé vice president: White House chief of staff to President Ford at age 34; then 10 years as the only congressman from Wyoming . . . briefly the No. 2 House Republican leader before being selected by Bush's father to be secretary of defense in 1989.[17]

It was well after Woodward published *Plan of Attack* that an administration insider wrote similarly of the philosophical battle that occurred during the first Bush term. Lawrence Wilkerson, another Republican internationalist-traditionalist and chief of staff for Secretary of State Colin Powell, called the connections a "cabal." One need not believe it was a conspiracy to recognize an ongoing ideological battle royal. Wilkerson penned an opinion piece for the *Los Angeles Times*. His enthusiasm for his old boss, Secretary Powell, was understandable. He nevertheless wrote this of the neoconservative nexus which he saw in operation first hand. Of the neoconservatives in the defense department and the vice president's office and their relationship with the State Department, Wilkerson wrote:

> The administration's performance during its first four years would have been even worse without Powell's damage control. At least once a week, it seemed, Powell trooped over to the Oval Office and cleaned all the dog poop off the carpet. He held a youthful, inexperienced president's hand. He told him everything would be all right because he, the secretary of state, would fix it. And he did—everything from a serious crisis with China when a U.S. reconnaissance aircraft was struck by a Chinese F-8 fighter jet in April 2001, to the secretary's constant reassurances to European leaders following the bitter breach in relations over the Iraq war.[18]

Wilkerson essentially said the same thing in a wide-ranging speech weeks earlier at the New America Foundation.[19]

The philosophical battle between the neoconservatives and the traditionalists touched on multiple issue areas. It included a general debate about "state sponsors of terror." That debate was somewhat obscured initially by Afghanistan. Afghanistan, after all, was a failed state rather than a state that sponsored terrorism. That Iraq had become part of the larger war on the global jihadis was evidenced in that the neoconservatives were unwilling to limit America's projection of power to jihadi threats only. One of the neoconservative rationales for toppling Saddam Hussein's regime was—whether he had weapons of mass destruction or simply sought them—the putative nexus between jihadis and rogue states. It was less than surprising when Iran and North Korea (two rogue states with WMD connections, relations with which neoconservatives passionately felt the Clinton administration had bungled) emerged as a part of the neoconservative agenda. President Bush included all three rogue states in his 2002 State of the Union speech, identifying them as "an axis of evil" and tyranny in the world. The president continued by characterizing each in neoconservative terms. President Bush said that such states constituted "an axis of evil, arming to threaten the peace of the world. By seeking weapons of mass destruction, these regimes pose a grave and growing danger. They could provide these arms to terrorists, giving them the means to match their hatred. They could attack our allies or attempt to blackmail the United States. In any of these cases, the price of indifference would be catastrophic."

The president's 2003 State of the Union speech reflected growing neoconservative influence even more that his 2002 speech. With respect to Iran, President Bush said the following:

> Different threats require different strategies. In Iran, we continue to see a government that represses its people, pursues weapons of mass destruction, and supports terror. We also see Iranian citizens risking intimidation and death as they speak out for liberty and human rights and democracy. Iranians, like all people, have a right to choose their own government and determine their own destiny, and the United States supports their aspirations to live in freedom.

Of the Democratic People's Republic of Korea (North Korea) and its leader, Kim Jong Il, whom the president had earlier called a "pygmy," Bush opined:

> On the Korean Peninsula, an oppressive regime rules a people living in fear and starvation. Throughout the 1990s, the United States relied on a negotiated framework to keep North Korea from gaining nuclear weapons. We now know that that regime was deceiving the world, and developing those weapons all along. And today the North Korean regime is using its nuclear program to incite fear and seek concessions. America and the world will not be blackmailed.[20]

Both the "mullahs" in Iran and the diminutive leader of North Korea were areas of contention between the traditionalists and the neoconservatives. That is not to say the traditionalists thought any better of the mullahs or Kim Jong Il; instead, they simply believed America's national security response to either required some nuance and patience versus simply more muscle.[21]

But Iraq was a special arena in which the philosophical battle played itself out in 2002–2003. Predictably, the neoconservatives believed the U.S. needed to topple the Hussein regime. They argued that the U.S. needed to "drain the swamp." Even reconstruction after the war became part of the ideological struggle. It was the neoconservatives generally (and Rumsfeld's commandos particularly) who became identified with Ahmed Chalabi,[22] flying the exile back to Iraq shortly after the U.S. invasion. In spring 2003, Robin Wright wrote: "The Pentagon favors Chalabi—a long-standing ally of Vice President Dick Cheney, Deputy Defense Secretary Paul Wolfowitz and influential neoconservative strategist Richard Perle—

particularly after the failure of possible alternative Iraqi leaders to emerge."[23] Perle too had served in the Reagan administration and while Perle was not among the signatories of the neoconservative manifesto cited above, he was a well-known neoconservative who held considerable sway in Washington's neoconservative circles.

However, perhaps the neoconservatives' most unifying theme was America's role with respect to peace in the Middle East and as friend of Israel. One report in spring 2003 noted the depth and breadth of the divide. "In the wake of the military victory in Iraq, the battle between the State Department and the Defense Department for control over U.S. foreign policy has intensified, . . . with skirmishes waged almost daily over policy toward North Korea, the Middle East peace process and the reconstruction of Iraq." Just weeks later, a reporter for the *Los Angeles Times* noted: "In the wake of war in Iraq, [President Bush's] behavior toward Israel will be seen as a litmus test of whether the United States really means what it has said about seeking democracy and peace throughout the Middle East." Powell and the traditionalists had been battling the neoconservatives over how to approach Middle East peace the entire previous year. The issues involved the administration's "road map," and the sequencing of events: which of the parties—Israel or the Palestinians—would concede something for whom and when? That is, who would make the first step? But even before the administration's "roadmap" for Middle East peace was formally "unveiled, some members of the president's core constituency" were "lining up against it." Many of the neoconservatives were "known to oppose it," according to the piece "primarily because they believe[d] the Palestinians should go first in making concessions."[24]

While peace in the Middle East and how to achieve it was integral to the philosophical tensions, the skirmishes carried over into all sorts of other areas. In preparing for a meeting in China (the so-called six-party talks on North Korea), the neoconservatives were alleged to have sabotaged Powell. "Just days before a meeting this week in Beijing between U.S. and North Korean officials, . . . the Defense Department pressed to have James A. Kelly, the head of the delegation and Powell's chief Asian expert, replaced by Undersecretary of State John R. Bolton, a Rumsfeld ally on North Korea. Powell rejected the suggestion."[25] John Bolton was a well-known neoconservative and "hardliner." In 2005, President Bush nominated John Bolton to be the U.S. ambassador to the United Nations. Disparaging comments about the efficacy of the United Nations were attributed to Bolton, causing many to wonder why Bush would nominate him to represent the United States there in the first place. (Indeed, the nomination encountered so much bipartisan difficulty in the Senate Committee on Foreign Relations—generally a fairly bipartisan committee—that the nomination was sent to the Senate floor without a recommendation. Ultimately, President Bush made Bolton a "recess appointment.")

The same article portrayed the links between certain Washington think tanks and policymakers inside the government. In 2003, Newt Gingrich had been working out of the American Enterprise Institute (AEI) in Washington, D.C. Though out of government, his connections to those currently in office remained important. Evidently, Gingrich had a major problem—as did many neoconservatives—with the state department's moderating influence on U.S. national security policy. Since neoconservatives generally believed that the U.S. needed to be more muscular, Gingrich and other neoconservatives typically shunned the sort of compromises common in diplomacy. "At the heart of many of the disputes" read one report, were "complaints by conservatives inside and outside the administration that the State Department bureaucracy is thwarting President Bush from carrying out a forceful agenda to stop terrorism and confront enemy states—a point that former House speaker Newt Gingrich (R-GA), a member of a Pentagon advisory committee who [was] close to Rumsfeld, plan[ed] to make in a speech . . . at the American Enterprise Institute." Gingrich's speech was memorable. Gingrich called "for major overhaul of the State Department, including hearings on Capitol Hill and an examination of the department by a task force of retired foreign service officers. He said he wanted to contrast the success of a transformed Defense Department with the 'failure of State,' which he described as 'six months of diplomatic failure followed by one month of military success now to be returned to diplomatic failure to exploit the victory fully.'" Tellingly, Gingrich also faulted "the State Department for advocating a 'road map' for peace in the Middle East."[26] Whoever may or may not have advocated it, President Bush announced and took credit for the "road map" once it was finally promulgated. It was therefore improper, strictly speaking, for Gingrich to have ascribed the road map to the state department alone. But proper had little to do with it; Gingrich was one neoconservative whose scorched-earth battles were legendary.

Following the "road map" skirmish, Iraq reappeared in the ideological debate. Reconstruction efforts there foundered as the insurgency grew. A debate arose in Washington over whose fault it was that reconstruction had not occurred as planned. One question revolved around stabilization efforts and how long the U.S. would need to stay in Iraq, in some form or another, to create a stable political climate. "There are also differences over how long the United States" would "remain in Iraq to provide aid, help restore a civilian Iraqi government, and hunt remnants of Mr. Hussein's forces. Many Pentagon officials want to withdraw as quickly as possible, while some State Department officials" voiced "concern that moving out too soon could destabilize the country."[27] Next, the question of who should lead the reconstruction efforts appeared. General Jay Garner was America's first overseer of Iraq, a retired general and a moderate. As quick military victory turned into plodding reconstruction and stabilization efforts the neoconservatives called for a more forceful presence. By 2003, neoconservative L. Paul "Jerry" Bremer, was called on to right the reconstruction ship. A piece in the *Washington Post* summarized Bremer's ideology as well as what he was expected to accomplish. It described Bremer as "a hard-nosed hawk" who was "close to the neoconservative wing of the Pentagon." Bremer was "supported by Rumsfeld and Deputy Defense Secretary Paul D. Wolfowitz." Importantly, it quoted aides as characterizing "the appointment" as affirming "Bush's satisfaction with Pentagon control over Iraq until a new government [was] in place."[28]

Case by case, the neoconservatives muscled the traditionalists out of the way. Controlling the military and demonstrating just how critical it was to the president by toppling the Taliban followed by Saddam's regime so quickly clearly endeared the neoconservatives to the president. Neoconservatives argued that the Pentagon was "ascendant" because it had "better internalized the president's worldview. The State Department, they say, [had] not succeeded in its main task of explaining U.S. policy to the world and winning support for it." One piece described the relationship between Secretaries Powell and Rumsfeld as "cordial." But there was no mistaking what the piece was about: an ideological, philosophical, and bureaucratic rivalry of incredible proportions. Secretary Rumsfeld was described as constantly sending missives to Secretary Powell offering the latter advice on this matter or that matter. State Department officials derisively called them "Rummygrams." And the secretary was said "to roll his eyes at the volume of 'Rummygrams' routinely sent his way that offer[ed] the defense secretary's views on foreign policy." The piece also noted the

multifrontal "attacks from neoconservatives" that state department officials believed were intended to "decapitate" Powell—one presumes figuratively only. That Gingrich's recent speech had resonated at the State
Department and "broken some china" was clear. The author noted, "Gingrich's speech triggered a bitter public response from the State Department." Powell was apparently fuming at Gingrich's swiping. During a
Senate hearing "Powell noted . . . that diplomats are supposed to craft alliances and find diplomatic solutions. 'That's what we do,' he said. 'We
do it damn well, and I am not going to apologize to anyone.' Powell's
deputy, Richard Armitage, helpfully characterized Gingrich as being off
his medication.[29]

Next, Iran reappeared as battleground for the administration's internal
ideological debates. Conventional wisdom held that two basic camps existed regarding Iranian politics: the moderate reformers (led by then-
President Khatami), who controlled the institutions of government or the
state; and the keepers of the revolution of 1979, often simply referred to
as the "mullahs." If the United States, who had no formal relationship
with Iran, wished to move Iran slowly from pariah status to the "community of nations," conventional wisdom held that U.S. diplomats
needed to carefully cultivate the reformers, more or less ignoring the
mullahs. Since the neoconservatives believed U.S. power ought to be
used to influence Iran, they saw no particular need to distinguish between
moderates and mullahs. Iran was Iran and American power really ought
to be able to make the Iranians see what was ultimately in their national
security interests, the neoconservatives argued. The subtleties of diplomacy were seen by the neoconservatives as a waste of American time and
resources. Both sides agreed that al Qaeda members had fled from
Afghanistan and traveled across Iranian territory to make their escapes.
The question then was how to respond to Iran, which may actually have
had information on al Qaeda members. Another was what to do if Iran actually allowed them sanctuary. President Bush, after all, was on record as
equating governments who harbored terrorists with terrorists and therefore subject to U.S. opprobrium and worse. "The State Department approach of trying to work with Tehran has prevailed with tentative support
from the White House, despite opposition among Pentagon policymakers
and condemnation from neoconservatives who would prefer to either
pressure or ignore Tehran." But for how long would the White House
continue to support the Department of State's approach, tentatively or

otherwise? Though not identified by agency or philosophy, someone inside the administration told Robin Wright "A lot of people [in the Department of State were] feeling betrayed. This dialogue [tentative diplomatic talks with reformers in Tehran] was based on the assumption that we can engage with the Iranians constructively on issues like Al Qaeda. If we can't trust that supposition anymore, we have to question this kind of exchange."[30] Clearly, Wright's source was suggesting yet again that the state department's approach with respect to Iran had yielded little measurable success. The implication was that defense needed to capture Tehran's attention one way or another.

Ultimately, the philosophical debate turned petty, even by Washington standards. As the once-popular war in Iraq turned into an insurgency with no end in sight, calls for investigations into intelligence failures became numerous. The CIA had always been seen by neoconservatives as nest of liberals and moderates who worked at cross-purposes to the neoconservative's agenda. In 2003, as increasing calls for investigations of intelligence were heard, those calls inevitably exacerbated the already intense ideological battles ongoing in the administration. By late spring 2003, with Saddam's putative WMD programs still unfound it became apparent that the CIA was contemplating undergoing an internal investigation to determine how accurate their intelligence was, in particular its main work product, the National Intelligence Estimate (NIEs). "The Central Intelligence Agency has begun a review to try to determine whether the American intelligence community erred in its prewar assessments of Saddam Hussein's government and Iraq's weapons programs," according to unidentified administration officials. "The CIA's review would come at a time of increasing tension between the Pentagon and CIA over the handling of intelligence."

> Intelligence officials said that several CIA analysts had quietly complained that senior Defense Department officials and other Bush administration officials sought to press them to produce reports that supported the administration's positions on Iraq. In addition, several current and former CIA officers who have been upset about what they believe has been the politicization of intelligence concerning Iraq were the first to disclose the existence of the new CIA review.

In an important revelation, the piece described friction between the CIA and the Pentagon's "office of special operations," a quasi-intelligence analysis center created by neoconservative Douglas Feith, another one of Secretary Rumsfeld's "roving commandos."

But other intelligence officials have said they believe that one source of the feuding between the CIA and Pentagon was the creation last year of a special Pentagon unit that reviewed intelligence reports concerning Iraq. That team was created in part as a result of the frustration some senior aides to Mr. Rumsfeld had felt over the way in which the CIA was handling the issue. . . .

Pentagon officials say the intelligence team did not produce its own reports, and instead reviewed the intelligence developed by other agencies, looking for links between Iraq and Al Qaeda that they did not believe had been sufficiently highlighted by other agencies. But the creation of the special unit created a furor within the intelligence community, after CIA analysts began to complain that the Pentagon's special unit was staffed by conservative ideologues eager to offer the Bush administration an alternative view of intelligence than that provided by the CIA.[31]

Shortly thereafter, evidence of other "neoconservative" commandos joining the fray appeared. Elliot Abrams, a neoconservative who had been indicted over the Iran-Contra affair years earlier and who wore his indictment as a badge of honor rejoined government service in the president's national security council. "Twelve years [after the Iran-Contra imbroglio], Abrams is helping to shape White House policies toward many of the world's trouble spots."

"Appointed . . . as President Bush's senior [NSC] adviser on the Middle East, his responsibilities extend from Algeria to Iran. But nowhere is his influence more evident than on the Arab-Israeli peace process." More than a Reaganite, Abrams was a hard-core neoconservative and his placement in the NSC meant neoconservatives had now infiltrated the NSC as well as the Pentagon and vice president's office.

A self-described "neo-conservative and neo-Reaganite" with strong ties to Jews and evangelical Christians, Abrams has become a flash point for the debate on how much pressure the Bush administration is prepared to apply to Israeli Prime Minister Ariel Sharon to reach an agreement with the Palestinians.

Administration rivals say Abrams worked behind the scenes to rewrite the road map on the basis of critiques drawn up by the American Israel Public Affairs Committee (AIPAC), a leading pro-Israel American lobby group. He fired off frequent e-mails to Rice and her deputy, Stephen Hadley, trying to reduce the role of international mediators in the peace process."[32]

Abrams had been waiting patiently to join the battle and he now found a propitious moment. By well into President Bush's second term, Abrams was using his position at the NSC to carry the neoconservative agenda forward. This meant clashing at times with Secretary of State Rice.[33]

Skirmishes continued as summer loomed. In late May Ron Brownstein published a piece in which he compared the maneuvers and countermaneuvers between the Israeli government under Sharon and the Palestinian Authority. "The politics of Middle East peace have become almost as complex in the United States as they are in the region itself," wrote Brownstein. "In the last month, President Bush has displayed more commitment and creativity in advancing the peace process between Israel and the Palestinians than at any point in his presidency. And that movement is kicking up swirls of political maneuvering, not only in Tel Aviv and the West Bank, but also in the United States." Brownstein introduced another wrinkle apart from the intra-Republican Party ideological battle. Brownstein opined that the president previously had been reluctant to confront Sharon when the U.S. and Sharon disagreed on some particular aspect of the "road map." The author noted that should Bush feel the need to do so now, Bush would be "confronting Sharon, whose Likud government ha[d] staunch support among two key elements of Bush's coalition: Christian conservatives and the neoconservative foreign policy thinkers—mostly Jewish and Catholic—who have the president's ear." To be clear, Brownstein suggested that if Bush confronted Sharon he would likely face "greater resistance to the renewed peace process . . . from within Bush's own coalition," according to Brownstein "by far."[34]

Iraq continued as a source of contention between the two ideological camps. In August, Ambassador Bremer (who replaced Jay Garner) decided to dissolve the Iraqi army with the stroke of a pen. Apparently, most neoconservatives were of the view that the Iraqi army was full of Baathist loyalist whom the United States would never be able to trust; therefore, the solution was to disband the military summarily. Traditionalists apparently believed that the U.S. coalition provisional authority—under the aegis of the defense department instead of the state department, which by itself was a source of contention—ought to build on the professional officers corps in the Iraqi military. The latter group argued that while some Baathist and Saddam loyalists doubtless existed in their ranks, careful vetting would permit the coalition authority to select the best from the military professionals for the new infrastructure of the future Iraqi military. Perhaps the most noteworthy information in the article, however, was mention of the Pentagon's influence. The office of special operations was characterized as being part of the debate over the Iraqi military and how to proceed.[35] In retrospect, that decision can be seen as one of the important decision junctures where, if "do-overs" were permissible, the U.S. might not have dissolved the entire Iraqi military.

The Pentagon's control of reconstruction efforts in Iraq persisted as an open political question. As the "occupation" after toppling of Saddam dragged on month after month, increasing numbers of complaints and criticisms appeared in the newspapers and on cable news. In October, President Bush began to have second thoughts and made a volte-face: he put then–NSC advisor Condoleezza Rice in charge of more of the Iraq occupation, apparently relieving the Pentagon of some of its hard-won responsibilities. For a time at least it appeared that Pentagon control of reconstruction had lost favor with President Bush. There was clearly confusion over the reasons Bush turned toward the NSC and Rice after relying on the Pentagon theretofore. And why, if Bush was demonstrating displeasure with the defense department, had Bush not turned to the state department and the capable Colin Powell? "From the start, the administration" had been "riven by ideological disputes on foreign policy. But both neoconservative hawks and mainstream Republican foreign policy realists" said "many of the administration's foreign policy headaches are directly related to the interagency process Rice oversees." A senior state Department official was quoted in the article as characterizing the entire decision-making process as "dysfunctional."[36] Whether it was NSC advisor Rice's fault alone is debatable—the secretary of defense had, after all, dominated the decisions made previously.

The president's change in heart may have had to do with Ahmed Chalabi. Prior to the war in Iraq, the Pentagon and the neoconservatives had globed onto Chalabi (or vice versa) as an *éminence grise*. (It would not be until much later, after the 9/11 final report and the Robb-Silberman report were published, that Chalabi was formally identified as a major source of intelligence for the Pentagon—and as those postmortems would determine, a source of poor intelligence.) The Pentagon believed Chalabi to be the sort of Iraqi exile whom the U.S. might be able to position in an important post–Iraq War role. Neither the state department nor the NSC agreed and policymakers from both argued Chalabi was trouble, dishonest, an inveterate self-promoter, and wanted for fraud in Jordan. Officials in both the NSC and the state department agitated against Chalabi, making Chalabi even more of a cause célèbre for the neoconservatives. In addition to characterizing the Bush administration's decision-making processes as "dysfunctional," the piece noted how confusing and politicized policymaking had become, with traditionalists on one side, neoconservatives on the other side, and the president subject to whomever he last heard.

Even members of Rice's staff expressed frustration. The NSC and State Department staffers were stunned to learn, for example, that the Pentagon, with the approval of the vice president, had flown controversial Iraqi exile leader Ahmed Chalabi into southern Iraq after Bush had opposed giving Chalabi special treatment.

Some of Powell's key lieutenants, who had gone along with the president's decision to give the Pentagon the principal postwar role, were frustrated first by the Defense Department's refusal to include them—and then Rice's unwillingness to intercede.

"Everything went back to Washington, where it became tangled up in the bureaucratic food fights," said the official who served in Iraq. "Absolutely everything."[37]

Newsweek published an article in November linking several of the threads discussed above together in one extraordinary investigative piece. It discussed the philosophical contest for the president's heart and mind. It described and analyzed the various programs begun by the defense department since neoconservatives found themselves back in policymaking positions: the office of special operations and others. It considered some of the ruthless backstabbing between the principals at the Pentagon, the NSC, and the state department. Importantly, it directed a bright spotlight on the role Vice President Cheney had been playing ever since 9/11.[38]

"Every Thursday, President George W. Bush and Vice President Dick Cheney have lunch together in a small dining room off the Oval Office. They eat alone; no aides are present. They have no fixed agenda, but it's a safe assumption that they often talk about intelligence—about what the United States knows, or doesn't know, about the terrorist threat." It continued: "As vice president, Cheney is free to roam about the various agencies, quizzing analysts and top spooks about terrorists and their global connections. 'This is a very important area. It's the one the president asked me to work on . . . I ask a lot of hard questions,' Cheney told NBC's Tim Russert last September [2003]. 'That's my job.'" The question is whether President Bush listened to the vice president and how closely. After all, George W. Bush, not Dick Cheney, was the president. The authors noted that the "president respects Cheney's judgment, say White House aides, and values the veep's long experience in the intelligence community (as President Gerald Ford's chief of staff, as a member of the House Intelligence Committee in the 1980s and as secretary of defense in the George H. W. Bush administration)."

Cheney's connection to Chalabi was the next issue *Newsweek* addressed, though it was hardly "news" by then.

> Writing recently in *The New Yorker*, investigative reporter Seymour Hersh alleged that Cheney had, in effect, become the dupe of a cabal of neoconservative full-mooners, the Pentagon's mysteriously named Office of Special Plans and the patsy of an alleged bank swindler and would-be ruler of Iraq, Ahmad Chalabi.[39]

With respect to Cheney's use of manufactured, politicized, or otherwise less-than-objective intelligence, the authors reported that it appeared "that Cheney has been susceptible to 'cherry-picking,' embracing those snippets of intelligence that support his dark prognosis while discarding others that don't. He is widely regarded in the intelligence community as an outlier, as a man who always goes for the worst-case scenario and sometimes overlooks less alarming or at least ambiguous signs." While the authors dutifully reported other sources who rejected such characterizations of Cheney, they also made it sound as though even Cheney promoters admitted that the vice president carved out a role as vice president that in some ways eclipsed the NSC advisor and/or secretary of state. Thus, even some of Cheney's admirers described the office of the vice president, "with its large and assertive staff, as a kind of free-floating power base that at times brushes aside the normal policymaking machinery under national security adviser Condoleezza Rice. On the road to war, Cheney in effect created a parallel government that became the real power center."[40]

Others confirmed Vice President Cheney's unusual influence. Still others confirmed Cheney's views of Secretary of State Powell. Woodward's

Plan of Attack asserted that President Bush had fully converted to the neo-conservative agenda sometime in 2002. There is evidence that he may have decided to invade Iraq as early as spring 2002, despite protestations to the contrary and Bush's efforts to get UN support, ironically using Secretary Powell as his instrument at the UN. There is also evidence that President Bush had not definitively decided until the 2002–2003 holiday period after consultations at his ranch in Crawford, Texas. Timing aside, Woodward wrote of a dinner party that was held at the Cheney household just after the invasion of Iraq had begun. Ken Adelman, another neoconservative who exerted influence from outside government, wrote an op-ed piece on April 10, 2003, entitled "Cakewalk Revisited," referring to an op-ed piece he published prior to the March invasion in which he argued Iraq would be a cakewalk. In "Cakewalk Revisited," Adelman reminded his readers that some fourteen months earlier he had predicted the quick victory all were now watching "more or less gloating." In Woodward's account, Vice President Cheney telephoned Adelman, who was then vacationing in Paris with his family. After telling Adelman what a clever column he had written, the vice president suggested that Adelman return to Washington posthaste. The vice president was holding a dinner party, whose guest comprised a veritable who's who of neoconservatives, to celebrate the administration's decision to topple Saddam Hussein. "Adelman realized it was Cheney's way of saying thank you, and he and his wife came back from Paris a day early to attend the dinner."

> When Adelman walked into the vice president's residence that Sunday night, he was so happy he broke into tears. He hugged Cheney for the first time in the 30 years he had known him. There had been reports in recent days of mass graves and abundant, graphic evidence of torture by Saddam Hussein's government, so there was a feeling that they had been part of a greater good, liberating 25 million people.
>
> "We're all together. There should be no protocol; let's just talk," Cheney said when they sat down to dinner.
>
> Wolfowitz embarked on a long review of the 1991 Persian Gulf War and what a mistake it had been to allow the Iraqis to fly helicopters after the armistice. Hussein had used them to put down uprisings [by Shiites and Kurds].

They turned to President Bush himself. Cheney had been at the president's elbow encouraging Bush on the proper course but Bush had ultimately made the decision. After a toast to the president and his leadership Cheney began speaking. "After Sept. 11, 2001, Cheney said, the president understood what had to be done. He [Bush] had to do Afghanistan first, sequence the attacks, but after Afghanistan—'soon thereafter'—the president knew he had to do Iraq. Cheney said he was confident after Sept. 11 that it would come out okay." Eventually "Scooter" Libby had his turn. Libby agreed it had all been a pretty remarkable thing the neoconservatives had pulled off against the stalwarts of Republican traditionalism. There had been Brent Scowcroft, "the pillar of establishment foreign policy, vocally on the other side, widely seen as a surrogate for the president's father." Then there had been "James A. Baker III, the former secretary of state [for George H. W. Bush], insisting on a larger coalition of nations." And last but not least had been "Lawrence Eagleburger, Baker's successor in the last half year of the first Bush administration, on television all the time saying war was justified only if there was evidence that Hussein was about to attack us." Indeed, "Eagleburger had accused Cheney of 'chest thumping.'" Finally, the group of happy neoconservatives focused in on their principal enemy, so it would appear from the conversation. Incredibly, given Powell's reputation and the stakes of war in Iraq, they "turned to the current secretary of state, Colin L. Powell, and there were chuckles around the table." Cheney said Powell "sure likes to be popular." Deputy Secretary Wolfowitz attempted to stick up for Powell and mentioned that Powell's UN speech on behalf of the president had been commendable. Woodward records the following response from Vice President Cheney: "Cheney shook his head, no. Powell was a problem. 'Colin always had major reservations about what *we were trying to do*.'"[41]

It was sometime difficult to discern where philosophical-ideological contests gave way to petty bureaucratic turf battles. Nor were the two mutually exclusive. That the neoconservatives were largely housed in the Pentagon's civilian leadership and the vice president's office and the traditionalists mostly housed in state (although either showed up in CIA and the NSC) made the lines even more confusing. By the time the president was re-elected in November 2004, it had more or less become a moot point whether a particular battle was ideologically driven, a bureaucratic turf war, or some combination of the two. Neoconservative objectives became apparent in President Bush's national security policy in 2003–2004. Per the neoconservative agenda, Bush eventually jettisoned Arafat as a partner to the U.S. in negotiating the "road map" for peace with Israel. President Bush increasingly gave Ariel Sharon a wide berth in how

Sharon reacted to Palestinian demands. In short, President Bush eventually assumed the neoconservative agenda on a case-by-case basis over the period.

By Bush's second inauguration, Colin Powell and Richard Armitage resigned their positions and the traditionalist-internationalist Republicans ascended in the Bush administration national security team. One traditionalist who left when Secretary Powell resigned, Lawrence Wilkerson, made news in 2005 but his charges have more or less been ignored by the White House. Three of the top neoconservatives in the administration have similarly left. Wolfowitz resigned in spring 2005 to head the World Bank—where he has been relatively popular and has enjoyed good media. Douglas Feith was rumored to be leaving in late 2004 and ultimately tendered his resignation in January 2005. I. Lewis "Scooter" Libby was indicted in the fall of 2005. Vice President Cheney remained the most powerful vice president ever, by virtually all accounts. Recently, evidence of a group of younger Republican activists has appeared, possibly mitigating the influence of the neoconservatives.[42] The Intelligence Reform and Terrorism Prevention Act is now law and while President Bush has some two years remaining in office, the November 7, 2006, midterm elections rendered Americans' judgment on Iraq. The opportunities for the neoconservatives to affect U.S. national security policy during the remainder of President Bush's time in office are likely fewer. Put differently, whatever damage or good the neoconservatives accomplished for U.S. security, their direct influence is mostly finished and only their reverberations will be noted in the future.

THE 9/11 VICTIMS' FAMILIES AS A SPECIAL-INTEREST GROUP THAT AFFECTED U.S. NATIONAL SECURITY POLICYMAKING

On November 27, 2002, the Intelligence Authorization Act became law. The statute (public law 107-306, also known as H.R. 4628) created what would become known as the 9/11 Commission. The act specifically created the National Commission on Terrorist Attacks upon the United States, a bipartisan panel formed to examine intelligence and policymaking failures related to the 9/11 attacks and to recommend changes for America's national security policymaking apparatuses.[43] The 9/11 Commission created a website for the Commission work and hearing schedules. Of the seven menu links, one was dedicated to the victims' families. A message there to the families read:

> Family members of 9-11 victims were instrumental in the creation of the 9-11 Commission. The Commissioners and staff are dedicated to working on behalf of the safety and security of the American people and the thousands of families who lost loved ones on September 11, 2001. The Commission strives to relate to family members and keep them apprised of the progress it makes during the course of its investigation into the attacks upon our Nation.[44]

From the beginning of the 9/11 Commission's investigation "the families" (shorthand for a collection of 9/11 victims' families) were adamantly interested in discovering why their loved ones had perished on 9/11. Indeed, though the families politically eclectic and different family groups eventually formed, the initial impulse of victims' families came together in a formidable special-interest group whose purpose was to determine the truth about how 9/11 happened and to seek justice for those responsible for 9/11. The families formed a Family Steering Committee for the 9/11 Commission to ensure that their interests were met.[45]

That the 9/11 families would follow the 9/11 Commission's work carefully was hardly surprising. They had already influenced the intelligence committees of both houses of Congress on behalf of the 9/11 victims' interests. The families had been instrumental in agitating for Congress to conduct the "Joint Inquiry," which produced a report that was released in late 2002. The nearly 900-page Joint Inquiry report had left many, including importantly the families, with more questions than answers. Apart from redactions in the report—most having to do with the Saudi royal family or sources and methods—the families and others believed the Joint Inquiry glossed over far too many topics.[46] The influence of the families as an interest group was readily apparent from 2002 into late 2005 when they commented on the 9/11 Commission's "report card."[47]

The families were not the only special-interest group interested in U.S. national security policymaking and intelligence reforms. In April 2003 a story appeared in the newspapers discussing how two seemingly disparate interest groups, "Jews and evangelical Christians" shared concerns and lobbied the Bush administration as well as Capitol Hill on issues having to do with Israel, Middle East peace, U.S. foreign policy toward the region, and in particular, the Bush administration's "road map" for Israeli-

Palestinian peace. The article noted how much more important such interest groups had become during an election cycle.[48]

The victims' families became a source of U.S. national security policy change, particularly influential in creating the Intelligence Reform and Terrorism Prevention Act. In May 2003, for example, then–Director of Central Intelligence, George Tenet, felt the families' wrath. Tenet had promised (October 2002) the families and Congress that he would "provide the names of agency officials responsible for one of the most glaring intelligence mistakes leading up to the attacks of Sept. 11." In spring 2003, Tenet had yet to do so. His failure had "angered some lawmakers and families of some of the attacks' victims," who had "wanted a more specific accounting of intelligence and law enforcement lapses." One of the failures about which the families were concerned "occurred in early January 2000, just before a Malaysia meeting of al Qaeda, when the CIA learned that Mr. Midhar (one of the 19 hijackers) had obtained a visa that allowed him repeated entry to the United States." The Joint Inquiry committee staff said it found no evidence that the FBI (responsible for investigating terrorism inside the United States) had received information from the CIA about the visa. "Mr. Midhar moved to San Diego, attended flight school and lived unnoticed in a building whose landlord was an informant for the FBI."[49] The Joint Inquiry consisted of the House Permanent Select Committee on Intelligence and the Senate Select Committee on Intelligence. "In a preamble to their statement of purpose, the committees said they would look thoroughly into the mistakes and lapses before Sept. 11 and far beyond—in memory of the victims of the attacks." The congressional committees justified their actions, in part, based on the families of the victims of 9/11. "The committees said they would 'search for facts to answer the many questions that their families and many Americans have raised and to lay a basis for assessing the accountability of institutions and officials of government.'"[50]

The families exerted influence year-round but often were behind the scenes. Many Americans had hardly ever seen the families in action. Unless one watched the hearings of the 9/11 Commission—where the families sat in the front rows of the audience section often stoically but occasionally with some animation—the only other time one could predict their appearance in the news was on anniversaries of 9/11. On the anniversary of 9/11 in 2003, for instance, many of the families read the names of their loved ones who had died on 9/11.[51] Nevertheless, the families became a salient societal source of national security change. Editorial and opinion writers penned commentaries increasing the general public's attention to the families. For example, E. J. Dionne Jr., a well-known *Washington Post* columnist, wrote a column praising the families, among other things.[52] The families and the media became potent societal forces for change as they lobbied for their interests.

One way in which the families affected national security policy was directly through their scrutiny of the 9/11 Commission and its personnel. In late 2003, a particularly contentious issue became public. The issue was the staff director of the 9/11 Commission. Philip Zelikow, a professor from University of Virginia, had been controversial for some time. His academic credentials were not in question. Rather, his professional connections to members of the Bush administration were. Though a scholar and presumably an objective observer of U.S. national security, his academic career had crossed paths with Dr. Condoleezza Rice. Some of the families wondered about the propriety of a former colleague of Dr. Rice investigating potential failures—intelligence and policymaking ones—during the Bush administration's tenure, during which Dr. Rice was a key adviser. "The executive director of a panel investigating the Sept. 11, 2001, terrorist attacks is at the center of an escalating fight between the commission and some relatives of attack victims, who have demanded that he remove himself from a broad part of the inquiry because of his ties to key national security officials." Many of the families suspected his impartiality due to his having been a colleague of Dr. Rice, whom he was now empowered to investigate. "The families wrote in an Oct. 3 letter to the Sept. 11 commission that executive director Philip D. Zelikow should recuse himself 'from any aspect of national security and executive branch negotiations and investigations' because of his past connections to the National Security Council and to key Bush administration officials." Dr. Zelikow stayed but a warning shot across the bow had been fired on the 9/11 Commission by the families.[53]

The families' influence manifested itself in numerous ways. In addition to the dustup over Dr. Zelikow and the 9/11 Commission, the families argued that the Joint Inquiry had been remiss. "Although a joint House-Senate committee found serious failings in U.S. intelligence, Congress ha[d] given no sign of 'even seriously examining the issue,' let alone investigating it, relatives of Sept. 11 victims said Monday." The families were determined to remedy that. They requested a meeting with Senate leaders of the intelligence committee (then chairman Pat Roberts of [R-KS] and vice chairman Jay Rockefeller [D-WV]) and their House counterparts (then-chairman Porter Goss [R-FL] and vice chair Jane Harman [D-CA]) as well as the White House. The Bush administration had only made minor adjustments thus far based on the recommendations made by the inquiry.

> The Bush administration has made some moves toward improving intelligence gathering and sharing. It created a Terrorist Threat Integration Center [known as TTIC] to bring together information gathered by the CIA, FBI and other agencies and made terrorism a primary focus of the FBI.

The article concluded with a reference to the Families' Steering Committee.[54]

It was clear that the influence of the families grew as President Bush's re-election neared. An issue that had arisen previously was the 9/11 Commission's right to see official records from the executive branch. At least one commissioner, former Senator Max Cleland (who left the 9/11 Commission shortly thereafter) strongly suggested that the White House was playing a game with documents. He argued that the White House knew that the Commission's mandate expired in May and he asserted that the White House fought tooth and nail over each and every document in an apparent attempt to run out the clock before deals could be negotiated over the documents. Among the families, the perception was that the White House was stonewalling. After Cleland's charge others began demanding that the White House surrender the documents. Republican Senator John McCain (R-AZ) suggested: 'If the families of the victims weighed in—and heavily, as they did before—then we'd have a chance of succeeding.' McCain further stated that, "given the 'obfuscation' of the administration in meeting document requests, McCain was ready to pursue an extension "if the commission feels it can't get its work done."[55] Clearly, the families had become a powerful societal influence whose wrath was felt on either end of Pennsylvania Avenue and among the 9/11 commissioners.

The families clearly contributed to the "independence" members of Congress were discovering as the election cycle approached. One report from the same period observed that key "members of Congress from both parties blasted the Bush administration . . . for refusing to turn over classified intelligence documents requested by the [9/11 Commission]." Senator Joe Lieberman (D-CN)—a moderate Democrat and a supporter of the war in Iraq—admitted White House stonewalling, saying that "the administration has 'resisted this inquiry at every turn.'" Another Republican maverick, Senator Chuck Hagel (R-NE), appeared on NBC's *Meet the Press* where as a member of the U.S. Senate Foreign Relations Committee and the Select Committee on Intelligence he "urged the administration to turn over the documents." Vice Chair of the Senate Select Intelligence Committee Senator Jay Rockefeller (D-WV) joined Hagel on *Meet the Press* where Rockefeller also suggested the Bush administration was stonewalling. One author wrote, "Tensions between the commission and the executive branch have waxed and waned during recent months. On Oct. 15, the commission announced that it had unanimously voted to subpoena documents from the Federal Aviation Administration. It said the FAA had displayed 'serious deficiencies in . . . production of critical documents.'" The reporter continued by observing that the FAA's delay had "significantly impeded the progress" of the 9/11 Commission.[56]

Other times, the families applied subtler pressure. For instance, they exerted their influence indirectly when editorial pieces of major newspapers highlighted their plight.

Today, a persistent strain of conspiracy theory overseas clouds the Sept. 11, 2001, terror attacks, usually claiming prior U.S. government knowledge of—even responsibility for—the attacks. That, and the peace of mind of 9/11 families, are both good reasons for the Bush administration to cooperate more freely with the 9/11 investigating panel headed by former New Jersey Gov. Thomas H. Kean. Unfortunately, relations have gotten so bad that Kean is threatening to subpoena certain White House records. Kean is reluctant to say what documents he is seeking, but they apparently include the daily presidential briefings compiled by the CIA on foreign affairs and threats.[57]

By year's end (2003) at least five things were clear with respect to the 9/11 Commission, the executive branch, and the families. One was that the families had discovered how much power they could wield when it came to holding the Bush administration's feet to the fire. The families proved a formidable source of accountability. Second, was that the Bush administration had consciously chosen to make a virtue of necessity. As the administration attempted to prevent the creation of the Commission in the first place, once it became clear that such a commission was demanded by the families, Congress, and many Americans, the administration wisely joined in in calling for the 9/11 Commission's creation. Third, the administration put on the public record its assertion of executive privilege — a long-held precedent but also a privilege that does not exist in the Constitution — and other similar devices to thwart or, if thwarting proved problematic, to delay the release of documents. Similarly, the Bush White House was initially against the extension of the Committee's time frame until public pressure made its extension an inevitability. Fourth, though no quid pro quo occurred, the administration apparently came to believe that by eventually making several compromises they would be excused in using 9/11 in the upcoming presidential election. What had once seemed sacrosanct in American politics — the tragedy of 9/11 — would subsequently become a basis on which the Bush administration would run in 2004. The Republican nomination convention was already scheduled for New York City, the site of the most of 9/11's carnage. Finally, it was clear that the families would become somewhat politicized during the election and become an election-year source of change in U.S. national security policy.

The families were perhaps most influential during 2004, when President Bush ran for reelection. As noted, in late 2003 the notion of extending the Commission's tenure a couple of extra months arose from time to time. It was not until early 2004 that it came up formally. The commissioners were well aware that the White House opposed any extension, especially one that overlapped an election year. "A growing number of commission members had concluded" that the panel needed "more time to prepare a thorough and credible accounting of missteps leading to the terrorist attacks on the World Trade Center and the Pentagon. But the White House and leading Republicans have informed the panel that they oppose any delay, which raises the possibility that Sept. 11–related controversies could emerge during the heat of the presidential campaign." Following its earlier precedent of resisting initially only to submit later, the White House attempted to put the kibosh on the extension idea. "President Bush and House Speaker J. Dennis Hastert (R-IL) have decided to oppose granting more time to an independent commission investigating the Sept. 11, 2001, attacks, virtually guaranteeing that the panel will have to complete its work by the end of May." The families were not amused. The entire deadline debacle angered the victims' families who argued "that the panel ha[d] not been aggressive enough in demanding more time and in seeking key documents and testimony from the Bush administration."[58] An election-year showdown was brewing. "Long-simmering tensions with the commission investigating the Sept. 11, 2001, terrorist attacks became a more immediate problem for the White House this week as the panel released a series of damaging revelations about missed opportunities to stop the al Qaeda hijackers and opposed the administration by asking for more time to complete its work."

The election year's influence may have been as important as the families themselves but the interaction between the two societal sources magnified both. The combined influence proved more than the simple sum of its whole. One author noted, for instance, that "several commission members and political analysts said yesterday that opposition to a proposal favored by many families of attack victims could hurt Bush, even as Democrats step[ped] up their criticism of the administration's use of intelligence before the Iraq war." Two moderate Democrats, Senators Joseph Lieberman (D-CN) and John Edwards (D-NC) (one a former vice presidential nominee and the other soon to be one), openly supported an extension of the deadline.[59] Apparently, the 9/11 Commission had unearthed evidence that indicated the Bush administration feared more embarrassing judgments not yet made public.

Whatever the merits of the thinly veiled indications of poor policymaking, the Bush administration once again began to feel the pressure created by the families. One article noted that "Republican strategists" were "worried that the report may be critical of the Bush administration—specifically, of failures by the White House to act on intelligence before Sept. 11 suggesting that a catastrophic terrorist attack might be imminent—and that it could damage the president's re-election hopes if presented in the middle of the campaign." The families responded. "Groups representing the families of victims of the attack have joined in calling for an extension, saying that it would be improper for the White House and Congressional Republicans to try to rush the commission into completing its work."[60] Within a week or so the White House, following its well-established precedent, relented.

"President Bush reversed himself yesterday and agreed to support a two-month extension of the deadline for completion of an independent investigation of the Sept. 11, 2001, terrorist attacks," read a piece in the *Washington Post*. "Yielding to pressure from the panel conducting the probe, the lawmakers who established it, and families of victims, the White House set a schedule that calls for release of the unclassified version of the report by July 26, a month before Republicans gather for their national political convention near Ground Zero in New York City." Clearly the White House felt the pressure from the families and elsewhere. That did not, however, make an extension inevitable since Congress created the Commission and its extension could only come by an act of Congress. "In announcing support for the delay, White House press secretary Scott McClellan said Bush wants the ten members of the [9/11 Commission] to 'have all the information they need to do a thorough job and complete their work in a timely manner.'" But adoption of the new deadline depended on how hard the White House pushed for it. "House Speaker J. Dennis Hastert (R-IL)" for instance continued "to believe the commission should stick to its original timetable," according to a source. The same piece noted: "The White House previously insisted that the bipartisan commission stick to its original plan and issue its report by May 27, saying the work should be completed as soon as possible. Privately, Republican officials said they wanted time for any politically damaging findings to blow over before the heat of the presidential campaign." It would not be the last battle over the Commission's work in the election year.[61]

Several members of Congress, including some Republicans, seemed in tune with the families and their concerns. Those members did not include the leadership. "House Speaker J. Dennis Hastert (R-IL)" read one report "hardened his opposition to extending the deadline for the independent commission studying the Sept. 11, 2001, attacks even as the panel's leaders pleaded yesterday for more time to complete their work." Speaker Hastert was left twisting alone in the wind when his Senate counterpart, Majority Leader Senator Bill Frist (R-TN) announced that he backed the extension.

Then came the hint of yet another looming battle. It had to do with a sitting NSC advisor and whether she ought to be called before a committee created by Congress. White House "officials announced . . . that national security adviser Condoleezza Rice . . . rejected an invitation to testify publicly in front of the panel. Several senior Bush and Clinton administration officials, including Defense Secretary Donald H. Rumsfeld and Secretary of State Colin L. Powell . . . have agreed to appear";[62] however, the White House drew the line at the NSC advisor. In fairness, the NSC advisor, unlike other national security advisers (the secretaries of state and defense), has never been subjected to the Senate's advice and consent provision. As discussed in chapter 4, the drafters of the 1947 NSA did not envision an NSC advisor. Rather, the position evolved out of the 1947 statute's executive secretary and the various ways different presidents used the NSC. Subsequent amendments intended for the NSC advisor, a personal adviser for each president, to be held above the political fray. Thus the administration had precedent on its side. In fact, Dr. Rice did ultimately testify in an open hearing in what was arguably the most controversial and gripping testimony in the entire hearings. It was during Dr. Rice's testimony that the infamous August 6, 2001, Presidential Daily Briefing memo became public (below). In the meantime, another wrinkle appeared in the process.

The reader may recall a former Bush administration "counterterrorism official," Mr. Richard Clarke. Mr. Clarke served previously in the Clinton administration as an NSC principal and had, in fact, served in the George H. W. Bush (41) administration in a relatively high position in the NSC staff. According to virtually all accounts, Mr. Clarke had been important in terms of U.S. counterterrorism policies. He and a small cadre of professional staffers (in the NSC and at the CIA and the FBI) helped to prevent a planned attack against America's homeland in the late 1990s. When Bush was elected Richard Clarke remained in his NSC staff position. In March 2004 the 9/11 Commission held a series of open hearings that truly became high political drama. First, it was an election year: it was a given that such hearings during a presidential reelection campaign would become politicized. Second, the 9/11 Commission was approaching its May deadline—though that was soon extended to July—increasing the pressure on the 9/11 Commission's work. Third, the general perception existed among some of the families that the Bush administration had attempted to thwart the 9/11 Commission at every turn, though after initial resistance the administration ultimately gave in to virtually every wish. Fourth, Americans were seeing for the first time policymakers grilled before the commissioners. Most Americans never see policymaking up close and personal; however, with the public hearings and cable news covering them live, anybody watching could see policymakers giving insider accounts of one of America's worst policymaking and intelligence failures. For these reasons and others, the March 2004 hearings became a particularly important time for the 9/11 Commission, the families, and the election campaign to converge into an important source of U.S. national security.

When Richard Clarke finally testified, the Capitol Hill room in which he testified was thick with drama. Richard Clarke left the Bush administration and had recently written a critical "insiders" book in the interim.

Its publication date, unsurprisingly, was timed by the publisher to accompany his testimony before the 9/11 Commission. Furthermore, previous hearings including high-level policymakers (former and present) had been made public by the time Richard Clarke testified; Secretaries Rumsfeld and Powell and DCI George Tenet had already testified. Clarke's appearance was at the eighth public hearing, March 23 through March 24, 2004. Media coverage characterized the setting this way: "It was Clarke's testimony that dominated the daylong commission hearings and prompted several audience members to applaud—and to call for Bush administration officials to be more forthcoming about their efforts prior to the Sept. 11 attacks." Many in the audience were family members of the victims. "Clarke opened his testimony with a stirring apology to the families of the victims of Sept. 11, who filled the front rows of the cavernous hearing room." Clarke was the first of all the administration's high-level policymakers to speak directly to the families and to apologize formally for his and the government's failures.

> "Your government failed you," [Clarke] said. "Those entrusted with protecting you failed you. And I failed you. We tried hard, but that doesn't matter because we failed. And for that failure, I would ask, once all the facts are out, for your understanding and for your forgiveness."
>
> Then, for more than an hour, Clarke summarized a litany of frustrations about what he said was the administration's almost-casual response to dire indications of a terrorist attack that would occur within U.S. borders or overseas.
>
> Clarke, a career government terrorism expert who left the administration a year ago, defended the thesis contained in his new book that administration officials had ignored dire warnings about Al Qaeda and missed one opportunity after another to counter the threat posed by Bin Laden's network.[63]

Clarke's testimony resonated across America. The families' representatives made the rounds in the media whereupon they lauded Clarke's honesty. Clarke's testimony apparently resonated with the White House as well, though less than harmoniously.

> As his advisers tell it, President Bush had tired of the White House playing defense on issue after issue. So this week, his aides turned the full power of the executive branch on Richard A. Clarke, formerly the administration's

top counterterrorism official, who charges in his new book that Bush responded lackadaisically in 2001 to repeated warnings of an impending terrorist attack.

Bush's aides unleashed a two-pronged strategy that called for preemptive strikes on Clarke before most people could have seen his book, coupled with saturation media appearances by administration aides. They questioned the truthfulness of Clarke's claims, his competence as an employee, the motives behind the book's timing, and even the sincerity of the pleasantries in his resignation letter and farewell photo session with Bush.

"The barrage was unusual for a White House that typically [ignored] its critics, and it was driven by White House calculations that Clarke would appear credible to average viewers" reported the *Washington Post*. "Bush's advisers [were] concerned that Clarke's assertions [were] capable of inflicting political damage on a president who [was] staking his claim for reelection in large measure on his fight against terrorism."

The administration had reason to be concerned if polling data were indicative. A Pew Poll conducted in the previous few days "found significant public interest in Clarke's criticisms, with nearly nine in 10 of the 1,065 Americans surveyed saying they had heard of Clarke's critique. Of those polled, 42 percent said they had heard 'a lot' about his claims and 47 percent said they had heard 'a little.'" As for the unusual "barrage" by the White House, President Bush's aides unleashed the two-pronged strategy just noted. Along with the maelstrom unleashed by Clarke's testimony was the resurrection of the issue of whether or not NSC advisor Rice would testify. The White House was frustrated and it was amid a reelection campaign. Furthermore, the U.S. was a year into a controversial war in Iraq that had increasingly become more unpopular. "National Security Advisor Condoleezza Rice, at the center of a controversy over her refusal to testify before the Sept. 11 commission, yesterday renewed her determination not to give public testimony and said she could not list anything she wished she had done differently in the months before the 2001 terrorist attacks." Dr. Rice may have made a mistake by going on the public airwaves to bat down Clarke's assertions about Rice's and President Bush's behavior with respect to 9/11. Many families of the victims wondered why Dr. Rice appeared on television criticizing Clarke's charges yet refused to testify before the 9/11 Commission. As for Clarke's apology to the families about his and others' decisions, Rice "brushed aside the notion that the U.S. government should apologize to Sept. 11 victims' families for not stopping the attacks, saying, 'It's important that we keep focused on who did this to us.' Rice asserted that 'we are safer today than we were on September 10,' and, asked whether there were any mistakes or misjudgments before the attacks, replied: 'I think we did what we knew how to do.'" Indeed, "Rice said she had 'absolutely nothing to hide' and 'would really like' to testify but will not because of the constitutional principle."[64]

Iraq's salience in the reelection campaign was increasing daily. Republicans, who controlled both houses of Congress, had been protective of the Bush administration; that airtight support was slipping. Many Republicans openly defended the Iraq decision during 2003 and had only recently begun to question the White House, understandably, since they felt their own reelection pressures. "Few congressional Republicans" were "willing to express publicly the frustration they speak of privately over the administration's reluctance to consult with Congress on its plans in Iraq." Moderate Republicans were under even more pressure. Senator Richard G. Lugar, the Indiana Republican who was chairman of the Senate's Foreign Relations Committee, had "been under growing pressure from congressional Democrats to hold hearings on the administration's plans."[65] Coming as it did while political fireworks were exploding in the 9/11 hearing rooms, these complaints added to pressure on the White House to do something.

The pressure was clearly building and the administration decided to unload its big guns. In the ninth 9/11 public hearing, just a little over a week after NSC advisor Rice defended her decision *not* to testify on principle, Dr. Rice became "the first national security advisor to journey to Capitol Hill to testify, in public and under oath" in order to testify before the 9/11 Commission, with many of the families in the audience. Reporters noted that Dr. Rice had to "defend her president and his actions on his most fundamental constitutional duty: protecting the nation's security." They further noted the building pressures: "Bush has made fighting terrorism the centerpiece of his presidency, and the war in Iraq is the centerpiece of his fight against terrorism. Yet American voters are expressing increasing doubts about his handling of the war as U.S. troops face deadly new attacks." Reporters used descriptions such as a "duel" between Clarke and Rice to characterize her testimony.[66] Whatever metaphor was most appropriate, Rice's testimony was extraordinary.

"In her long-awaited appearance before the bipartisan commission investigating the Sept. 11 attacks, Ms. Rice insisted under sometimes sharp questioning that Mr. Bush 'understood the threat, and he understood its importance,' as she put it in her opening statement." Describing one series of exchanges that became critical for getting the August 6, 2001, Presidential Daily Briefing (PDB) memo released, "Ms. Rice faced tough early questioning from Richard Ben-Veniste, a Democratic commission member and former Watergate prosecutor. In sometimes testy and confrontational exchanges, he pressed [Rice] on whether she had told the president about her knowledge of the presence of al Qaeda cells in the United States, which had been passed on to her by Richard A. Clarke, President Bush's former counterterrorism director." Rice gave as much as she took. During one exchange with former Senator Bob Kerrey (the replacement for Max Cleland) Kerrey "preceded his questioning by saying that he believed the war on terrorism was a war on radical Islam. He added that the United States did not understand how it was viewed by Muslims, and that he was very worried that the 'military tactics' being used in Iraq 'are going to do a number of things, and they're all bad,' including a civil war," eliciting applause from the audience. Rice riposted. "In answer to a question from Mr. Kerrey about why the United States had not responded militarily to the attack on the destroyer *Cole* in Yemen, Ms. Rice quoted from a Kerrey speech saying that the best response to the attack would perhaps be to deal with 'the threat of Saddam Hussein.'" In other words, she used former Senator Kerrey's own words following the 2000 USS *Cole* attack against the senator now questioning her. Kerrey was undeterred and focused on the still-classified memo, the August 6, 2001, PDB. "She did not mention the charges lodged recently by Mr. Clarke, who had been a counterterrorism official in both administrations, that the Bush administration was slow to awake to al Qaeda and, even after Sept. 11, 2001, was almost inexplicably preoccupied with Iraq." Rather, "Rice described Mr. Clarke as having worked closely with the Bush White House to develop a comprehensive antiterrorism approach and to promote antiterrorism measures that had lain dormant. Rice continued: 'While we were developing this new strategy to deal with al Qaeda, we also made decisions on a number of specific anti–al Qaeda initiatives that had been proposed by Dick Clarke,' she said. 'Many of these ideas had been deferred by the last administration, and some had been on the table since 1998.'" However, "on the critical question of what the Bush White House did in response to those warnings, Rice's performance was markedly less effective. Repeatedly, she described a White House inner circle that spent its time on broad strategy and left it up to the bureaucracy to decide how to meet the escalating threat, with no real follow-up from the White House."

The media ultimately focused on the news of the memo and Rice's apparent attempt to dodge it. Repeatedly, "Rice told the commission that warnings and memos that reached her desk—including a critical Aug. 6 CIA report on al Qaeda plans to attack the United States—were too vague to permit concrete action." Yet another description raised the classified memo in this way: "That piece of the puzzle remained in dispute in part because of questions about a key classified document that detailed terror threats to Bush about a month before the Sept. 11, 2001, attacks. Commissioners called on the White House to make the document public, which [seemed] certain to keep the investigation in the headlines."[67]

Before addressing the memo, we should note that the controversy was not merely over a particular memo, though this one was arguably explosive. Instead, it was over President Bush's general stewardship of national security. Some families and members of Congress believed that Bush was too aloof, worrying more about his vacation time than threats to U.S. national security. After Richard Clarke's charges and Dr. Rice's attempts at rebuttal, it was a certainty that the 9/11 Commission was going to address them directly. "When the Washington investigative machinery" got rolling, wrote one reporter, it took "a major event to stop it. National security Advisor Condoleezza Rice's defense of the Bush antiterrorism effort at yesterday's hearing before the 9/11 commission was not enough." On the issue of whether or not Bush was too aloof, "many [Democrats] felt that Rice's testimony pushed the trail of blame directly to Bush. 'Just one month before terrorists claimed the lives of 3,000 Americans at the World Trade Center and the Pentagon, President Bush was on a 30-day vacation in Crawford, Texas,' said Rep. Elijah E. Cummings (D-MD), chairman of the Congressional Black Caucus." Cummings also charged, thus conflating the two issues, that Bush's government received warning of al Qaeda's plans to attack while Bush cleared brush in Crawford, Texas.

What was the memo? It was clear that the memo had to do with warnings that went to the White House about 9/11 that apparently went unanswered. The central question was what did President Bush and his senior advisers know in the summer of 2001 about a flurry of terrorist threats picked up by intelligence services, and what did they do about it. Or apropos of Mr. Ben-Veniste's former Watergate experience, what did President Bush know and when did he know it? As noted above, Mr. Ben-Veniste sparred with Rice over the memo, attempting to bait her. As a member of the Commission, Ben-Veniste knew the contents of the memo but was bound by oath not to discuss directly its contents. He instead attempted to get Dr. Rice to discuss it before the public. Though watching it live was most dramatic, quoting the transcript actually gives a decent sense of how tense the exchanges were.

> I want to ask you some questions about the August 6, 2001, PDB. We had been advised in writing by the CIA on March 19, 2004, that the August 6 PDB was prepared and self generated by a CIA employee. Following Director Tenet's testimony on March 26 before us, the CIA clarified its version of events, saying that questions by the President prompted them to prepare the August 6 PDB. You have said to us in our meeting together earlier, in February, that the President directed the CIA to prepare the August 6 PDB.

Rice responded to the bait. "You said, did it not warn of attacks? It did not warn of attacks inside the United States. It was historical information based on old reporting. There was no new threat information, and it did not, in fact, warn of any coming attacks inside the United States." Mr. Ben Veniste continued:

> Now, you knew by August 2001 of al Qaeda involvement in the first World Trade Center bombing. Is that correct?
>   You knew that in 1999, late '99, in the Millennium threat period, that [the U.S. government] had thwarted an al Qaeda attempt to blow up Los Angeles International Airport and thwarted cells operating in Brooklyn, New York, and Boston, Massachusetts.
>   As of the August 6th briefing, you learned that al Qaeda members [had] resided or traveled to the United States for years and maintained a support system in the United States. And you learned that FBI information since the 1998 blind sheik warning of hijackings to free the blind sheik indicated a pattern of suspicious activity in the country, up until August 6th, consistent with preparation for hijackings. Isn't that so?

Rice asked Ben-Veniste whether he wished her to answer questions in a series, showing some frustration and perhaps a lack of experience with being interrogated. Mr. Ben-Veniste pressed further:

> You have indicated here that this was some historical document. And I am asking you whether it is not the case that you learned in the PDB memo of

August 6th that the FBI was saying that it had information suggesting that preparations—not historically, but ongoing, along with these numerous full-field investigations against al Qaeda cells—that preparations were being made consistent with hijackings within the United States.

Continuing to appear flustered, Rice said "What the August 6th PDB said—and perhaps I should read it to you," at which point Ben-Veniste zeroed in: "We would be happy to have it declassified in full at this time—(applause)—including its title." The audience in the hearing room erupted in applause, including several representatives of the families. After a couple of additional short exchanges in which Ben-Veniste attempted to push his advantage and Rice continued to regain her composure, Rice responded in a lengthy colloquy.

> May I address the question, sir? The fact is that this August 6th PDB was in response to the president's questions about whether or not something might happen or something might be planned by al Qaeda inside the United States. He asked because all of the threat reporting, or the threat reporting that was actionable, was about the threats abroad, not about the United States.
>
> This particular PDB had a long section on what bin Laden had wanted to do—speculative, much of it—in '97, '98, that he had in fact liked the results of the 1993 bombing. It had a number of discussions of—it had a discussion of whether or not they might use hijacking to try and free a prisoner who was being held in the United States, Rassam. It reported that the FBI had full field investigations underway. And we checked on the issue of whether or not there was something going on with surveillance of buildings, and we were told, I believe, that the issue was the courthouse in which this might take place.
>
> Commissioner, this was not a warning. This was a historic memo—historical memo prepared by the agency because the President was asking questions about what we knew about the inside.

Ben-Veniste again asked Dr. Rice if she would not wish to declassify the PDB so others could read for themselves whether it was "historical" or "dire."

> I want to repeat that when this document was presented, it was presented as, yes, there were some frightening things—and by the way, I was not at Crawford, but the president and I were in contact, and I might have even been, though I can't remember, with him by video link during that time.

The president was told this is historical information—I'm told he was told this is historical information. And there was nothing actionable in this. The president knew that the FBI was pursuing this issue. The president knew that the director of Central Intelligence was pursuing this issue. And there was no new threat information in this document to pursue.

Mr. Ben-Veniste then asked Rice effectively whether she thought the president had taken the warning seriously. Had the administration done something actionable, could not at least part of 9/11 been avoided? Rice's response is again worth quoting in full.

My view, Commissioner Ben-Veniste, as I said to Chairman Kean, is that, first of all, the director of Central Intelligence and the director of the FBI, given the level of threat, were doing what they thought they could do to deal with the threat that we faced. There was no threat reporting of any substance about an attack coming in the United States. And the director of the FBI and the director of the CIA, had they received information, I am quite certain, given that the director of the CIA met frequently face to face with the President of the United States, that he would have made that available to the President or to me.

I do not believe that it is a good analysis to go back and assume that somehow maybe we would have gotten lucky by, quote, "shaking the trees." Dick Clarke was shaking the trees, director of Central Intelligence was shaking the trees, director of the FBI was shaking the trees. We had a structural problem in the United States.[68]

So there it was. The federal government, not the Bush administration in particular, had a structural problem. That guaranteed the memo would be released. And soon it provided additional fodder for the families and critics who felt the Bush administration had failed. In fact the memo was released the following day but not without Mr. Ben-Veniste prompting Dr. Rice to repeat the title of the memo: "Bin Laden Determined to Strike in U.S."

A few days later veteran *Washington Post* reporter Dana Priest wrote a column which began: "By the time a CIA briefer gave President Bush the Aug. 6, 2001, President's Daily Brief headlined 'Bin Laden Determined To Strike in US,' the president had seen a stream of alarming reports on al Qaeda's intentions." Additionally, the president's top advisers had seen the same "stream of alarming reports." "So had Vice President Cheney and Bush's top national security team, according to newly declassified information released yesterday by the commission investigating the Sept. 11, 2001, attacks." Priest reported that the PDB "ended with two paragraphs of circumstantial evidence that al Qaeda operatives might already be in the United States preparing 'for hijackings or other types of attacks' and that the FBI and the CIA were investigating a call to the U.S. Embassy in the United Arab Emirates in May 'saying that a group of Bin Laden supporters was in the US planning attacks with explosives.'"[69]

On the same day the *New York Times* reported on then-DCI George Tenet's testimony before the 9/11 Commission. Though his testimony was somewhat less explosive, Tenet did admit that the CIA had made mistakes. He also testified that the "light was blinking red" and he and the CIA kicked up their efforts; alas, their efforts were not enough.[70] Tenet's assertion of increased activity on behalf of the CIA was backed up within 24 hours. Douglas Jehl reported that in December 1998—during the Clinton administration—Director Tenet himself had declared "war" on al Qaeda. Disappointingly, however, the "directive had 'little overall effect' within the Central Intelligence Agency and the rest of the $30 billion intelligence community, spread across more than a dozen agencies, according to a staff report by the presidential commission looking into the Sept. 11 attacks."[71]

Interestingly, the Bush administration's response may have reflected precisely President Bush's and Vice President Cheney's view of executive power and the view that showing remorse equaled showing weakness. That perception continued to dog the administration through the elections and well into 2006. In what would become an uncomfortable reaction from Bush during the presidential debates later that year, President Bush reportedly consciously neglected some five opportunities "to offer regrets" for the administration's behavior with respect to 9/11. Though it is impossible to be precise in attributing how much the administration's unwillingness to express remorse exacerbated the families' anger, the effect was substantial.

SUMMARY

In this chapter multiple societal influences following 9/11 were considered. They included the philosophical debate at the heart of America's response to 9/11 and what became the Iraq War. The debate occurred outside the government in society at large, but it also, importantly, occurred inside the halls of U.S. national security policymaking. One of the most important philosophical debates was between moderate, traditionalist Republican internationalists and their fellow Republican neoconservatives. The former George H. W. Bush administration was staffed with many from the former camp and they reappeared in the George W. Bush administration quite naturally. However, the neoconservatives, many of whom also were former Bush administration policymakers, also appeared in the George W. Bush administration. They had probably been relatively active in the first George H. W. Bush administration but they grew in importance following eight years of the Clinton presidency. They believed that President Clinton's years in office represented foreign policy drift. They believed, as well, that the time had come for their agenda to be tested in the Bush (43) administration to correct years of what they saw as neglect. Their timing was important as it intersected with the events of 9/11 and what followed. They used 9/11, justly in their minds, to foster their neoconservative national security agenda and to promote Western democratic values globally.

We also considered another critical societal input that hastened the Intelligence Reform and Terrorism Prevention Act. That societal input was the victims' families as a special-interest group. Special-interest groups are often seen negatively. Here, no such connotation was intended. America is, at its heart, a pluralistic society in which competing demands employ special-interest groups—often comprised of former policymakers—to lobby for their respective interests. To generalize about any single group would be foolhardy. For our purposes, the special-interest group of the families was not considered good or bad; rather it was simply considered a potent force whose influence grew over time and especially during an election year. Clearly, not all the families were in lockstep politically, culturally, economically, or in any other way. But they did have one thing that drew them together: they all had suffered personal tragedies on 9/11 when their family members' lives were taken. In a dramatic and profound event such as 9/11, the personal tragedies were synergistic. The families became an emotive political force in U.S. national security and they influenced the remaking of U.S. national security policy in 9/11's wake.

In the next chapter, we examine government itself as a source of U.S. national security policy. The huge national security bureaucracy that was built up during the Cold War became an important input to policymaking:

rejection of isolationism forever and in its place *Pax Americana*. That Cold War machinery was relatively successful at thwarting what its masters saw as Soviet tyranny. Following the demise of the Soviet Union, however, the machinery was not disassembled; instead, it persisted, doing what it had done for generations. When 9/11 occurred the machinery was not entirely prepared to deal with it. The world had changed considerably and governmental bureaucracies and institutions created to protect America were ill-equipped for those changes. Following 9/11, the bureaucracy was forced to respond.

NOTES

1. George W. Bush, "The President's State of the Union Address," January 28, 2003, *op cit*. (The three lines quoted from the speech resulted in applauses counted in the transcript as numbers 45 and 46.)

2. Alan Sipress, "Policy Divide Thwarts Powell in Mideast Effort," *Washington Post*, April 26, 2002. The quote was actually: "With Powell back from the [Middle East], Bush has yet to resolve what a former State Department official called the 'battle royal' between Defense and State, delaying the adoption of a plan on how to proceed." But the piece made clear that while the specific issue was Israel and how hard Bush would lean on Prime Minister Ariel Sharon, the battle was much broader and covered a range of issues. Moreover, while the piece suggested the "battle" was simply between the State and Defense Departments the entire article made it clear that neoconservatives were strategically located in the vice president's office as well as the NSC in addition to the Pentagon.

3. The appellation neoconservatives (or simply neocons) was ascribed these foreign policy intellectuals and elites by the media. They have more or less accepted the name. However, in the late 1980s and early 1990s several of the foreign policy elites who had served under Presidents Reagan and George H.W. Bush, many of whom would go on to serve George W. Bush, called themselves the Vulcans. See David Rothkopf, *Running the World*, *op cit*., 220.

4. Project for the New American Century, "Statement of Principles," June 3, 1997, http://www.new-americancentury.org/statementofprinciples.htm (accessed February 5, 2004), This organization is known by the acronym initialization PNAC.

5. Project for the New American Century, "Statement of Principles," June 3, 1997.

6. Alan Sipress, "Policy Divide Thwarts Powell in Mideast Effort," *Washington Post*, April 26, 2002.

7. Alan Sipress, "Policy Divide Thwarts Powell in Mideast Effort," With respect to the ideological rift being described, it was discussed in M. Kent Bolton, *U.S. Foreign Policy and International Politics: George W. Bush, 9/11, and the Global-Terrorist Hydra* (Englewood Cliffs, NJ: Prentice Hall, 2005). However, when most of the research for that book was done in 2002, a good deal of evidence about squabbles between traditional competitors, the Departments of State and Defense, was unearthed. Little then had surfaced on the

vice president's office and its connection to other neoconservatives in the Pentagon. The vice president was frequently described as "powerful" or even the "most powerful" vice president in recent memory but the degree to which he orchestrated his positions at the NSC principals level was not generally known then. Consequently, *U.S. Foreign Policy and International Politics* underestimated the influence of the vice president and his advisers, notably I. Lewis "Scooter" Libby, David Addington, and a couple of others.

8. To be clear, there were other signatures on PNAC's statement of principles, but here only those who served in the Bush 43 Administration were identified.

9. As George W. Bush campaigned against Vice President Al Gore in 2000, he often suggested in campaign speeches that the Clinton-Gore team had had their chance to solve the big issues plaguing America and had failed. "On all the big issues facing this country, our message on November 7 will be loud and clear: you've had your chance. You have not led, and we will," said candidate Bush on November 3, 2000. He repeated the same many times after becoming president.

10. Elizabeth Becker and James Dao, under the general heading of Hearts and Minds, "Bush Will Keep Wartime Office Promoting U.S." *New York Times*, February 19, 2002.

11. At this writing, former PM Ariel Sharon remains in a coma and Hamas has replaced Fatah as the democratically elected leader of the Palestinian people. Yasser Arafat died in fall 2004.

12. Alan Sipress, "Policy Divide Thwarts Powell in Mideast Effort."

13. Alan Sipress, "Policy Divide Thwarts Powell in Mideast Effort."

14. Thom Shanker and Eric Schmitt, "Rumsfeld Seeks Consensus Through Jousting," *New York Times*, March 19, 2003.

15. Thom Shanker and Eric Schmitt, "Rumsfeld Seeks Consensus Through Jousting," *New York Times*. During the Gerald R. Ford administration, Donald Rumsfeld replaced James Schlesinger as secretary of defense; also a young Republican rising star named Dick Cheney served as President Ford's chief of staff.

16. Bob Woodward, *Plan of Attack* (New York: Simon and Schuster, 2004), 29.

17. Bob Woodward, *Plan of Attack,* 27–28.

18. Lawrence B. Wilkerson, "The White House Cabal," *Los Angeles Times*, October 25, 2005, http://www.latimes.com/news/opinion/commentary/la-oe-wilkerson25oct25,0, 7455395.story?coll=la-news-comment-opinions.

19. Lawrence B. Wilkerson, "Weighing the Uniqueness of the Bush Administration's National Security Decision-Making Process: Boon or Danger to America?" (speech, New America Foundation, American Strategy Program Policy Forum, October 19, 2005), http://www.newamerica.net/Download_Docs/pdfs/Doc_File_2644_1.pdf (accessed November 12, 2005).

20. For quotes from Bush's 2002 State of the Union speech see George W. Bush, "The President's State of the Union Address," January 29, 2002, http://www.whitehouse.gov/ news/releases/2002/01/20020129-11.html (accessed February 1, 2002); for quotes from his 2003 speech see George W. Bush, "The President's State of the Union Address," January 28, 2003, http://www.whitehouse.gov/news/releases/2003/01/print/20030128-19 .html (accessed January 29, 2003). For the president's characterization of Kim Jong Il as a pygmy, see *Newsweek*, May 19, 2002, http://www.msnbc.com/news/754330.asp (accessed December 21, 2002).

21. It is empirically arguable whether the neoconservative's reliance on muscular foreign policy has actually changed things for the better. Clearly, the ultimate results of the Iraq War will not be known for some time. A current snapshot does not bode well for neoconservative thinking. If a democracy of sorts eventually emerges in Iraq then the Iraq War may well prove worth its exorbitant costs. During this writing, Iran's surrogate in Lebanon, Hezbollah, fought the Israelis using Lebanon and its population as cover. Israel's image as having a highly vaunted military was questioned by Israelis as a result. Finally, a recent opinion piece by the *New York Times'* Nicholas Kristof challenged the claim of the Bush administration policy's effectiveness with respect to North Korea. See Nicolas D. Kristof, "Talking to Evil," *New York Times*, August 13, 2006, http://select.nytimes.com/2006/08/13/opinion/13kristof.html.

22. Chalabi's name is variously spelled Ahmed and Ahmad.

23. Robin Wright, "White House Divided over Reconstruction," *Los Angeles Times*, April 2, 2003, http://www.latimes.com/news/nationworld/iraq/homefront/la-war-postwar 2apr02,1,7358865.story? coll=la%2Dhome%2Dheadlines.

24. Glenn Kessler, "State-Defense Policy Rivalry Intensifying," *Washington Post*, April 22, 2003; Maura Reynolds, "Bush Commitment Is Key to 'Road Map' for Mideast," *Los Angeles Times*, April 30, 2003, http://www.latimes.com/news/nationworld/nation/ la-fg-bush30apr30001423,1,2491552.story ?coll=la%2Dheadlines%2Dnation.

25. Glenn Kessler, "State-Defense Policy Rivalry Intensifying."

26. Glenn Kessler, "State-Defense Policy Rivalry Intensifying."

27. New York Times, "Rumsfeld Denies the U.S. Has Plans for Permanent Iraq Bases," *New York Times*, April 22, 2003, http://www.nytimes.com/2003/04/22/international/world-special/22PENT.html.

28. Mike Allen, "Expert on Terrorism to Direct Rebuilding," *Washington Post*, May 1, 2003, http://www.washingtonpost.com/ac2/wp-dyn/A2950-2003May1.html.

29. Sonni Efron, "Diplomats on the Defensive," *Los Angeles Times*, May 8, 2003, http://www.latimes.com/news/nationworld/world/la-fg-state8may08,1,467133.story?coll =la%2Dhome%2Dheadlines.

30. Robin Wright, "U.S. Ends Talks with Iran over Al Qaeda Links," *Los Angeles Times*, May 21, 2003, http://www.latimes.com/news/nationworld/world/la-fg-usiran 21may21,1,3914095.story?coll= la%2Dheadlines%2Dworld.

31. James Risen, "Prewar Views of Iraq Threat Are Under Review by CIA," *New York Times*, May 22, 2003.

32. Michael Dobbs, "Back in Political Forefront," *Washington Post*, May 27, 2003.

33. Helene Cooper, "Rice's Hurdles on Middle East Begin at Home," *New York Times*, August 10, 2006, http://www.nytimes.com/2006/08/10/washington/10rice.html. To quote the piece briefly: "On her recent trips to the Middle East, Ms. Rice was accompanied by two men with very different outlooks on the conflict: Elliott Abrams, senior director at the National Security Council, and C. David Welch, a career diplomat and former ambassador to Egypt who is assistant secretary of state for Near East affairs." Then "Mr. Welch represents the traditional State Department view that the United States should serve as a neutral broker in the Middle East. Mr. Abrams, a neoconservative with strong ties to Mr. Cheney, has pushed the administration to throw its support behind Israel." Interestingly,

Cooper quoted "one senior administration official" as saying "'The genius of Elliott Abrams is that he's Elliott Abrams,' one senior administration official said. 'How can he be accused of not sufficiently supporting Israel?'"

34. Ronald Brownstein, "Maneuvering Over 'Road Map' for the Mideast," *Los Angeles Times*, May 26, 2003, http://www.latimes.com/news/nationworld/nation/la-na-out look26may26,1,7828987.column? coll=la%2Dheadlines%2Dnation (my emphasis).

35. Mark Fineman, Warren Vieth, and Robin Wright, "Dissolving Iraqi Army Seen by Many as a Costly Move," *Los Angeles Times*, August 23, 2003, http://www.latimes .com/news/nationworld/world/la-fg-iraqarmy24aug24002421,1,6880219.story?coll =la-headlines-world.

36. Glenn Kessler and Peter Slevin, "Rice Fails to Repair Rifts, Officials Say: Cabinet Rivalries Complicate Her Role," *Washington Post*, October 12, 2003.

37. Glenn Kessler and Peter Slevin, "Rice Fails to Repair Rifts, Officials Say."

38. Mark Hosenball, Michael Isikoff, and Evan Thomas, "Cheney's Long Path to War," *Newsweek*, November 8, 2003: http://www.msnbc.com/news/991211.asp.

39. Mark Hosenball, Michael Isikoff, and Evan Thomas, "Cheney's Long Path to War," (my emphasis).

40. Mark Hosenball, Michael Isikoff and Evan Thomas, "Cheney's Long Path to War," (my emphasis).

41. Bob Woodward, *Plan of Attack*, (New York: Simon and Schuster, 2004), 409–411 in the "Epilogue." Also see the same account in Bob Woodward, "Cheney Was Unwavering in Desire to Go to War," *Washington Post*, April 20, 2004, http://www.washingtonpost .com/wp-dyn/articles/A25550-2004Apr19.html.

42. On Cheney's damage from the Libby case and other issues, see Paul Richter, "Cheney Still in Background, but Not Unscathed," *Los Angles Times*, October 29, 2005, http://www.latimes.com/news/nationworld/nation/la-na-cheney29oct29,1,3843933 .story?coll=la-headlines-nation. Also see Elisabeth Bumiller and Eric Schmitt, "The Vice President," *New York Times*, October 30, 2005, http://nytimes.com/2005/10/30/politics/ 30cheney.html. For evidence of the waning power of the "old guard," in this case simply a cognate for the neoconservatives who had gained power during Bush's first term: "The new civilian leadership team that has moved into place under Defense Secretary Donald H. Rumsfeld over the past few months is shaping up to be less ideological, more balanced, and more attuned to Congress than the first-term group it has succeeded, according to defense analysts and lawmakers," In Bradley Graham, "At Pentagon, Less Ideology, More Balance," *Washington Post*, August 22, 2005, http://www.washing-tonpost.com/wp-dyn/ content/article/2005/08/21/AR2005082100800.html. Also see Peter Baker and Jim Vande-Hei, "Bush Team Rethinks Its Plan for Recovery," *Washington Post*, December 29, 2005, http://www.washingtonpost.com/wp-dyn/content/article/2005/12/28/AR2005122801517 .html. Bush advisers worried that Bush's legacy would be Iraq only, which caused a high-level political debate in Washington. Accordingly, "White House counselor Dan Bartlett and communications director Nicolle Wallace counseled a more textured approach. The same-old Bush was not enough, they said; he needed to be more detailed about his strategy in Iraq and, most of all, more open in admitting mistakes—something that does not come easily to Bush." Josh Bolten, who eventually replaced Andrew Card as Bush's second chief of staff, reportedly is more attuned to bolstering the president's legacy.

43. *Intelligence Authorization Act for Fiscal Year 2003*, Public Law 107–306, H.R. 4628, 107th Cong., 2nd sess.,116 Statute 2383, Title VI, p, 26. The initial act set a deadline for the committee's work of eighteen months. Subsequently, the 108th Congress, 2nd session amended the original statute lengthening the committee's deadline by two months or a total of twenty months. (See Public Law 108-207.)

44. See http://www.9-11commission.gov/family/index.htm, a link in perpetuity now under the control of the National Archives (accessed July 24, 2004).

45. "Statement of the Family Steering Committee for The 9/11 Commission," 9/11 CitizensWatch, March 8, 2004, http://www.911citizenswatch.org/modules.php?op =modload&name=News&file=article&sid=110&mode=thread&order=0&thold=0 (accessed July 27, 2004).

46. The Joint Inquiry may be found at: http://www.gpoaccess.gov/serialset/creports/pdf/fullreport.pdf (accessed in January 2003). The address was checked again in January 2006, at which time the full report was still available online.

47. The 9/11 Public Discourse Project, "Final Report Card on 9/11 Commission Recommendations," December 5, 2005, http://www.9-11pdp.org. For the Families Steering Committee's frustrations, see John Prados, "Slow Walked and Stonewalled," *The Bulletin of the Atomic Scientists*, March/April 2003, http://www.thebulletin.org/article.php?art_ ofn=ma03prados. For the families' comments on the 9/11 Commission's Final Report see 9/11 CitizensWatch, "Citizens Critique of Flawed 9/11 Commission Process," July 24, 2004, http://www.911citizens-watch.org/modules.php?op=modload&name=News&file= article&sid=353&mode=thread&order=0& thold=0 (accessed December 19, 2004).

48. Maura Reynolds, "Bush Commitment Is Key to 'Road Map' for Mideast," *Los Angeles Times*, April 30, 2003, http://www.latimes.com/news/nationworld/nation/la-fg-bush 30apr30001423,1,2491552.story? coll=la%2Dheadlines%2Dnation.

49. Jeff Gerth, "Officials Who Failed to Put Hijackers on Watch List Not Named," *New York Times*, May 15, 2003, http://www.nytimes.com/2003/05/15/international/worldspecial/ 15INTE.html.

50. David Johnson and Don Van Natta Jr., "Congressional Inquiry into 9/11 Will Look back as Far as 1986," *New York Times*, June 5, 2002, http://www.nytimes.com/2002/06/ 05/politics/05INQU.html.

51. Kirk Semple, "Ceremonies Nationwide Commemorate Sept. 11 Attacks," *New York Times*, September 11, 2003, http://www.nytimes.com/2003/09/11/national/11CND-ATTA .html; Michael Powell and Dale Russakoff, "In New York, Roll of Names Is Part of Quiet Remembrance," *Washington Post*, September 11, 2003, http://www.washingtonpost.com/ ac2/wp-dyn?pagename=article&contentId=A59167-2003Sep11.

52. E.J. Dionne, Jr., "To Honor Service," *Washington Post*, September 12, 2003, http://www.washingtonpost. com/ac2/wp-dyn/A63094-2003Sep11.html.

53. Dan Eggen, "Sept. 11 Panel Defends Director's Impartiality: Concerns of Victims' Relatives over Zelikow's National Security Ties Are Dismissed," *Washington Post*, October 14, 2003.

54. Laurence Arnold, "9-11 Families Press for Intel Changes," Associated Press, October 20, 2003.

55. Philip Shenon, "9/11 Commission Could Subpoena Oval Office Files," *New York Times*, October 26, 2003, http://www.nytimes.com/2003/10/26/national/26KEAN.html.

56. Ken Silverstein, "Congress Presses White House for 9/11 Papers," *Los Angeles Times*, October 27, 2003, http://www.latimes.com/news/nationworld/nation/la-na-commish 27oct27,1,6597578.story?coll=la-headlines-nation; Ceci Connolly, "Senators Call on White House to Share Records With 9/11 Panel," *Washington Post*, October 27, 2003. Senator Joe Lieberman ran for reelection for his senate Seat in the primary elections in August 2006. For being too close to the Bush administration Lieberman was successfully challenged by political newcomer Ned Lamont who ran on an anti–Iraq War platform.

57. Editorial, "Silence Feeds 9/11 Theories," *Los Angeles Times*, October 28, 2003, http://www.latimes.com/news/opinion/editorials/la-ed-withhold28oct28,1,1355905 .story?coll=la-news-alert.

58. Dan Eggen, "9/11 Panel Unlikely to Get Later Deadline," *Washington Post*, January 19, 2004, http://www.washingtonpost.com/ac2/wp-dyn/A28025-2004Jan18.html (my emphasis).

59. Dan Eggen, "Battle Over 9/11 Panel's Deadline Intensifies," *Washington Post*, January 29, 2004, http://www.washingtonpost.com/ac2/wp-dyn/A58200-2004Jan28.html.

60. Philip Shenon, "Senators to Request Extension for 9/11 Panel," *New York Times*, January 30, 2004, http://www.nytimes.com/2004/01/30/politics/30TERR.html.

61. Mike Allen and Dan Eggen, "Extension of 9/11 Probe Backed," *Washington Post*, February 5, 2004, http://www.washingtonpost.com/wp-dyn/articles/A13964-2004Feb4 .html.

62. Dan Eggen, "Hastert Still against Giving 9/11 Panel More Time," *Washington Post*, February 26, 2004, http://www.washingtonpost.com/wp-dyn/articles/A6948-2004 Feb25.html.

63. Josh Meyer, "Terror Not a Bush Priority before 9/11, Witness Says," *Los Angeles Times*, March 25, 2004, http://www.latimes.com/news/nationworld/nation/ la-na-commish25mar25,1,7704823.story?coll=la-headlines-nation.

64. Dana Milbank and Walter Pincus, "Rice Defends Refusal to Testify," *Washington Post*, March 29, 2004, http://www.washingtonpost.com/ac2/wp-dyn/A31904-2004Mar28 .html

65. Mary Curtius, "Congress Wants Answers on Bush's Plans for Iraq," *Los Angeles Times*, April 19, 2004, http://www.latimes.com/news/nationworld/iraq/la-na-congiraq 19apr19,1,2678079.story?coll=la-home-headlines.

66. Maura Reynolds, "A Chance to Erase Doubts, or Raise Them," *Los Angeles Times*, April 7, 2004, http://www.latimes.com/news/nationworld/nation/la-na-rice7apr07,1 ,3642779.story?coll=la-headlines-nation.

67. David Stout, "Bush Understood Threat Posed by Al Qaeda, Rice Tells Panel," *New York Times*, April 8, 2004, http://www.nytimes.com/2004/04/08/politics/08CND-PANE .html. The second and third quotes respectively are Maura Reynolds, "Testimony Paints Image of Passive Inner Circle," *Los Angeles Times*, April 8, 2004, http://www.latimes.com/ news/nationworld/nation/la-na-assess9apr09,1,3756594.story? coll=la-headlines-nation; and David Von Drehle, "Zeroing In on One Classified Document," *Washington Post*, April 9, 2004, http://www.washingtonpost.com/ac2/wp-dyn/A62481-2004Apr8.html.

68. National Commission on Terrorist Attacks upon The United States, *Ninth Public Hearing*, witness Dr. Condoleezza Rice, April 8, 2004, http://www.9-11commission

.gov/archive/hearing9/9-11Commission_Hearing_2004-04-08.pdf (accessed on July 30, 2004).

69. Dana Priest, "Panel Says Bush Saw Repeated Warnings," *Washington Post*, April 14, 2004, http://www.washingtonpost.com/ac2/wp-dyn/A9642-2004Apr13.html.

70. Terence Neilan, "CIA Chief Defends Agency but Allows 'We Made Mistakes,'" *New York Times*, April 14, 2004, http://www.nytimes.com/2004/04/14/politics/14CND-PANE .html.

71. Douglas Jehl, "Terror Memo Disregarded, Report Says," *New York Times*, April 15, 2004, http://www.nytimes.com/2004/04/15/politics/15INTE.html.

CHAPTER 8

Governmental Postmortems and U.S. National Security Policymaking

Responding to widespread criticism of the government's handling of terrorist threats, President Bush called tonight for the creation of a cabinet department for domestic defense that would combine 22 federal agencies into a single one intended to prevent attacks against the United States.

Mr. Bush's proposal, which included changes he resisted last fall when he appointed Gov. Tom Ridge of Pennsylvania to coordinate domestic security from the White House, would place the Customs Service, the Secret Service, the Immigration and Naturalization Service, and the Coast Guard in a new Department of Homeland Security with an initial annual budget of $37.5 billion.

—Elisabeth Bumiller and David E. Sanger,
"Bush, as Terror Inquiry Swirls, Seeks Cabinet Post on Security,"
New York Times, June 7, 2002

It is well-established that the intelligence community's structure and practices prior to the September 11 attacks were simply not up to the task of waging a global war on terror and protecting the homeland. The systemic intelligence community deficiencies during the "Summer of Threat" leading up to the attacks were summed up by the 9/11 Commission in two short sentences: "Information was not shared . . . Analysis was not pooled."

—The Commission on The Intelligence Capabilities of the
United States Regarding Weapons of Mass Destruction
(Robb-Silberman WMD Commission),
Report to the President of the United States, March 31, 2005

Following the attacks of 9/11, Americans predictably rallied around the flag in a display of national unity rarely seen in America. In chapter 3, we discussed the unity of purpose or Cold War consensus that formed near the beginning of the Cold War. Did a similar post-9/11 consensus form following 9/11 and its aftermath? At first glance, the answer appears to be a firm yes. Indeed, most Americans regardless of their specific politics unified around the president, the federal government, and the U.S. military, and around policies most Americans understood would be forthcoming: namely, a punitive attack against the nebulous al Qaeda network in retaliation for 9/11 and to forestall a repeat of its successful attacks. Though unified, it is unlikely that very many Americans fully comprehended what the eventual retaliation would entail. In fact, evidence exists that the Bush administration did not fully appreciate how vast the war on terror would become.

America had been attacked; the attackers represented an ideology that was clearly antithetical to America's way of life. Whatever the objective facts, many Americans vaguely perceived their country as a paragon of freedom and liberty and as appropriately associated with those virtues in international politics. Most Americans believed that America stood for something good (political freedom defined in a peculiarly American way) and thwarting its opposite (tyranny). Political freedom and opposition of tyranny were integral elements of America's origins and, therefore, a part of the American ethos and mythology that evolved while the U.S. was still an isolationist country. When transposed to America's behavior internationally, America's ethos has repeatedly revolved around finding an appropriate role in the world. Though America's appropriate role has always included the same mythology and ethos, only in the twentieth century did America's appropriate role include actively using America's vast resources and power to thwart tyranny internationally. Thus, the Cold War was precisely congruent with America's ethos.

Following 9/11, however, more than simply an American post-9/11 consensus existed; in fact, many of America's principal allies also felt compelled to draw together against the jihadis who attacked the U.S. on 9/11. America's relations with Europe and the European Union have always experienced ups and downs. While allies during the Cold War, the French and British both decided to create their own nuclear deterrence, calculating that America would be unlikely to risk its own existence over

London or Paris. They were doubtlessly correct. Comparing Europe's bygone grand past versus America's new superpower status has proved popular in Europe, ever since the U.S. became a superpower or "hegemonic power" as many Europeans perceived it. Nevertheless, the impetus to resist jihadi terror unleashed against the U.S. was somewhat generalized among America's allies. It was similarly understandable that eventually it would pass as America and Europe considered over time their different approaches. After 9/11, however, a consensus rarely ever seen briefly existed between the United States, as the victims of 9/11, and America's principal allies. On September 12, the French daily *Le Monde*—far from a booster for American hegemony—published a famous headline: "We are all Americans! We are all New Yorkers."[1] If America could be attacked with such devastating consequences from an amorphous non-state actor (al Qaeda), surely the British, French, Germans, and others could similarly be attacked.

Just as surely as 9/11 created a new post-9/11 consensus, its shelf life would ultimately deteriorate over time, absent another attack.[2] Indicators of both the national and international unity continued through much of 2002. Using the White House transcript of President Bush's State of the Union speech on January, 28, 2003, as a barometer, the president continued to elicit manifold applause lines before a Joint Session of Congress. (No fewer than seventy-five separate applauses were recorded on the transcript.)[3] Despite President Bush's political capital, by the time the commander in chief ordered U.S. troops to invade Iraq, the post-9/11 unity had begun to fragment internationally and even domestically.

Unity is associated with stasis: when the peoples of any pluralistic society are unified behind their government, few incentives exist for that government to change. Absent consensus, demands for change become more frequent. Though President George W. Bush was reelected in November 2004, he was, ironically, reelected with a mandate to change America's national security bureaucracy! Why? What changed the post-9/11 consensus forged in the crucible of the horrific attacks of 9/11? In chapter 6, we examined some external sources of change and how those helped to erode the consensus President Bush helped to create after 9/11. In chapter 7, we examined societal sources of change that created the demand for change. Insofar as dramatic change in a complex democracy is necessarily slow, consensus suffered as change appeared to languish. In this chapter we examine governmental inputs that caused increasing disunity as opposed to consensus. We argue that said government inputs hastened the reorganization of America's national security bureaucracies. Societal pressure created an impetus for the government to scrutinize itself. Those multiple postmortems thereby created an impetus for what became the Intelligence Reform and Terrorism Prevention Act, the first major reorganization of the president-NSC-policymaking model since the 1947 National Security Act.

COMMISSIONS, PANELS, AND OTHER GOVERNMENTAL SOURCES OF U.S. NATIONAL SECURITY CHANGE

We have repeatedly referred to the various postmortems, in particular, the so-called 9/11 Commission that came together to dissect failure associated with 9/11. Indeed, the 9/11 Commission would become the "Mother of All Postmortems." In what follows we examine three important formal postmortems and one informal one. The three formal ones were the Joint Inquiry (JI) conducted by the U.S. House Permanent Select Intelligence and the Senate Select Intelligence Committees, the 9/11 Commission, and the Robb-Silberman WMD Commission. One internal and far less disseminated postmortem was the Iraqi Survey Group's so-called "Duelfer Report." It too will be examined briefly.[4] How did these postmortems affect all the levels of government that determine and implement U.S. national security policymaking? And how did the postmortems result in the IRTPA?

Joint Inquiry

Shortly after 9/11, consensus existed in the United States and elsewhere with respect to President Bush's declared war against al Qaeda, what the president repeatedly called "evil." It may not be fair to suggest that consensus existed broadly vis-à-vis thwarting "evil." But consensus existed with respect to punishing al Qaeda and proactively altering U.S. national security policy to accomplish that goal in order to forestall additional attacks. President Bush had been president a mere nine months when the 9/11 attacks were launched. Nonetheless, within months pressure was being felt in Congress to discover what had led to the attacks. Had policymakers known about the threat and failed to act? Was America's intelligence community properly organized for the new transnational, non-state actors and the threats they now represented to America's national security? Over time, questions of policymaking errors followed. The intelligence community more or less evolved from the 1947 National Security Act with the tides of the Cold War as did the NSC, the president-NSC-policymaking model, and other national security institutions. The intelligence community was structured to collect intelligence on enemy *states* rather than non-state actors. The National Security Council and the president-NSC-policymaking model were similarly structured to help the president make policy based on timely intelligence about state actors. It was therefore necessary for Americans, the Bush (43) administration, and Congress to consider whether reforms needed to be made in light of the 9/11 attacks and the new transnational entities that launched them as well as the "failures" that permitted the attacks to succeed.

The Joint Inquiry sought to explore these questions and others. According to then-Senator Bob Graham (D-FL), former chair of the Senate Select Intelligence Committee, the Joint Inquiry included "both findings of fact and 19 recommendations for reform." The senator thanked his colleagues who had helped create the recommendations, his then-cochairman Senator Richard Shelby (R-AL), as well as the chairman and vice chairman of the House Intelligence Committee, then-Congressman Porter Goss (R-GA) and Congresswoman Jane Harman (D-CA), respectively. Interestingly, the original 1947 National Security Act (NSA) gave the then-DCI relatively muscular authorities over the intelligence community but for a multiplicity of reasons—not the least of which was the Department of Defense's budgetary control over large parts of the intelligence community—the DCI never became more than the nominal head of the intelligence community. The Joint Inquiry and the other postmortems attempted to change that.

Almost exactly one year before the 9/11 Commission released its final report, Senator Bob Graham, speaking of the Joint Inquiry, said that the Joint Inquiry fulfilled "the commitment that was made to the American people and particularly to the families of those who perished in" the 9/11 tragedy. What was the Joint Inquiry's commitment about which the Senator Graham spoke? "The commitment was to conduct a thorough search for the truth about what our intelligence agencies knew or should have known about al-Qaida[5] and its intentions prior to September 11." Beyond the search for facts, the Joint Inquiry "was then to apply the lessons learned from that experience to reform the intelligence community in such a way as to mitigate the likelihood of a repetition of September 11." Senator Graham reported back to President Bush, the 9/11 victims' families, and the American people that the Joint Inquiry's work was completed in summer 2003.[6] The Joint Inquiry set "three principal goals" for its work: 1) to "conduct a factual review of what the Intelligence Community knew or should have known prior to September 11, 2001, regarding the international terrorist threat to the United States, to include the scope and nature of any possible international terrorist attacks against the United States and its interests"; 2) to "identify and examine any systemic problems that may have impeded the Intelligence Community in learning of or preventing these attacks in advance"; and 3) to "make recommendations to improve the Intelligence Community's ability to identify and prevent future international terrorist attacks."[7] In theory, each of the three was a measurable objective. Inasmuch as none of the goals addressed potential policymaking errors, it was a certainty that the Joint Inquiry would be followed by other postmortems.

The Joint Inquiry published its initial report in late 2002. When the Joint Inquiry was published online in December 2002, the report created an understandable stir among the public and particularly among families of the 9/11 victims. Some 860 pages of analysis—a number of which were redacted—produced a report of intelligence failures in spades. Apart from the redactions the Joint Inquiry was enormously useful for purposes of subsequent postmortems. That proved fortuitous as the Joint Inquiry raised nearly as many questions as it answered. The Joint Inquiry made a number of substantive recommendations which ultimately ended up being recommended again in the 9/11 Commission's final report and echoed yet again in the so-called Robb-Silberman report. Since the recommendations will be considered below, they need not be discussed in depth here.[8] However, it is worth considering a few of the Joint Inquiry's more substantive findings as those findings created an impetus for change as well as an impetus for additional postmortems.

Under "Systemic Findings," the Joint Inquiry's first finding was that prior to 9/11, the intelligence community (IC) was neither well-organized nor well-equipped, and did not adequately adapt to meet the challenge posed by global terrorists focused on targets within the domestic United States. Serious gaps existed, according to the Joint Inquiry, between the collection coverage provided by U.S. foreign and domestic intelligence capabilities. Put simply, the intelligence community that evolved from the 1947 NSA through the Cold War through the post–Cold War era was not properly organized for a transnational threat such as al Qaeda. The result, according to the Joint Inquiry, was that "these problems greatly exacerbated the nation's vulnerability to an increasingly dangerous and immediate international terrorist threat inside the United States." Second, neither the U.S. government nor the intelligence community had a comprehensive counterterrorist strategy for combating the threats posed by Osama bin Laden's al Qaeda or similar threats. The director of central intelligence (DCI) was either unwilling or unable "to marshal the full range of Intelligence Community resources necessary to combat the growing threat to the United States." In other words, despite DCI Tenet's "declaration of war" on al Qaeda in 1998, little substantive action followed the declaration, which ultimately made the declaration ring hollow.

Another substantive finding concerned the analytic focus of the intelligence community. Analysis and analysts lacked incentives and the positions were seen as dead-end jobs in the community. There "was a dearth of creative, aggressive analysis targeting [bin Laden] and a persistent inability to comprehend the collective significance of individual pieces of intelligence." The lack of incentives resulted in a serious undermining of "the ability of U.S. policymakers to understand the full nature of the threat, and to make fully informed decisions." Similarly, the U.S. intelligence community lacked trained linguists in Arabic and other languages in which al Qaeda operatives and other terrorists might be monitored. Consequently, reams of intelligence data in languages other than English stacked up without being translated in a timely way. "Agencies within the Intelligence Community experienced backlogs in material awaiting translation, a shortage of language specialists and language-qualified field officers, and a readiness level of only 30 percent in the most critical terrorism-related languages used by terrorists." Another important finding concerned the National Security Agency (NSA), so secret that in the 1980s many still referred it "no such agency." That once secret and high-tech agency failed to modernize over time making its raw data unusable by the larger intelligence community. Additionally, the NSA was reluctant to share its data across the community. The NSA's purview, signals intelligence, was meaningless unless it was converted to usable data, processed, translated, and then passed along to agencies that could use "actionable" intelligence to stop terrorists (or for that matter state enemies) from doing America harm. Specifically, the Joint Inquiry charged that the NSA and the FBI did not work well together. In other words, turf battles between the two agencies hampered their overall cooperation for America's national security. More generally, the Joint Inquiry found "serious problems" in the sharing of information among various intelligence agencies. "Serious problems in information sharing . . . persisted, prior to September 11, between the Intelligence Community and relevant non–Intelligence Community agencies" including other federal, state, and local authorities. Importantly, that included information sharing at the highest level—the president-NSC-policymaking model and the president's NSC principals. The report implied that part of the problem was the lack of a central clearinghouse for intelligence. The federal government did not have a central place or site to which all types of intelligence and counterintelligence information could go for the entire government to access it. The report noted that the CIA had earlier created the Counterterrorism Center but that the CTC was limited to external threats only, as the CIA was proscribed by law from spying domestically. The Joint Inquiry was concerned that no such center existed *in* the U.S. leaving the U.S. at a clear disadvantage in the new era of non-state, transnational threats.

Another of the Joint Inquiry's findings was that al Qaeda and similar transnational organizations raised funds in a variety of ways—not typical of states—and the federal government had been remiss in finding new instruments to keep up with the global financial nexus, particularly the raft of methods used by non-state actors to transfer money globally. The next finding was rather stunning. It was that intelligence reporting from 1998 through the summer of 2001 was rife with warnings that al Qaeda intended to strike in the U.S. homeland! With the exception of the 1993 World Trade Center attacks, al Qaeda's previous attacks were directed at U.S. assets worldwide but not at the American homeland. The Joint Inquiry discovered information that suggested, in fact, that ample intelligence existed that al Qaeda devoted considerable energy to finding a way to attack the United States homeland. As the information came in, the federal government did virtually nothing to prepare for that eventuality.[9]

A *USA Today* article that accompanied the release of the Joint Inquiry's report summarized the Joint Inquiry's findings this way. "Among the persistent problems uncovered by" the Joint Inquiry were "lack of information sharing," "poor analysis," and "lopsided intelligence budgets." With respect to the latter, out of the estimated 30-plus billion dollars devoted to intelligence each year, some 80–85 percent of it was controlled by the Pentagon rather than the specific intelligence agency that collected and analyzed intelligence. As several of the intelligence community's assets were non–defense department assets, the relatively robust budget was not getting to the agencies that needed it. To cite the most obvious, the CIA, America's premiere human intelligence agency, had to wrest its share of intelligence budget from the 20–25 percent of the total budget not controlled by the defense department. Noting that the onus was on the intelligence community itself to stop resisting reform, the peroration of the *USA Today* piece read, "If the intelligence agencies won't seize the initiative to develop an effective master plan, then someone else will have to, in spite of all the risks that might entail."[10]

The findings were understandably shocking to many Americans. Americans who had never heard of al Qaeda or Osama bin Laden before 9/11 now learned that al Qaeda's designs against the U.S. homeland were not wholly unanticipated events.[11] The U.S. government generally and the intelligence community specifically had known for years that Osama bin Laden hated the United States and that al Qaeda trained *tens of thousands* of recruits over the course of several years. Indeed, al Qaeda and fellow travelers were connected to the first attack on the Twin Towers in 1993. Since 1993, bin Laden and others had been preparing to loose their thousands of recruits on America and its assets worldwide. In the interim, these same persons had attacked American embassies in Africa (1998), American civilian and military assets in Saudi Arabia (1996), and the USS *Cole* (2000) and had made no secret that these actions were leading to a some sort of spectacular attack on the U.S. homeland.

The Joint Inquiry report made clear that *al Qaeda had considered a variety of different ways of using airplanes to attack America.* For instance, the Joint Inquiry outlined the Bojinka Plot in which al Qaeda operatives including Khalid Sheik Mohammad (KSM), one of the principal "masterminds" in 9/11, planned to explode transpacific airliners.[12] KSM was the major planner and facilitator of the 9/11 attacks. He recruited the particular hijackers from the thousands of al Qaeda recruits. He worked out the logistical details for their activities in Afghanistan and Europe, their various trips to the U.S. during which they entered at different times and through different ports of entry, and acted as the main liaison between the hijackers (particularly Mohammad Atta) and Osama bin Laden. (Recently, during the spring of 2006, Khalid Sheik Mohammad's interviews from interrogations were used in the Zacarias Moussaoui trial in which KSM divulged that a "second wave" of attacks was planned for after 9/11, though the planning was far less advanced when America struck Afghanistan.)[13]

Clearly, the Joint Inquiry performed a valuable service. The committee looked through some one million documents and interviewed some 500 persons. The Joint Inquiry unearthed links that were known generally in the intelligence community but about which most Americans had never heard and against whom little preparation was made. How could this have happened? Part of the answer was, of course, in the Joint Inquiry's findings: the government had not evolved for the post–Cold War world; bureaucratic turf battles prevented large parts of the national security bureaucracy (first created by the 1947 NSA) from preparing for the non-state actors who threatened the United States in the post–Cold War era; and simply put, neither the Clinton nor Bush administrations created the necessary impetuses to counter effectively bureaucratic inertia. The Joint Inquiry also raised more questions than it answered; it thereby provided an impetus for subsequent postmortems. As noted, *USA Today*'s editorial board predicted that someone else would have to emerge to actually perform the massive job of reorganizing national security institutions whose incredible inertia had increased over the fifty-plus years of their lifetime. That someone else would be the so-called 9/11 Commission.

The 9/11 Commission: "The Mother of All Postmortems"

"Yielding to intense pressure from families of Sept. 11 victims, the White House agreed last night to a congressional compromise that would create an independent commission to investigate the terrorist attacks" read one article just about one month prior to the Joint Inquiry's online publication of its own report. At this early date, few could have guessed just how definitive, comprehensive, and insightful the 9/11 Commission's final work product would be. Before the 9/11 Commission finished its work, it would interview some 1200 persons in ten different nations and it would review some 2.5 million pages of documents. Nothing like it had ever been seen. Its final report was shorter than Joint Inquiry's (roughly 600 pages) but its disclosures, findings, and recommendations would go much further. It would become, in short, the "Mother of All Postmortems" in U.S. national security history. So popular did it become that it actually made the *New York Times* bestseller list for nonfiction—no mean feat for a government commission. Governmental prose and bureaucratese are normally excruciatingly painful to read.

The 9/11 Commission (officially, The National Commission on Terrorist Attacks upon the United States) almost did not see the light of day. Only the confluence of the victims' families and other factors created the 9/11 Commission. The 9/11 Commission's purview was nothing short of the entire president-NSC-policymaking model created and evolved from the 1947 NSA. The "wrangling" that preceded the Commission's creation was described as follows: the agreement put "an end to several months of wrangling between Congress and the Bush administration, which had objected to details of the commission's makeup. Senator Tom Daschle, the [then] Democratic leader, said earlier Thursday that the administration was stalling on the plan because it could not control the commission's eventual findings." Interestingly, a Republican Senator, John McCain (R-AZ), pressured the Bush White House to relent, allowing the creation of the Commission. McCain made a central compromise, giving the Committee a more bipartisan appearance. "The key to the compromise was allowing Senator John McCain, Republican of Arizona, to appoint one of the Republican slots. Mr. McCain had fought zealously for the Commission for months, leveling bitter criticism at the White House for stonewalling the 9/11 Commission's creation; victims' families' representatives as well as Democrats believed Senator McCain would appoint someone who would be aggressive in questioning public officials. At the same time, the White House was satisfied that Mr. McCain's appointment would not be partisan in nature."[14]

Once created, the Commission assumed an expansive and comprehensive mandate, describing its own scope as "sweeping." "The law directed us to investigate 'facts and circumstances relating to the terrorist attacks of September 11, 2001,' including those relating to intelligence agencies, law enforcement agencies, diplomacy, immigration issues and border control, the flow of assets to terrorist organizations, commercial aviation, the role of congressional oversight and resource allocation, and other areas determined relevant by the Commission." Much of the discussion in 2002 and 2003 had been on intelligence failures; clearly, intelligence failures remained a central piece of the puzzle. However, the 9/11 Commission's mandate permitted the ten commissioners (five Republicans and five Democrats) to investigate the facts and circumstances relating to the attacks including diplomacy, congressional oversight, funding of America's national security bureaucracy—in short, policymaking and policy implementation—and specifically the president-NSC-policymaking model. When the Commission published its final report in July 2004, it would ultimately make scores of recommendations for restructuring the entire national security bureaucracy created by the 1947 National Security Act. It would become the most sweeping reorganization of the U.S. government's national security policymaking in over a half century.

Once the 9/11 Commission was created, bureaucratic scrambles to get out in front of the Commission were considerable and seen at the highest levels of government as the president and other executive national security agencies sought to outflank the Commission's work. "President Bush said tonight that he would create a Terrorist Threat Integration Center to merge units at the CIA, FBI, and other agencies into a single government unit intended to strengthen the collection and analysis of foreign and domestic terror threats."[15] The Joint Inquiry had already published its recommendation for the same a month earlier. President Bush knew that the 9/11 Commission's work was ongoing. Furthermore, the president was in the middle of planning to invade Iraq and had informed his "war cabinet" (his NSC principals), the Saudis, and perhaps others of his intentions; clearly it was a busy time for the president. "President Bush's decision to create a new threat assessment center could dramatically remake the way the U.S. government analyzes and responds to terrorist threats, *but it is also aimed at heading off even more drastic changes sought by some lawmakers.*"

> The plan [was] a clear response from Bush to rising demands in Congress and the recommendations of various terrorism panels for improved information-sharing between federal agencies. The FBI and CIA, in particular, [came] under heavy criticism for failing to communicate information that some lawmakers have said might have helped thwart the Sept. 11, 2001, terrorist attacks.[16]

Presaging what would become the National Counterterrorism Center (NCTC) under the Intelligence Reform and Terrorism Prevention Act (the IRTPA), President Bush wisely contemplated using his executive power to shake things up significantly. "For the first time, one group" would have the "task of analyzing data gathered by U.S. agents in this country and overseas. The analysts will pore over transcripts of tape-recorded conversations, assess tips from FBI informants, scrutinize satellite photos of overseas weapons labs, study terrorism updates from foreign security agencies and read the confessions of al Qaeda prisoners."[17] On the other hand, Bush clearly could not have known with certainty that the 9/11 Commission would recommend the replacement of the director of central intelligence with a new director of national intelligence. "The new center is aimed at helping to eliminate remaining barriers between the nation's intelligence agencies, particularly the CIA and FBI, over sharing and analyzing intelligence. The center will be placed directly under the supervision of Director of Central Intelligence George J. Tenet, reinforcing Tenet's role as Bush's senior intelligence adviser, officials said."[18] Though President Bush understandably failed to anticipate all of the 9/11 Commission's subsequent recommendations, Bush clearly anticipated that major changes lay ahead whether he directed them or whether they came from the 9/11 Commission. Therefore, his proposal of an interagency terrorist threat integration center made good political sense given the circumstances.

The president was not the only one attempting to forestall even bigger changes and reorganizations. The CIA and the FBI had pointed fingers at each other since 9/11. With reorganization in the air, their storied rivalry turned ugly. "The rivalry between the CIA and the FBI for the lead role in U.S. intelligence" had been "one of the longest-running turf wars in government, the subject of storied comic routines and *New Yorker* parodies. Before Sept. 11, 2001, a mutual stalemate had the CIA in charge of foreign intelligence, the FBI in charge of domestic law enforcement, and nebulous uncertainty about how to handle threats that traverse[d] the borders." Now both seemed up for grabs. "Putting the CIA in the driver's seat of the proposed center—whose responsibility appears to have grown to include a centralizing of all counterterrorism information in a single location—led to suspicions that Bush's trust in the FBI had waned after a series of damaging revelations and the FBI's inability to change itself from a law enforcement to an intelligence agency."[19]

It was time for the FBI, whose image the Joint Inquiry had scrutinized and which had taken a beating for months, to return bureaucratic fire. In a preemptive move of its own the FBI issued a press release: "As part of its ongoing reorganization efforts, the FBI has put in place for the first time a formal structure to prioritize intelligence exploitation and to establish strategic plans for intelligence collection, analysis and dissemination. Through a series of organizational initiatives, the FBI is elevating the analytical process above the individual case or investigation to an overall effort to analyze intelligence. New executive-level officers will be accountable for ensuring that the FBI has optimum intelligence strategies, structure, and policies in place to address evolving threats."[20] The point was that the looming reorganization encountered bureaucratic inertia and plenty of it. Fifty years of doing things one way (namely, fighting the Cold War) would not be changed easily or quickly, nor was a single commission's recommendations enough to effect the monumental changes that were required.

Though the full recommendations of the 9/11 Commission included some forty recommendations, the following were the proposals then publicly discussed. First, the 9/11 Commission proposed a director of national intelligence (DNI) with significant budget and tasking authorities. Second, it recommended establishing a national counterterrorism center as a central clearinghouse of intelligence and counterintelligence for the federal government working with states and local law enforcement (what became the NCTC). Third, it recommended establishing a domestic nuclear detection office (what became the DNDO) inside the Department of Homeland Security, a department which had only been created after 9/11. Fourth, was the proposal to establish a strong civil liberties protection mechanism within the new office of the director of national intelligence (the civil liberties oversight board in the ODNI). Fifth, they recommended the creation of a terrorist screening center. Sixth, the 9/11 Commission insisted that the FBI had to be reorganized "into an agency focused on preventing terrorist attacks through intelligence collection and other key efforts, while improving its ability to perform its traditional role as a world-class law-enforcement agency." Proposals seven through ten were all related to screening America's borders and border security: strengthening transportation security through screening and prevention, improving border screening and security through the US-VISIT entry-exit system, and establishing the National Targeting Center to screen all imported cargo and to improve shipping security. Another recommendation was the creation of a biological-chemical-radiological weapons shield. The final recommendations were the creation of new instruments to target terrorism financing and better cooperation with America's partners in the war against terrorism.[21] The Commission's recommendations were eventually codified in law; they became part of the IRTPA, which we examine in chapter 9. Two additional postmortems that must be considered are the CIA's Iraqi Survey Group report and the Robb-Silberman Committee report. We turn to them next in that order.

The Iraqi Survey Group: The Duelfer Reports

One of the principal justifications for invading Iraq was the administration's belief that Saddam Hussein held and stockpiled weapons of mass destruction (WMDs). To cite just a couple of examples indicative of the administration's charges, President Bush gave a speech to the American Enterprise Institute on February 26, 2003, just weeks before the invasion of Iraq. Amid the august conservative scholars and journalist assembled at the AEI, President Bush made the following declaration about Saddam Hussein.

> In Iraq, a dictator is building and hiding weapons that could enable him to dominate the Middle East and intimidate the civilized world—and we will not allow it. This same tyrant has close ties to terrorist organizations, and could supply them with the terrible means to strike this country—and America will not permit it. The danger posed by Saddam Hussein and his weapons cannot be ignored or wished away. The danger must be confronted. We hope that the Iraqi regime will meet the demands of the United Nations and disarm, fully and peacefully. If it does not, we are prepared to disarm Iraq by force. Either way, this danger will be removed.
>
> The safety of the American people depends on ending this direct and growing threat. Acting against the danger will also contribute greatly to the long-term safety and stability of our world . . .[22]

Parts of the president's first paragraph were patently inaccurate and the president and his NSC principals surely must have known of at least some of those inaccuracies by late February 2003.

One reason they must have known was the CIA's own internal examination: the Iraqi Survey Group's Duelfer reports. President Bush gave a series of stump speeches the previous fall during the midterm elections on behalf of Republican candidates in major races the White House was keenly watching. Without taking the time to quote each one, a fair summary is that each of eleven speeches delivered in seven days had President Bush asserting (with varying verb tenses, confusing his message somewhat) that Saddam Hussein had WMDs *and* known links to al Qaeda.[23] Nor was President Bush the only NSC principal involved. Vice President Cheney told a friendly Veterans of Foreign Wars audience in August 2002 that "we now know that Saddam has resumed his efforts to acquire nuclear weapons. Among other sources, we've gotten this from the firsthand testimony of defectors—including Saddam's own son-in-law, who was

subsequently murdered at Saddam's direction." Just as the Iraq War began, Vice President Cheney told Tim Russert on NBC's *Meet the Press*:

> But we also have to address the question of where might these terrorists ac-
> quire weapons of mass destruction, chemical weapons, biological weapons,
> nuclear weapons? And Saddam Hussein becomes a prime suspect in that re-
> gard . . . . We know he's reconstituted these programs since the Gulf War.
> We know he's out trying once again to produce nuclear weapons and we
> know that he has a long-standing relationship with various terrorist groups,
> including the al Qaeda organization.[24]

In fact, virtually every one of the vice president's assertions was a matter
of intense debate within the intelligence community and, hence, the NSC
principals. The intelligence community had retreated from its earlier view
that their evidence proved Saddam Hussein's intentions. It is implausible
to think, given the vice president's and his staff's direct involvement, that
the vice president was unaware of the debate within the intelligence community. What is more, both then–Secretary of Defense Donald Rumsfeld
and NSC advisor Condoleezza Rice were similarly on record as having alleged that Saddam Hussein's Iraq held WMDs—hyperbole about mushroom clouds and so forth. They too were inarguably aware of the internal
debate regarding the bill of particulars against the Iraqi dictator's regime.

For the record, it is our view that most of the administration's policymakers believed their own rhetoric. The intelligence agencies of many of
America's principal allies similarly held that Saddam Hussein *may have*
reconstituted said WMD programs. The Bush administration, therefore,
was not alone in its stubborn resolve to accept only the worst about Hussein. In any case, various administration members' individual motives are
less than germane to present purposes. Our own view is that the administration may reasonably be charged with extreme hubris regarding their
certainty of Iraq's WMD program. Evidence subsequently arose that the
administration "cherry-picked" intelligence to fit their preconceived notions about Iraq. However, a clear distinction should be made between
hubris—the arrogance that comes with power and the belief in one's own
rhetoric—and callous prevarication or outright lies. To believe the administration went to war in Iraq without believing its own rhetoric seems un-
supportable by the facts. The evidence does support, however, that the administration suffered from a fatal flaw that so many others have suffered

over history. While a definitive answer must necessarily await future scrutiny, we tentatively accept that poor intelligence, arrogance of power, ideological blind spots, and hubris led the administration to believe its own "spin."

Nevertheless, the administration made the charge that Iraq held WMDs and was seeking to increase its stockpiles thereof in late 2002 and early 2003. It is also the case that no WMDs were found in Iraq after America's intervention. One result of this dramatic misreading of the evidence is that shortly after toppling the Hussein regime, the U.S. government immediately set about attempting to find evidence of what the administration charged with such certainty prior to the war. On September 30, 2004, the Iraqi Survey Group (ISG), a creation of the CIA intended to discover WMDs, filed its final report on the matter. The history of the ISG report is rather long and somewhat convoluted. Suffice it to say that what began as a search for WMDs under Dr. David Kay ended with his former assistant, Charles Duelfer, releasing three volumes documenting what the ISG found after Hussein had been removed from power.[25] (Mr. Duelfer submitted an additional addendum in spring 2005.)[26]

In some 1,000 pages (three volumes) of analysis, the ISG's WMD report on Iraq found no evidence of extant WMD programs. Among its findings were that Saddam Hussein had sought WMDs for many years and had successfully produced WMD programs (chemical and biological) in the 1990s. The Duefler report also noted that Saddam was a totalitarian leader whose decisions were effectively Iraq's decisions. No committees or panels made Iraq's choices to seek such weapons. Ultimately, accordingly to the Iraqi Survey Group,

> Saddam wanted to recreate Iraq's WMD capability—which was essentially destroyed in 1991—after sanctions were removed and Iraq's economy stabilized, but probably with a different mix of capabilities to that which previously existed. Saddam aspired to develop a nuclear capability—in an incremental fashion, irrespective of international pressure and the resulting economic risks—but he intended to focus on ballistic missile and tactical chemical warfare (CW) capabilities.

(How Mr. Duelfer determined precisely what Saddam Hussein's intentions were shall be left to others with epistemological skills similar to Mr. Duelfer's.) The Duelfer report noted that Saddam's desire to end UN sanctions and inspections (the very device that ended his WMD ambitions) took precedence over his ambition to obtain WMDs. "As with other WMD areas, Saddam's ambitions in the nuclear area were secondary to his prime objective of ending UN sanctions." While the report found evidence of intentions and material evidence of violations of sanctions on missile delivery systems (something needed to deliver WMDs), no evidence of WMD stockpiles was found. Put differently, the mushroom clouds and other horrific images conjured by the administration to justify invading Iraq were untrue. Moreover, Duelfer's documentation indirectly raised anew the issue of whether Saddam could have been contained as he had been during the George H.W. Bush and Clinton administrations.

Clearly, the admission proved humiliating to the CIA and the broader intelligence community. One may quibble with some of the Duelfer report's assertions: namely, that Saddam Hussein had "ambitions" to reconstitute WMDs. After all, ascertaining an individual's intentions or ambitions is far from a certain science. On balance, however, the Duelfer report provided Americans with an important compendium of evidence documenting Saddam Hussein's sordid history with WMDs and the use thereof on Iraqis and Iranians. Finally, the Duelfer report reopened charges that the Bush administration "ginned up" its intelligence; that is, that the Bush administration planned to go to war in Iraq whether or not WMDs existed and that the administration was simply waiting for a convenient pretext. As of this writing, the 109th Congress has neglected to investigate charges of politicization of prewar intelligence. Perhaps the 110th Congress will exercise its oversight duty sometime after the Democrats take control in January 2007. Until then, the reader is left to determine his or her own confidence level about the Congress or the administration. It may prove difficult to determine definitively whether or not the administration politicized intelligence. Nor would it likely change, fundamentally, the reorganizations and reforms already undertaken. The IRTPA and the Robb-Silberman Commission both assumed that such politicization was possible if not likely. They therefore made their respective recommendations with that assumption in mind. The Robb-Silberman WMD Commission is the final commission examined as a governmental source of U.S. national security and a source of the reorganization hastened by the postmortems' findings.

Robb-Silberman WMD Report

The Commission on the Intelligence Capabilities of the United States Regarding Weapons of Mass Destruction (known as the Robb-Silberman WMD Commission) was asked by the Bush administration "to evaluate comprehensively the quality of U.S. intelligence on WMD and related 21st Century threats—whether from state actors or transnational terrorist networks—and to provide specific recommendations for ensuring that the Intelligence Community [was] prepared to identify and warn the United States Government about such threats in the future." Despite the fact that its final work product was published *after* the passage of the Intelligence Reform and Terrorism Prevention Act, much of the Robb-Silberman work was coterminous with the work of lawmakers who drafted the IRTPA. Furthermore, since the creation of the new director of national intelligence and the reorganization of the president-NSC policymaking model, DNI John Negroponte used the Robb-Silberman Commission Report as a blueprint for the manifold reorganizations that Negroponte ultimately implemented. The Robb-Silberman Commission was therefore another important governmental source of change. The institutional changes that official and unofficial governmental postmortems recommended were memorialized in the IRTPA and the reorganization begun by it.

Unlike the 9/11 Commission, much of whose work was open to the public, the Robb-Silberman Commission's work was principally in executive sessions, meaning it was not open to the public's viewing. Whereas the 9/11 Commission was negotiated between the White House and Congress, the Robb-Silberman Commission was the result of an executive order signed by President Bush on February 6, 2004, just months prior to the 9/11 Commission's July publication of its final report and during the time President Bush and Congress were arguing over the extension of the 9/11 Commission's tenure. Nevertheless, the Robb-Silberman Commission sought to keep the public informed of its work and solicited input from the public and the intelligence community. The Robb-Silberman Commission produced its final report and gave it to the president on March 31, 2005.

"The commission called for dramatic change to prevent future failures" in U.S. policymaking and in the intelligence community. The Robb-Silberman Commission took for granted obvious and manifold failures of imagination surrounding 9/11 *and* the invasion of Iraq. Rather than simply duplicate the 9/11 Commission, who focused almost entirely on 9/11, the Robb-Silberman commission looked "at *why* U.S. spy agencies mistakenly concluded that Iraq had stockpiles of weapons of mass destruction, one of the administration's main justifications for invading in March 2003." The Robb-Silberman report made seventy-four recommendations under multiple headings (nuclear, biological, chemical, and so forth). It noted, moreover, that President Bush could implement many of its recommendations via executive order. Importantly, Robb-Silberman "urged Bush to give broader powers to John Negroponte, the new director of national intelligence (DNI), to deal with challenges to his authority from the CIA, Defense Department or other elements of the nation's 15 spy agencies." Clearly, the release of the Robb-Silberman report came too late to substantially affect the Intelligence Reform and Terrorism Prevention Act. However, the Robb-Silberman report "was the latest somber assessment of intelligence shortfalls that a series of investigative panels have made since the terrorist attacks of Sept. 11, 2001. Numerous investigations [had already] concluded that spy agencies had serious intelligence failures before the Sept. 11, 2001, terror attacks against the United States."[27] The Robb-Silberman recommendations have proved especially important, since the still-fluid reorganization of America's national security institutions and bureaucracies has continued through early 2007.

Wholly new bureaucracies are not particularly easy to create. For instance, bureaucratic resistance from agencies whose power is being raided must be carefully considered. Changes to the intelligence community began before the IRTPA was passed into law; said changes were therefore memorialized by the IRTPA and continued into early 2007. Similar to the 1947 National Security Act, adjustments and evolutions may be expected to continue well after the IRTPA was signed into law. The institutions created by the IRTPA are likely to undergo significant evolution over the next decade or more.

Of the seventy-four recommendations made by the Robb-Silberman Commission, the Bush administration claimed to have implemented 70 by mid 2005. "The Administration endorsed 70 of the 74 recommendations of the WMD Commission," and committed to study further "three of the recommendations." The White House reported on June 29, 2005 that one classified recommendation would not be implemented. At that time President Bush announced additional actions to implement the recommendations of the Robb-Silberman WMD Commission; interestingly, the president announced his actions to make America "safer" and to "ensure" that

America's intelligence community was prepared for the threats of the twenty-first century.[28] One of its most important recommendations, from our perspective, was its strong endorsement of the position of director of national intelligence. As shall be seen in the chapter 9, which focuses on the actual language of the IRTPA, the new legislation amended the former 1947 NSA in order to create the director of national intelligence in law. The new DNI, former U.S. Ambassador to Iraq John Negroponte, appeared to be moving in the direction urged by both the 9/11 Commission and the Robb-Silberman WMD reports as he attempted to maneuver between his new bureaucratic creation and its biggest rival, the Department of Defense (chapter 10). The Robb-Silberman Commission endorsed the position and strongly urged the president to make the position far more than simply another layer of bureaucracy. Another of the Robb-Silberman Commission's contributions to the process of change was that it "officially" declared what the Duelfer report had already discovered and attempted to disseminate to a broad audience. Insofar as Robb-Silberman was comprised of Washington's "wise" men and women from both major political parties, it gave an official federal government imprimatur to the Robb-Silberman conclusions and recommendations.

> We conclude that the Intelligence Community was *dead wrong* in almost all of its prewar judgments about Iraq's weapons of mass destruction. This was a major intelligence failure. Its principal causes were the Intelligence Community's inability to collect good information about Iraq's WMD programs, serious errors in analyzing what information it could gather, and a failure to make clear just how much of its analysis was based on assumptions, rather than good evidence. On a matter of this importance, we simply cannot afford failures of this magnitude.[29]

An additional contribution was Robb-Silberman commissioners' willingness to wade, albeit tentatively, into the waters of whether or not the Bush administration politicized intelligence. As seen above, the Joint Inquiry avoided that question on the theory that it would be inappropriate to delve into the politicization of intelligence question due to the proximity of the election cycle. What the Senate Select Intelligence Committee called "phase two" of its investigation would reportedly wait until after the 2004 presidential election—it is still waiting as of early 2007. The Robb-Silberman Commission, by contrast, was a bipartisan commission whose work continued during and after the election. With respect to politicization, Robb-Silberman "found no indication that spy agencies distorted the evidence they had concerning Iraq's alleged weapons of mass destruction, a charge raised against the administration during 2004's presidential campaign."[30] What Robb-Silberman neglected to address was whether or not the White House politicized the intelligence.

Ruling that intelligence had not been noticeably politicized did not equate to avoiding controversy. Indeed, the Robb-Silberman Commission made recommendations that were controversial—not controversial to most Americans, but controversial inside the government bureaucracy. Perhaps the most controversial was its proposal to reorganize the Federal Bureau of Investigation. The FBI, as most readers know, existed before the national security bureaucracy created by the 1947 NSA. In fact, the FBI's storied history dated to the late 1930s. The Robb-Silberman commission recommended "restructuring the FBI's counterterrorism and counterintelligence operations and analysis under one director, and having that individual report *both* to the new director of national intelligence as well as to the FBI director." Existing as it had for years before the 1947 NSA, the FBI evolved principally as a crime-investigation and crime-solving institution and, as such, was always housed in the Department of Justice. The Department of Justice, of course, had a bureaucratic identity and mission quite apart from national security institutions. Over time, the FBI evolved into an institution or agency within the larger Cold War mission of U.S. foreign policy. As is the case with any other bureaucracy, though, the FBI's national security functions (counterintelligence and eventually intelligence), became well-entrenched with patrons on Capitol Hill whose oversight responsibilities and committee chairmanships became dependent on the FBI growing into a full-fledged Cold War institution. It was less than surprising, therefore, that the Robb-Silberman Commission's recommendations about altering the FBI would elicit particularly reactionary complaints from those persons slated to be affected by the Commission's recommendations.

First, a wall between crime investigation, domestic intelligence, and foreign intelligence had come to exist. Civil libertarians worried that blurring the distinction between domestic and foreign intelligence approached a dangerous precipice. As veteran *Washington Post* reporter Walter Pincus reported, "Kate Martin of the Center for National Security Studies, who had been briefed by FBI sources on the proposal, said that giving the DNI, whose prime concern is foreign intelligence, a role in domestic counterterrorism operations could create civil liberties issues." Second, many within the FBI believed their institution had already reformed considerably since 9/11. "Several current and former intelligence officials, who had access to part or all of the report, praised many of its findings and recommendations but said the panel at times ignored changes instituted since the attacks of Sept. 11, 2001. They also criticized the commission for failing to take into consideration complexities of the intelligence business."[31]

The FBI was far from the only institution that came under the harsh glare of the Robb-Silberman Commission's critique. The Robb-Silberman panel chronicled occasion after occasion where the CIA got it wrong, "dead wrong." The problems appeared systemic. Going back more than ten years, the panel noted that the CIA carried forward erroneous assumptions without any mechanism to challenge a particular assumption's validity. Thus, misjudgments made perhaps fifteen years earlier formed the basis of subsequent analyses, which necessarily resulted in recurrent misjudgments. Similarly, the CIA and others used sources from foreign intelligence agencies, sources that as it turned out were of dubious legitimacy. In one case—a case whose story was published by the *Los Angles Times* prior to the release of the Commission's findings but confirmed in Robb-Silberman—a German source called "Curveball" fled Iraq to Germany and fed erroneous information to the CIA third and fourth hand. After attempting to receive asylum in Germany for roughly a year, Curveball began telling German intelligence of mobile biological-chemical labs in Saddam Hussein's arsenal. The Bush administration already believed such mobile labs existed. Curveball fabricated a tall tale in which he claimed to have had evidence of mobile labs in Iraq on which he allegedly worked. That fabrication became one of the bases for the Bush administration to justify going to war in Iraq. The irony was that the administration actually had an insider in Saddam's policymaking circles whose information refuted Curveball, but many analysts and policymakers believed the worst about Saddam anyway.

In June 2006 a story in the *Washington Post* added some context to the sordid Curveball story. Apparently, just prior to Secretary of State Powell's recitation of evidence before the United Nations on February 5, 2003, Secretary Powell's last attempt to inform the UN of that evidence that the administration believed it had, a CIA official with appropriate expertise was tasked with going over the secretary's speech to check it for accuracy. The CIA expert apparently recognized a huge inaccuracy. "In late January

2003, as Secretary of State Colin Powell prepared to argue the Bush administration's case against Iraq at the United Nations, veteran CIA officer Tyler Drumheller sat down with a classified draft of Powell's speech to look for errors. He found a whopper: a claim about mobile biological labs built by Iraq for germ warfare." The sentence about the mobile labs, Drumheller later asserted, took Drumheller by complete surprise as he believed he had excised the information earlier. How had it found its way back into the speech that Secretary Powell delivered before the UN and the world? According to Drumheller, he personally

> called the office of John E. McLaughlin, then the CIA deputy director, and was told to come there immediately. Drumheller said he sat across from McLaughlin and an aide in a small conference room and spelled out his concerns.
>
> McLaughlin responded with alarm and said Curveball was "the only tangible source" for the mobile lab story, Drumheller recalled, adding that the deputy director promised to quickly investigate [*sic*].

Split infinitive aside, what happened after that is unclear. Drumheller remained adamant that he brought the situation to the attention of the CIA's top people, McLaughlin and then-DCI George Tenet. In fact, the exchange is mentioned in the Robb-Silberman Commission's final report, though it does not mention Drumheller by name. Apparently, someone at CIA—or possibly at the White House—decided to include the comment despite their awareness of problems with Curveball as a source. Neither George Tenet nor John McLaughlin recalled the exchange with Drumheller when the *Washington Post* published its story. Secretary Powell's chief of staff, Lawrence Wilkerson, recalled that both Wilkerson and Secretary Powell were suspicious of the evidence and asked George Tenet about its veracity. Either Tenet or someone sufficiently senior assured Secretary Powell that the Curveball evidence was solid.[32]

Finally, the Robb-Silberman panel criticized the executive and legislative branches of the federal government for "leaking." Leaks in Washington D.C. are a cottage industry. At least since Watergate, a cozy relationship has evolved between reporters of the nation's premier newspapers with "leakers" in all branches of government. As of this writing, two major intelligence investigations were ongoing in the country. One involved the leak of a CIA operative's name, a leak that reportedly came from the

White House and was allegedly intended to smear her husband, former ambassador Joe Wilson, a critic of Bush foreign policy. In fall 2005, Vice President Cheney's former national security advisor and chief of staff, I. Lewis "Scooter" Libby was indicted for lying to the special prosecutor charged with investigating the leak. A second ongoing investigation is trying to determine who leaked news that the National Security Agency (NSA) tapped electronic communications without court warrants. In the latter case, the leak presumably again came from the executive branch, perhaps a disaffected NSA employee or former employee. One article reported that Judge Silberman and former Senator Robb were "shocked to learn of the loss of critical intelligence assets over the past 20 years as a result of leaks to the news media." It was the nonsecret that everyone in Washington knew, but here was a presidential commission making an issue of it and explicitly stating that such behavior was antithetical to national security. The *New York Times* quoted Judge Silberman, cochair of the panel, as saying, "We were stunned even in the war on terror to find out how leaks had so hampered" legitimate U.S. national security secrets. Apparently, the panel discussed possible remedies to the problem of leaks but could not agree on the solution.[33]

The Robb-Silberman Commission proved invaluable to the ongoing reorganization following the passage of the IRTPA into law. Ambassador Negroponte attempted to maneuver his new bureaucratic entity (the ODNI) into a position in which he could truly lead the intelligence community, in place of disparate agencies all implementing their own missions. At this writing the bureaucratic posturing is still rampant. The concluding chapter (chapter 10) will discuss some of the details of that posturing. Suffice it for now to note that DNI Negroponte has used the new law (the IRTPA) and the Robb-Silberman report as levers by which to move his office's mission and America's national security interests forward in an age during which non-state, transnational actors such as al Qaeda and its affiliates attempt to do harm to those same interests.

SUMMARY

Governmental commissions and panels have often played an important role in the creation of public policy, including U.S. national security policy. Two important examples come to mind well before the failures surrounding 9/11 and the Iraq War justifications. In 1986, the Tower Commission report, cochaired by former Senator John Tower (R-TX) and Republican journeyman Brent Scowcroft, influenced both the executive (subsequently prohibiting the NSC staff from acting operationally in government policy) and the legislative branches. A decade earlier the so-called Church commission (named after former Senator Frank Church [D-ID]) resulted in major changes in law proscribing the CIA's involvement in assassinations of disagreeable foreign leaders. Since 9/11, however, the sheer number of different commissions and panels created by the federal government has been unprecedented. As seen in this chapter, their collective imprimatur vis-à-vis America's national security bureaucracy has been integral in facilitating the reorganization of the intelligence community and the president-NSC-policymaking model. We next turn to an examination of the specific and direct reorganizations that resulted from these commissions. The IRTPA has wrought significant changes on virtually all parts of the federal bureaucracy entrusted with policymaking and implementation of U.S national security policy.

NOTES

1. Jean-Marie Colombani, "We are all Americans! We are all New Yorkers," *Le Monde* (Paris), September 12, 2001.

2. We have contended elsewhere that should another attack occur, which is quite likely, the post-9/11 consensus shall truly become a fixture of U.S. foreign policy. The metaphor used was "a second shoe dropping." M. Kent Bolton, "The London Attacks: What Do They Mean for America?" *San Diego Union-Tribune*, July 13, 2005. Also see M. Kent Bolton, *U.S. Foreign Policy and International Relations*, 184–186.

3. George W. Bush, "The President's State of the Union Address," January 28, 2003, http://www.whitehouse.gov/news/releases/2003/01/print/20030128-19.html.

4. The House Permanent Select Committee on Intelligence and the Senate Select Committee on Intelligence, Report of the Joint Inquiry into the Terrorist Attacks of September 11, 2001, 107th Cong., 2d sess., http://intelligence.senate.gov/iraqreport2.pdf (accessed on February 12, 2003), hereafter cited as the Joint Inquiry; National Commission on Terrorist Attacks upon the United States, Final Report, published online on July 24, 2004, http://www.9-11commission.gov/, hereafter cited as 9/11 Commission; The Commission on the Intelligence Capabilities of the United States Regarding Weapons of Mass Destruction, report to the President of the United States, published online on March 31, 2005, http://www.wmd.gov/report/wmd_report.pdf, hereafter cited as the Robb-Silberman report; Central Intelligence Agency, Iraqi Survey Group, Charles Duelfer, Comprehensive Report of the Special Advisor to the DCI on Iraq's WMD (Washington D.C., 30 September 2004), hereafter cited as the Duelfer report.

5. Arabic spellings arise time and again in these pages. Any language whose alphabet does not easily translate into the English alphabet is a language that must be transliterated. As with many such languages, Arabic is transliterated differently by different transliteration systems. Al Qaeda is sometimes spelled al-Qaida, al-Qai'da, and even al Qida in older government documents.

6. Senator Bob Graham, "Joint Intelligence Report—Post 9/11," Congressional Record (Senate), July 24, 2003, S9887–S9888. Also see the Federation of American Scientists, http://www.fas.org/irp/congress /2003_cr/s072403.html (accessed July 23, 2005). For an Acrobat formatted copy of the Joint Inquiry Report, see "The Joint Inquiry into the Terrorist Attacks of September 11, 2001," by the House Permanent Select Committee on Intelligence and the Senate Select Committee on Intelligence, Senate Report Number 107-351, House Report Number 107-792, 107th Cong., 2d sess., December 20, 2002, http://intelligence. senate.gov/iraqreport2.pdf. The report may also be found at http://news .findlaw.com/hdocs/docs/911rpt/ (accessed July 2004).

7. Joint Inquiry, "Introduction," 1 (Acrobat Reader pagination, 33).

8. The recommendations of the Joint Inquiry, some sixteen pages in total, are set apart from the full report in the recommendation appendix. See http://intelligence.senate.gov/ recommendations.pdf.

9. It is worth noting that Lawrence Wright published in 2006 a book on al Qaeda and 9/11 in which the author argued, among other things, that had law enforcement worked together in a coordinated fashion, 9/11 might have been stoppable. His thesis flies in the face of the criticisms leveled against the Clinton administration's law-enforcement approach. Lawrence Wright, *The Looming Tower: Al-Qaeda and the Road to 9/11* (New York: Knopf Publishing, 2006). Conservative George Will (a traditional rather than neoconservative) wrote the following about Wright's argument. "The London plot against civil aviation confirmed a theme of an illuminating new book" Looming Tower. "The theme is that better law enforcement, which probably could have prevented Sept. 11, is central to combating terrorism. F-16s are not useful tools against terrorism that issues from places such as Hamburg (where Mohamed Atta lived before dying in the North Tower of the World Trade Center) and High Wycombe, England." George W. Will, "The Triumph of Unrealism," *Washington Post*, August 15, 2006, http://www.washingtonpost.com/wp-dyn/content/article/ 2006/08/14/AR2006081401163.html.

10. Editorial, "Intelligence Agencies Close Minds to Suggested Reforms," *USA Today*, December 12, 2002, http://www.usatoday.com/news/opinion/editorials/2002-12-12-13 -edit-usat_x.htm [accessed August 4, 2004].

11. To be clear, the precise nature of the 9/11 attacks did surprise policymakers, scholars, journalists, and the American people alike. As scholars and professors of U.S. foreign policy, many of us had been predicting an al Qaeda attack on a major American city in our classes for years. However, on 9/11 I was completely stunned and remained stunned for days after. I had fully expected some sort of chemical or, more likely I thought, biological attacks. Similarly, many governmental officials generally believed al Qaeda was planning to attack the U.S. and probably in a major city. Hence, while policymakers generally understood there was some amorphous threat out there called al Qaeda (headed by Osama bin Laden), it is this text's position that the attacks on New York and Washington on 9/11 came as an utter surprise nonetheless.

12. See, for example, Joint Inquiry, 30–31 (Acrobat Reader pagination, pp. 60–63). Also see "Khalid Shaykh Mohammad: The Mastermind of 9/11," Joint Inquiry, 309–324 (Acrobat Reader pagination, 361–376). (As seen throughout this text, multiple spellings of the same name occur due to different transliteration systems.)

13. For example, see Jerry Markon and Timothy Dwyer, "Moussaoui Says He Was to Fly 5th Plane," Washington Post, March 28, 2006, http://www.washingtonpost.com/wp-dyn/content/article/2006/03/ 27/AR2006032700148.html; Jerry Markon and Timothy Dwyer, "Operative's Role Unclear," Washington Post, March 28, 2006, http://www.washingtonpost.com/wp-dyn/content/article/2006/03/27/AR2006032702056.html.

14. David Firestone, "White House Gives Way On a Sept. 11 Commission: Congress Is Set to Create It," New York Times, November 15, 2002.

15. David Johnston, "CIA Director Will Lead Terror Center," New York Times, January 29, 2003, http://www.nytimes.com/2003/01/29/politics/29TERR.html (my emphasis).

16. Dan Eggen and John Mintz, "Agency to Concentrate Intelligence Analysis," Washington Post, January 30, 2003.

17. Dan Eggen and John Mintz, "Agency to Concentrate Intelligence Analysis."

18. Walter Pincus and Mike Allen, "Terrorism Agency Planned," Washington Post, January 29, 2003.

19. Drew Clark, "Intelligence Reorganization Spotlights Fabled FBI-CIA Rift," Government Executive, March 17, 2003, http://www.govexec.com/dailyfed/0303/031703cdam1.htm.

20. Federal Bureau of Investigation, "FBI Creates Structure to Support Intelligence Mission" (press release, April 3, 2003), http://www.fbi.gov/pressrel/pressrel03/mueller040303.htm.

21. White House, "Protecting the Homeland," December 5, 2005, http://www.whitehouse.gov/news /releases/2005/12/20051205-5.html (accessed January 6, 2005).

22. George W. Bush, "President Discusses the Future of Iraq" (press release on speech to the American Enterprise Institute, Washington Hilton Hotel, February 26, 2003), http://www.whitehouse.gov/news/releases/ 2003/02/20030226-11.html.

23. George W. Bush, "Remarks by the President at New Mexico Welcome," October 28, 2002, http://www. whitehouse.gov/news/releases/2002/10/print/20021028-4.html; George W. Bush, "Remarks by the President in Colorado Welcome," October 28, 2002, http://www.whitehouse.gov/news/releases/2002/10/print/20021028-5.html; George W. Bush, "Remarks by the President at South Dakota Welcome," October 31, 2002, http://www.whitehouse.gov /news/releases/2002/10/print/20021031-1.html; George W. Bush, "Remarks by the President at New Hampshire Welcome," November 1, 2002, http://www.whitehouse.gov/news/ releases/2002/11/print/20021101-5.html; George W. Bush. "Remarks by the President in Florida Welcome," November 2, 2002, http://www.whitehouse.gov/news/releases/ 2002/11/print/20021102-8.html; George W. Bush, "Remarks by the President in Atlanta, Georgia Welcome," November 2, 2002, http://www.whitehouse.gov/news/releases/ 2002/11/print/20021102-3.html; George W. Bush, "Remarks by the President at Tennessee Welcome," November 2, 2002, http://www.whitehouse.gov/news/releases/2002/11/ 20021102-2.html; George W. Bush, "Remarks by the President at Tennessee Welcome," November 2, 2002, http://www.whitehouse.gov/news/releases/2002/11/20021102-2.html; George W. Bush, "Remarks by the President in Minnesota Welcome," November 3, 2002,

http://www.whitehouse.gov/news/releases/2002/11/20021103-2.html; George W. Bush, "Remarks by the President at Arkansas Welcome," November 4, 2002, http://www.whitehouse.gov/news/ releases/2002/11/20021104-5.html; and George W. Bush, "Remarks by the President in Texas Welcome," November 4, 2002, http://www.whitehouse.gov/ news/releases/2002/11/print/20021104-9.html.

24. Dick Cheney, "Remarks by the Vice President to the Veterans of Foreign Wars 103rd National Convention," August 26, 2002, http://www.whitehouse.gov/news/releases/ 2002/08/20020826.html; Dick Cheney, interview, "Meet the Press," NBC, March 16, 2003.(my emphasis).

25. Charles Duelfer, Iraqi Survey Group, Central Intelligence Agency, Comprehensive Report of the Special Advisor to the DCI on Iraq's WMD, October 10, 2004, http:/ www.cia.gov/cia/reports/iraq_wmd_2004/index.html (accessed on January 16, 2006).

26. Charles Duelfer, Iraqi Survey Group, Central Intelligence Agency, Comprehensive Report, of the Special Advisor to the DCI on Iraq's WMD, September 30, 2004, http:// www.foia.cia.gov/duelfer/Iraqs_WMD_Vol1.pdf.

27. Walter Pincus and Peter Baker, "Data on Iraqi Arms Flawed, Panel Says" *Washington Post*, April 1, 2005, http://www.washingtonpost.com/wp-dyn/articles/A15184-2005 Mar31.html.

28. White House, "Bush Administration Implements WMD Commission Recommendations: Actions to Implement WMD Commission Recommendations," (press release, June 29, 2005) http://www.whitehouse.gov/news/releases/2005/06/20050629-2.html.

29. Commission on the Intelligence Capabilities of the United States Regarding Weapons of Mass Destruction (letter of transmittal attached to the report) March 31, 2005, unnumbered front matter http://www.wmd.gov/report/wmd_report.pdf (accessed on March 31, 2005)(my emphasis).

30. Katherin Shrader, "WMD Commission Releases Scathing Report," Associated Press in *Washington Post*, March 31, 2005, http://www.washingtonpost.com/wp-dyn/ articles/A15184-2005Mar31.html.

31. Walter Pincus, "Intelligence Panel's Findings Criticized: Experts Call Suggestions Uniformed," *Washington Post*, March 31, 2005, http://www.washingtonpost.com/wp-dyn/ articles/A14104-2005Mar30.html.

32. Joby Warrick, "Warnings on WMD 'Fabricator' Were Ignored, Ex-CIA Aide Says," *Washington Post*, June 25, 2006, http://www.washingtonpost.com/wp-dyn/content/article/ 2006/06/24/AR2006062401081. html. For the relevant coverage in the Robb-Silberman report see "Biological Warfare Finding 4," 94–105 (Acrobat Reader pagination, 110–121).

33. Scott Shane, "CIA Answers Criticism with Pledge to Do Better," New York Times, April 2, 2005. For an excellent piece on the art of leaking in Washington DC, see E. J. Dionne ,Jr., "All the President's Leaks," *Washington Post*, April 11, 2006, http://www.washingtonpost.com/wp-dyn/content/article/2006/04/10/AR2006041001049 .html. Also see Dana Milbank, "On the Subject of Leaks a Talkative President Runs Dry," *Washington Post*, April 11, 2006, http://www.washingtonpost.com/wp-dyn/content/article/ 2006/04/10/AR2006041001500.html; David E. Sanger and David Johnston, "White House Memo," *New York Times*, April 11, 2006, http://www.nytimes.com/2006/04/11/ washington/ 11leak.html.

The Intelligence Reform and Terrorism Prevention Act of 2004

In previous chapters we have examined the passage of the National Security Act of 1947 (NSA) and the profound changes that the 1947 statute and its subsequent amendments made to America's national security bureaucracy. In fact, it is somewhat misleading to discuss a U.S. national security bureaucracy as if it is a single entity. The reality is far more complex. Since the 1947 NSA, a host of different policymaking, war fighting, diplomatic, and other national security institutions, as well as intelligence-collection and intelligence-analysis bureaucracies, have all evolved into ever more complex entities over time. Some of the disparate agencies simply evolved according to bureaucratic laws: inertia, momentum, turf battles, and so forth. Other times, Congress exercised its oversight responsibilities and mandated change. On rare occasions, events external to the U.S. have forced quick changes to protect America's national security interests. Whatever the original source or reason, in the sixty years since the 1947 NSA became law, America's national security state has emerged as the world's largest, most complex, and most sophisticated layered bureaucracy, the *sine qua non* of the world's most formidable hegemony.

What remains to be analyzed is how all the recommendations became codified in U.S. law as the Intelligence Reform and Terrorism Prevention Act (IRTPA). At this preliminary point, only inferences may be made regarding the ultimate effects to U.S. national security policy. Policymaking is an iterative process that is constantly absorbing additional inputs and responding accordingly. We have repeatedly asserted that the process of national security policymaking is iterative; nevertheless, it rarely yields demonstrable changes from year to year or even from administration to administration. Rather, all the sources of U.S. national security policy typically result in incremental, less-than-dramatic changes. Using the 1947 NSA as precedent, it is a safe bet that the effects of 9/11 may be manifested over decades, perhaps generations. Initially, as happened following the 1947 NSA, many changes occurred rapidly. Following those initial changes, incremental and evolutionary changes occurred. Incremental change will likely be the case with what the IRTPA mandated too. Some initial observations may be made regarding the immediate changes that the IRTPA caused. In what follows, we reexamine the recommendations made by the commissions discussed in chapter 9 with a different focus: what ended up being changed in law.

NATIONAL INTELLIGENCE BUDGET: THE NIP, THE JMIP, AND TIARA

Before examining the IRTPA, a primer on America's intelligence budget is necessary. The federal government distinguishes three principal categories. At the risk of adding more confusion to an already confusing alphabet soup of acronyms and initializations, it is important to understand that national intelligence is categorized for organizational and operational purposes as follows. "The U.S. Intelligence Community is a federation of executive branch agencies and organizations that work—both together and separately—to conduct intelligence activities necessary for the conduct of foreign relations and the protection of the national security of the United States."[1] This "federation" is further operationalized according to a threefold division. The first, and the one that was most affected by the postmortems considered herein was the National Intelligence Program (NIP). "The agencies and organizations whose resources are included as part of the NIP include the CIA, NSA, DIA, NGA, NRO, and the intelligence elements of the Department of State, Department of Justice, Department of Energy, and Department of the Treasury."[2] The Defense Intelligence Agency (DIA), the National Security Agency (NSA), the National Geospatial-Intelligence Agency (NGA), and the National Reconnaissance Office (NRO) were historically under the defense department, and essentially remain so today, though as will be seen, the DNI has been given authorities related to each. This is an important point as will be seen. Additionally, national intelligence is divided into another category called the Joint Military Intelligence Program (JMIP). "The JMIP falls under the authority of the Secretary of Defense. JMIP resources support multiple defense organizations across functional boundaries and mission areas. Many of the programs under JMIP *parallel* those in the NIP. As a result, some agencies, like NGA, receive funding from both the NIP and JMIP budgets, making both management by the new DNI problematic and oversight redundant. Finally, the third category is called Tactical Intelligence and Related Activities (TIARA), pronounced as is the adornment worn on some heads. TIARA has historically existed under the aegis of the defense department. JMIP encompasses military-intelligence activities intended to support defense-wide objectives versus particular military-services objectives. In other words, the JMIP category of national intelligence is for defense department objectives that transcend the objectives of say the army or marines in a particular theater of operations. TIARA functions, by contrast, are explicitly those activities that represent "an aggregation of intelligence activities funded by each of the military services and the Special Operations Command to meet their specific requirements."[3] Parts of both JMIP and TIARA were and remain under the authority, ostensibly, of the Department of Defense.

For budgetary purposes, the IRTPA placed the new DNI at the head of the NIP: the DNI was tasked to provide guidance, based on the president's priorities (or in consultation with the White House, including the NSC), to the various heads of the manifold intelligence agencies included in the NIP, after which the NIP's priorities would be fixed, monies earmarked for particular priorities, and the process continued through its appropriations for that fiscal year. Congress, of course, must appropriate those monies and may decrease or increase the actual amount as determined by the president, the DNI, and the agency heads. Though the appropriations committees of Congress ultimately provide oversight, so too do the Senate Select Committee on Intelligence and the House Permanent Select Committee on Intelligence. In any case, though multiple defense department–related entities are included in the process, the DNI *ostensibly has budgetary control* as well as programmatic authority over the NIP.[4]

The budgets of both the JMIP and TIARA, by contrast, are enacted somewhat differently. First, the Department of Defense's budget is normally appropriated—after consultations and budget priorities are forwarded from the White House and its Office of Management and Budget (OMB) to different oversight committees in Congress—by the Senate Armed Services Committee and its House equivalent, the House Committee on Armed Services. (In fact, the appropriations committees of either body are involved in the budget appropriations, but the national intelligence budget receives additional oversight by the intelligence committees and the armed services committees on either side of Congress, thus the earlier assertion of redundancy.) Therefore, the defense department's budget and oversight is subject to one process while the national intelligence budget is subject to another. Yet, since the JMIP and TIARA are both part of the larger annual intelligence budget processes, defense is subject to different oversight committees in Congress for different parts of its budget. Second, and despite the fact that parts of the intelligence budget are under the Department of Defense instead of the office of the DNI (ODNI), the budgets of the JMIP and TIARA are both enacted through a different mechanism than the DNI's NIP. The JMIP budget, for instance, is enacted by the undersecretary of defense for intelligence, until recently Dr. Stephen A. Cambone, whereas the TIARA apparently is under the deputy secretary of defense, currently Gordon England (formerly Paul Wolfowitz), whose immediate boss is the secretary of defense. To make matters even more confusing, the IRTPA apparently intentionally drafted somewhat ambiguous language with respect to the aforementioned. As noted in the Robb-Silberman report, the "DNI will also *participate* in the development of JMIP and TIARA budgets managed by the Secretary of Defense including providing budget guidance to those elements of the Intelligence Community not within the NIP."

Prior to the IRTPA being passed by Congress, political showdowns were seen between powerful members (particularly in the House but in the Senate as well) who sat on the respective armed services committees. Fortunately, they were ultimately resolved via compromise. One of the residual results, however, was that the IRTPA left its language ambiguous if not intentionally obtuse: in a sort of reverse Solomon solution, it attempted to fuse the two mothers of the same baby together. The result has been a bureaucratic "food fight," with DNI Negroponte increasingly attempting to assume the authorities (budgetary and otherwise) given him by the IRTPA, while Undersecretary Cambone and Secretary Rumsfeld effectively attempted to thwart his success.[5]

The intelligence community was traditionally and continues to be subject to oversight by both Congress and the executive branch. The NSC is a primary source of oversight for the intelligence community in the executive branch. The NSC was envisioned originally to provide "guidance for and direction to the conduct of national foreign intelligence and counterintelligence activities. The statutory members of the NSC are the President, the Vice President, the Secretary of State, and the Secretary of Defense."

Though not mentioned in the Robb-Silberman Report, we differentiated between statutory principals and ad hoc principals, both of whom are important, depending upon the administration in office. Additionally, the President's Foreign Intelligence Advisory Board (PFIAB), since its inception under President Eisenhower in 1956, has provided executive oversight. Specifically, in addition to its input on the legality of actions taken by a president with respect to intelligence, the "PFIAB . . . assesses the adequacy of management, personnel, and organization in the intelligence agencies and makes recommendations to the President for actions to improve U.S. intelligence efforts. The Intelligence Oversight Board is a standing committee of the PFIAB and is the White House entity with oversight responsibility for the legality and propriety of intelligence activities." Of course, as briefly noted above, the Office of Management and Budget also exercises general budgetary oversight for purposes of the executive branch.[6]

Though somewhat perplexing and confusing, it was important for the reader to understand the complexity of what is typically called "the intelligence budget." The reality is that multiple intelligence budgets exist. Moreover, the intelligence community serves multiple bosses including Congress, the president, the military and other intelligence consumers, and the NSC principals, both statutory and ad hoc. With that admittedly head-spinning bookkeeping disposed of, we may now consider the IRTPA. How did its drafters seek to incorporate the 9/11 Commission's recommendations? And how did they seek to respond to the array of rumors swirling around the Robb-Silberman Commission's work as the two overlapped in mid to late 2004? How did the IRTPA's drafters seek to resolve—sometimes paper over—the conflicting sentiments about to whom various creations of the IPRTA would answer and so forth?

FROM RECOMMENDATION TO STATUTE: THE INTELLIGENCE REFORM AND TERRORISM PREVENTION ACT

The Intelligence Reform and Terrorism Prevention Act: Title I

The IRTPA became law in December 2004. In its Acrobat Reader (.pdf) formatted version it was fewer than 250 pages of legalese. It is divided into eight major sections or titles:

I. Reform of the Intelligence Community
II. Federal Bureau of Investigation

III. Security Clearances
IV. Transportation Security
V. Border Protection, Immigration, and Visa Matters
VI. *Terrorism Prevention*
VII. *Implementation of the 9/11 Commission Recommendations*
VIII. Other Matters.[7]

For our purposes Titles I, II, VI, and VII—the titles italicized above—are of particular concern. Under "Reform of the Intelligence Community," the IRTPA created a director of national intelligence (known as the DNI) who would "be appointed by the President," by and "with the advice and consent of the Senate." The IPRTA dictated that any person whom the president ultimately nominated as the director of national intelligence (DNI), "shall have extensive national security expertise," seemingly a reasonable demand.

It is important to note that the DNI, created by the IRTPA, is subject to congressional advice and consent. One recurring criticism of the NSC advisor is that (s)he has never been subject to congressional oversight. Traditionally, the reasoning held that the NSC advisor was the president's personal advisor on national security affairs and, as such, needed to have the president's full confidence. Moreover, the original NSA did not envision what then was called only an executive secretary becoming such an influential person in American national security policymaking. Over time, the NSC advisor evolved into arguably the most important adviser to the president on national security. None of the amendments to the 1947 NSA, including the IRTPA, which amended multiple parts of that statute, have ever changed the fundamental status of the president's NSC advisor. However, the DNI, envisaged as more robust and attentive to the president and the country's intelligence and national security needs and also conceived as a close advisor to a given president, *was* made subject to the Senate's advice and consent prerogatives, a distinction that may well prove important in time.

In creating the DNI, legislators were cognizant that the 1947 NSA had previously created a director of central intelligence (DCI) who oversaw the intelligence community, which was, in fact, quite small at the beginning of the Cold War. Over the years, the community had truly blossomed, evolving into a multiplicity of intelligence-collection and/or intelligence-analysis agencies. Prior to 9/11, the intelligence community consisted of separate intelligence agencies for the U.S. (1) Air Force, (2) the Army, (3) the Coast Guard, (4) the Marine Corps, and (5) Navy Intelligence, all part of the TIARA category discussed above, as well as (6) the Defense Intelligence Agency, (7) the National Geospatial-Intelligence Agency, (8) the National Reconnaissance Office, and (10) the National Security Agency, all more or less under the aegis of the defense department and part of both the JMIP and NIP budget categories. The community also included (11) the state department's Bureau of Intelligence and Research (INR), 12) the Department of Energy's Intelligence and Security, (13) the Federal Bureau of Investigation (justice department), and (14) an intelligence entity under the Department of the Treasury, all categorized primarily as NIP for budgetary purposes. After 9/11, the Department of Homeland Security (DHS) was created, with its own internal intelligence, making a total of fifteen disparate agencies that comprised the intelligence community between 9/11 and the passage of the IRTPA. The statute amended the 1947 NSA, supplanting the DCI with the new DNI, the director of the intelligence-community constellation with budgetary and tasking responsibilities over technically the entire intelligence community. Legislators consciously proscribed the DNI from holding dual positions in the intelligence community and they proscribed co-location of the DNI "within the Executive Office of the President." The IRTPA explicitly stated that the DNI shall serve as the "head" of the intelligence community. It further stated that the DNI would "act as the *principal adviser to the President*, to the *National Security Council*, and the *Homeland Security Council* for intelligence matters related to the national security."[8]

Under "Responsibilities and Authorities," the IRTPA enumerated several responsibilities and authorities for the DNI. The DNI was "responsible for ensuring that national intelligence is provided to the President," and other "heads of departments and agencies in the Executive Branch," as well as to "the Chairman of the Joint Chiefs of Staff" (CJCS), "senior military commanders," and others whom the DNI determined were "appropriate." The defense department was estimated to control some eighty percent of the intelligence budget. The IRTPA arguably remedied that: it made the NIP "based on the priorities set by the President," with the DNI providing "guidance" on the principal intelligence budget for the community. The IRTPA appeared to leave the budget authority somewhat ambiguous. It provided the DNI with the basis for *super* authority but it left subject to interpretation the following key phrase: the DNI "shall *participate in the development* by the Secretary of Defense of the annual budgets of the Joint Military Intelligence Program and for Tactical Intelligence and Related Activities,"[9] (i.e., the JMIP and TIARA).

Under the heading of "Responsibility of the Director of National Intelligence Program Budget Concerning the Department of Defense," the IRTPA noted: "subject to the direction of the President" the DNI "shall, *after consultation* with the Secretary of Defense, *ensure* that the National Intelligence Program [NIP] budgeted for the elements of the intelligence community that are within the Department of Defense *are adequate* to satisfy the national intelligence needs of the Department of Defense, including the needs of the Chairman of the Joints Chiefs of Staff and the commanders of the unified and specified commands, and wherever such elements of the unified and specified commands, and wherever such elements are performing Government-wide functions, the needs of other federal departments and/or agencies."[10] The question may still properly be asked: to what extent does the DNI "participate in" creation of the TIARA budget and, perhaps to lesser extent, the JMIP budget? Clearly, the IRTPA wished for the DNI to participate in the budgets of the entire intelligence community; it instructed the DNI to ensure that the NIP budgeted for both the JMIP and TIARA budgets. However, insofar as Congress and its oversight responsibilities are subject to a patronage system, the DNI is left to carve out his own turf and find his own patrons.

Under "Tasking and Other Authorities," the DNI was instructed to "establish objectives, priorities, and guidance for the intelligence community to ensure timely and effective collection, processing, analysis, and dissemination" of its intelligence product. Under the office of the DNI (ODNI) the IRTPA created the National Counterterrorism Center (NCTC). In a subparagraph reminiscent of the subparagraph that led to the CIA's paramilitary follies in the past, the IRTPA stated that the DNI was to "perform such other functions as the President may direct." The DNI, in short, is envisioned as integrating the formerly far-flung intelligence empire of the president and his NSC principals. The ambiguities in the legislative language were a product of compromise and powerful congresspeople protecting the defense department's "turf" (including aspects that overlapped with intelligence) and other congresspeople who pushed for the more radical reforms.[11] The former attempted effectively to thwart the DNI's success while the latter attempted to give the DNI leverage.

The IRTPA created a relationship between the DNI and the NSC statutory principals as well between the Joint Intelligence Community Council and the NSC. A search of the legislation indicated only three occurrences of "National Security Council" as a search string, yet it amended the 1947 NSA that created the NSC over 30 times. By contrast, the Robb-Silberman report discussed the NSC repeatedly, referring to the NSC in many chapters throughout the report.[12] Nevertheless, the IRTPA created a parallel entity—perhaps similar to the Homeland Security Council (HSC)—that it called the Joint Intelligence Community Council (JICC).[13] The IRTPA implicitly recognized the potential for the JICC to become an important new locus of U.S. national security policymaking over time. That is not to suggest that the JICC, as conceived, was intended to supplant the NSC itself but, rather, it is important to note the similar composition of the JICC and the NSC and the ambiguity left unspecified: namely, how the NSC and JICC are intended to interact in the future. Given bureaucratic imperatives for survival—bureaucracies are assumed to expand their mandate and budget and where necessary to absorb rival bureaucracies—we simply note this new bureaucratic entity created by the IRTPA. It is also important for future analysts and scholars to watch the JICC and how it ultimately gets fitted and arranged into the larger national security bureaucracy and the president-NSC-policymaking model. Therefore, a brief description of the JICC created by IRTPA is appropriate.

"Title I of the National Security Act of 1947 (50 U.S.C. 402 et seq.) is amended by inserting after section 101 the following new section." The insertion read: "There is a Joint Intelligence Community Council" and that it "shall consist" of "the Director of National Intelligence" whom the law specified "shall chair the Council." Hence, the DNI is a statutory NSC principal as well as the chair of the JICC. The JICC's additional membership included the secretary of state, secretary of defense, secretary of homeland security, attorney general, secretaries of the treasury and energy, and such "other officers of the United States Government as the President may designate from time to time."[14] Notably, the legislation excluded the NSC adviser from the JICC. Neither were the president nor the vice president, both NSC principals in the 1947 NSA, included on the JICC. The new legislation was also silent on two "advisers" (recall the 1947 NSA and 1949 amendments divided the principals into "members" and "advisers"), the Director of Central Intelligence—who has been supplanted by the DNI, therefore his absence is understandable—and a representative of the Joint Chiefs of Staff of the military. The Goldwater-Nichols Act (1986) created the modern chairman of the joint chiefs of staff (CJCS) whose chain of command is separate from the Joint Chiefs and the combatant commanders. Historically, however, various presidents included the CJCS and/or various other military chiefs or a personal presidential military adviser in NSC principals committee settings, in both statutory and ad hoc configurations. Other administrations excluded said military representation in the NSC principals setting. (See chapter 4.) Precisely how integral to national security policymaking the JICC principals will become remains to be seen.[15]

After IRTPA became law, the Robb-Silberman Committee wrote this: "The JICC as currently composed does not include a representative from the Executive Office of the President, or other parts of the Executive Branch that do not include elements of the Intelligence Community. The President could easily solve the problem of no White House representation by making the Special Assistant to the President for National Security Affairs [i.e., the NSC advisor] a member of the Council [the JICC]."[16] Further, Robb-Silberman concluded of the JICC that although "not a perfectly representative group of consumers, the JICC should provide the DNI with valuable feedback on intelligence products." Finally, Robb-Silberman noted a potential conflict of interest within the JICC. "We do not think, however, that the JICC is the appropriate body to perform more sustained oversight of the Intelligence Community. Since the DNI chairs the JICC, and the members of the JICC are heads of departments containing intelligence components, the body would have a 'conflict of interest' that would impair its ability to play an independent oversight role."[17] Moreover, as we noted elsewhere, the NSC, the NSC advisor, the PFIAB, the OMB, and relevant congressional committees were all intended to provide oversight of intelligence collection and analysis and its efficacy for America's national security interests. The Robb-Silberman report referred to the PFIAB in its discussion of the new DNI and general oversight matters on intelligence. Accordingly, Robb-Silberman called for strengthened oversight of the intelligence community as reorganized under the IRTPA. Presumably, the authors of Robb-Silberman perceived the potential for intelligence abuse in their recommendations to strengthen and reform the intelligence community. The PFIAB also is intended to oversee the legality of community functions, including espionage and other covert matters. Hence, presumably, the IRTPA made a conscious attempt to create redundancy in oversight in order to protect Americans' civil liberties.

During the Cold War, the CIA and the FBI both were accused of over-stepping their statutory mandates. President Nixon, for instance, used America's intelligence agencies for personal reasons. The end result was the publication of the so-called Church Committee and Pike Committee reports on intelligence abuses.[18] Both investigations subsequently led to charges of the CIA, for instance, acting like a rogue agency. In the after-math of 9/11, of course, the consensus was that America's intelligence community needed to be strengthened substantially so that another 9/11 never caught America again unawares. However, knowing the delicate balance needed in the U.S. between personal liberties and fourth amend-ment (and other) protections, the commissioners of the various post-mortems and the IRTPA drafters all sought to strike that balance by creat-ing a civil liberties entity within the office of the DNI (ODNI). The Robb-Silberman report suggested that PFIAB continue to function but recommended an even "more vigorous" role with respect to the commu-nity. Interestingly, Robb-Silberman lamented that the PFIAB was insuffi-ciently equipped to conduct all of its responsibilities.[19] In a bit of irony that demonstrated the prescience of the Robb-Silberman report, in late 2005, the *New York Times* broke a story, subsequently confirmed by the White House, that the national security agency (NSA) was collecting sig-nal intelligence on jihadi groups and in so doing collected information on Americans. If the opposite end of an al Qaeda or other jihadi phone call, email, or other signal intelligence terminated with an American, the NSA intercepted and possibly used it.[20] Apparently, the commissioners of Robb-Silberman were correct in their anticipation of potential problems.

The section in the IRTPA that created the NCTC in the ODNI fell un-der the same title (Title I—Reform of the Intelligence Community). Sub-title B actually created the NCTC and a National Counterproliferation Center (NCPC) as well as the National Intelligence Centers (NICs).[21] The NCTC's primary mission was to "serve as the primary organization in the United States Government for analyzing and integrating all intelligence possessed or acquired by the United States Government pertaining to ter-rorism and counterterrorism." The law qualified NCTC's responsibilities only slightly in terms of domestic intelligence. The law stated that the NCTC's purview is total "excepting intelligence pertaining exclusively to domestic terrorist and domestic counterterrorism," presumably still the domain of the FBI,[22] inasmuch as a wholly separate domestic intelligence agency was not created by the IRTPA.

In an early 2006 speech made by DNI John Negroponte, the importance of the NCTC was implied by its new boss, the DNI. Mr. Negroponte was honored by Georgetown University in February 2006 as the recipient of the Trainor Endowment's award for exemplary diplomacy. On the occasion, Mr. Negroponte gave a short speech then answered questions from the audience, mostly Georgetown students and faculty. In response to one questioner who wished to know the differences between "centers" established by the IRTPA and "mission managers," something recommended by Robb-Silberman and implemented by the new DNI, Negroponte said the following: "Of course the centers are pretty much bricks and mortar, aren't they. The National Counterterrorism Center is an institution with several hundred people in it."[23] Mr. Negroponte revealed the overall importance of the NCTC in the Bush administration's war against global jihadis. He also roughly revealed how big the new bureaucracy was: several hundred persons, a sizable bureaucracy for one that was created so recently.

The NCPC's mission, according to the drafters of the IRTPA, was to "halt the proliferation of weapons of mass destruction, their delivery systems, and related materials and technologies."[24] The NICs appeared to be a device at the DNI's discretion for prioritizing intelligence. "The Director of National Intelligence may establish one or more national intelligence centers to address intelligence priorities, including, but not limited to, regional issues."[25] In his Georgetown remarks, Mr. Negroponte also mentioned new information on the NCPC. Of the NCPC, Negroponte said "the National Counterproliferation Center also has 60, 70 people in it." And though the Robb-Silberman report did not mandate how many persons should be seconded to the NCPC, it in fact suggested "fewer than 100" persons for the counterproliferation center. The IRTPA envisioned the NCPC as "a central feature of counter proliferation activities, consistent with the President's *Proliferation Security Initiative*," and suggested it "should include the physical interdiction, by air, sea, or land, of weapons of mass destruction, their delivery systems, and related materials and technologies, and enhanced law enforcement activities to identify and disrupt proliferation networks, activities, organizations, and persons."[26]

It would appear that the DNI is envisaged as a parallel officer to the president's NSC advisor and homeland security adviser. If we accept the NSC's evolution over time as precedent, there is every reason to believe that the DNI will also become a powerful presidential adviser who may well accumulate more influence over time, particularly as campaigns against transnational threats unfold over coming years if not decades.[27] It is plausible to assume that the drafters of the IRTPA were attempting to provide the new DNI with a realistic chance to form a powerful bureaucratic power base in the executive office, apart from the NSC advisor. Given the natural bureaucratic rivalry of the secretaries of state and defense, two exceptionally powerful bureaucratic actors who sit on both the JICC and the NSC principals, it is further reasonable to believe that the drafters of IRTPA wished to carve out a bureaucratic perch for the DNI as the arbiter between the parochial differences that are likely to occur between the secretaries of state and defense. Conceivably, it occurred to the drafters of IRTPA that the DNI would potentially be in a position to build coalitions, say with the state department if and when the defense department attempted to thwart an initiative or priority of the DNI. In any case, the JICC may prove an important barometer of how powerful the DNI becomes over time and therefore is a worthwhile unit of analysis for future studies.

The Intelligence Reform and Terrorism Prevention Act: Title II

Title II of the IRTPA is devoted to the Federal Bureau of Investigation (FBI). The first subtitle reads, "Improvement of Intelligence Capabilities of the Federal Bureau of Investigation." It is difficult to interpret Title II as anything other than a sharp rebuke of the FBI's domestic intelligence efforts with respect to 9/11. Though not alone in its faults, the FBI was notorious for keeping its own council and not sharing information with CIA and other intelligence agencies. Part of the reason was undoubtedly the fact that the FBI had a broad twofold mandate: it was both a crime fighting agency and an intelligence collection and analysis agency. Nevertheless, as both the 9/11 Commission final report and the Robb-Silberman WMD report made clear, the FBI dropped the domestic intelligence ball. Further, despite FBI director Robert S. Mueller's efforts, apparently far too little had been done to improve the FBI's systemic and institutional problems by the time the IRTPA was drafted; clearly, the FBI came in for harsh criticism in 2005 by Robb-Silberman. The IRTPA commenced its "improvements" and reorganizations by reminding its consumers, the executive and legislative branches as well as the public, of the following. First, the 9/11 Commission's final report "stated that, under Director

Robert Mueller, the Federal Bureau of Investigation ha[d] made significant progress in improving its intelligence capabilities." Second, in "the report, the members of the Commission also urged that the Federal Bureau of Investigation fully institutionalize the shift of the Bureau to a preventive counterterrorism posture."[28]

From there the IRTPA directed specific instructions for the FBI in order to change fundamentally the FBI's orientation and culture. "The Director of the Federal Bureau of Investigation shall continue efforts to improve the intelligence capabilities of the Federal Bureau of Investigation and to develop and maintain within the Bureau a national intelligence workforce." The FBI director was ordered to:

> develop and maintain a specialized and integrated national intelligence workforce consisting of agents, analysts, linguists, and surveillance specialists who are recruited, trained, and rewarded in a manner which ensures the existence within the Federal Bureau of Investigation an institutional culture with substantial expertise in, and commitment to, the intelligence mission of the Bureau.

The IRTPA instructed the FBI director to ensure that each agent employed thereafter received training not only in the FBI's traditional "criminal justice matters" but also in national intelligence matters. Subsequently, the IRTPA instructed the FBI director to implement a host of specific actions to improve training and career enhancement, to reorient the culture and to incentivize nontraditional career paths traditionally left unrewarded in the FBI, to enact advanced training programs, and generally to improve the intelligence capabilities of the FBI.[29] A subsequent section of the IRTPA instructed the FBI to reorient its Office of Intelligence, beginning with a change in nomenclature. Thereafter, it would become the Directorate of Intelligence of the FBI. The Directorate was instructed to undertake actions needed to meet the intelligence and counterintelligence functions of the FBI's traditional turf (domestic intelligence), but also to enhance its intelligence capabilities abroad. Finally, two subparagraphs of the section instructed the FBI to ensure its compliance with the IRTPA by: (1) FBI Director Mueller working with the head of the Directorate of Intelligence and (2) the FBI Director enacting the reforms "under the joint guidance of the Attorney General," the FBI's historical boss, as well as the DNI, the FBI's newly created boss.[30]

Since the Robb-Silberman report was published *after* the IRTPA was drafted, it therefore had a less direct role in shaping the IRTPA's recommendation than did the 9/11 Committee recommendations. Nevertheless, the Robb-Silberman Report became a blueprint for DNI Negroponte as he built his new bureaucratic empire. Both reports, of course, recommended the creation of the DNI, who would henceforth replace the director of the CIA in the NSC principals and other important policymaking settings. Moreover, the DNI was given budget and programmatic authorities that the DCI either never had or never exercised. (Recall that the Robb-Silberman recommendations dealing directly with covert actions—the historical purview of the CIA—were all classified. Consequently, no assessment of those recommendations was possible.)

The CIA was also directed to change itself. "The CIA Director should emphasize (a) rebuilding the CIA's analytic capabilities; (b) transforming the clandestine service by building its human intelligence capabilities; (c) developing a stronger language program, with high standards and sufficient financial incentives; (d) renewing emphasis on recruiting diversity among operations officers so they can blend more easily in foreign cities; (e) ensuring a seamless relationship between human source collection and signals collection at the operational level; and (f) stressing a better balance between unilateral and liaison operations."[31] The IRTPA memorialized other reorganizations and changes in procedures for the CIA, some of which transcended the CIA alone and focused on the relationship between it and its intelligence community competitors. The IRTPA instructed the CIA and the Department of Defense to work better together in coordinating their respective intelligence domains. With respect to the CIA and the new DNI, the IRTPA instructed the following: "The [DNI], in consultation with the Secretary of Defense and the *Director of the Central Intelligence Agency*, shall develop joint procedures to be used by the Department of Defense and the Central Intelligence Agency to improve the coordination and deconfliction [*sic*] of operations that involve elements of both the Armed Forces and the Central Intelligence Agency consistent with national security and the protection of human intelligence sources and methods." Deconfliction notwithstanding, the IRTPA apparently intended to force smoother coordination to obviate bureaucratic turf battles. Since the Department of Defense controlled some 80 percent of the entire intelligence budget prior to the IRTPA, one might imagine that defense exercised its bureaucratic prerogatives with some zeal.[32] By contrast, the CIA was a relatively minor bureaucratic actor—at least if annual budgets are used as the basis of bureaucratic prowess. The IRTPA, hence, identified several ways in which defense and the CIA might better coordinate their activities in the future and attempted to give the new DNI a fighting chance to seize the day.[33]

One of Washington insiders' favorite parlor games is that of leaks and counter-leaks. Reports of turmoil in the CIA appeared in the nation's newspapers in 2005. Director Porter Goss, who replaced George Tenet in 2004, previously had sniped at the CIA from his congressional seat in the House committee that oversaw the CIA. In 2005, Director Porter Goss attempted to create a new identity for the CIA following its reorganization—some apparently thought emasculation—by the IRTPA. Regardless of the correct description of the IRTPA's effects, poor morale was said to characterize America's once-premier intelligence agency. "A year after taking charge of the Central Intelligence Agency, Porter J. Goss is still struggling to rebuild morale and assert leadership within an institution shaken by recent failures and buffeted by change," according to the ubiquitous but anonymous congressional, White House, and intelligence community sources. A light appeared at the end of the tunnel and, for the first time in a long time, the light was not a train hurdling its way toward the CIA. "The CIA and its human spying operations are expected to benefit from changes in next year's [fiscal year 2006] intelligence budget, under classified plans being drawn up by the House and Senate Intelligence Committees, including a version approved by the Senate panel Thursday."[34] About a month after that news appeared, the *Washington Post* reported the following:

> The CIA will retain its role as chief coordinator of overseas spying by U.S. intelligence agencies under a plan approved by the White House that sources said was scheduled to be announced today.
>
> The plan envision[ed] creation of a National Clandestine Service within the CIA under Director Porter J. Goss, sources said. The chief of the new service will supervise the CIA's human intelligence operations and coordinate—but not direct—similar activities undertaken abroad by other parts of the intelligence community, including the FBI and Defense Department agencies.

The same piece noted that a mounted effort on Capitol Hill had nearly taken away the CIA's historical clandestine authority as a result of its poor performance and intelligence failures dating from before but certainly including 9/11. "The Senate Select Committee on Intelligence—citing past

CIA failures in averting the Sept. 11, 2001, attacks and in overstating Iraq's weapons of mass destruction—recently concluded in a report that coordination of human intelligence should be moved to the office of the director of national intelligence, John D. Negroponte." Had that happened, an already demoralized CIA would have suffered significantly. "If the coordinating role had not remained in the CIA, it would have been bad for agency morale," which already was 'down,' a former senior intelligence official said yesterday." Apparently having some difficulty interpreting "deconfliction," the same author reported:

> As currently envisioned, the clandestine services director will have a deputy who would not only coordinate overseas spying operations, but also ensure that agencies do not overlap one another in recruitment or operations, described by one official as "deconflicting" activities in the community. The deputy will also supervise establishment of common standards for training all human intelligence collectors in tradecraft, including the recruitment, vetting and handling of sources.[35]

Therefore, while the IRTPA prescribed few specific changes and did little to rehabilitate the CIA's standing in the reorganized intelligence community that the IRTPA created, the IRTPA took for granted that the CIA would continue to be the lead agency in HUMINT and clandestine operations. In late 2005, the Office of the DNI announced the following with respect to the CIA. "Today, the Director of National Intelligence (DNI) and the Director of the Central Intelligence Agency announced the President's approval of the establishment of the National Clandestine Service (NCS) within the CIA." Confusing an already confusing alphabet soup of policymaking acronyms even more, the National Clandestine Service was announced as reporting "directly to the Director of the CIA" and as working "with the Office of the Director of National Intelligence to implement all of the DNI's statutory authorities."[36]

The Intelligence Reform and Terrorism Prevention Act: Title VI

In Title VI of the IRTPA, the drafters created a set of new laws to prevent future acts of terrorism, the "terrorism prevention" part of the legislation. The first matter they addressed was the now infamous Foreign Intelligence Surveillance Act (FISA). Already noted above was the story that broke in late 2005 in which the *New York Times* scooped its competition with a story in which President Bush was said to be circumventing FISA. The administration admitted that it indeed had, following 9/11, begun using the NSA (then under Director General Michael V. Hayden, who subsequently was appointed as the first principal deputy DNI) to spy on what the administration promised was signal intelligence of al Qaeda or other terrorist organizations. Since to date the full breadth of the program is only known by a few members of Congress, it is impossible to confirm the administration's charge that only al Qaeda's and other jihadi organizations' signals were being tapped. Few Americans seemed concerned about spying on al Qaeda; indeed most Americans apparently approved of it in the post-9/11 world. The problem arose insofar as some of the signal intelligence terminated somewhere in the U.S., and some of these intercepts were bound to include American citizens.[37] Judged by how few complaints followed the scoop, if American citizens were working with al Qaeda and/or its affiliates, few Americans worried that such Americans' civil rights might be violated. The devil was, as is so often the case, in the details of the program. And the administration refused to disclose them.

Subtitle A under Title VI was entitled "Individual Terrorist as Agents of Foreign Powers." Therein the IPRTA amended the 1978 FISA legislation with the language "engages in international terrorism or preparation thereof," slightly reorienting FISA for today's global jihadi threats. The legislation also directed the attorney general to report to the relevant committees of Congress on a "semiannual" basis "the aggregate number of persons targeted" under FISA.[38] This provision too proved difficult for the Bush administration to comply with, as the *New York Times* story and subsequent reporting determined. The relevant congressional committees, according to the IRTPA, were both the U.S. House Permanent Select Committee on Intelligence and the Senate Select Intelligence Committee as well as the respective judiciary committees on either side of Congress. The administration had not even squared its actions with Foreign Intelligence Surveillance Court, as was discovered in late 2005 when Judge Colleen Kollar-Kotelly, the federal judge who oversaw the Federal Intelligence Surveillance Court, questioned the Justice Department as to whether NSA intercepts were being properly used according to FISA.[39]

Under another subsection of Title VI, the drafters of IRTPA provided for financial instruments for the proactive attacking of foreign terrorism.

As with any criminal enterprise, money is needed to implement terrorism plans. Following 9/11, much was learned about al Qaeda financing, much of which came from charitable organizations—some witting, some unwitting—raising money for Islamic causes. In fact, following 9/11 the federal government cracked down dramatically on Islamic charities operating in the United States, which had hitherto been left mostly unencumbered. That costly lesson translated itself in a series of executive orders as well as legislation. Under "Money Laundering and Financial Crimes Strategies Reauthorization," the IRTPA sought to obviate terrorism financing. Indeed, the IRTPA devoted several pages and sections to attacking the financing that enabled terrorists to strike the U.S. and to ensure that any future activity along those lines was made incredibly more difficult. While those provisions were, doubtlessly, exceptionally important and well worth reading, in-depth analysis is beyond the current scope. However, the reader is encouraged to assess the manifold financial instruments created by IRTPA.[40] It is worth noting that the 9/11 Public Discourse Project's "report card" gave its only high mark to date to this aspect of the post-9/11 reforms and reorganizations.[41] Additionally, in June 2006 the media broke another story—again it was the *New York Times* that scooped the others—in which it reported that the U.S. had effectively used a financial consortium, known as SWIFT in Brussels, to stymie al Qaeda's efforts. The Bush administration complained bitterly about the disclosure, arguing that it had helped the enemy to know what tools were being used against it. We shall leave the judgment of whether the *New York Times* behaved irresponsibly to others. Suffice it to say that much of what was reported could be found simply by reading the IRTPA.

Two additional subsections under Title VI are worth brief mention. Both deal with weapons of mass destruction (WMD): biological, chemical, radiological, and nuclear.[42] Both Subtitle I (the letter "I"), entitled "Weapons of Mass Destruction Prohibition Improvement Act of 2004" and Subtitle J "Prevention of Terrorist Access to Destructive Weapons Act of 2004" were relatively sensible provisions in law criminalizing development and trafficking in said weapons. Clearly, the IRTPA accepted the premise of President Bush's speeches in 2002 (and since) in which he identified the intersection of jihadis with the world's most dangerous weapons as the biggest threat to the U.S. and the Western world for the foreseeable future.[43]

**The Intelligence Reform and Terrorism Prevention Act:
Miscellaneous**

The IRTPA devoted nearly 100 pages to "Implementation of 9/11 Commission Recommendations."[44] In those pages, it is clear, the legislators who drafted the IRTPA attempted to follow the 9/11 Commission recommendations essentially in total. Very few items recommended by the 9/11 Commission did not find their way into the IRTPA. Some of the most interesting sections are entitled "Diplomacy, Foreign Aid, and the Military in the War on Terrorism" (at § 7001 subtitle A), "United States Policy toward Dictatorships" (at § 7107), "Promotion of Free Media and other American Values" (at § 7108), and "Public Diplomacy Responsibilities of the Department of State," that is, the State Department's propaganda responsibilities (at § 7109). The main subtitles enumerated under Title VII are clear indicators that the IRTPA codified the 9/11 report's recommendations in law. Included were: "Subtitle B—Terrorist Travel and Effective Screening," "Subtitle C—National Preparedness," "Subtitle D—Homeland Security," "Subtitle F—Presidential Transition," and others. Much of the language in IRTPA appears intentionally obtuse; in fairness it should be said that U.S. legal code is written in legalese and, perhaps, is the language that only lawyers may fully appreciate. Nevertheless, once deciphered they appear to be largely sensible provisions now part of U.S. law that shall hopefully be useful to the president and his NSC policymakers in preventing future 9/11s.

SUMMARY

The IRTPA constituted historic reorganization of America's national security bureaucracy. The reorganization was on a level that approached the 1947 reorganizations discussed throughout this book. The reorganizations directed are well underway and some have been completed, both of which *should* prove beneficial to U.S. national security. We have acknowledged that the 9/11 Commission was exceptionally successful in seeing its recommendations codified in law. The Bush administration endorsed virtually all of its recommendations. Following the passage of the IRTPA into law, the Bush administration and the new DNI have complied with virtually all the recommendations made by the 9/11 and Robb-Silberman commissions. The president, of course, signed the IPRTA on December 17,

2004, giving his official blessing to the legislation. The Robb-Silberman Commission's influence was somewhat less direct in terms of the IPRTA itself but its recommendations have been used in whole by the DNI during his nearly 24 months as the head of American's intelligence community. Of all the many recommendations offered by both, only one substantive, measurable recommendation—at least of those that were unclassified—was not endorsed by the president. The commissions recommended disclosure of America's annual intelligence budget. The budget is not exactly a carefully guarded secret. In fact, it was all but known that the intelligence budget was roughly $30 billion annually prior to 9/11. It is now known that the budget increased markedly following 9/11. As cited previously the intelligence community's overall appropriation for fiscal year 2005, which passed Congress and was signed by the president, was $44 billion.[45]

The IRTPA represented a significant reorganization to the institutions that create and implement U.S. national security policies. It structurally changed the U.S. intelligence community. The new DNI was empowered with authorities that the DCI never had or used. Those authorities and others have now been vested in the DNI. Time will tell how deft a bureaucratic actor DNI Negroponte and his successors prove to be. Early indications are mixed; Mr. Negroponte is encountering predictable bureaucratic resistance, particularly in the Department of Defense. Recently, for instance, a former CIA official expressed his concerns that the ODNI might not be up to the task. Mr. John O. Brennan, who was the interim director of the National Counterterrorism Center (NCTC) until July 2005, said he still did not detect any "overarching framework" that would assign roles and responsibilities in a systematic way, delineating who was responsible for what precisely. "His concerns are widely echoed in Washington, where John D. Negroponte [approached] the end of his first year as the first director of national intelligence, a job created by Congress in response to the Sept. 11 attacks." Mr. Brennan further suggested that "he did not believe that Mr. Negroponte had moved decisively enough to limit efforts by the Pentagon," which the reporter noted still controlled "80 percent of the intelligence budget, to expand its role in spying."[46]

Another piece specifically cited the defense department as Mr. Negroponte's biggest bureaucratic obstacle. Since the Pentagon historically controlled so much of the intelligence budget, it is no surprise that a bureaucratic rivalry has appeared. "One test for Director of National Intelligence

John D. Negroponte in his first year in office was how, as President Bush's top intelligence adviser, he would meet challenges to his authority that came from Defense Secretary Donald H. Rumsfeld." According to the same piece, the IRTPA *gave the DNI roughly 70 percent of the intelligence budget*. Since the intelligence budget is by definition a zero-sum process, the DNI's 70 percent came at the expense of the Pentagon's historical 80 percent. In an extraordinary exchange between Senator Susan Collins (R-MN), one of the drafters of the IRTPA, with DNI Negroponte testifying before the Senate Armed Services Committee, Collins queried Negroponte "whether a recent Defense Department directive placing authority over the Pentagon intelligence activities with Undersecretary of Defense for Intelligence Stephen A. Cambone created any 'concerns' that the DNI's authority was being subverted." Negroponte responded that "he had worked with Cambone on the directive for three months, that there was 'constant dialogue,' and that every change he suggested was accepted." In a moment of perhaps unusual candor for so seasoned a diplomat as Mr. Negroponte, he "suggested that there may have been a bit of conflict, after all: 'One area that we're working on now—and I don't mean to invite help, because I think we'll work our way through it quite well—is the area of personnel. And what you have there are intelligence-community personnel who are also in a Cabinet-level department. And we look at those people as intelligence people, and the secretary [of defense] certainly looks upon those as DOD folks.'"[47] Clearly, the jury is still out on how well DNI Negroponte has fared against Secretary Rumsfeld, his lieutenants such as Dr. Cambone, and their replacements.

More positively, from a reorganization and reform perspective, the IRTPA created both the National Counterterrorism Center (the NCTC) and the National Counterproliferation Center (NCPC) and as was seen, hundreds of persons are now working in these new institutions, presumably fortifying the U.S.'s capabilities against the global jihadi threat *as well* as traditional state actors (Iran, North Korea, China, and so on). The numbers revealed by Negroponte in his Georgetown University speech (discussed above) were for a "few hundred" persons at the NCTC and sixty or seventy persons at the NCPC. Furthermore, the National Intelligence Centers or NICs were noted. Those centers are operating and, if working as envisioned by the 9/11 and Robb-Silberman commissioners, they should be providing interagency intelligence analysis and advice.

Early in 2006, DNI Negroponte announced the creation and staffing of the position of director for mission managers, a concept articulated in the Robb-Silberman WMD Report and apparently linked with the NICs. A sense of interagency functionality of the mission managers may be gathered from reading the press release announcing them. First, a general summary was provided.

> The DNI created four Mission Managers: one for counterterrorism, the Director of the National Counterterrorism Center; one for counterproliferation, the Director of the National Counterproliferation Center; and one each for the countries of Iran and North Korea. Mission Managers will not directly manage operations or analysis, but will instead lead the Intelligence Community at a strategic level.

An even clearer picture emerges when reading the descriptions of specific mission managers. For example, under the mission manager created for North Korea, the press release observed, "Ambassador [Joseph] DeTrani is responsible for integrating collection and analysis on North Korea across the Intelligence Community, identifying and filling gaps in intelligence, and planning and ensuring the implementation of strategies, among other duties." One may presume that said transfunctionality is what is meant by a "strategic level."[48]

In sum, many changes have been made to the president-NSC-policymaking model as well as the how the intelligence community interacts with it. The IRTPA is comprehensive legislation aimed at thwarting future surprise attacks against the United States and its allies. It attempted to accomplish its goals via multiple avenues. The main one was to reform significantly the intelligence community and how it moved intelligence data from agencies to policymakers. Integral to this process in the future shall likely be the Joint Intelligence Community Council. In the final chapter we turn to some of the implications that follow from the changes discussed in this chapter. In so doing we shall attempt to assess how well the changes wrought by the IRTPA have fared.

NOTES

1. Robb-Silberman, 579 (Acrobat Reader pagination, 595).
2. Robb-Silberman, 587 (Acrobat Reader pagination, 603).

3. Robb-Silberman, 588 (Acrobat Reader pagination, 604).

4. Robb-Silberman, 588–589 (Acrobat Reader pagination, 604–605).

5. Secretary of Defense Donald Rumsfeld and Undersecretary of Defense for Intelligence Stephen Cambone, resigned and announced plans to retire, respectively, following the November 7, 2006, midterm elections. See William Branigin, "Rumsfeld to Step Down as Defense," *Washington Post*, November 8, 2006, http://www.washingtonpost.com/wp-dyn/content/article/2006/11/08/AR2006110801180.html; for Cambone, see Washington in Brief, "Pentagon Official to Resign," *Washington Post*, December 2, 2006, http://www.washingtonpost.com/wp-dyn/content/article/2006/12/01/AR2006120101471.html.

6. Robb-Silberman, 589 (Acrobat Reader pagination, 605) (my emphasis).

7. *Intelligence Reform and Terrorist Prevention Act of 2004,* Public Law 108-455 (December 17, 2004), http://frwebgate.access.gpo.gov/cgi-bin/getdoc.cgi?dbname=108_cong_public_laws&docid=f:publ458.108.pdf (accessed on October 12, 2005). The original copy used for this manuscript was found at the C-SPAN Web site http://c-span.org/pdf/2004IntelAct.pdf (accessed on December 30 2004). Hereafter referred to as the IRTPA, with section and Acrobat Reader pagination, the latter in parentheses.

8. IRTPA, Title I, "Reform of the Intelligence Community," at § 1011 (Acrobat Reader pagination, 8). (Note, the Acrobat version has only the pagination provided by the Acrobat reader; hereafter a page number refers to the Acrobat Reader's automatic pagination system designated by Acrobat, in this case, page 8 of 236 or simply 8.)

9. IRTPA, Title I, "Reform of the Intelligence Community," at § 1011, adding 102–3(A), (Adobe Reader pagination, 9).

10. IRTPA, Title I, "Reform of the Intelligence Community," at § 1011, (Adobe Reader pagination, 18).

11. IRTPA, Title I, "Reform of the Intelligence Community," at § 1011 (Adobe Reader pagination, 12 and 14).

12. Inasmuch as both reports were published in Acrobat format, a simple search using "National Security Council" and "NSC" may be done. The Robb-Silberman report cites the National Security Council some 26 times dispersed widely throughout the report.

13. As will be seen presently, the IPRTA accounted for the continuation of the President's Foreign Intelligence Advisory Board; the JICC is significantly different inasmuch as its principals are the heads of major intelligence and homeland security bureaucracies.

14. IRTPA, Title I, "Reform of the Intelligence Community," at § 1022 (Adobe Reader pagination, 41–42).

15. The IRTPA legislation designates the Joint Intelligence Community Council as responsible for advising the DNI on "establishing requirements . . . and monitoring and evaluating the performance of the Intelligence Community." IRTPA, Title I, Subtitle C, at § 1031 (Adobe Reader pagination, 41).

16. Robb-Silberman, endnote 27, 350 (Acrobat Reader pagination, 366).

17. Robb-Silberman, 336 (Acrobat Reader pagination, 352).

18. The Church Committee findings may be found at the AARC Public Library Contents Web site at http://www.aarclibrary.org/publib/church/reports/contents.htm. The Pike Committee work and analysis thereof may be found at Muskingum College, New Concord

Ohio: http://intellit.muskingum.edu/cia_folder/ cia70s_folder/cia70sinvu-z.html (accessed in January 2006).

19. Robb-Silberman, 337 (Acrobat Reader pagination, 353).

20. James Risen and Eric Lichtblau, "Bush Lets U.S. Spy on Callers without Courts," *New York Times*, December 16, 2005, http://nytimes.com/2005/12/16/politics/16program.html. This article broke the NSA warrant-less spying story. Since then literally scores of pieces have been published. Also, since then an additional dustup occurred over the news that the NSA, along with privately owned telephone companies in America, collected data on phone calls including those of Americans.

21. IRTPA, Title I, Subtitle B, "National Counterterrorism Center, the National Counter Proliferation Center, and the National Intelligence Centers," at § 1021, 1022, and 1023 (Acrobat Reader pagination, 36–41).

22. IRTPA, Title I, Subtitle B, Ibid at § 1021 (Acrobat Reader pagination, 37).

23. John D. Negroponte, "Intelligence Reform: Challenges and Opportunities," (speech, Georgetown University, February 17, 2006), http://www.dni.gov/dni_remarks_georgetown_20060217.html (accessed February 18, 2006).

24. IRTPA, Title I, Subtitle B, Ibid at § 1022 (Acrobat Reader pagination, 39).

25. IRTPA, Title I, Subtitle B, Ibid at § 1022 (Acrobat Reader pagination, 39).

26. IRTPA, Title I, Subtitle B, Ibid at § 1022 (Acrobat Reader pagination, 40).

27. The current author has made the argument elsewhere that the global war against ji-hadi extremists shall likely be a multi-decade, if not multi-generational, matter. See M. Kent Bolton, *U.S. Foreign Policy and International Politics*, *op cit*. That argument has been carried over into this book as well. However, it should be noted that persons inside and outside the Bush administration also perceive the struggle against those who wish to reestablish the caliphate system versus modernity as long-term. Here we have quoted the president and others in the administration to that effect. But even critics of the administration have argued similarly. See Center for American Progress and the Council on Foreign Relations, *The Terrorism Index*, (July 28, 2006), http://www.americanprogress.org/site/pp.aspx? c=biJRJ8OVF&b= 1826603&printmode=1 (accessed July 29, 2006). One of the two co-sponsors of the report was the Center for American Progress, a progressive group that has been relatively hostile to the Bush administration.

28. IRTPA, Title III, at § 2001 (Acrobat Reader pagination, 64).

29. IRTPA, Title III, at § 2001 (Acrobat Reader pagination, 64–65).

30. IRTPA, Title III, at § 2002 (Acrobat Reader pagination, 66). For a view of how well the FBI has done in its efforts to reorient the FBI and integrate its mission with that of the ODNI, see Sari Horwitz, "Old-School Academy in Post-9/11 World: New Focus Is on Terrorism, but Training Is Struggling to Keep Up," *Washington Post*, August 17, 2006, http://www.washingtonpost.com/wp-dyn/content/article/2006/08/16/ AR2006081601622 .html.

31. 9/11 Commission, 414 (Acrobat Reader pagination, 432).

32. The 9/11 Commission report, for instance, documented battles between Defense and the CIA prior to 9/11 over the then-secret Predator drone which the CIA had configured to fire hellfire missiles — missiles the CIA could only get from Defense. The result included, arguably, at least one attempt to kill Osama bin Laden prior to 9/11 that never took

place due to debates about who controlled the Predator and who would pay for the missiles. See 9/11 Commission, Chapter 6 "From Threat to Threat," especially sections "Afghan Eyes," and "Considering a Response."

33. IRTPA, Title I, at § 1013 (Acrobat Reader pagination, 26–27).

34. Douglas Jehl, "After a Year Leading CIA, Goss Is Struggling, Some Say," *New York Times*, September 23, 2005, http://www.nytimes.com/2005/09/23/politics/23intel.html.

35. Walter Pincus, "CIA to Remain Coordinator of Overseas Spying," *Washington Post*, October 13, 2005, http://www.washingtonpost.com/wp-dyn/content/article/2005/10/12/AR2005101202174.html.

36. Office of the Director of National Intelligence, "Establishment of the National Clandestine Service (NCS)," ODNI News Release No. 3–05, October 13, 2005, http://www.dni.gov/ release_letter_101305.html (accessed December 5, 2005) (my emphasis).

37. See James Risen and Eric Lichtblau, "Bush Lets U.S. Spy on Callers without Courts," *New York Times*, December 16, 2005, http://nytimes.com/2005/12/16/politics/16program.html, *supra*. While it is beyond the current scope, the reader may wonder why Americans might get exercised about the NSA spying on al Qaeda members and affiliates even if one end of the signals intelligence being intercepted terminated in America. Indeed, some Americans may believe that if Americans are helping al Qaeda they should have their e-mail and phone calls as well as other electronic intelligence intercepted. As far we are concerned, that is a reasonable sentiment. The problem arises, however, when the president or his agents are deciding who and what constitutes al Qaeda and affiliates. Moreover, what constitutes an interceptable signal? For instance, we have previously researched al Qaeda and other jihadi groups. While an Academic Fellow for the Foundation for the Defense of Democracies, we were sent to the Middle East in summer 2005. Were our Internet searches that attempted to find more about al Qaeda subject to interception? The point is that without a court warrant, there exist no guarantees that such a program is not abused, even by well-intentioned officials.

38. IRTPA, Title III, at § 6001 (Acrobat Reader pagination, 106–107).

39. James Risen and Eric Lichtblau, "Bush Lets U.S. Spy on Callers Without Courts," December 16, 2005, http://nytimes.com/2005/12/16/politics/16program.html; Dan Eggen and Charles Lane, "On Hill, Anger and Calls for Hearings Greet News of Stateside Surveillance," *Washington Post*, December 17,2005, http://www.washingtonpost.com/wp-dyn/content/article/2005/12/16/AR2005121601825.html. Especially see Carol D. Leonnig, "Surveillance Court Is Seeking Answers: Judges Were Unaware of Eavesdropping," *Washington Post*, January 5, 2006, http://www.washingtonpost.com/wp-dyn/content/article/2006 /01/04/AR2006010401864.html.

40. IRTPA, Title VI, at § 6002, 6101, 6102, and 6201 through 6205 as well as § 6601-6604 (Acrobat Reader pagination, 108–112 and 25–128).

41. 9/11 Public Discourse Project, "Final Report on 9/11 Commission Recommendations," December 5, 2005.

42. It should be noted that the media traditionally refer to such weapons as WMDs. Some agencies within the U.S. government, academics, and specialists in the area refer to the same weapons by the initialization CBRN for chemical, biological, radiological, and nuclear.

43. IRTPA, Title VI, at § 6801–6911 (Acrobat Reader pagination, 130–139).

44. IRTPA, Title VII, at § 7001–7804 (Acrobat Reader pagination, 139–228).

45. Scott Shane, "Official Reveals Budget for U.S. Intelligence," *New York Times*, November 8, 2005, http://www.nytimes.com/2005/11/08/politics/08budget.html. Also see footnote above where other sources for the intelligence budget are cited.

46. Scott Shane, "Year into Revamped Spying, Troubles and Some Progress," *New York Times*, February 28, 2006, http://www.nytimes.com/2006/02/28/politics/28terror.html.

47. Walter Pincus, "Negroponte's Battle for Authority," *Washington Post*, March 6, 2006, http://www.washingtonpost.com/wp-dyn/content/article/2006/03/05/AR2006030500817.html.

48. Office of the Director of National Intelligence, "ODNI Announces Mission Managers and Senior Leadership Position" (news release, January 11, 2006) http://www.dni.gov/release_letter_011106.html

CHAPTER 10

The Future of U.S. National Security Policymaking

Achieving this goal is the work of generations. The United States is in the early years of a long struggle, similar to what our country faced in the early years of the Cold War. The twentieth century witnessed the triumph of freedom over the threats of fascism and communism. Yet a new totalitarian ideology now threatens, an ideology grounded not in secular philosophy but in the perversion of a proud religion. Its content may be different from the ideologies of the last century, but its means are similar: intolerance, murder, terror, enslavement, and repression.

—George W. Bush, preamble to *The National Security Strategy of the United States, March 2006.*

It is the policy of the United States to seek and support democratic movements and institutions in every nation and culture, with the ultimate goal of ending tyranny in our world. In the world today, the fundamental character of regimes matters as much as the distribution of power among them. The goal of our statecraft is to help create a world of democratic, well-governed states that can meet the needs of their citizens and conduct themselves responsibly in the international system. This is the best way to provide enduring security for the American people.

—White House, *The National Security Strategy of the United States, March 2006.*

September 11th, 2001, was one of those rare external stimuli—a foreign policy crisis—that permitted policymakers to shape U.S. national security policy directly and demonstrably. That may, at first glance, appear a rather unremarkable statement. However, presidents and other national security policymakers do not normally affect U.S. national security policy directly and demonstrably. Rather, societal and governmental sources typically result in continuity in U.S. national security policy over time. Presidents often enter office thinking that they directly affect foreign policy only to discover that the bureaucracy entrusted with implementing policy as well as inertial societal, governmental, and role sources constrain a given president's direct influences. If the president's direct influence is constrained, then so too is the influence of the president-NSC-policymaking model. As a foreign policy crisis, 9/11 began an important reorganization of the very institutions and bureaucracies that normally implement U.S. national security policy, including the president-NSC-policymaking model. Since 9/11, external, societal, and governmental inputs have continued the reorganization begun by 9/11.

A foreign policy crisis is a rare but critical stimulus that permits individual decision makers to circumvent standardized, established routines and 9/11 most certainly permitted the circumvention of routine procedures. The primary purpose of this book has been to explain those manifold changes. The last time U.S. foreign policy was so dramatically affected was as the Cold War commenced. Though *not* a foreign policy crisis, the series of cataclysmic events (from Turkey to the Korean War) was perceived by policymakers as if they collectively constituted a foreign policy crisis. The result of those perceptions was the passage of landmark legislation that thereafter shaped America's foreign policy for some sixty years. That legislation, the 1947 National Security Act, created the president-NSC-policymaking model, the modern intelligence community, and an array of accoutrements that have comprised *Pax Americana* ever since. Those institutions, including the NSC, the CIA, and the unified Department of Defense, became inseparable from America's change of national security trajectory, which became the Cold War and containment of the Soviet Union. Even after the Soviet Union ceased to exist, the Cold War institutions created by the 1947 NSA persisted in doing what they had done since their creation: contained various nation-state enemies, invariably defined as global tyrannies, as they appeared on U.S. policymakers' radar screens.

The 9/11 attacks were perceived by policymakers and most Americans as an extreme existential threat to the U.S. security. As such 9/11 compelled decision makers to take significant action in response. Additionally, 9/11 surprised U.S. policymakers. Policymakers are probably surprised by events more often than is comforting to those of us who study U.S. national security policy. However, surprise in combination with grave threat and short time in which to respond is a relatively infrequent circumstance for U.S. policymakers. Since policymakers perceived themselves as having only a small window of time in which to respond to 9/11 before additional attacks occurred (i.e., before a horrific day actually worsened), policymakers quickly responded. In responding hastily the president and his NSC principals circumvented normal operating procedures and the larger expertise normally provided by the vast bureaucracy created by the 1947 NSA. The surprise of 9/11 meant that policymakers had not considered specific contingency plans—the lifeblood of bureaucratic operations—and therefore those policymakers were compelled to improvise, which they certainly did. Some of their improvisations turned out well; others turned out less well. Improvisation may lead to exceptionally creative policymaking or it may lead to disaster. The outcome is neither guaranteed nor generalizable. The only thing guaranteed by a foreign policy crisis is that the policymaking processes will deviate from routine policymaking processes.

The outcome of 9/11 was a change in U.S. national security policy, no small accomplishment: containment was supplanted by preventive (arguably preemptive) strikes as the national security instrument of choice by which other U.S. national security goals (survival of America, promotion of democracy as a valued preference, protection of America's important allies, and global trade) would thereafter be achieved. In other words, an essentially defensive policy—containment and nuclear deterrence—was replaced by a proactive, offensive policy that sought to anticipate threats a priori and then to thwart them before they fully materialized. Containment had served the U.S. and its Western allies since the early 1950s. Following 9/11, containment was immediately dismissed as inadequate to the neutralization of the new transnational, non-state threats: global jihadis. Some version of containment and nuclear deterrence doubtless continues in U.S. national security policy for more traditional, state-actor threats but only time will tell whether and how often the U.S. continues to rely on either and for which threats.

As discussed in chapters 2 and 3, democracy has always been a foreign policy goal for the U.S. to one extent or another. However, during America's isolationist past, American policymakers contented themselves with demonstrating the virtues of democracy by example. During American's isolationist past, U.S. policymakers were willing to use America's democratic governance as an example to others, "that shining city on a hill." Nevertheless, we have seen that having democracy as a goal did not forestall U.S. policymakers from entering into alliances, from time to time, with rather undemocratic partners. During the Cold War, for instance, U.S. policymakers formed alliances of expediency with authoritarian, nondemocratic regimes. The greater good of thwarting Soviet tyranny made such alliances, as U.S policymakers perceived them, the lesser of two evils and, therefore, congruent with America's ethos and mythology.

U.S. foreign policy has been internationalist or globalist in its orientation ever since the U.S. jettisoned isolationism following World War II. Today, U.S. foreign policy may properly be characterized as interventionist rather than simply internationalist. Even when U.S. national security policy consisted principally of containment, America intervened in the affairs of other sovereign nations. However, during the Cold War the U.S. intervened in other nations' sovereign affairs nearly always as part and parcel of containment of the Soviet Union—those interventions were widely known as proxy wars. In the post-9/11 environment the Bush administration—and we argue that what began under Bush will largely be adopted by his successors and will only undergo incremental refinement—launched the United States, for its foreseeable future, on a course of neointerventionism, including "regime change" when deemed necessary. Since its origins America has recurrently sought an appropriate role in world politics. Since World War II, leading the democratic world has been seen as America's appropriate role by most U.S. national security policymakers. It became the U.S. foreign policy consensus or orthodoxy of both major political parties in America. Since 9/11, the Bush administration has promoted democracy as an explicit U.S. foreign policy objective and has sought to lead the world in achieving that objective. Promoting democratic governance has therefore become an explicit objective of U.S. national security, along with America's previous objectives of commercial liberalism and other similar goals. Consequently, attenuating or thwarting nondemocratic governance has also become a fundamental goal of U.S. national security policy. The Bush administration changed democracy from a value or preference that underlay American objectives to an explicit national security goal. As an epigraph to this chapter suggested, the Bush administration's unabashed advancement of democracy is materially different than previous administrations. Following the preamble that began the *National Security Strategy of the United States*, March 2006, the NSC drafters of the document wrote the following:

> It is the policy of the United States to seek and support democratic movements and institutions in every nation and culture, with the ultimate goal of ending tyranny in our world. In the world today, the fundamental character of regimes matters as much as the distribution of power among them. The goal of our statecraft is to help create a world of democratic, well-governed states that can meet the needs of their citizens and conduct themselves responsibly in the international system. This is the best way to provide enduring security for the American people.

The paragraph formed the predicate for the entire document and for national security strategy of the United States according to President George W. Bush's National Security Council and its staffers. The fifty-page document used the word "democracy" no fewer than 52 times.[1]

As new goals and objectives replaced older ones, new policymaking machinery, processes, and institutions necessarily followed. President Bush and future presidents will have new national security institutions to help them navigate an increasingly complex international environment. Just as containment of the Soviet Union necessitated creation of a unified Department of Defense and a comprehensive set of military institutions, the CIA and other intelligence community assets, an enhanced Department of State with multiple and layered applications of diplomacy, and the U.S. National Security Council (NSC), new bureaucratic creations have accompanied America's most recent change in trajectory. Many new institutions and processes were created by the president by fiat, through executive orders. Others examined in this book were created via complex negotiation and compromise between the executive and the legislative branches. However they were created, the new institutions, bureaucracies, and procedures will hereafter accompany America's sojourn into a future of both state and non-state threats and increasingly ubiquitous weapons of mass destruction.

We have considered the genesis of the new institutions and machinery. Many of them were created by Congress and paralleled the 1947 National Security Act. We devoted an entire chapter to what the 1947 NSA created and another chapter to the successor legislation that resulted from 9/11 and its aftermath, the IRTPA. Over time, one should expect to see incremental evolution in institutions quickly created by Congress in the aftermath of 9/11. Other creations were improvised by President Bush, who was given wide berth by the American people and Congress during the early months following 9/11.[2] Whether created by Congress or the president, the post-9/11 consensus was a requisite for these changes. As the Cold War consensus made change possible during the late 1940s and early 1950s, the post-9/11 consensus was requisite for the manifold changes enacted since 9/11. America, the EU, China, and India will increasingly compete for the world's finite resources as each continues its respective advancement in the twenty-first century. Therefore, while we have conceded that jihadi extremism is an existential threat to America and the West, state threats will also continue. Future presidential administrations shall have to contend with both concomitantly, lest they become obsessed with transnational threats and neglect developments in traditional state threats.

PROCESS

In these final pages, we wish to review some of the changes documented in previous chapters. To do so we return to the issue of process, something discussed early in chapter 2. Recall the cluster of inputs (exogenous or X variables) that were effectively held constant while considering a particular cluster of inputs. When societal inputs were considered, for example, governmental, individual, role, and external inputs were held constant in order to focus on societal. Similarly, when governmental inputs were considered, external, societal, individual, and role inputs were held constant. In this chapter, we make no attempt to hold independent variables constant. Process is perhaps most difficult for an analyst to get right. It requires considering all the inputs simultaneously given a particular setting or issue area. Process presumes that all the inputs affect foreign policy-making, according to time, context, and issue area.

Without considering process, U.S. national security policymaking might seem far too organized and clean. Policymaking is invariably a messy process. In order to examine process the analyst must employ a conceptual construct or framework for considering all of the multiple inputs in some meaningful way. First, a brief review of the changes discussed in detail in earlier chapters will be summarized. Our review intentionally compares the two significant legislative acts that shaped America's national security policymaking institutions, procedures, and processes during the Cold War through September 11, 2001, and following 9/11 respectively. Then two thematic criteria are articulated and employed to analyze process as it relates to the reorganizations herein analyzed.

The Changes Resulting from 9/11 and Its Aftermath

New NSC entities were created that need to be represented in any organization chart of America's reorganized national security institutions and in the president-NSC-policymaking model. They are the Department of Homeland Security; its NSC cognate, the NSC Homeland Security Council; and the Joint Intelligence Community Council. We are aware that the JICC, strictly speaking, is not a policymaking bureaucracy. On the other hand, neither was the NSC created by the 1947 NSA, yet the president-NSC-policymaking model evolved nevertheless. The president and the president alone is the commander in chief by virtue of Article II of the U.S. Constitution. The NSC was created originally as a purely advisory body. In reality, it became a policymaking institution with vast power and influence and a staff who, from time to time at least, became policymakers on the ground in interesting parts of the world. NSC staff members have less frequently become policymakers in America's history, but we previously noted that the NSC staffer Richard Clarke became a policymaker and NSC principal. The following represents an approximation of today's version of the president-NSC-policymaking model. It is expected to evolve over time as did the original version.

The NSC principals committee has changed only slightly in composition from the original 1947 National Security Act. Since the IRTPA, the NSC

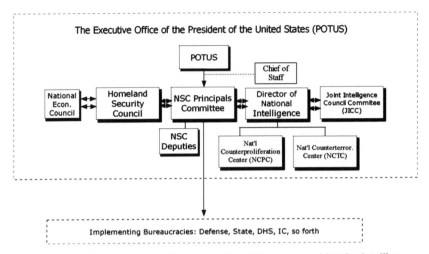

Figure 10.1. The Executive Office of the Presidency created by the Intelligence Reform and Terrorism Prevention Act. The main tier represents policymaking and advising. It may include ad hoc members such as the president's Homeland Security Advisor, Ms. Townsend; the secretary of DHS (currently Michael Chertoff); and the chairman of the Joint Chiefs of Staff (currently General Peter Pace, U.S. Marines). The primary locus of policymaking has become substantially larger than in the original president-NSC-policymaking model discussed in chapter 4.

principals may be identified as the president, the vice president, the secretaries of state and defense, the new director of national intelligence (DNI), the chairman of the Joint Chiefs of Staff (an adviser), and, probably, the president's adviser for homeland security. In the graphic above, the level of advising and policymaking that used to be occupied singly by the NSC during most of the Cold War (and by the president-cabinet model before the Cold War) has expanded considerably despite the fact that the NSC principals have changed only marginally. Indeed, the graphic arguably underrepresents the vast and complex myriad of structures beneath the JICC, the NSC, and the Homeland Security Council.

The National Economic Council was formally made part of the NSC policymaking level under President Bill Clinton. It was largely adopted as such under the current President, George W. Bush, though since 9/11, very little has been written about it. The National Economic Council's actual importance has been difficult to estimate accurately since 9/11; it has never formally been demoted or changed under the Bush administration, but 9/11 has likely caused it to atrophy bureaucratically. That it continues to exist suggests it will continue in future presidencies as well, even as

some of the other policy-line agencies accrue more bureaucratic influence. President George W. Bush's former director of the office of management and budget (OMB), Joshua Bolten, was recently made President
Bush's second chief of staff and was given more policymaking and management authority. Presumably, OMB director Joshua Bolten was represented on the National Economic Council prior to 9/11. As President
Bush's new chief of staff, Joshua Bolten, likely sits on multiple first-tier
policymaking committees.

Under the director of national intelligence (DNI) is yet another new bureaucratic institution not represented above. Since the 9/11 Committee
completed its work, DNI Negroponte used many of the recommendations
of the Robb-Silberman Commission to adjust, incrementally, a wholly
new bureaucratic creation which he, as the newest NSC principal, directs.
There is every reason to believe that incremental change will continue as
the Office of the DNI (ODNI) attempts to meet its new tasks and to coordinate effective intelligence collection and intelligence analysis into a
seamless product used by the NSC principals. Beyond collection and
analysis, DNI Negroponte will have to battle with powerful institutions
whose turf was made into a competitive field of bureaucratic rivalry by
the IRTPA. Who ultimately controls the playing field may become apparent over time. Over time, scholars, analysts, and policymakers will scrutinize its efficacy and more will be learned about it. Time will tell whether
the ODNI becomes simply another bureaucratic layer or an important bureaucratic actor in U.S. national security policymaking. If the former, then
the DNI is likely to lose any clout he gained through the IRTPA's designation of him as an NSC principal.

Multiple questions remain to be answered. Will the new DNI prove the
very influential person envisaged by the IRTPA? Will DNI Negroponte
and his successors marshal the intelligence community sufficiently such
that the intelligence community gathers intelligence and shares it across
the community? Insofar as they do, the DNI may truly be characterized as
a significant change in the way the president-NSC-policymaking model
operates: it would have directly affected policymaking at the NSC principals level. Will the DNI—whether Negroponte or his successors—prove
up to their bureaucratic disadvantages when compared to the Department
of Defense (to name the most obvious bureaucratic challenge)? Will the
DNI prove able to command the necessary attention from the NSC principals in order to balance a strong secretary of defense in the future? Will

the historically critical Department of State reemerge as the influential actor it was in years past? In short, will the DNI integrate itself effectively in future U.S. foreign and national security policymaking?

Additional questions about the reorganized president-NSC-policymaking structure should be posed. How will the JICC integrate itself and its intelligence product into the NSC principals committee setting? Will the congressional committees (and subcommittees) reorganize themselves as recommended in the 9/11 Commission and Robb-Silberman reports so as to create effective oversight of the reorganized structures? Will congressional oversight help to ensure the DNI's influence in the NSC principals while also ensuring the DNI's impartiality? If the DNI becomes captive to any presidential administration rather than to the presidency and America's security interests, the new DNI may potentially prove harmful to America's security interests. Will the director of CIA—no longer the DCI as the DNI has usurped those authorities—regain the reputation that the CIA historically enjoyed in America's Cold War history? Will the Department of Defense continue its forays into clandestine operations—something for which it is not particularly well-suited?[3]

What of the vice president and the NSC principals? We have argued that Vice President Cheney has become, inarguably, the most powerful vice president since the end of World War II—perhaps in all of America's history. Will the vice president also become a permanent force in the NSC principals? Will the next vice president—taking for granted that (s)he will not prove as powerful as Vice President Cheney in the George W. Bush administration—continue to flex bureaucratic muscle? These and many more questions must ultimately be answered by subsequent scholarship. However, some tentative assessment may be made based on evidence to date.

The Post-9/11 President-NSC-Policymaking Model: A Tentative Assessment of the Integration of the IRTPA's Provisions

Director Negroponte and his first principal deputy, General Michael V. Hayden, have made some reorganizations of their own since the IRTPA became law and Negroponte became America's first DNI. Director Negroponte chose to use the Robb-Silberman recommendations as his template or blueprint. For instance, a National Counterterrorism Center (NCTC) was created. Since Negroponte's appointment, the new DNI has created a similar center for counterproliferation. Thus, the NCPC is organized as a separate center at the same level that the NCTC exists. General Michael Hayden joined the ODNI as Negroponte's principal deputy director of national intelligence. Before he was appointed as Negroponte's principal deputy, General Hayden directed the National Security Agency (NSA). Interestingly, the NSA historically fell under the aegis of the defense department. (Its budget, for instance, was part of what chapter 9 called the Joint Military Intelligence Program [JMIP] budget.) Presumably, it is now funded through both the JMIP and the National Intelligence Program. General Hayden joined the ODNI as an active U.S. Air Force General. (Since his appointment as America's first principal deputy director of national intelligence, General Hayden was nominated and approved by President Bush and Congress to direct the Central Intelligence Agency. The implications of that appointment are discussed below.)

The 9/11 Commission recommended and the DNI has announced the composition of multiple mission managers. Two known mission managers were announced by the ODNI in early 2006. Both mission managers were announced as being "responsible for integrating collection and analysis" for their respective missions "across the Intelligence Community, identifying and filling gaps in intelligence, and planning and ensuring the implementation of strategies, among other duties."[4] Precisely how and where they fit in the ODNI's organization chart is not clear, but they probably fit somewhere in line with or slightly below the NCPC and the NCTC. The Bush administration's approach to Iran and North Korea has been the subject of a raft of media coverage in 2006. America's relations with both countries have not been satisfactorily resolved. Whether and to what extent the mission managers appointed by DNI Negroponte have been involved has received virtually no media attention. The mission managers may prove an important bellwether of how well the DNI is doing bureaucratically. DNI Negroponte appears to consider the mission managers as small regionally- or functionally-based shops whose overarching organizational theme is interagency or trans-agency operations. How successfully mission managers integrate themselves into the post-IRTPA template must also await future scholarship.

In the following examination of how well the DNI and reorganized intelligence community have been grafted onto the president-NSC-policymaking model, two criteria shall be employed. Both are thematic. Both consider process rather than individual clusters of inputs. Furthermore, both criteria allow the reader to consider the IRTPA's creations in terms of the mission the IRTPA set as its objective for the newly adjusted intelligence community, with the director of national intelligence at its apex. As we have seen, the drafters of the IRTPA sought to re-create an intelligence community answering to one bureaucratic master who also served as an NSC principal, and so they must accomplish two main tasks. The first task shall be to transmit to the president and his other NSC principals objective, best-estimate, unvarnished intelligence and to do so even when said intelligence is not what other NSC principals wish to hear. The second is to integrate the newly created intelligence community into a vast bureaucratic behemoth created to fight the Cold War.

Integrating the Intelligence Community Seamlessly with
Policymaking: "Speaking Truth to Power"

In 2006 the *Oxford English Dictionary* defined a cliché as a "stereotyped expression, a commonplace phrase; also, a stereotyped character, style, etc."[5] A cliché is, in other words, a shop-worn phrase used to capture some sentiment that lacks precision but that is nevertheless repeated time and again as it has some kernel of generalizable knowledge understandable to many. Following 9/11 and the various postmortems examined herein, one cliché that appeared time and again was "to speak truth to power." As with most clichés, it captured some essence of reality: it represented the failure of the intelligence community and others to tell policymakers, particularly President Bush's NSC principals or war cabinet, what they needed to hear, rather than what they wished to hear. Fairly or not, the cliché was applied to agencies such as the CIA, the FBI, and the NSA, all of whom failed to say no to the president and his top policymakers. When the president and his principal policymakers—that is, Vice President Dick Cheney and Secretary of Defense Donald Rumsfeld—believed that Saddam Hussein had reconstituted Saddam's WMD program, despite evidence to the contrary, then-DCI George Tenet failed to tell the president that there existed evidence to the contrary. Tenet's failure to listen to his own agency, who told him the CIA had a high-level defector *inside* Saddam Hussein's inner circle who unequivocally confirmed that Saddam Hussein had not reconstituted his WMD, became an example of the failure to "speak truth to power." Instead of listening to his own specialist, who believed the informant in Saddam's inner circle, DCI Tenet accepted another so-called intelligence asset: "Curveball." Curveball's information contradicted the informant known to be inside Hussein's inner circle. Curveball was an Iraqi defector to Germany whom the CIA never interviewed directly. Nevertheless, George Tenet listened to Curveball's inaccurate affirmation that mobile biological labs existed—a belief the administration, particularly the administration's neoconservatives, insisted was true—over the information provided by Saddam Hussein's foreign minister, Naji Sabri.[6] Specialists at the CIA who had a bona fide informant's knowledge, for many reasons, failed to speak truth to power. In fairness to them, speaking truth to power would have involved high-level CIA analysts challenging Vice President Cheney's (and prominent neoconservatives in the vice president's office, Lewis I. "Scooter" Libby and David Addington among them) and Secretary Rumsfeld's (and prominent neoconservatives in the Department of Defense, Paul Wolfowitz and Douglas Fieth among them) long-held belief that mobile biological labs existed.

Though overly generalizable and a cliché and, moreover, a cliché that has been used ad nauseam in the post-9/11 period, "speaking truth to power" was precisely what the DNI position was created to do in order to reestablish the intelligence community's bona fides. DNI Negroponte must reestablish the reputation of the National Intelligence Estimates (NIEs) as a credible and reliable basis on which U.S. policymakers rely. DNI Negroponte need not prove that NIEs are always right. Rather, Negroponte must reestablish that his intelligence community's National Intelligence Estimates are the best estimate the intelligence community can make given all the uncertainty involved at a given time. For DNI Negroponte and the new intelligence structure to be successful they must expose their own assumptions, the underlying assumptions that are always made when attempting to predict phenomena, to the light of day as well as making those assumptions clear to the president and his NSC principals. DNI Negroponte and the other elements of the intelligence community must be prepared to tell subsequent NSC principals and presidents the reality versus what policymakers may believe is the reality.

Negroponte will have to tell the administration's ideologues when the intelligence community's best estimates do not support strongly held preconceived notions. Similarly, Negroponte must be able to tell them yes when the evidence does support a president and his NSC principals' beliefs. It will likely mean Negroponte (and perhaps his principal deputy)[7] may have to butt heads with powerful policymakers in order to protect the intelligence community's reputation but, more importantly, to ensure that a seamless transition exists between intelligence and policymaking at the NSC principals level. In early 2006, multiple indicators that Negroponte was butting heads bureaucratically with powerful institutions and their powerful cabinet officers appeared in the print media.

A potentially positive indicator of DNI Negroponte's bureaucratic acumen appeared as 2006 began. (Though positive in terms of "speaking truth to power," it may have augured poorly from a civil liberties perspective.) First, recall that the *New York Times* broke the story in fall 2005 about the National Security Agency eavesdropping on international signals data. That story, predictably, led to outcries of "Big Brother" and misuse of authorities by the intelligence community and policymakers. Specifically, the question turned on who determined whether an electronic signal—e-mail, telephone calls, and the like—could be gathered. The administration held (and apparently based on that understanding began gathering information shortly after 9/11) that if one end of the signal was a member of al Qaeda or another jihadi organization (or presumably other transnational threats), that was sufficient reason to gather it. On its face it appeared a reasonable enough position; however, it raised all manner of questions about abuse, safeguards, and oversight. Understandably, many Americans were concerned that the administration apparently felt no need to comply with the Foreign Intelligence Surveillance Act (FISA) provisions of obtaining a warrant in order to gather signals intercepts. The NSA historically has been restricted from collecting domestic SIGINT.[8] The administration took the position that *it*—with no FISA court or congressional oversight—could determine whether probable cause existed absent a FISA court warrant. Indeed, the administration contended that they need not obtain a warrant even *ex poste facto*, a relatively radical departure from past practices. The intrepid Walter Pincus began 2006 with an assessment of how the National Security Agency shared its information with other intelligence agencies, something the 9/11 Commission and Robb-Silberman reports lamented as not having happened prior to 9/11. Pincus suggested that the new intelligence community structure under DNI Negroponte was at least working well and sharing its work product.[9] If true, it meant that Negroponte had been able to wrest control of an agency historically under the Department of Defense's control, the NSA. (Though it is beyond the present scope, the number of agencies with whom the NSA shared its intercepts presented a potential for abuse. If, for instance, it shared its intercepts with IRS or DEA, that would be an abuse many Americans would likely find discomforting. Neither the IRS nor the DEA are frontline institutions in the war against the global jihadis, the justification for the intercepts in the first place.) Just days later another piece reported that DNI Negroponte's principal deputy, General Michael V. Hayden, in response to a letter from minority leader Nancy Pelosi (D-CA), explained to Representative Pelosi that he and the DNI had authorized parts of the same basic program under their own authority.[10] This was potentially important inasmuch as it demonstrated that the DNI and his principal deputy were exerting influence over NSA, a long-time Department of Defense operation and an agency that was known as reluctant to share the data it collected. Setting the issue of the potential for abuse aside, it appeared that Negroponte had followed the integration plans of both the 9/11 and Robb-Silberman WMD commissions. On that count, it provided positive evidence that DNI Negroponte was willing to exert his own influence.

Conversely, since it also suggested an overreach by President Bush, that is, failure to obtain a FISA warrant, it may also have demonstrated a failure by Negroponte and his principal deputy to tell the administration no when it was potentially violating U.S. law. On that count, it may have suggested that the DNI failed to speak truth to power. It may be too early to know definitively as the story continues to engulf the Washington media. New twists and turns appear in the media regularly at this writing. Following the historic November 7, 2006, midterm elections in which the Democrats seized power in both the House and Senate, the *New York Times* published a story in which the Bush White House was said to be consciously contemplating a showdown over the wiretapping program with the incoming Democrat-led Congress.[11] The matter appeared far from settled.

In May 2006, new revelations about the program appeared in which the NSA was reported to have purchased the phone-record data from major U.S. phone companies for the period of shortly after 9/11 through 2006. Very little at this point is known. The White House confirmed the program's existence but refused to divulge details publicly. The administration apparently briefed the relevant intelligence committees or their key members. In May, a week to the day after Porter Goss resigned from the CIA (discussed below), the story broke that the NSA also had collected phone-record data from millions of American phone calls and that the world's largest database was constructed from them. Understandably, a political maelstrom accompanied that revelation. From reports, it would appear that the administration used the same justification it used for by-passing FISA, namely, preventing another 9/11. Also according to reports, only broad parameters of the data were collected (the number calling and the number dialed, the time the call was placed, duration of the call, and so on), not the actual phone calls. The administration made the decision and the NSA complied. That suggested that DNI Negroponte was consulted and on board though his name has rarely appeared in press accounts of the revelation.[12] Reports claimed the NSA created the largest database in the world! Reports also suggested that the intelligence community, specifically the NSA, planned or had used statistical analysis of the records data in order to discover patterns.[13] The data analysis sounds suspiciously like data mining. If so, the questions shall include what deductive assumptions were made in mining data. Or was it inductive? Did they simply use statistical algorithms to find patterns from which they later made generalizations? The accounts have raised many questions. In one account, Vice President Cheney was reportedly an influential voice in convincing the president that it was incumbent on President Bush to authorize the program and the database construction.[14] It is difficult at this early point to conclude anything definitively about whether abuse has occurred and, if so, whether DNI Negroponte was part of it. If the reports of Cheney favoring the program and influencing its adoption are true, it may well augur poorly for the DNI in terms of speaking truth to power. Only as more information becomes available shall it be possible to make definitive statements about DNI Negroponte's role.

As noted above, early in 2006 DNI Negroponte created two new "mission managers," the interagency device recommended to Negroponte by the Robb-Silberman report. "The director of national intelligence, John D. Negroponte . . . created new 'mission managers' for Iran and North Korea, adding those two countries to a short list of top-priority challenges for American intelligence agencies," reported the *New York Times*.[15] The piece suggested that Negroponte was exerting control over his new fiefdom, created by the IRTPA. In theory, the mission managers may prove to be powerful transcommunity power centers that ensure critical husbandry of resources and areas of expertise across the intelligence community. DNI Negroponte noted them upon receiving the Trainor Award for exemplary diplomatic service in spring 2006 at Georgetown University. In his prepared remarks he said, "We have named mission managers for Iran and North Korea. These new posts are occupied by senior intelligence professionals whose job is to make the decisions and take the actions that I myself would take if I could spend all my time working on a single issue or a single country." Subsequently, in the question and answer period that followed he responded to a question about what criteria are used to establish different mission managers.[16] Negroponte's impromptu remarks support the view that the mission managers appear to have the ability to cull information from across the intelligence community. If so, questions must be asked as to what sort of cooperation they have received from the defense department's traditional intelligence community agencies.

In short, at this early time in the ODNI's history, whether the DNI and those whom he entrusts to speak for him were willing to speak truth to power seems questionable at best. On the one hand, it may turn out that the NSA's warrant-less collection of telephone records, including many domestic ones, which were then shared across the intelligence community was suggestive that "stovepipes" had come down. That was something both the 9/11 and Robb-Silberman commissions hoped to facilitate. On the other hand, if rumors of Vice President Cheney's role in the imbroglio are true and if Negroponte simply bowed to the will of a strong vice president who appeared to have influenced the president unduly, real substantive questions of the DNI's independence are necessarily raised. Though we hasten to add that it may be too early to judge fairly the DNI's behavior with respect to his superiors, our tentative conclusion is that the ODNI *has not spoken truth to power*!

Since the NSA warrant-less spy story broke in December 2005, dribs and drabs about the program continued to leak over several months. General Hayden took a leading role in explaining the program and assuring the public that it was legal. As noted above, the program consisted of the collection of signals intelligence (phone calls, e-mails, and the like) in which one of the ends was reported to have terminated with an al Qaeda (or affiliate) member. Thus, the program was described as limited and the public was assured that the NSA was not, for example, spying on regular Americans; that is to say, Americans who had no contact with jihadi groups elsewhere. In May 2006, *USA Today* broke the story that the NSA's warrant-less program was vastly greater than Americans had been led to believe in late 2005 and early 2006.[17] That revelation began days of literally scores of articles attempting to catch up with *USA Today*'s scoop. For present purposes, let us simply recall that a week earlier Porter Goss had tendered his resignation but was identified widely as having been fired—that happened "abruptly" on May 7, 2006. By Monday, May 10, 2006, President Bush, with DNI Negroponte on his right side and Deputy DNI General Michael Hayden on his left, announced that Bush had nominated Hayden to direct the CIA. Hayden's nomination to direct the CIA (spring 2006) resurrected many of the statements Hayden had made in behalf of the warrant-less NSA spy program in the previous months.

On Thursday, May 18, 2006, the Senate Select Intelligence Committee held its first hearing on General Hayden's nomination to take over the CIA. The first half of the day was a public hearing that was broadcast later that night on C-SPAN, but anyone with Internet access could have watched it live as it unfolded. The hearing, unsurprisingly, produced sparks as U.S. senators vented their frustration over the administration's failure to brief the intelligence committee members until the day before Hayden's hearing (March 17, 2006) and Hayden's questionable briefings and statements to date on NSA spying. However, the hearing was worth watching for scholars who wished to understand whether the ODNI was willing to give his congressional overseers the best assessments the intelligence community could produce, irrespective of potential political pressures exerted by the White House. The transcript, including not just General Hayden's prepared remarks but the entire question and answer session that followed them, was published on the DNI's Web site the next day.

Normally, the ranking Democrat on the Senate Select Intelligence Committee would have been Senator Jay Rockefeller (D-WV) who had recently had surgery and was unable to attend the hearing. In his absence, the ranking Democrat was Senator Carl Levin (D-MI). As one might expect, the hearing was about many things, perhaps least about General Hayden's qualifications for directing the CIA or even why he might be interested in doing so rather than staying on officially as the deputy DNI. Nevertheless, the participants occasionally posed useful questions and the witness, General Hayden, responded with what appeared to be genuine frankness. Senator Levin, for instance, reminded General Hayden that the intelligence community's job—and Hayden's job if confirmed—was to give policymakers the unvarnished truth: to speak truth to power, as it were. Senator Levin said the "next director must right this ship and restore the CIA to its critically important position. To do so, the highest priority of the new director must be to ensure that intelligence which is provided to the president and to the Congress is, in the words of the new reform law, quote, 'Timely, objective and independent of political considerations.'"[18]

As the senator's comments were rhetorical, the general did not get the chance to answer him then. However, in his prepared comments General Hayden had anticipated similar questions. With respect to how he saw his job, if confirmed, General Hayden said, "I will indeed lead CIA analysts by example. I will—as I expect every analyst will—always give our nation's leaders our best analytic judgment."[19] Perhaps that is what the reader would expect him to say, but it did put him, under oath, on the record as saying he would not allow the CIA, were he confirmed its director, to be partial to political considerations in its work product. General Hayden also provided some details of the NSA program he implemented that were not publicly known. For example, he noted that it began on October 6, 2001, fewer than thirty days after the 9/11 attacks.[20] The hearing raised the issue of objective analysis in multiple ways worth considering briefly here.

General Hayden eventually got a chance to answer Senator Levin's question directly. At one point Levin again raised the problem of the intelligence community resisting powerful men who wanted to push a theory then search for evidence of it. Senator Levin cited former director of CIA Porter Goss in a previous hearing.

> During the confirmation hearings of Porter Goss, I asked him whether or not he would correct the public statement of a policymaker if that public statement went beyond the intelligence. And here's what Mr. Goss said: "If I were confronted with that kind of a hypothetical, where I felt that a policymaker was getting beyond what the intelligence said, I think I would advise the person involved. I do believe that would be a case that would put me into action, if I were confirmed, yes, sir."

When Senator Levin asked General Hayden if Hayden agreed with Goss' position, Hayden said "Yes, sir, I think that's a pretty good statement."[21] Even more pointedly, Senator Levin reminded General Hayden of the Pentagon's shop for special operations, the ad hoc intelligence analysis shop in the defense department that used the same intelligence the community had but concluded from it that there was evidence of Saddam's

WMDs as well as evidence that Saddam had connections to al Qaeda. "Feith," Senator Levin noted, referring to Douglas Feith, "established an intelligence analysis cell within his policy office at the Defense Department. While the intelligence community was consistently dubious about links between Iraq and al Qaeda, Mr. Feith produced an alternative analysis asserting that there was a strong connection." Senator Levin then asked Hayden whether he was comfortable with Douglas Feith's intelligence unit in the Pentagon. Hayden replied, "No, sir, I wasn't. And I wasn't aware of a lot of the activity going on, you know, when it was contemporaneous with running up to the war. No, sir, I wasn't comfortable."[22] Arguably, General Hayden should have said more about his apparent unease at the time; however, that he was willing to state his feelings and potentially burn bridges with a powerful defense secretary in so open a hearing perhaps augured well for his willingness in the future to tell powerful policymakers no when they think yes. One final comment General Hayden made in the hearing is worth consideration here. General Hayden told the hearing that there were two ways to approach intelligence.

> There's an approach to the world in which you begin with first principles, and then you work your way down to specifics. And then there's an inductive approach to the world in which you start out there with all the data and work yourself up to general principles. They are both legitimate. But the only one I'm allowed [as director of CIA] to do is induction.[23]

General Hayden's presentation was impressive. He came off as smart, self-assured, thoroughly convinced of the IRTPA-mandated reforms, and genuine. While smooth, he did not appear slick. When addressing uncomfortable issues he adopted diplomatic language but his body language showed his actual feelings. If the hearings were any indication of General Hayden's personal ethics, we would amend our earlier tentative conclusion. While DNI Negroponte has not, as yet, demonstrated a willingness to say no to powerful policymakers, his deputy perhaps has. Furthermore, that DNI Negroponte has so relied on Hayden and apparently prevailed on Hayden to accept the nomination for a lateral move as director of CIA may indicate that DNI Negroponte is prepared to speak truth to power. Though a hackneyed cliché, it is precisely what the DNI and the new director of CIA must do in order to integrate the former into the larger policymaking–intelligence community nexus. It is also what the new director of CIA must do to restore the CIA's once-vaunted reputation.

Integrating the Intelligence Community with Policymaking

In addition to being prepared to tell policymakers that their preconceived notions are wrong when evidence dose not support them, the DNI must gain operational control of the vast intelligence community's various institutions under him. DNI Negroponte and his intelligence empire must integrate itself with the policymaking structure (the NSC principals), and will have to butt heads with other important bureaucrats. First, DNI Negroponte must wrest operational control of the Department of Defense's contributions to the intelligence community: principally, the National Security Agency, the Defense Intelligence Agency, the National Recognizance Organization, and the National Geospatial-Intelligence Agency. The various service branches' intelligence agencies will likely continue to operate primarily for tactical battlefield needs and are therefore less important for Negroponte to control (the TIARA components in chapter 9). Other cabinet-level intelligence branches must also be integrated but they will likely be more natural allies with the DNI against the perceived bureaucratic power of Department of Defense. For instance, the U.S. State Department's intelligence analysis branch (INR) could prove a natural ally against the Department of Defense. Defense has rapidly grown more powerful primarily at the expense of the Department of State so the latter may have a natural inclination to form alliances with the DNI's new structure. Moreover, the INR has acquired a reputation for independence from some of the other agencies in the intelligence community, again making it a likely partner for the ODNI. The energy department's intelligence apparatus may also find similar reasons to partner with the ODNI. Additionally, the U.S. Justice Department's FBI—America's closest thing to a domestic-intelligence agency—may well be inclined to form alliances. The new cabinet agency, the Department of Homeland Security, similarly, may have bureaucratic reasons to partner with the ODNI. Though the FBI has historically neglected to share its data with CIA and vice versa its best bureaucratic bet is to form alliances with the ODNI rather than attempt to stand independently against the ODNI or, even more problematically, the defense department. Consequently, the task of integrating the ODNI's new structure with the defense department's bureaucratically robust structure will involve integrating two sets of existing institutions. First, DNI Negroponte will need to gain control of those structures enumerated above as defense department intelligence institutions, at least the ones not dedicated principally to tactical intelligence.

This will likely be a difficult matter for DNI Negroponte and his deputies to effect. Already, the Department of Defense's undersecretary of defense for intelligence, Dr. Stephen Cambone, has created obstacles; or more precisely, former Secretary of Defense Donald Rumsfeld instructed Cambone to erect obstacles. For instance, in February 2006, at least one report noted that "congressional specialists" specified "a Nov. 23, 2005, Rumsfeld directive interpreted by some officials as a challenge to Negroponte's authority. It outlined responsibilities for Rumsfeld's [then] undersecretary for intelligence, Stephen A. Cambone." Among the challenges Rumsfeld's defense department had erected while Negroponte had been putting his own team together, "Rumsfeld ha[d] been expanding [DOD's] intelligence activities"[24] on his own. (Elsewhere, we noted that both Secretary Rumsfeld and Undersecretary Cambone have respectively resigned and announced plans to leave their Pentagon positions following the November 7, 2006, midterm elections.)

Second, DNI Negroponte must force the CIA to integrate itself into the new structure. Over the course of the Cold War and prior to the IRTPA, the CIA always perceived itself differently than other intelligence agencies. For one thing, in addition to analyzing intelligence and formerly producing the national intelligence estimates for the NSC principals, the CIA also had a storied history of spycraft and allure dating back to its creation in 1947 when "Wild Bill" Donovan created a clandestine cloak-and-dagger operation whose qualities included high drama and *esprit de corps*, a history of cadres with Ivy League educations, and a good bit of mythology about its accomplishments. The CIA developed two main branches: the Directorate of Analysis and the Directorate of Operations. Since at least Eisenhower, presidents have used the latter to topple governments the U.S. perceived as Soviet pawns, to conduct covert operations that American presidents wished to be able to deny "plausibly," and to conduct paramilitary operations of various kinds. With human intelligence (HUMINT) as one of its primary tools, the CIA considered itself outside the normal strictures of other intelligence community entities and often outside the oversight prerogatives of the legislative branch. Finally, the CIA was its own executive department—not part of defense, justice, treasury, state, or some other cabinet agency.

Around the same time DNI Negroponte was receiving the Trainor Award at Georgetown, one reporter asserted that Negroponte had attempted to bring the Department of Defense's strategic-intelligence institutions under his control. After 9/11, the Pentagon began an information collection system called the Counterintelligence Field Activity agency (CIFA) which was said to produce Talon reports, in which soldiers and other government employees who were trained to spot suspicious activities created reports of those activities that were then archived in the bowels of the Pentagon in some database or other. Potentially suggestive of Negroponte taking on the defense department's bureaucratic power directly, the *Washington Post* reported that a "spokesman for Director of National Intelligence John D. Negroponte said the [National Counterterrorism Center], which is under his control, was 'playing the primary role in seeking to establish common standards' across the intelligence community, and added: 'There are various suspicious-activity reporting systems, and it is NCTC's role to improve and coordinate the way they are done.'" The piece cited one of Negroponte's main nemeses at the defense department, Stephen Cambone, then undersecretary of defense for intelligence and bureaucratic operator par excellence as well as then-Secretary Rumsfeld's "roving commando" as the point person dealing with the new DNI.[25]

In spring 2006, some indications appeared of the ongoing machinations of Secretary of Defense Rumsfeld and Undersecretary Cambone. This may have indicated that they were feeling Negroponte's pressure or anticipating his next moves. First were the reports that the defense department was combining data collected from the NSA program, already highly suspect since the *New York Times* broke the warrant-less program the previous December, with the Pentagon's own CIFA and Talon reports as well as with the Northern Command in the U.S.[26] The reporting began relatively benignly. The NSA warrant-less wiretaps had accumulated signals intelligence since shortly after 9/11. Since the NSA was under the Pentagon, it was unsurprising that information generated by NSA might be used by other Pentagon intelligence-collection and/or intelligence-analysis institutions. However, since the IRTPA was passed, DNI Negroponte's ODNI ought to have been the office through which sharing of NSA's work product was coordinated. Instead, "[i]nformation captured by the National Security Agency's secret eavesdropping on communications between the United States and overseas has been passed on to other government agencies, which cross-check the information with tips and information collected in other databases," according to unnamed current and former administration officials. Databases that cross-checked information from NSA with "tips and information" collected elsewhere sounded suspiciously similar to CIFA. The piece further reported that the "NSA has turned such information over to the Defense Intelligence Agency (DIA) and to other government entities," the information again coming from unnamed sources. Agencies reported to be "allowed" to request such information were identified as "the FBI, DIA, CIA, and Department of Homeland Security." The report noted that at least one intelligence community consumer, the Defense Intelligence Agency (DIA), had "used NSA information as the basis for carrying out surveillance of people in the country suspected of posing a threat." In other words, it sounded as though the DIA was stumbling into the FBI's traditional turf.

> DIA personnel stationed inside the United States went further on occasion, conducting physical surveillance of people or vehicles identified as a result of NSA intercepts, said two sources familiar with the operations, *although the DIA said it does not conduct such activities.*
>
> The military personnel—some of whose findings were reported to the Northern Command in Colorado—were employed as part of the Pentagon's growing post-Sept. 11, 2001 domestic intelligence activity based on the need to protect Defense Department facilities and personnel from terrorist attacks, the sources said.

Clearly, the Defense Department and the DIA *did* conduct "such activities" despite protestations to the contrary. The author cleverly implied that Cambone's CIFA and Talon reports were entangled somehow with the NSA's collections. For instance, the article noted that the Pentagon was a "system that civilian and military personnel" used "to report suspicious activities around military installations. Information from these reports is fed into a database known as the Joint Protection Enterprise Network, which is managed, as is the Talon system, by the Counterintelligence Field Activity [CIFA], the newest Defense Department intelligence agency to focus primarily on counterterrorism."[27] Nowhere in this article were the newly created National Counterterrorism Center (NCTC) or DNI Negroponte mentioned. It appeared, at the very least, that the defense department was circumventing the structure created by Congress in December 2004 (though opposed by Rumsfeld prior to the law's passage). It also appeared that the Department of Defense was crossing the HUMINT line, effectively usurping the CIA's traditional turf as well as the FBI's. (The CIA has traditionally been prohibited from operations inside the United States where the FBI typically has authorities and responsibilities.)

DNI Negroponte gave a speech to the World Affairs Council in Philadelphia just days after the NSA-Pentagon circumvention of him and his office was reported. He did not address the implications of Rumsfeld's Department of Defense ignoring Negroponte. It would hardly have been expected for the DNI to call out the defense secretary in such a public forum. However, Negroponte did raise a couple of interesting points. For one thing, he crossed bureaucratic swords with the CIA. Negroponte mentioned that prior to the IRTPA, the then-DCI was overextended. Mr. Negroponte lamented that "the Director of the CIA was dual-hatted: he also was Director of Central Intelligence, coordinating and guiding 14 other intelligence agencies." DNI Negroponte implied rather obviously that since he had consolidated power in the ODNI, the CIA could go about its traditional mission (HUMINT) freed from the shackles of managing the entire constellation of intelligence entities, presumably allowing the CIA to contribute more robustly to the overall intelligence community DNI Negroponte directed. It was an oblique swipe at CIA director Porter Goss. That Goss and Negroponte were fighting an internecine bureaucratic battle would become much clearer a couple of months later when Goss was forced to resign. Additionally, Negroponte pointed out that prior to the IRTPA, the intelligence community generally and the CIA specifically were poorly structured to fight al Qaeda and other jihadi groups. Negroponte said "the Intelligence Community had a structural challenge: it wasn't well-organized previously to respond to transnational threats confronting the homeland."

The second interesting point made by Negroponte concerned two Pentagon-related issues. First, Negroponte explained how he viewed his own job as DNI. Negroponte said his office was "assembled to do four things:

> preside over the Intelligence Community's strategy, policies, standards, and budgets. Again four things: strategy, policies, standards, and budgets. And the Directorate of National Intelligence is not here to manage the Intelligence Community's individual business units—their own leadership can do that—it is here to *integrate—this is a real watchword for us—to integrate* them into what President Bush has called for. That is to say, an intelligence enterprise that is "more unified, coordinated, and effective."

Again, it was an oblique reference, but given the media reports of bureaucratic turf wars around the time of his speech, Negroponte seemingly threw a fairly deft jab at Rumsfeld. A few paragraphs later in the same speech, Negroponte recounted his accomplishments to date. He cited several, a few of which were specific instructions from the Robb-Silberman Commission examined in a previous chapter. But Negroponte then noted that so far the ODNI had begun "the development of an integrated human capital plan" that included "both jointness requirements—somewhat along the lines of the Goldwater-Nichols legislation as it applied to our military a generation ago—so that intelligence officers obtain[ed] experience outside of their own agencies." The Goldwater-Nichols Act was specifically directed at the Pentagon and its *interactions with the NSC principals*. Here, DNI Negroponte apparently used Goldwater Nichols as a surrogate for the defense department, again subtly reminding the defense department (read Rumsfeld and Cambone) of the IRTPA. Finally, Negroponte noted that he had established "strong relations with the Department of Defense by rationalizing budgetary decision making for national and defense-related budgets."[28]

In a bureaucratic turf battle with Defense, Negroponte was at a distinct disadvantage. To begin with, the Department of Defense's budget dwarfed Negroponte's budget. Even after the IRTPA, the Defense Department had control of part of Negroponte's budget by virtue of the fact that it funded the National Security Agency (NSA), the Defense Intelligence Agency (DIA), and the National Reconnaissance Office (NRO) as well as the budgets of the individual militaries' intelligence functions (TIARA and JMIP). "Other Pentagon agencies have sizable budgets—the National Geospatial-Intelligence Agency, the department's mapping office, has a budget of about $3 billion, and the Defense Intelligence Agency gets $1 billion to $3 billion annually." In total, the intelligence community's entire budget—both those institutions funded under the defense department's budgetary process and those funded separately under Negroponte's intelligence community budget—was estimated to be in the low $40 billions. The article reminded readers of Negroponte's March Senate hearing during which Negroponte called the intelligence budget "his key weapon" and a "powerful integrating force." By controlling "which agencies and which programs are funded" Negroponte told the Senate, Negroponte could force separate agencies toward greater collaboration or jointness.

Still, Negroponte acknowledged at a Senate hearing in March, there had been open conflict with the Pentagon over at least one issue: personnel. The law setting up his job [the IRTPA] gave Negroponte the authority to transfer professionals from individual intelligence agencies into joint centers or other agencies to make the integration process work. But the Pentagon has made that process difficult, officials said, in part by issuing a directive that any such transfer required the "concurrence" of its intelligence chief, [Stephen] Cambone.[29]

A month earlier, Walter Pincus noted that one test for DNI Negroponte "was how, as President Bush's top intelligence adviser, he would meet challenges to his authority that came from Defense Secretary Donald H. Rumsfeld."[30] By spring 2006, the evidence demonstrated that Negroponte had engaged his bureaucratic rival if not quite brought the Department of Defense's intelligence managers to heel.

Interestingly, in the meantime, Rumsfeld found himself in trouble over the Pentagon's move into the clandestine HUMINT world, something outside the Pentagon's historical purview; Rumsfeld's failure to work well with other cabinet secretaries, specifically Secretary Rice; and *importantly*, for the mini-mutiny of retired and even uniformed officers who called for Rumsfeld's head. With respect to Secretary of State Rice, a week or so earlier she told reporters that she and the administration had made thousands of "tactical" mistakes with respect to the Iraq War. When asked to comment, Secretary Rumsfeld said "he did not know what Secretary of State Condoleezza Rice was talking about when she said last week that the United States had made thousands of 'tactical errors' in handling the war in Iraq."[31] Next, a report surfaced that suggested that the Pentagon's CIFA and Talon reports had potentially run amok.[32] Ever since Douglas Feith's counterterrorism evaluation group emerged in the Pentagon as an intelligence-analysis arm of the civilian leaders in the Department of Defense in the run-up to the Iraq War, Secretary Rumsfeld was under some pressure for his Department of Defense's perceived encroachments on the intelligence community's turf. Moreover, since shortly after the Iraq War began in March 2003, stories of Feith's "shop" manufacturing and/or cherry-picking intelligence abounded. Thus, as the *Washington Post* continued to report on Pentagon's activities related to intelligence in 2006, it put Rumsfeld on the defensive. At the time of this writing Secretary of Defense Rumsfeld's "resignation" was only months old and his former commando, Undersecretary Stephen Cambone's, decision to leave by the end of 2006 was only weeks old. Rumsfeld's impact, however, will likely be felt for some time.

In 2006 a PBS *Frontline* special entitled "The Dark Side" confirmed the nature of Douglas Feith's special group in the defense department and how and why it came into being. If anything, it demonstrated far more nefarious origins. In the transcript to the special, the narrator portrayed Vice President Cheney as having one searing memory from his time as secretary of defense for President George H.W. Bush. The memory was that the CIA seldom got things right—mostly an unfair conclusion. In fact, "The Dark Side" demonstrated that the CIA was well ahead of the curve in Afghanistan following the 9/11 attacks: the CIA, not defense department special operations, was described as successfully pursuing al Qaeda for a month before the defense department could get anything meaningful underway in Afghanistan. In any event, the narrators said, quoting a brief portion of the transcript, "Cheney wanted information that linked Osama bin Laden and Saddam Hussein." Next NSA expert James Bamford was quoted as saying "they [Cheney, Rumsfeld, et al.] weren't getting that information from the CIA. And so [Cheney] put pressure, I think, on Rumsfeld and on the Pentagon to come up with their own estimates." The narrator then noted that inside "the Pentagon bureaucracy, Rumsfeld could easily and quietly grow a nearly invisible operation." Next, Melvin Goodman (a former CIA agent) was quoted as saying, "They needed an office that would produce the intelligence that the CIA wouldn't produce. Rumsfeld said, 'I can solve your problem,' and he put Douglas Feith on that issue." Finally, a former Clinton NSC staffer, Daniel Benjamin, was quoted as follows: "So they're going to do their own analysis. They're going to show what the CIA's been missing all along about the true relationship between Saddam and al Qaeda."[33] "The Dark Side" affirmed what others have described as a "cabal" between Cheney and Rumsfeld and their respective lieutenants.

It was the spring mutiny, however, that placed Secretary Rumsfeld in unusually hot water. Typically it was Rumsfeld and/or Rumsfeld's lieutenants who lambasted others; they were unaccustomed to being lambasted themselves. At the beginning of April, that quickly changed. "The retired commander of key forces in Iraq called yesterday for Donald H. Rumsfeld to step down, joining several other former top military commanders who have harshly criticized the defense secretary's authoritarian style for making the military's job more difficult." As early as the 2003 invasion of Iraq, professional military and military intellectuals questioned whether Secretary Rumsfeld's notions of war fighting adequately accounted for the needs of the military after Saddam was removed and for the military generally, as it would conceivably get pinned down in Iraq for some time. Recall that then-General Eric K. Shinseki, a former commander in America's peacekeeping efforts in Bosnia, was asked by a reporter before the invasion how many troops it would take to invade and topple Iraq. Shinseki opined that several hundred thousand troops would be needed to change the regime and to secure the peace thereafter. The then–Undersecretary of Defense, Paul Wolfowitz characterized the general's views as "wildly off the mark."[34] Ever since, a tit-for-tat series of leaks and counterleaks and official comments had gone round the subject repeatedly. Those intradepartmental battles raged with renewed vigor in 2006.

Whether the U.S. entered Iraq with enough troops and whether the secretary of defense and his civilian colleagues were competent to run the Pentagon had been the subject of repeated news stories. When the debate reappeared openly in 2006, Rumsfeld must have felt the ground shifting beneath him. One of the generals who called for Rumsfeld's head had worked for Rumsfeld in Iraq. His words were said to resonate particularly among other U.S. Army brass. One report put it this way:

> It is widely known there [the Pentagon] that [retired Army Major General John Batiste] was offered a promotion to three-star rank to return to Iraq and be the No. 2 U.S. military officer there but he declined because he no longer wished to serve under Rumsfeld. Also, before going to Iraq, he worked at the highest level of the Pentagon, serving as the senior military assistant to Paul D. Wolfowitz, then the deputy secretary of defense.

Early in 2006, two former military analysts wrote a book about the tactical war-fighting mistakes that characterized the Bush administration's foray into Iraq. Former Marine General and MSNBC analyst Bernard Trainor and Michael B. Gordon wrote a book titled *Cobra II*, and the book became must-read curriculum for students of U.S. national security. Among other things the book alleged that President Bush, on the advice of his secretary of defense, had made manifold "tactical" mistakes,[35] something that Secretary of State Rice also admitted. It began an open-ended freeform debate in Washington and on the cable news channels.

Former Ambassador Bremer, whom we identified as a neoconservative in an earlier chapter, weighed in on the political fray. Bremer published his own memoirs of his time as Ambassador to Iraq. "In a new book, the official, L. Paul Bremer III, wrote that he had voiced his concerns personally to Mr. Bush and other administration officials, even writing a formal message in May 2004 to Defense Secretary Donald H. Rumsfeld." The same piece reported that Bremer "stated that 'the deterioration of the security situation' made it clear that 'we were trying to cover too many fronts with too few resources.'" Perhaps the most damning charge, however, was that "Mr. Bremer also criticized Mr. Rumsfeld for 'pumping up' the number of new Iraqi security forces to 'justify a drawdown of [U.S.] forces,'" that is, publicly telling Congress and the American people that more Iraqi troops were trained than in fact were.[36] By mid April what had begun relatively exclusively inside military circles turned into a wide-ranging donnybrook over the secretary's tenure.

Major General John Batiste, among others, was again quoted to the effect that the military needed "leadership up there that respects the military as they expect the military to respect them. And that leadership needs to understand teamwork,"[37] presaging events that followed the midterm elections. Following the 2006 midterm elections, we learned that President Bush had begun considering firing Rumsfeld in spring 2006. Ironically, the spring "mutiny" reportedly caused the president to hold off until a time during which it would not appear that he had responded to the officers' complaints. "Oddly enough, it was the generals who helped keep Rumsfeld in his job," wrote David Ignatius only days after the resignation. He noted that President Bush made the decision that Rumsfeld would have to go the previous spring. However, the "generals' revolt," as Ignatius characterized it, "erupted on newspaper op-ed pages, with former officers lining up to denounce their ex-boss." The White House "decided it couldn't appear to bow to pressure and retreated."[38]

Negroponte's next bureaucratic impediment was the CIA and its director of some eighteen months, Porter Goss. Prior to becoming DCI, then director of CIA when the IRTPA demoted the DCI, Porter Goss served in the U.S. House of Representatives. Representative Goss served on the House Permanent Select Committee on intelligence; in fact, he chaired the committee when Republicans became the majority party. Prior to serving in the House, Porter Goss served in the CIA during its glory days. Goss was said to be the favorite of Vice President Cheney when former DCI George

Tenet resigned.[39] The question was how to get the venerable institution, always a bastion of unconventional thinking, to integrate better into the broader intelligence community. Despite the defense department's apparent forays into clandestine HUMINT, the CIA was America's premiere HUMINT institution, but it was said to be demoralized after some eighteen months of Porter Goss's leadership. When the position was changed under the IRTPA, Goss was reported to have wanted out as he reportedly found it difficult to operate under Negroponte. In May 2006, CIA director Porter Goss was reported to have resigned "abruptly" midday on a Friday, clearly an unplanned event. While he may have resigned—though that is far from clear—he was also reportedly fired. Moreover, Negroponte was reported to have told President Bush that Bush needed to fire Goss in order for Negroponte to do Negroponte's job effectively. David Ignatius wrote this about Goss's Friday (May 5, 2006) resignation: "Goss was dumped by a president who doesn't like to fire anyone. That was a sign of how badly off track things had gotten at the CIA. Goss and his aides were feuding with the agency's staff and with officials of the Office of the Director of National Intelligence (DNI), the new bureaucratic canopy that overlays the CIA and 14 other intelligence agencies." The same columnist noted "Director of National Intelligence John Negroponte, who favored replacing Goss, similarly spoke of 'transition and reform.'" "That's a gentle way of describing the past year of reorganization, which intelligence veterans say has been closer to chaos and disintegration," wrote Ignatius.[40] Two reporters at the *Los Angeles Times* similarly wrote of Negroponte's dissatisfaction with Goss and how it led to Goss's demise. But they also noted the important bureaucratic turf battle between Negroponte as DNI and Secretary of Defense Rumsfeld.[41]

As a deft bureaucratic operator, DNI Negroponte might have been expected to take advantage of Rumsfeld's bleeding. Instead, just as Rumsfeld's travails multiplied, reports reappeared that suggested the ODNI was in disarray. In an early 2006 piece, Negroponte was whispered about on Capitol Hill. Power and proximity to power are Washington D.C.'s lifeblood. In early February, an article was published that read:

Several members of Congress who played major roles in creating Negroponte's job said that—while it is still too early to draw final judgments—they worry that he has started too slowly in working to lead and coordinate the government's 15 intelligence agencies. They are particularly focused on whether, in his first 10 months, Negroponte has been able to exert effective control over the Pentagon, which under Defense Secretary Donald H. Rumsfeld is playing a growing role in gathering and analyzing intelligence.[42]

Roughly translated, "while it is too early to draw final judgments" meant the sources of the story had likely already drawn their judgments but such initial judgments were never final and always subject to later revision. The clever countermove in the bureaucratic pas de deux may always be used to justify a complete volte-face later if needed. The phrase "particularly focused" on whether Negroponte had moved quickly enough to present the Department of Defense with a fait accompli roughly translated as the Pentagon had demonstrated more bureaucratic muscle. It meant, moreover, that Negroponte was struggling to integrate his IRTPA-mandated components of the defense department under his complete control. Based on the IRTPA itself, Negroponte may have had some bureaucratic and legal cover to strike preemptively against Rumsfeld. Whether he did so or not was another matter. In fact, at nearly the same time Rumsfeld was being skewered publicly, Negroponte came in for harsh bipartisan criticism. "In an April 6 report, the Intelligence Committee warned that Mr. Negroponte's office could end up not as a streamlined coordinator but as "another layer of large, unintended, and unnecessary bureaucracy." The committee went so far as to withhold part of Mr. Negroponte's budget request until he convinced members he had a workable plan."[43]

It appeared that both Negroponte and Rumsfeld—both veterans of bureaucratic turf battles dating back to Nixon and Ford administrations—had sources in the media to whom they leaked juicy tidbits that highlighted the other's foibles. Both men had worked with the likes of former Secretary of State Henry Kissinger; both had learned how to use sharp elbows against bureaucratic rivals. Both were consummate bureaucratic operators. And then there were reporters, who probably echoed sentiments of Congress where many wished Negroponte well and others wished him less than well. Some of the sources were concerned by Negroponte's apparent unwillingness to go for Rumsfeld's jugular. The Pentagon was already well out in front of Negroponte's intelligence community in terms of domestic intelligence gathering—something slightly questionable in any case due to the Posse Comitatus Act[44]—which meant that Negroponte's future actions were already depreciated by some extent. The implied conclusion, therefore, was that Mr. Negroponte would need more than simple good luck to outmaneuver Secretary Rumsfeld.

DNI Negroponte needed a benefactor of sufficiently recognized gravitas to run interference for him in against Rumsfeld. He shortly would be given a slight reprieve from an unlikely source: a former high CIA official whose bona fides were solid and who was critical of Cheney and Rumsfeld and their actions with respect to intelligence in the run-up to the Iraq War. Paul Pillar, the "former CIA official who coordinated U.S. intelligence on the Middle East until last year . . . accused the Bush administration of 'cherry-picking' intelligence on Iraq to justify a decision it had already reached to go to war, and of ignoring warnings that the country could easily fall into violence and chaos after an invasion to overthrow Saddam Hussein."[45] Pillar published a piece in *Foreign Affairs* which caused a stir. *Foreign Affairs* is published by and represents the Council on Foreign Relations, an organization with plenty of gravitas in Washington. The Council has traditionally represented U.S. foreign policy orthodoxy over many decades. CFR's membership included former Democratic, Republican, and even neoconservative policymakers, keeping it relatively immune from charges of partisanship.

> The most serious problem with U.S. intelligence today is that its relationship with the policymaking process is broken and badly needs repair. In the wake of the Iraq War, it has become clear that official intelligence analysis was not relied on in making even the most significant national security decisions, that intelligence was misused publicly to justify decisions already made, that damaging ill will developed between policymakers and intelligence officers, and that the intelligence community's own work was politicized. As the national intelligence officer responsible for the Middle East from 2000 to 2005, I witnessed all of these disturbing developments.

Thus, the former CIA intelligence officer responsible for the Middle East, Paul Pillar, fired a salvo directly at the Cheney-Rumsfeld-neoconservative nexus that led America and President Bush into war with Iraq. Pillar aimed his salvo at the White House and the vice president as well as the Department of Defense and clearly, by implication, Secretary Rumsfeld. Fired squarely at neoconservatives, whom Pillar believed forgot about Republican traditionalist realpolitik, Pillar noted:

> the White House also inadvertently pointed out the real problem: intelligence on Iraqi weapons programs *did not drive its decision to go to war*. A view broadly held in the United States and even more so overseas was that deterrence of Iraq was working, that Saddam was being kept "in his box,"

and that the best way to deal with the weapons problem was through an aggressive inspections program to supplement the sanctions already in place. That the administration arrived at so different a policy solution indicate[d] that its decision to topple Saddam was driven by other factors—namely, the desire to shake up the sclerotic power structures of the Middle East and hasten the spread of more liberal politics and economics in the region.

Vice President Cheney, a person not lacking gravitas himself, was also the target of Pillar's opprobrium.

The Bush administration deviated from the professional standard not only in using policy to drive intelligence, but also in aggressively using intelligence to win public support for its decision to go to war. This meant selectively adducing data—"cherry-picking"—rather than using the intelligence community's own analytic judgments . . . In an August 2002 speech, for example, Vice President Dick Cheney observed that "intelligence is an uncertain business" and noted how intelligence analysts had underestimated how close Iraq had been to developing a nuclear weapon before the 1991 Persian Gulf War. [Cheney's] conclusion—at odds with that of the intelligence community—was that 'many of us are convinced that Saddam will acquire nuclear weapons fairly soon.'"[46]

Pillar's piece provided Negroponte cover, unintentionally and presumably unsolicited. It meant, among other things, that Negroponte would live to fight another day and that despite the odds against balancing the relationship envisaged in the IRTPA between the DNI and the defense department, Negroponte still had some room to maneuver and some time in which to accomplish such maneuvering.

Another shot across the administration's neoconservative bow, this one from FBI sources who had fared badly under scrutiny in both the 9/11 and Robb-Silberman Commissions, was about to be fired directly at Rumsfeld's Pentagon and Rumsfeld's leadership by implication. E-mail messages unearthed by the American Civil Liberties Union in a lawsuit against the defense department's treatment of "enemy combatants" showed that the FBI had actually raised the issue of abuse repeatedly with Washington FBI headquarters. Accordingly, the documents also contained "numerous complaints from FBI agents working at the U.S. detention facility at Guantánamo Bay, Cuba. The agents said that military interrogators used abusive, ineffective and potentially illegal methods. One e-mail described an interrogation in which a prisoner was put under a strobe light and shown gay pornographic films." Moreover, the report alleged that documents and e-mails "suggest[ed] that harsh interrogation methods were approved of and encouraged by high-ranking Pentagon officials and commanders. In an internal FBI memo dated May 2004, an unidentified bureau official complained that defense secretary Donald H. Rumsfeld's public pronouncements about interrogation policies were misleading."[47] A similar sort of critique of Rumsfeld's defense department was published just two days later. It suggested that defense was tone deaf to the debates ongoing in the public square of ideas with respect to how America's military treated prisoners of war (POWs), whatever nomenclature was used to characterize them.

By early spring 2006, DNI Negroponte could look back on his first year in office and compare the positives and the negatives, what he had accomplished, and what remained for him to accomplish. The print media were there to help out, scoring winners and losers.

> A year after a sweeping government reorganization began, the agencies charged with protecting the United States against terrorist attacks remain troubled by high-level turnover, overlapping responsibilities and bureaucratic rivalry, former and current officials say.
>
> Progress has been made, most of the officials say, toward one critical goal: the sharing of terrorist threat information from all agencies at the National Counterterrorism Center. But many argue that the biggest restructuring of spy agencies in half a century has bloated the bureaucracy, adding boxes to the government organization chart without producing clearly defined roles . . .
>
> Senator Susan Collins, a Maine Republican who played a central role in negotiating the intelligence reorganization, said she was "very concerned" about what she viewed as Mr. Negroponte's passivity in the face of assertive moves by Defense Secretary Donald H. Rumsfeld.
>
> "I think Director Negroponte has battles to fight within the bureaucracy, and particularly with the Department of Defense," Ms. Collins said. "DOD is refusing to recognize that the director of national intelligence is in charge of the intelligence community."

All agreed that information sharing was much improved from the bad old days when the CIA refused to share with the FBI and the NSA refused to share with either the FBI or the CIA.[48] Since this book was begun (2005) other bureaucratic turf battles have been fought. Not all of them involved the new DNI directly. If fact, two battles that have played out before Americans have involved the defense department and the reorganizations at the CIA respectively. Neither explicitly involved DNI Negroponte. Nor are the myriad turf battles, budget skirmishes, and parochial clashes, much less the personality fracases, likely to be completed anytime soon. As seen with the 1947 National Security Act, such parochialism and simple evolution continued for decades. There is no reason to expect the IRTPA amendments to the 1947 NSA to take less time to play themselves out fully. President Bush's tenure runs until January 2009. In all likelihood, evolutions and adjustments will continue well into the next president's term(s) in office.

Earlier, we discussed a confirmation hearing in 2006 for General Michael V. Hayden. We return briefly to that May 18, 2006, hearing to demonstrate that Negroponte's first deputy DNI (now the CIA's new director) used bureaucratic elbows with the best of them. First, General Hayden noted in his response to Senator Kit Bond (R-MS) that it was no small matter that DNI Negroponte made the CIA the lead intelligence community agency in human intelligence (HUMINT). In other words, *the CIA was to reestablish its prominence as the primary clandestine service in the intelligence community constellation*, despite the Department of Defense's efforts at forays into clandestine operations. General Hayden said: "And I think it's singularly significant that Ambassador Negroponte made the director of CIA [then Porter Goss] the national HUMINT manager."[49] Senator Bond noted that he had recently spoken with Secretary Rumsfeld about the ambiguity in the IRTPA over intelligence community assets that were ostensibly under both the Department of Defense and ODNI. "Yesterday at the Defense appropriations hearing, Secretary Rumsfeld assured us that there's total complete working interoperability and cooperation between the Department of Defense and the CIA and other agencies in human intelligence. Has that been achieved, or is that a work in process, a goal towards which we are working? And what do you think really about the relationships between the FBI, NSA, Department of Defense in the clandestine service?" queried Senator Bond. Very forthrightly, or so it appeared, General Hayden responded, "I think it's best described as a process that needs to be continually managed." General Hayden continued, "You've got folks out there [at the Department of Defense], quite legitimately, but for slightly different purposes, they should be using common tradecraft, they should be using common standards, they should be using the same standards to validate a source, they should be using the same language in the same format when they make reports. Those are the things that the national HUMINT manager should ensure." There was no doubt as to who Hayden believed should be setting those standards. General Hayden talked about a "bright line" that needed to be created between the defense department's and ODNI's functions. "They get kind of merged, so that the actions are actually on the ground, in reality, indistinguishable, even though their *sources of tasking and sources of authority* come from different places . . . *That's where we need to manage this*. That's where this needs to be done well." The "we" about whom General Hayden spoke was the DNI, not the secretary of defense.[50]

General Hayden continued to answer Senator Bond's and other senators' questions. But near the end of his response to Senator Bond, General Hayden made some interesting and broad observations about how he saw the ODNI and the CIA's roles in the "long war" against terrorism. For example, General Hayden suggested that the struggle against jihadis was far from simply a military matter. "But this is a long war," said General Hayden. And it was "not just going to be won with *heat, blast, and fragmentation*. It is fundamentally a war of ideas." General Hayden then observed that foreign policymaking and national security policymaking, as always, came down to allocating scarce resources. "That's the tough decision—how best to allocate our resources and then apportion it organizationally, so you keep up this high ops tempo that has al Qaeda on its back foot right now, while still underpinning all the other efforts of the U.S. government that over the long term—over the long term—cuts the production rate of those who want to kill us and those who hate us, rather than simply dealing with those who already have that view."[51] General Hayden's view of the war against global jihadis suggested that military might was only one weapon; many other weapons would necessarily be deployed against jihadis, the new, nontraditional, non-state actor, and those weapons would likely need to be deployed over the long term.

Finally, in the exchange with Senator Levin discussed above, General Hayden admitted the tensions between the ODNI and the Department of Defense. As already seen, General Hayden admitted he was uncomfortable with Douglas Feith's activities while Feith was still at the Department of Defense running, among other things, special operations and a quasi-intelligence-analysis shop in the Pentagon. Senator Levin pushed General Hayden on the relationship between the defense department and the ODNI. Levin queried, reaching beyond the now retired Feith, to then-Secretary

Rumsfeld's point man on intelligence for the Department of Defense. "There's been press reports that you had some disagreements with Secretary Rumsfeld and Undersecretary Cambone with respect to the reform legislation that we were looking at relating to DNI and other intelligence-related matters." Senator Levin continued: "Can you tell us whether or not that is accurate, there were disagreements between you and the Defense secretary [*sic*]? Because some people say you're just going to be the instrument of the Defense secretary." Senator Levin's concern involved the fact that General Hayden was still an officer of the United States Air Force and as a result Levin and others wondered whether confusion in the chains of command might result. General Hayden immediately disabused the Senate Select Intelligence Committee, Senator Levin, and other senators of that notion. Hayden chose his words carefully. "Sir," he responded to Senator Levin, "let me recharacterize them [*sic*]. The secretary and I did discuss this. I think it's what diplomats would call that frank and wide-ranging exchange of views." Though seemingly already answered, Senator Levin rephrased the same question again. "Is it fair to say that on some of those issues there were differences between you and Secretary Rumsfeld?" General Hayden's answer this time was direct. "Yes, sir."[52] While only so much may be reasonably gleaned from congressional testimony, General Hayden's testimony made clear that he understood the Department of Defense's encroachments into the clandestine operations arena. Moreover, he saw a delineation—a "bright line"—between those areas in which the Department of Defense's actions were legitimate and those that were the ODNI's turf. If this testimony accurately reflected General Hayden's views, and we presume it did as he was under oath, General Hayden acquitted himself well. What is more, as he was then DNI Negroponte's number two—in addition already to being nominated to direct the CIA—his performance suggested that the ONDI understood the bureaucratic battle in front of it and was prepared for it. Taken together with other evidence presented here, the ODNI's office appeared as well-prepared as can reasonably be expected at this early point for the long struggle ahead—both in terms of the war against jihadis and the war against bureaucratic rivals.

We offer another tentative conclusion about Negroponte's bureaucratic acumen and his ability to integrate the newly reorganized intelligence community. Here, the evidence seems to support the conclusion that DNI Negroponte has engaged his bureaucratic nemeses directly. That does not guarantee his success. But more concern would be raised had he simply chosen to avoid bureaucratic conflicts that must inevitably be thrashed out. DNI Negroponte appeared willing to cross bureaucratic swords with the Department of Defense and others in order to integrate the reorganized intelligence community per IRTPA.

Negroponte recently demonstrated that he recognized the lingering problems at the CIA; moreover, he has moved relatively decisively to ameliorate the situation at the CIA. Negroponte's apparent willingness to take his concerns regarding former CIA director Porter Goss directly to the White House demonstrated that he was not timid about enlisting the White House's clout on something he considered important. Negroponte's maneuvering of his principal deputy, General Michael V. Hayden, to direct the CIA demonstrated that Negroponte knew he needed a CIA director whose loyalty to Negroponte was well-established. Further, Negroponte tempered what otherwise might have seemed simple ambition by quickly announcing that in order to reassure the beleaguered CIA under his and Hayden's new leadership, Negroponte was willing to bring back a popular CIA manager—someone who had been purged under Porter Goss—to boost the morale and esprit de corps of the CIA. It would appear that Negroponte understands the CIA's comparative advantage against the defense department. By reestablishing the CIA's lead role in HUMINT under Negroponte's direct leadership, he may be attempting to thwart the defense department's encroachment into the CIA's historical turf. If so, Negroponte had demonstrated deft bureaucratic instincts. If, on top of his bureaucratic instincts, Negroponte demonstrates a willingness to tell the truth to the NSC principals, of which he is now a member by virtue of the IRTPA, and to the president in the daily briefings of which Negroponte wisely took command in 2005, Negroponte's moves auger well for the future of the ODNI. If so, Negroponte may be seen as a particularly good selection for America's first DNI in retrospect. Only time will tell.

SUMMARY AND CONCLUDING OBSERVATIONS

Handicapping the ODNI: Speaking Truth to Power and Integration of the ODNI with the President-NSC-Policymaking Model

This chapter was about process rather than simply particular inputs. U.S. foreign policy inputs—external-systemic as well as societal and governmental—were examined in detail in previous chapters. In this chapter, it was assumed that the messy business—process—whereby all the inputs come together at given times and in given situational contexts trumped individual analysis of the various sources of U.S. foreign policy. Thematically, two criteria were used to discuss process. The first was a shop-worn cliché: speak truth to power. A cliché to be sure, but its essence is an important indicator of whether the 9/11 reforms have been successful so far and whether they will be successful in the future. Only if the new bureaucratic layer created by the IRTPA is willing to tell policymakers (and we assume the new DNI will evolve into a policymaker as did the NSC advisor) what they need to hear versus what they wish to hear can the IRTPA reforms be seen over time as successful. The second criterion involved the process of integration of the ODNI into the intelligence community and at the apex of its interaction with the president-NSC policymaking model. Namely, we examined whether a wholly new bureaucracy can hold its own against powerful, long-established bureaucratic institutions that instinctively resist change. Inertia and momentum characterize bureaucratic behavior during most times. That 9/11 was a foreign policy crisis allowed the confluence of several important foreign policy inputs permitting the creations of new institutions, something existing institutions would be expected to resist. On the first criterion, the tentative conclusion was that Negroponte has yet to establish that he is willing to tell policymakers what they need to hear versus what they wish to hear. That is not to say that Negroponte or future DNIs will not establish such a willingness eventually. Unfortunately, to date we could not find enough evidence to support the affirmative conclusion for the DNI. On the second criterion, we concluded that DNI Negroponte has demonstrated acute awareness of the bureaucratic obstacles erected by existing institutions to hinder integration of new institutions with old Cold War ones. Furthermore, we have found evidence that he has engaged those obstacles repeatedly.

The President-NSC-Policymaking Model in the Post-9/11 Environment

What can be said with certainty is that the president-NSC-policymaking model has been modified demonstrably since 9/11. The DNI is a cabinet-level actor, in theory, on par with the secretaries of defense, state, homeland security, and any other cabinet agency who might serve as an ad hoc principal. The IRTPA created the position and the DNI's office (ODNI) such that it has the power in law to force the intelligence community to work together and to eschew previously parochial missions. The IRTPA mandated the secretary of defense to coordinate his vast bureaucratic empire—at least those parts of the empire that collect and analyze intelligence—with the ODNI. The IRTPA notwithstanding, the Department of Defense has evolved into a cabinet agency above all others in terms of its budget and number of employees. The Office of the DNI is a new agency that must flex its bureaucratic muscle in order to force the Department of Defense to integrate in the ways directed by the drafters of the IRTPA. Whether the modifications prove themselves to be simply added layers of bureaucracy or whether they prove themselves imperative for America's national security interest in the twenty-first century must await future judgments. If the DNI proves incapable of using the IRTPA to bend the Department of Defense (and others) to the DNI's and the IRTPA's will, it will not be due to a lack of legal authority. It is worth recalling, however, that the director of central intelligence (DCI) was similarly given wide authority in the 1947 National Security Act, yet the DCI never directed the intelligence community in the ways envisioned by the NSA's creators.

A natural comparison arises; we have attempted to make a good deal about that comparison. The 1947 NSA gave broad power to the then-DCI to command and control the intelligence community and filter its entire work product to the NSC principals, a key unit of analysis of the president-NSC-policymaking model. It never gave the DCI the necessary budgetary instruments to effect that change. The IRTPA gave the DNI budgetary and programmatic authorities that the DCI might have envied. Legislative tools alone do not make powerful bureaucratic institutions. Were that the case, the Department of Defense would not have become the bureaucratic hegemon it has become. Instead, leadership, vision, bureaucratic acuity, and serendipity all play a part. Given the latter, it becomes a problematic endeavor to predict what will ultimately become of the ODNI and the DNI, in ten years, in a generation, perhaps in two generations (approximately the amount of time over which the Cold War occurred).

Director of National Intelligence Negroponte has demonstrated some good instincts. Unfortunately, however, Negroponte has been oddly absent from the NSA warrant-less wiretapping and domestic phone-record data revelations. Though the story continued to break while this text was being written, at first blush his absence from the controversy did not augur well for a DNI who was willing to tell powerful persons (in this case, specifically President Bush and Vice President Cheney) that the IRTPA also envisioned a civil liberties balance with the increased powers and authorities created for the ODNI. Surely, DNI Negroponte knows that the IRTPA explicitly included sections (titles) on FISA and on civil liberties. That the National Security Agency was the alleged culprit raised interesting questions. The NSA, recall, remained ostensibly under dual control of its long-time bureaucratic home, the Department of Defense, and its new bureaucratic home, the ODNI. In fairness to the DNI and his office, the controversial program began well before the IRTPA created his position and before he arrived on the scene. However, at some point after becoming the DNI and after former NSA director General Hayden became the deputy DNI (i.e, sometime in 2005) DNI Negroponte had to have learned of the program's existence. It is inconceivable that the NSA was instructed to conduct an intelligence collection program of which DNI Negroponte was intentionally kept uninformed. It is even more inconceivable that his principal deputy—who was aware of its authorization by President Bush in late 2001—would have not fully briefed the DNI on the program's existence.

The entire sequence of events, of course, has yet to be revealed publicly. Perhaps when its details are known, a benign explanation of DNI Negroponte's and his then–Deputy DNI Hayden's involvement will be offered. Whatever the involvement of the DNI, we cannot help but wonder how the controversial program bodes for the DNI as the newest NSC principal in the president-NSC-policymaking model. If DNI Negroponte has become an NSC principal as mandated in the IRTPA, it is difficult to understand how such a program could have proceeded well into 2006 without the slightest indication of oversight by FISA and/or PFIAB and/or the ODNI's own civil liberties entities. Regrettably, two possibilities occur to us, neither hopeful in terms of the IRTPA's ultimate success in reorganizing the federal government to better fight transnational threats. DNI Negroponte was designated as a statutory NSC principal by virtue of the IRTPA; one possibility therefore is that DNI Negroponte has become an NSC principal in name only. (The IRTPA envisioned the DNI as an NSC principal in reality, not just nominally.) Another possibility was DNI Negroponte was fully briefed; if true, it would appear that the DNI acquiesced to other powerful NSC principals. If either of the two possibilities proves accurate, then DNI Negroponte failed an early-but-major test of the IRTPA and the integration its drafters envisaged. We have not attempted to suggest that we have exhausted all possibilities—others probably exist. Perhaps the answers to these questions and other possibilities will be known in the relatively near future.[53]

While our focus has been the institutional, bureaucratic, and operational changes unleashed by 9/11 and its aftermath on America's national security institutions, a few comments about America's foreign policy (the policy itself, not the institutions charged with making and implementing it) are in order here in the conclusion. Whatever one thinks about President George W. Bush and the commitment he has made for generations of Americans in the name of defeating jihadi terrorism and extremist ideology, it cannot be said that he did so without acknowledging that it would be a long and dangerous journey. He repeatedly told Americans, Congress, and policymaking elites that America's war against the jihadis would be a long-term investment, that it would be costly, and that it would not always go well. He said so shortly after 9/11 and he has repeated it (or his NSC has repeated it) in the president's most recent national security strategy.

Achieving this goal is the work of generations. The United States is in the early years of a long struggle, similar to what our country faced in the early years of the Cold War. The twentieth century witnessed the triumph of freedom over the threats of fascism and communism. Yet a new totalitarian ideology now threatens, an ideology grounded not in secular philosophy but in the perversion of a proud religion. Its content may be different from the ideologies of the last century, but its means are similar: intolerance, murder, terror, enslavement, and repression.

He continued, noting that like those who drafted the 1947 National Security Act, the United States government "must lay the foundations and build the institutions that our country needs to meet the challenges we face."[54] In that sense, the Bush administration, perhaps even more than those who faced down the Soviet Union in the late 1940s, has extrapolated from past experience the lengthy commitment the president's decisions have set for America's national security for the foreseeable future.

One may reasonably question, however, whether his decision to invade Iraq as part of the war against global jihadi extremism was a necessary one. Similarly, one might argue whether it was a wise decision politically and strategically. It is our view that the answer to the first question is no. All the evidence accumulated since the March 2003 invasion suggests that Saddam Hussein could have been contained. Sanctions and inspections kept him from reconstituting his WMD program and there is little reason to believe that increased sanctions and inspections would have yielded demonstrably different results. Similarly, our view is that it was unwise strategically to invade Iraq. (Politically, it may have greatly enhanced President Bush's reelection—but at a horrendous price.) Having made clear our own views, it should be noted that Saddam Hussein has been removed from power and that might ultimately accrue positively in the long-term for America and its allies, including the so-called "friendly royals" in the Middle East. In time, hopefully, it will accrue positively for Iraq as well. It seems inarguable at this point that the war has been far more costly than President Bush and some of his top policymakers calculated. Exceeding 3000 deaths, tens of thousands of maimed troops, and countless numbers of noncombatant Iraqis, the cost of invading Iraq in U.S. blood has exceeded the cost of America's intelligence failures pre-9/11. Many of us worried that invading Iraq might divert the administration's and America's attention away from more critical tasks: pursuing al Qaeda to every corner of the globe where the jihadi organization used failed states or weak states to carry out its anti-Western, anti-modern deeds and pursing similar jihadi groups whose very existence and future plans are antithetical to Western democracy and modernity. At present, it would appear that those of us who worried about the administration diverting its attention away from more imperative tasks may have been correct. Still, should the "unity government" in Iraq bring stability in the next 6–12 months, though a high price will have been paid, democracy in Iraq might prove a remarkably transformative event for the region. Democracy is far more than the procedural democracy (elections characterized by universal suffrage over a certain age) thus far seen. Democracy includes elections and representative government of the majority who respect rights of the minority and respect the rule of law. It would also include some commitment to tolerance of religious and ideological differences. That has not happened thus far though we remain hopeful that it will. Rather, so far the decision to invade Iraq—and the way the aftermath of this decision was implemented—has been a pluperfect blunder.

Finally, we would be remiss were we not to offer some way of gauging whether some of the speculation and guesses made in these pages prove prescient or dead wrong. A few concrete indicators come to mind. First, should the DNI simply turn out to be another version of America's former DCI—that is, should the DNI not seize the day and the authority the IRTPA gave him—at least part of our speculation would prove inaccurate. We have argued that the IRTPA is significant; indeed, we argued that the IRTPA constituted the most significant national-security policy legislation passed in the U.S. since the 1947 National Security Act. The institutions created by the IRTPA, therefore, should be expected to parallel the institutional growth of bureaucracies created by the 1947 NSA. That growth includes the DNI (and the ODNI) rising to an important and prominent role in the future war against transnational phenomena (al Qaeda and beyond al Qaeda) as well as future state threats. Indication of the DNI doing so would include his complete integration as an NSC principal, not just during the Bush administration's remaining time but in the next administration's time and the one following that, and so on. An indicator that we got it wrong would be a rejection of substantial portions of that to which President Bush has committed the U.S. when the next president is inaugurated in January 2009. If the new president, for instance, characterized President Bush's response to 9/11 as overwrought and wrongheaded, clearly, the thesis of this book could properly be criticized. We suspect, however, that while the next president may well characterize the diversion in Iraq as wrongheaded,[55] the war against the global jihadi hydra will continue to motivate and animate the next president in largely similar ways to the ways in which it has animated President George W. Bush.

By similar logic, were the next president to call for wholesale changes in America's promotion of democracy, the arguments made here might well be challenged. It is our contention that America has always stood in principle for democracy even though it has not always behaved as though it stood for that laudable principle. President George W. Bush made it an explicit part of America's national security objectives. It is our contention that while his successor may attempt to temporize on democratization, it will be difficult to jettison it outright. Subsequent administrations may hedge on it, or incrementally demote it in times of expediency, but will not abandon it as a U.S. objective. Similarly, it is our view that U.S. national security policy, under future presidents, will continue to project America's power globally and intervene when they believe it is in its national security interests to do so. The reader may properly say that such a statement is self-evident. We, however, argued that for the foreseeable future subsequent presidents will intervene (sometime perhaps for naked self-interest) but will do so using the language of democracy for justification of said interventions.

Finally, we described a post-9/11 consensus that we argued developed following the trauma of 9/11. In fact, we argued that the post-9/11 consensus in many ways paralleled the Cold War consensus. We shall conclude with some observations about the post-9/11 consensus. Since it was argued that said consensus made possible the changes this book has attempted to document, it should therefore be delineated clearly. Following 9/11, policymaking elites of both main political parties agreed that the global jihadis were something the U.S. and the West would need to face for many years, and perhaps generations, to come. That consensus made President Bush's decision to topple the Taliban regime and (and perhaps unwittingly scatter al Qaeda) absolutely imperative for most policymaking elites and palatable to those few who did not agree it was imperative. The reader may recall that the international community—Russia, France, Germany, Britain, an array of Middle East allies, even the Islamic Republic of Iran and others—rallied around America in a display of international solidarity seldom seen. What became consensus among policymaking elites spread among the attentive public and, thence, to the mass public. Conservatives, liberals, environmentalists, and persons of virtually every political persuasion accepted that America must punish Afghanistan, attempt to destroy al Qaeda, hold the Taliban responsible for harboring al Qaeda and, furthermore, pursue al Qaeda and its complex affiliates to every corner of the globe lest the global jihadis attack America or America's allies again.

The post-9/11 consensus, it seems to us, consists of the following tenets. The U.S. has the global responsibilities as well as the military and economic resources to defeat the jihadi ideology globally wherever it may be found. That the U.S. was attacked made it clear to policymaking elites and the public that America was the jihadis' principal target but also that America's allies were likely targets as well. The consensus also included the horrific realization that it was probably only a matter of time before America and its allies would be attacked again and, perhaps, in more spectacular ways than 9/11. Specifically, the post-9/11 consensus coalesced around the belief that weapons of mass destruction—biological, chemical, radiological, and possibly nuclear—are almost inevitably going to be used by global jihadis. The questions is where and when. The consensus also included the notion that—and President Bush and his administration deserve some credit for this—the campaigns ahead will necessarily last many years. After 9/11, policymakers and the mass public alike believed that much of America's national security future would be integrally connected with fighting a long and difficult war against new transnational threats. Jihadis were the most obvious target, but policymakers and others realized that other non-state actors may well come to challenge America's position in world affairs as well as America's very way of life. Though less clear, the consensus has involved the slow realization among many policymakers that while transnational threats are the most proximate threat America and the West face, traditional state actors too would persist and therefore U.S. national security policy would have to learn how to do multiple things simultaneously.

The post-9/11 consensus *did not* include the belief that the U.S. necessarily had to invade Iraq. Indeed, both the mass public and the policymaking elites appeared almost equally divided on whether Iraq was the next logical step in the war against global extremist ideologies. Insofar as the invasion was carried out quickly and relatively painlessly, even persons who disagreed that Iraq was the next logical step came to support it at least nominally. Many who had disagreed with the decision to topple Saddam Hussein next believed that America's resources—both in treasure and blood—ought to be used only to pursue known areas where al Qaeda was regrouping and reorganizing. Thus, a split in public opinion reflected in innumerable polls has demonstrated that President Bush squandered some of the good will he had accrued following 9/11 and the punitive strikes against al Qaeda in Afghanistan. Nevertheless, even those of us who disagreed with Iraq as the next logical step believed that once committed there America had the responsibility, minimally, to prevent Iraq from becoming a failed state such as Afghanistan was prior to 9/11.

It is therefore important to distinguish those who have become disenchanted with Iraq from the post-9/11 consensus. They are not, to be sure, mutually exclusive. Indeed the contrary is true. They are compatible sentiments and therefore continue to reflect the post-9/11 consensus. Recall, for example, how many policymaking elites differed over particular campaigns in the long struggle of the Cold War. People differed over how to handle Korea. President Truman was punished at the ballot box for handling the Korean War in a way considered less-than-successful by most Americans. President Eisenhower, by contrast, was elected largely because most Americans believed he would remedy the stalemate there. Similarly, from Presidents Truman to Ford, six presidents were involved in the Vietnam War, another of the many campaigns that comprised the Cold War. Presidents Truman, Kennedy, and Johnson represented the Democratic Party and one approach to the Vietnam War within the larger context of the Cold War struggle. Presidents Eisenhower, Nixon, and Ford represented the Republican Party and another approach to the Vietnam War within the larger context of the Cold War struggle. *The Cold War consensus was the societal requisite* for both parties' approaches to Vietnam within the Cold War context. One should not expect any less of the current post-9/11 consensus.

If, by contrast, the post-9/11 consensus broke down and devolved into something else, then our theses may appropriately be criticized. Were Americans to take the position—and it would necessarily need to be represented broadly among the public and policymaking elites—that 9/11 was simply one of those awful but unpredictable things that befall great countries from time to time, that would suggest that this book's arguments are inaccurate. If Americans broadly demanded that a large portion of America's Defense budget be reprogrammed (for instance, diverted to domestic programs) because most Americans came to believe that no serious existential transnational threat to America existed, that too would indicate this book's arguments were misguided. It is our belief, however, that those things will not happen. America will continue on the path set by President George W. Bush following 9/11 for good or ill. Only incremental change will characterize future changes in the direction, tenor, and contours of U.S. national security policy. Unless and until another foreign policy crisis happens, U.S foreign policy is likely to continue following the trajectory it took following 9/11 for the foreseeable future. Indeed, and sadly, we suspect that another attack against America and/or its allies is quite likely in the future. It may occur before the next president of the United States is inaugurated in January 2009. It may occur after that inauguration. In either case, it is likely, we fear, to be even more horrific than 9/11. It may well involve weapons of mass destruction and many more lives than did 9/11. When it happens—and we argue that it is a matter of when rather than if—the post-9/11 consensus is likely to be greatly refortified.

Until then, however, we remain hopeful that some of the changes enacted since 9/11, as well as the 9/11 Commission's and the Robb-Silberman Commission's WMD reports, have made the U.S. at least slightly less vulnerable to future jihadi attacks and/or other transnational extremist ideologies and, with any luck, less vulnerable to the kind of state-actor threats America will surely encounter in its future. Insofar as America continues to be the world's single hegemonic power, America will necessarily continue to be the target of choice for state and non-state threats of all kinds.

NOTES

1. White House, *National Security Strategy of the United States, March 2006*, White House, http://www.whitehouse.gov/nsc/2006/nss206.pdf, "Preamble," i–ii, "Introduction," 1 (accessed on March 16, 2006)(my emphasis). That is, "democracy" was mentioned about once per page.

2. A recent review of 9/11 and its aftermath read as follows: "the frantic first few months after the Sept. 11, 2001, attacks, the Bush administration created what amounted to a new secret side of the government, based on an expansive view of the president's authority to wage the war on terror. From secret C.I.A. prisons and harsh interrogation tactics overseas to warrant-less eavesdropping at home, the new counter-terror structure was established with little Congressional oversight or legal scrutiny" a variation on what we have written repeatedly in this analysis. James Risen, "The War on Terror, Under New Scrutiny," *New York Times*, December 3, 2006, http://www.nytimes.com/2006/12/03/weekinreview/03risen.html.

3. To cite but the most obvious reason, certain clandestine actions are predicated on America's presidents being able to deny plausibly a particular action. Invariably, future clandestine operators shall be captured or worse. If captured and identified as a member of the U.S. uniformed forces, plausible deniability would become problematic at best.

4. Office of the Director of National Intelligence, "ODNI Announces Mission Managers and Senior," ODNI News Release No. 2–06, January 11, 2006, http://www.dni.gov/release_letter_011106.html (accessed February 12, 2006).

5. *Oxford English Dictionary* online edition, http://www.oed.com/, s.v. "Cliché" (accessed May 14, 2006).

6. Scott Shane, "Iraqi Official, Paid by CIA, Gave Account of Weapons," *New York Times*, March 22, 2006, http://www.nytimes.com/2006/03/22/politics/22intel.html; Walter Pincus, "Ex-Iraqi Official Unveiled as Spy," *Washington Post*, March 23, 2006, http://www.washingtonpost.com/wp-dyn/content/article/2006/03/22/AR2006032202103.html.

7. Until quite recently General Hayden's name appeared as the principal deputy DNI on the ODNI web site. Recently, an "acting" principal deputy DNI's name has appeared: Lieutenant General Ronald L. Burgess, Jr. Deputy DNI Michael Hayden was appointed to direct the CIA in 2006 (discussed below).

8. James Risen and Eric Lichtblau, "Bush Lets U.S. Spy on Callers without Courts," *New York Times*, December 16, 2005, http://nytimes.com/2005/12/16/politics/16program.html. This was the original story that "scooped" other newspapers. Others followed

quickly. See Dan Eggen, "Bush Authorized Domestic Spying" *Washington Post*, December 16, 2005, http://www.washingtonpost.com/wp-dyn/content/article/2005/12/16/AR2005121600021.html; David S. Cloud, "Pentagon Is Said to Mishandle a Counterterrorism Database," *New York Times*, December 16, 2005, http://www.nytimes.com/2005/12/16/politics/16pent-agon.html; David Sanger, "In Speech, Bush Says He Ordered Domestic Spying," *New York Times*, December 17, 2005, http://nytimes.com/2005/12/18/politics/18bush.html; Peter Baker and Lexie Verdon, "President Acknowledges Approving Secretive Eavesdropping," *Washington Post*, December 17, 2005, http://www.washingtonpost.com/wp-dyn/content/article/2005/12/17/AR2005121700456.html; Eric Lichtblau and James Risen, "Eavesdropping Effort Began Soon After Sept. 11 Attacks," *New York Times*, December 18, 2005, http://www.nytimes.com/2005/12/18/politics/18spy.html.

9. Walter Pincus, "NSA Gave Other U.S. Agencies Information from Surveillance," *Washington Post*, January 1, 2006, http://www.washingtonpost.com/wp-dyn/content/article/2005/12/31/AR2005123100808.html.

10. Eric Lichtblau and Scott Shane, "Files Say Agency Initiated Growth of Spying Effort," *New York Times*, January 4, 2006, http://nytimes.com/2006/01/04/politics/04nsa.html.

11. Eric Licthblau, "With Power Set to Be Split, Wiretaps Re-emerge as Issue," *New York Times*, November 10, 2006, http://www.nytimes.com/2006/11/10/us/politics/10nsa.html.

12. On Monday, May 15, 2006, three full days (and news cycles) into the controversy, Negroponte's name appeared prominently. "When he was asked about the National Security Agency's controversial domestic surveillance program last Monday, U.S. intelligence chief John D. Negroponte objected to the question and said the government was 'absolutely not' monitoring domestic calls without warrants. Three days after Negroponte responded, the story of NSA collecting millions of domestic phone records broke in *USA Today*. 'This is about international terrorism and telephone calls between people thought to be working for international terrorism and people here in the United States,' Negroponte told reporters." Dan Eggen, "Negroponte Had Denied Domestic Call Monitoring," *Washington Post*, May 15, 2006, http://www.washingtonpost.com/wp-dyn/content/article/2006/05/14/AR2006051400762.html.

13. The story first broke in *USA Today* on Friday, May 12, 2006. *USA Today* was not one of the papers we read and archived daily for this project; therefore, the following days' reporting from the papers used in this book are cited on the program. See John Markoff, "Questions Raised for Phone Giants in Spy Data Furor," *New York Times*, May 13, 2006, http://www.nytimes.com/2006/05/13/washington/13phone.html; David G. Savage, "Phone Firms Questioned," *Los Angeles Times*, May 13, 2006, http://www.latimes.com/news/nationworld/nation/la-na-nsa13may13,0,7842766.story?coll=la-home-headlines; Arshad Mohammed and Terence O'Hara, "NSA Program Further Blurs Line on Privacy," *Washington Post*, May 13, 2006, http://www.washingtonpost.com/wp-dyn/content/article/2006/05/12/AR2006051202048.html.

14. Scott Shane and Eric Lichtblau, "Cheney Pushed U.S. to Widen Eavesdropping," *New York Times*, May 14, 2006 http://www.nytimes.com/2006/05/14/washington/14nsa.html.

15. Douglas Jehl, "North Korea and Iran Win Special Notice at Spy Center," *New York Times*, January 12, 2006, http://www.nytimes.com/2006/01/12/politics/12intel.html.

16. John D. Negroponte, "Intelligence Reform: Challenges and Opportunities," (speech, Georgetown University, February 17, 2006), http://www.dni.gov/dni_remarks_georgetown_20060217.html (accessed February 18, 2006).

17. Leslie Cauley, "NSA Has Massive Database of Americans' Phone Calls," *USA Today*, May 12, 2006, http://www.usatoday.com/news/washington/2006-05-10-nsa_x.htm.

18. Senate Select Committee on Intelligence, *Hearing on the Nomination of General Michael V. Hayden to Be The Director of The Central Intelligence Agency*, May 18, 2006 as posted on May 19, 2006 on the Office of the Director of National Intelligence, http://dni.gov/testimonies/20060518_testimony_2.pdf (accessed on May 19, 2006). (Hereafter, Hayden CIA Confirmation Hearing.)

19. Hayden CIA Confirmation Hearing, 13.

20. Hayden CIA Confirmation Hearing, 26.

21. Hayden CIA Confirmation Hearing, 36.

22. Hayden CIA Confirmation Hearing, 36.

23. Hayden CIA Confirmation Hearing, 37–38.

24. Walter Pincus, "Some Lawmakers Doubt DNI Has Taken Intelligence Reins," *Washington Post*, February 2, 2006, http://www.washingtonpost.com/wp-dyn/content/article/2006/02/01/AR2006020102215.html.

25. Walter Pincus, "Corralling Domestic Intelligence: Standards in the Works for Reports of Suspicious Activity," *Washington Post*, January 13, 2006, http://www.washingtonpost.com/wp-dyn/content/article /2006/01/12/AR2006011201852.html.

26. The Northern Command, known as NORTHCOM, was reinvigorated following 9/11. Then–Deputy Secretary of Defense Paul Wolfowitz, discussed at length elsewhere in these pages, visited NORTHCOM in Colorado. He said the following: "We must be prepared for attacks on our territory and our people, whether from organized armed forces or networks of global terrorists. A fundamental way in which we'll remain prepared for uncertainty is through the commitment of the men and women of Northern Command, who, today, shoulder a great responsibility on behalf of our nation." See Paul Wolfowitz, "Standup of U.S. Northern Command" (prepared remarks, Peterson Air Force Base, Colorado Springs, CO, October 1, 2002), http://www.dod.gov/speeches/2002/s20021001-depsecdef1.html (accessed January 13, 2006).

27. Walter Pincus, "NSA Gave Other U.S. Agencies Information from Surveillance," *Washington Post*, January 1, 2006, http://www.washingtonpost.com/wp-dyn/content/article/2005/12/31/ AR2005123100808.html (my emphasis). The piece mentioned General Michael V. Hayden, Negroponte's principal deputy director of national intelligence, but in defense of the NSA warrant-less program, not CIFA or Talon.

28. John D. Negroponte (remarks to the World Affairs Councils of Americas, Philadelphia, PA, January 18, 2006), http://www.dni.gov/World_Affairs_Council.htm (accessed January 20, 2006).

29. Doyle McManus and Peter Spiegel, "Spy Czar, Rumsfeld in a Turf War," *Los Angeles Times*, May 6, 2006, http://www.latimes.com/news/nationworld/nation/la-na-ciaassess6may06,0,1094951.story?coll=la-home-headlines.

30. Walter Pincus, "Negroponte's Battle for Authority," *Washington Post*, March 6, 2006, http://www.washingtonpost.com/wp-dyn/content/article/2006/03/05/AR20060305 00817.html.

31. Joel Brinkley, "Rice, in England, Concedes U.S. 'Tactical Errors' in Iraq," *New York Times*, April 1, 2006, http://www.nytimes.com/2006/04/01/world/middleeast/01rice .html; Josh White, "Rumsfeld Challenges Rice on 'Tactical Errors' in Iraq," *Washington Post*, April 6, 2006, http://www.washingtonpost.com/wp-dyn/content/article/2006/04/05/ AR2006040502269.html.

32. "Pentagon Wrongly Kept Reports in Threat Files," in Washington in Brief, *Washington Post*, April 6, 2006, http://www.washingtonpost.com/wp-dyn/content/article/ 2006/04/05/AR2006040502102.html.

33. "The Dark Side," by Michael Kirk, *Frontline*, PBS, June 29, 2006, http://www .pbs.org/wgbh/pages/frontline/darkside/etc/script.html (accessed June 30, 2006).

34. Eric Schmitt, "Pentagon Contradicts General on Iraq Occupation Force's Size," *New York Times*, February 28, 2003.

35. Michael B. Gordon and Bernard Trainor, *Cobra II: The Inside Story of the Invasion and Occupation of Iraq* (NY: Pantheon, 2006).

36. Thom Shanker, "Bremer Says He Sought Rise in U.S. Troop Strength in Iraq," *New York Times*, January 10, 2006, http://www.nytimes.com/2006/01/10/politics/10bremer .html; Bradley Graham and Thomas E. Ricks, "In a New Book, Bremer Defends His Year in Iraq," *Washington Post*, January 10, 2006, http://www.washingtonpost.com/wp-dyn/ content/article/2006/01/09/AR2006010900614.html.

37. Thomas E. Ricks, "Rumsfeld Rebuked by Retired Generals: Ex-Iraq Commander Calls for Resignation," *Washington Post*, April 13, 2006, http://www.washingtonpost .com/wp-dyn/content/article/2006/04/12/AR2006041201114.html; Peter Spiegel and Paul Richter, "Anti-Rumsfeld Chorus Grows," *Los Angeles Times*, April 13, 2006, http://www.latimes.com/news/nationworld/nation/la-na-general13apr13,0,3539237 .story?coll=la-home.

38. David Ignatius, "The Defense Secretary We Had," *Washington Post*, November 9, 2006, http:// www.washingtonpost.com/wp-dyn/content/article/2006/11/08/AR200611080 2084.html.

39. References to the Goss-Cheney friendship and Goss's perceived change of behavior in order to curry favor with Cheney in particular may be found in 2004, an election year and the year the IRTPA was passed. See Mike Allen and Walter Pincus, "Bush Considers Goss for CIA Director," *Washington Post*, June 25, 2004, http://www.washingtonpost .com/wp-dyn/articles/A3960-2004Jun24.html; Mike Allen, Fred Barbash, and Walter Pincus, "Picks Rep. Goss for Director of CIA," *Washington Post*, August 10, 2004, http:// www.washingtonpost.com/wp-dyn/articles/A53253-2004Aug10.html; Mike Allen and Walter Pincus, "Democrats Respond to Goss Nomination With Caution," *Washington Post*, August 11, 2004, http://www.washingtonpost.com/wp-dyn/articles/A54947-2004Aug10 .html; Joel Brinkley and James Risen, "On Other Side of the Aisle, Bruised Feelings Linger," *New York Times*, August 11, 2004, http://www.nytimes.com/2004/08/11/politics/ 11goss.html.

40. David Ignatius, "The CIA at Rock Bottom," *Washington Post*, May 7, 2006, http://www.washing-tonpost.com/wp-dyn/content/article/2006/05/05/AR2006050501660.html.

41. Doyle McManus and Peter Spiegel, "Spy Czar, Rumsfeld in a Turf War" *Los Angeles Times*, May 6, 2006, http://www.latimes.com/news/nationworld/nation/la-na-ciaassess6may06,0,1094951.story?coll=la-home-headlines.

42. Walter Pincus, "Some Lawmakers Doubt DNI Has Taken Intelligence Reins," *Washington Post*, February 2, 2006, http://www.washingtonpost.com/wp-dyn/content/article/2006/02/01/AR2006020102215.html.

43. Scott Shane, "In New Job, Spymaster Draws Bipartisan Criticism," *New York Times*, April 20, 2006, http://www.nytimes.com/2006/04/20/washington/20intel.html.

44. Traditionally, the Posse Comitatus Act has been interpreted as proscribing America's military forces from deploying as such for domestic security purposes. One legal scholar in particular from the Judge Advocate General's Corps argued in a provocative piece he published on the Internet that in fact the military may be used for domestic security. See Craig T. Trebilcock, "The Myth of Posse Comitatus," October 2000, http://www.homelandsecurity.org/journal/articles/Trebilcock.htm (accessed April 16, 2006). Trebilcock's opinion notwithstanding, the traditional view held sway.

45. Walter Pincus, "Ex-CIA Official Faults Use of Data on Iraq," *Washington Post*, February 10, 2005, http://www.washingtonpost.com/wp-dyn/content/article/2006/02/09/AR2006020902418.html.

46. Paul R. Pillar, "Intelligence, Policy, and the War in Iraq," *Foreign Affairs*, March–April, 2006, http://www.foreignaffairs.org/20060301faessay85202/paul-r-pillar/intelligence-policy-and-the-war-in-iraq.html (accessed April 3, 2006)(my emphasis).

47. Greg Miller, "E-Mails Show FBI Agents Fretted about Prisoner Abuse," *Los Angeles Times*, February 24, 2006, http://www.latimes.com/news/nationworld/nation/la-na-abuse24feb24,1,5488026.story?coll=la-headlines-nation (my emphasis); Josh White, "FBI Interrogators in Cuba Opposed Aggressive Tactics," *Washington Post*, February 24, 2006, http://www.washingtonpost.com/wp-dyn/content/article/2006/02/23/AR2006022301813.html.

48. Scott Shane, "Year into Revamped Spying, Troubles and Some Progress," *New York Times*, February 28, 2006, http://www.nytimes.com/2006/02/28/politics/28terror.html.

49. Hayden CIA Confirmation Hearing, 28.

50. Hayden CIA Confirmation Hearing, 29–30.

51. Hayden CIA Confirmation Hearing, 31.

52. Hayden CIA Confirmation Hearing, 39.

53. *The New York Times*, the *Washington Post*, and the *Los Angeles Times* each reported on May 17, 2006 that the White House decided to brief fully the relevant committees in both the House and the Senate. Unfortunately, the reason the White House decided to do so was, reportedly, that they got caught running the programs and because the hope to preempt any efforts to derail General Michael V. Hayden's confirmation for director of the CIA. See The New York Times, "Full Panels to Get Surveillance Briefing," *New York Times*, May 17, 2006, http://www.nytimes.com/2006/05/17/washington/

17intel.html; Charles Babington and Dafna Linzer, "More Lawmakers to Be Privy to Classified Briefings," *Washington Post*, May 17, 2006, http://www.washingtonpost .com/wp-dyn/content/article/2006/05/16/AR2006051601609.html; and Gregg Miller and Joseph Menn, "President Backs Off Wiretap Secrecy," *Los Angeles Times*, May 17, 2006, http://www.latimes.com/news/nationworld/nation/la-na-nsa17may-17,1,7523163 .story?coll=la-headlines-nation.

54. White House, *National Security Strategy of the United States, March 2006*, White House, http://www.whitehouse.gov/nsc/2006/nss206.pdf (Acrobat Reader pagination, 6).

55. We admit that our suspicion here is scarcely a "scoop." Already, the Democratic Party has rejected the Iraq War as a fool's errand and parts of the Republican Party have begun to distance themselves from the decision to invade Iraq. No one in either party, as far as we are aware, has questioned President Bush's reponse to 9/11, and for good reason.

Bibliography

Abramowitz, Michael, and Spencer S. Hsu. 2006. "Cheney Rejects Idea of Iraq Withdrawal." *Washington Post*, November 18, 2006. http://www.washington post.com/wp-dyn/content/article/2006/11/17/AR2006111701638.html.

Abramowitz, Michael, and Glenn Kessler. 2006. "Hawks Bolster Skeptical President." *Washington Post*, December 10, 2006. http://www.washingtonpost.com /wp-dyn/content/article/2006/12/09/AR2006120900443.html.

Adler, Mortimer J., ed. 1966. "American State Papers, The Federalists, J. S. Mills." *Britannica Great Book Series*. Vol. 40. Chicago: Encyclopedia Britannica.

Allen, Mike. 2003. "Expert on Terrorism to Direct Rebuilding." *Washington Post*, May 1, 2003. http://www.washingtonpost.com/ac2/wp-dyn/A2950-2003May1 .html.

Allen, Mike, Fred Barbash, and Walter Pincus. 2004. "Picks Rep. Goss for Director of CIA." *Washington Post*, August 2004. http://www.washingtonpost .com/wp-dyn/articles/A53253-2004Aug10.html.

Allen, Mike, and Dan Eggen. 2004. "Extension of 9/11 Probe Backed." *Washington Post*, February 5, 2004. http://www.washingtonpost.com/wp-dyn/ articles/A13964-2004Feb4.html.

Allen, Mike, and Walter Pincus. 2004. "Bush Considers Goss for CIA Director." *Washington Post*, June 25, 2004. http://www.washingtonpost.com/wp-dyn/ articles/A3960-2004Jun24.html.

———. 2004. "Democrats Respond to Goss Nomination With Caution." *Washington Post*, August 11, 2004. http://www.washingtonpost.com/wp-dyn/ articles/A54947-2004Aug10.html.

Allison, Graham. 1972. *Essence of Decision: Explaining the Cuban Missile Crisis*. New York: Little Brown & Co.

Ambrose, Stephen E. 1983. *Eisenhower: Soldier and President*. New York: Simon and Schuster.

———. 1984. *Eisenhower: Soldier, General of the Army, President-Elect, 1890–1952*. New York: Simon and Schuster.

Anderson, John Ward. 2005. "E.U. Leaders and Public Differ on Pullout in Iraq." *Washington Post*, December 9, 2005. http://www.washingtonpost.com/wp-dyn/content/article/2005/12/08/AR2005120801914.html.

Andrews, Edmund L., and Terence Neilan. 2003. "Attack Injures 7 U.S. Soldiers in Angry Iraqi City." *New York Times*, May 1, 2003. http://www.nytimes.com/2003/05/01/international/worldspecial/01CND-IRAQ.html.

Arnold, Lawrence. 2003. "9-11 Families Press for Intel Changes." *Associated Press*, October 20, 2003. Associated Press Wire Service (accessed October 20, 2003).

The Assassination Archives and Research Center. Church Committee Reports. http://www.aarclibrary.org/publib/church/reports/contents.htm (accessed March 2005).

Associated Press. 2003. "Blix Doesn't Expect Capture to Yield Banned Weapons." *Los Angeles Times*, December 17, 2003. http://www.latimes.com/news/nationworld/world/la-fg-blix17dec17,1,5294922.story?coll=la-headlines-world.

———. 2003. "Car Bomb Wounds 41 U.S. Troops in Iraq." *New York Times*, December 9, 2003. http://www.nytimes.com/aponline/international/AP-Iraq.html.

———. 2003. "Officials: N. Korea Test-Fires Missile." *USA Today*, April 1, 2003. http://www.usatoday.com/news/world/2003-04-01-nkorea-japan_x.htm.

———. 2004. "Bush's Iraq and Overall Job Ratings at New Lows" *Los Angeles Times*, April 6, 2004. http://www.latimes.com/news/nationworld/world/la-fg-poll6apr06,1,7885369.story?coll=la-headlines-world.

———. 2004. "Insurgents Lure Police to House, Kill Dozens." *Los Angeles Times*, December 29, 2004. http://www.latimes.com/news/nationworld/iraq/la-122904iraq_ wr,0,1262650.story?coll=la-home-headlines.

———. 2004. "U.S. Commander Says Qaeda Working in Iraq." *New York Times*, January 29, 2004. http://www.nytimes.com/aponline/international/AP-Iraq.html.

———. 2005. "$82 Billion OKd in Emergency Spending." *Los Angeles Times*, May 11, 2005. http://www.latimes.com/news/nationworld/nation/la-na-spending11may11,1,6383767.story?coll=la-headlines-nation.

———. 2005. "Senate Approves $50 Billion for War Efforts." *Los Angeles Times*, October 8, 2005. http://www.latimes.com/news/nationworld/world/la-fg-iraqbill8oct08,1,6709172.story?coll=la-headlines-world.

———. 2006. "Protesters Rampage in 2 Pakistani Cities." *New York Times*, February 14, 2006. http://www.nytimes.com/aponline/international/AP-Prophet-Drawings.html.

Babington, Charles, and Dafna Linzer. 2006. "More Lawmakers to Be Privy to Classified Briefings." *Washington Post*, May 17, 2006. http://www.washingtonpost.com/wp-dyn/content/article/2006/05/ 16/AR2006051601609.html.

Baker, Peter, and Jim VandeHei. 2005. "Bush Team Rethinks Its Plan for Recovery." *Washington Post*, December 29, 2005. http://www.washingtonpost.com/ wp-dyn/content/article/2005/12/28/AR2005122801517.html.

Baker, Peter, and Lexie Verdon. 2005. "President Acknowledges Approving Secretive Eavesdropping." *Washington Post*, December 17, 2005. http://www.washingtonpost.com/wp-dyn/content/article/2005/12/17/AR2005121700456.html.

The Baker-Hamilton Group. 2006. "The Iraq Study Group Report." *New York Times*, December 6, 2006. http://graphics8.nytimes.com/packages/pdf/international/20061206_btext.pdf (accessed December 6, 2006).

Balz, Dan. 2006. "White House Shifts Into Survival Mode." *Washington Post*, April 28, 2006. http://www.washingtonpost.com/wp-dyn/content/article/2006/04/19/AR2006041902517.html.

Becker, Becker, and James Dao. 2002. "Bush Will Keep Wartime Office Promoting U.S." *New York Times*, February 19, 2002.

Benjamin, Daniel. 2004. "President Cheney: His Office Really Does Run National Security." *Slate.com*, November 7, 2005. http://www.slate.com/id/2129686/ (accessed December 24, 2005).

Benjamin, Daniel, and Steven Simon. 2002. *Age of Sacred Terror*. New York: Random House.

Bolton, M. Kent. 1992. "How Decision Time and Degree of Anticipation Affect the Decisionmaking Process as U.S. Decisionmakers Confront Various Foreign Policy Challenges." PhD diss., the Ohio State University.

——. 2001. "*Pas de Trois*: The Synergism of Surprise, Threat, and Response Time and its Effects on U.S. Foreign-Policy Behavior." *Conflict Management and Peace Science* 18(2): 175–212.

——. 2005. *U.S. Foreign Policy and International Politics: George W. Bush, 9/11, and the Global-Terrorist Hydra*. New York: Prentice Hall.

Bonner, Raymond. 2003. "Indonesia Accuses Muslim Cleric of Plot to Oust Government." *New York Times*, April 14, 2003. http://www.nytimes.com/2003/04/14/international /asia/14CND-INDO.html

Boot, Max. 2005. "Our Extreme Makeover" *Los Angeles Times*, June 27, 2005. http://www.latimes.com/news/opinion/commentary/la-oe-boot27jul27,0,1437541.column?coll=la-news-comment-opinions.

Bowman, Karlyn H. 2003. American Enterprise Institute for Public Policy, "America after 9/11: Public Opinion on the War on Terrorism and the War with Iraq." September 2003. http://www.ciaonet.org/wps/bok01/. (For her full findings, see http://www.ciaonet.org/wps /bok01/bok01.pdf.)

Branigin, William. 2004. "Al Qaeda Trying to Spark a 'Civil War' in Iraq, U.S. Says." *Washington Post*, February 9, 2004. http://www.washingtonpost.com/wp-dyn/articles/A25736-2004Feb9.html.

———. 2006. "CIA Director Porter Goss Resigns." *Washington Post*, May 5, 2006. http://www.washingtonpost.com/wp-dyn/content/article/2006/05/05/AR2006050500937.html.

———. 2006. "Rumsfeld to Step Down as Defense Secretary." *Washington Post*. November 8, 2006: http://www.washingtonpost.com/wp-dyn/content/article/2006/11/08/AR 2006110801180.html.

Brinkley, Joel. 2006. "Rice, in England, Concedes U.S. 'Tactical Errors' in Iraq." *New York Times*, April 1, 2006. http://www.nytimes.com/2006/04/01/world/middleeast/01rice.html.

Brinkley, Joel, and James Risen. 2004. "On Other Side of the Aisle, Bruised Feelings Linger." *New York Times*, August 11, 2004. http://www.nytimes.com/2004/08/11/politics/11goss.html.

Brownstein, Ronald. 2003. "Maneuvering Over 'Road Map' for the Mideast." *Los Angeles Times*, May 26, 2003. http://www.latimes.com/news/nationworld/nation/la-na-outlook26may26,1,7828987.column?coll=la%2Dheadlines%2Dnation.

———. 2006. "Bush's Ratings Sink, but Trust Remains." *Los Angeles Times*, January 26, 2006. http://www.latimes.com/news/nationworld/nation/la-na-poll 27jan27,0,510814.story?coll=la-home-headlines.

Bumiller, Elisabeth. 2006. "Rove Is Giving Up Daily Policy Post to Focus on Vote." *New York Times*, April 20, 2006. http://www.nytimes.com/2006/04/20/washington/20bush.html.

Bumiller, Elisabeth, and Eric Schmitt. 2005. "The Vice President." *New York Times*, October 30, 2005. http://nytimes.com/2005/10/30/politics/30cheney.html.

Burns, John F. 2003. "Insurgents Use Rockets on Donkey Carts to Hit Sites in Iraqi Capital." *New York Times*, November 21, 2003. http://www.nytimes.com/2003/11/22/international/middleeast/22IRAQ.html.

———. 2003. "US Strike Hits Insurgent at Safe House." *New York Times*, June 8, 2006. http://www.nytimes.com/2006/06/08/world/middleeast/08cnd-iraq .html

Burns, John F., and Christine Hauser. 2004. "Bremer Is Increasing Pressure for a Quick End to Iraqi Uprisings." *New York Times*, April 19, 2004. http://www.nytimes.com/2004/04/18/international/middleeast/18CND-IRAQ.html.

Bush, George H. W., and Brent Scowcroft. 1989. *A World Transformed*. New York: Alfred A. Knopf.

Bush, George W. 1999. "A Distinctly American Internationalism." Ronald Reagan Library, Simi, California, November 19, 1999.

————. 2000. Mount Holyoke College's, International Relations Program Website. http://www.mtholyoke.edu/acad/intrel/bush/wspeech.htm (accessed February 23, 2006).

————. 2002. "Remarks by the President at Arkansas Welcome." November 4, 2002. http://www.whitehouse.gov/news/releases/2002/11/20021104-5.html.

————. 2002. "Remarks by the President at New Hampshire Welcome." November 1, 2002. http://www.whitehouse.gov/news/releases/2002/11/print/20021101-5.html.

————. 2002. "Remarks by the President at New Mexico Welcome." October 28, 2002. http://www.whithouse.gov/news/releases/2002/10/print/20021028-4.html.

————. 2002. "Remarks by the President at South Dakota Welcome." October 31, 2002. http://www.whitehouse.gov/news/releases/2002/10/print/20021031-1.html.

————. 2002. "Remarks by the President at Tennessee Welcome." November 2, 2002. http://www.whitehouse.gov/news/releases/2002/11/ 20021102-2.html.

————. 2002. "Remarks by the President in Atlanta, Georgia Welcome." November 2, 2002. http://www.whitehouse.gov/news/releases/2002/11/print/20021102-3.html.

————. 2002. "Remarks by the President in Colorado Welcome." October, 28, 2002. http://www.whitehouse.gov/news/releases/2002/10/print/20021028-5.html.

————. 2002. "Remarks by the President in Florida Welcome." November 2, 2002. http://www.whitehouse.gov/news/releases/ 2002/11/print/20021102-8.html.

————. 2002. "Remarks by the President in Minnesota Welcome." November 3, 2002. http://www.whitehouse.gov/news/releases/2002/11/20021103-2.html.

————. 2002. "Remarks by the President in Texas Welcome." November 4, 2002. http://www.whitehouse.gov/news/releases/2002/11/print/20021104-9.html.

————. 2003. "President Discusses the Future of Iraq." Speech to the American Enterprise Institute. Washington DC: Hilton Hotel. February 26, 2003. http://www.whitehouse.gov/news/releases/ 2003/02/20030226-11.html.

Cauley, Leslie. 2006. "NSA Has Massive Database of Americans' Phone Calls." *USA Today*, May 12, 2006. http://www.usatoday.com/news/washington/2006-05-10-nsa_x.htm.

Chan, Sewell. 2004. "U.S. Civilians Mutilated in Iraq Attack." *Washington Post*, April 1, 2004.

Chan, Sewell, and Thomas E. Ricks. 2004. "Army Girds to Confront Radical Cleric." *Washington Post*, April 14, 2004.

Chandrasekaran, Rajiv. 2004. "Anti-U.S. Uprising Widens in Iraq; Marines Push Deeper Into Fallujah." *Washington Post*, April 8, 2004.

Chandrasekaran, Rajiv, Mike Allen, and Doug Struck. 2004. "U.S. Transfers Political Authority in Iraq." *Washington Post*, June 28, 2004. http://www.washingtonpost.com/wp-dyn/articles/A10917-2004Jun28.html.

Chandrasekaran, Rajiv, and Susan B. Glasser. 2003. "Ground War Starts, Airstrikes Continue as U.S. Keeps Focus on Iraq's Leaders." *Washington Post*, March 21, 2003.

Chandrasekaran, Rajiv, and Anthony Shadid. 2003. "Ministry, Hotels in Baghdad Attacked." *Washington Post*, November 22, 2003.

Chen, Edward. 2003. "A Hands-Off President Jumps In." *Los Angeles Times*, March 21, 2003. http://www.latimes.com/news/nationworld/iraq/battle/la-war-bushday21mar21,1,3216193.story?coll=la%2Dhome%2Dheadlines.

Cheney, Dick. 2002. "Remarks by the Vice President to the Veterans of Foreign Wars 103rd National Convention." August 26, 2002. http://www.whitehouse.gov/news/releases/2002/08/20020826.html.

Clark, Drew. 2003. Daily Briefing. "Intelligence Reorganization Spotlights Fabled FBI-CIA Rift." GovExe.com, March 17, 2003. http://www.govexec.com/dailyfed/0303/031703cdam1.htm.

Cloud, David S. 2005. "Pentagon Is Said to Mishandle a Counterterrorism Database." *New York Times*, December 16, 2005. http://www.nytimes.com/2005/12/16/politics/16pent-agon.html;

CNN Cable Network, 2001.Archive. "The Big Story: High Stakes in Standoff." April 6, 2001. http://archives.cnn.com/2001/WORLD/asiapcf/east/04/06/china.big.picture/ (accessed August 2004).

Coll, Steve. 2003. "Hussein Was Sure of Own Survival." *Washington Post*, November 10, 2003.

Colombani, Jean-Marie. 2002. "We are all Americans! We are all New Yorkers." *Le Monde*, September 12, 2001.

The Commission on the Intelligence Capabilities of the United States Regarding Weapons of Mass Destruction, Report to the President of the United States. 2005. Report to the President of the United States, March 31, 2005. http://www.wmd.gov/report/wmd_report.pdf (accessed on March 31, 2005).

Connolly, Ceci. 2003. "Senators Call on White House to Share Records with 9/11 Panel." *Washington Post*, October 27, 2003.

Cooper, Helene. 2003. "Rice's Hurdles on Middle East Begin at Home." *New York Times*. August 10, 2006: http://www.nytimes.com/2006/08/10/washington/10rice.html.

Cornell University Law Collection. 2006. http://www.law.cornell.edu/uscode/html/uscode50/usc_sec_50_00000401——000-notes.html (accessed September 19, 2004).

Cowell, Allan. 2003. "British Muslims Are Seen Moving Into Mideast Terrorism." *New York Times*, May 1, 2003. http://www.nytimes.com/2003/05/01/international/ europe/01CND-BOMB.html.

Crabb.Cecil V., and Kevin Mulcahy. (1986). *Presidents and Foreign Policy Making: From FDR to Reagan*. Baton Rouge, LA: Louisiana State University Press.

Curtius, Mary. 2004. "Congress Wants Answers on Bush's Plans for Iraq." *Los Angeles Times*, April 19, 2004. http://www.latimes.com/news/nationworld/iraq/la-na-congiraq19apr19,1,2678079.story?coll=la-home-headlines.

Daniszewski, John. 2003. "Shiite Cleric Could Make or Break Transition." *Los Angeles Times*, November 24, 2003. http://www.latimes.com/news/nationworld/world/la-fg-sadr24nov24,1,5093743.story?coll=la-headlines-world.

———. 2003. "Time of Recovery for Baghdad." *Los Angeles Times*, April 14, 2003. http://www.latimes.com/news/nationworld/world/la-war-baghdad14apr14004417,1,3097500.story?coll= la%2 Dheadlines%2Dworld.

———. 2003. "Troops Tell of Street Fight With Dogged Foe." *Los Angeles Times*, December 2, 2003. http://www.latimes.com/news/nationworld/world/la-fg-samarra2dec02,1,7960049.story?coll=la-headlines-world.

Daniszewski, John, and Tyler Marshall. 2003. "Disarray in Iraq Threatens U.S. Goals." *Los Angeles Times*, May 25, 2003. http://www.latimes.com/ news/nationworld/world/la-fg-rebuild25may25235423,1,743970.story?coll=la%2 Dheadlines%2Dworld.

Daragahi, Borzou. 2006. "Clerics Take Lead After Iraq Bombing." *Los Angeles Times*, February 24, 2006. http://www.latimes.com/news/nationworld/world/la-fg-clerics24feb24,0,405063.story?coll=la-home-headlines.

Deane, Claudia. 2005. "Opinions Mixed on Next Four Years." *Washington Post*, January 22, 2005. http://www.washingtonpost.com/wp-dyn/articles/A27538-2005Jan21.html

Dionne, E.J., Jr. 2003. "To Honor Service." *Washington Post*, September 12, 2003. http://www.washingtonpost. com/ac2/wp-dyn/A63094-2003Sep11.html.

———. 2005. "All the President's Leaks." *Washington Post*, April 11, 2006. http://www.washingtonpost.com/wp-dyn/content/article/2006/04/10/AR2006041001049.html.

Dixon, Robyn. 2003. "Basra Could Boil Over Again." *Los Angeles Times*, August 12, 2003. http://www.latimes.com/news/nationworld/world/la-fg-basra12aug12,1,249768.story?coll=la-headlines-world.

Dobbs, Michael. 2003. "Back in Political Forefront." *Washington Post*, May 27, 2003.

Dowd, Maureen. 2006. "A Come-to-Daddy Moment." *New York Times*, November 9, 2006. http://select.nytimes.com/2006/11/09/opinion/09dowd.html.

Duelfer, Charles. 2004. Special Advisor to the Director of Central Intelligence, "Comprehensive Report of the Special Advisor to the DCI on Iraq's WMD." Central Intelligence Agency. Iraqi Survey Group, October 10, 2004. http://www.cia.gov/cia/reports/iraq_wmd_2004/index.html (accessed in October 2004).

Efron, Sonni. 2003. "Diplomats on the Defensive." *Los Angeles Times*, May 8, 2003. http://www.latimes.com /news/nationworld/world/la-fg-state8may 08,1,467133.story?coll=la%2Dhome%2Dheadlines.

Efron, Sonni, and Alissa J. Rubin. 2004. "U.S. Asks U.N. to Go to Iraq, Assess Feasibility of Vote." *Los Angeles Times*, January 20, 2004. http://www.latimes .com/news/nationworld/world/la-fg-uniraq20jan20,1,6457296.story?coll= la-headlines-world.

Eggen, Dan. 2003. "Sept. 11 Panel Defends Director's Impartiality: Concerns of Victims' Relatives Over Zelikow's National Security Ties Are Dismissed." *Washington Post*, October 14, 2003.

———. 2004. "9/11 Panel Unlikely to Get Later Deadline." *Washington Post*, January 19, 2004. http://www.washingtonpost.com/ac2/wp-dyn/A28025-2004Jan18 .html.

———. 2004. "Battle Over 9/11 Panel's Deadline Intensifies." *Washington Post*, January 29, 2004. http://www.washingtonpost.com/ac2/wp-dyn/A58200-2004 Jan28.html.

———. 2004. "Hastert Still against Giving 9/11 Panel More Time." *Washington Post*, February 26, 2004. http://www.washingtonpost.com/wp-dyn/articles/ A6948-2004Feb25.html.

———. 2005. "Bush Authorized Domestic Spying" *Washington Post*, December 16, 2005. http://www.washingtonpost.com/wp-dyn/content/article/2005/12/16/ AR2005121600021.html.

———. 2006. "Negroponte Had Denied Domestic Call Monitoring." *Washington Post*, May 15, 2006. http://www.washingtonpost.com/wp-dyn/content/article/ 2006/05/14/AR2006051400762.html.

Eggen, Dan, and Charles Lane. 2005. "On Hill, Anger and Calls for Hearings Greet News of Stateside Surveillance." *Washington Post*, December 17,2005. http://www.washingtonpost.com/wp-dyn/content/article/2005/12/16/ AR2005121601825.html.

Eggen, Dan, and John Mintz. 2003. "Agency to Concentrate Intelligence Analysis." *Washington Post*, January 30, 2003.

Fallows, James. 2004. "Blind into Baghdad." *Atlantic Monthly*, January–February, 2004. http://www.theatlantic.com/issues/2004/01/fallows.htm (accessed May 6, 2004).

Farley, Maggie. 2004. "U.N. Endorses Iraq's Interim Government." *Los Angeles Times*, June 9, 2004. http://www.latimes.com/news/nationworld/iraq/la-fg-un 9jun09,1,563648.story?coll=la-home-headlines.

Fattah, Hassan M. 2006. "As News Spreads of Deaths in South, Anger Boils Over Into Demonstrations in Beirut." *New York Times*, July 31, 2006. http://www.ny-times.com/2006/07/31/world/middleeast/31beirut.html.

Federal Bureau of Investigation. 2003. Press Release. "FBI Creates Structure to Support Intelligence Mission." April 3, 2003. http://www.fbi.gov/pressrel/ pressrel03/mueller040303.htm.

The Federation of American Scientists. "The October 2002 National Intelligence Estimate on Iraq." http://www.fas.org/irp/cia/product/iraq-wmd.pdf (accessed July 2005).

——. Senator Bob Graham's Letter. http://www.fas.org/irp/congress/2003_cr/ s072403.html (accessed July 23, 2005).

Filkins, Dexter. 2004. "New Government Is Formed in Iraq as Attacks Go On." *New York Times*, June 2, 2004. http://nytimes.com/004/06/02/international/ middleeast/02IRAQ.html.

——. 2004. "U.S. Says Files Seek Qaeda Aid in Iraq Conflict." *New York Times*, February 9, 2004. http://www.nytimes.com/2004/02/09/international/ middleeast/09INTE.html.

Filkins, Dexter, and Ian Fisher. 2003. "U.S. Is Now in Battle for Peace after Winning the War in Iraq." *New York Times*, May 3, 2003. http://www.nytimes.com/ 2003/05/03/international/worldspecial/03IRAQ.html.

Filkins, Dexter, and Kirk Semple. 2004. "9 Militias to Disband in Iraq, but Not Rebel Cleric's Force." *New York Times*, June 7, 2004. http://www.nytimes .com/2004/06/07/international/middleeast/07CND-IRAQ.html.

Fineman, Mark, Warren Vieth, and Robin Wright. 2003. "Dissolving Iraqi Army Seen by Many as a Costly Move." *Los Angeles Times*, August 23, 2003. http://www.latimes.com/news/nationworld/world/la-fg-iraqarmy24aug 24002421,1,6880219.story?coll=la-headlines-world.

Finer, Jonathan, and Bassam Sebti. 2006. "Sectarian Violence Kills Over 100 in Iraq." *Washington Post*, February 24, 2006. http://www.washingtonpost.com/ wp-dyn/content/article/2006/02/23/ AR2006022300216.html.

Finn, Peter, and Susan Schmidt. 2003. "Al Qaeda Is Trying to Open Iraq Front." *Washington Post*, September 7, 2003.

Firestone, David. 2006. "White House Gives Way On a Sept. 11 Commission: Congress Is Set to Create It." *New York Times*, November 15, 2002.

Fisher, Ian. 2003. "Suicide Bombers Strike at 2 U.S. Bases, Wounding Dozens of G.I.'s." *New York Times*, December 10, 2003. http://www.nytimes.com/2003/ 12/10/international/middleeast/10IRAQ.html.

Fisher, Ian, and Dexter Filkins. 2003. "Bombers Kill 14 in Iraq; Missile Hits Civilian Plane." *New York Times*, November 23, 2003. http://www.nytimes .com/2003/11/23/international/ middleeast/23IRAQ.html.

Fleishman, Jeffrey. 2003. "Ansar Fighters Surrender to Kurds: Denied Refuge in Iran, Hundreds Have Agreed to Turn Themselves in, A Commander Says." *Los Angeles Times*, April 7, 2003. http://www.latimes.com/news/

nationworld/iraq/battle/la-war-ansar7apr07,1,4955785.story?coll=la%2
Diraq%2Dbattle.

———. 2004. "Iraqi Melting Pot Nears Boiling Point." *Los Angeles Times*, January 26, 2004. http://www.latimes.com/news/nationworld/world/la-fg-kirkuk26
jan26,1,7309277.story?coll=la-headlines-world.

Fleishman, Jeffrey, and Edmund Sanders. 2004. "Clashes Go On as Radical Shiite Hints at Accord." *Los Angeles Times*, April 14, 2004. http://www.latimes
.com/news/nationworld/world/la-fg-iraq14apr14,1,1358176.story?coll=
la-headlines-world.

Ford, Gerald R. 1979. *A Time to Heal: The Autobiography of Gerald R. Ford.*
New York: Harper and Row Publishers.

Froomkin, Dan. 2005. "Insider Lashes Out." *Washington Post*, October 20, 2005.
http://www.washingtonpost.com/wp-dyn/content/blog/2005/10/20/
BL2005102001131.html.

The Future of Freedom Foundation. 1821. "Warning Against the Search for
'Monsters to Destroy.'" http://www.fff.org/comment/AdamsPolicy.asp (accessed January 22, 2006).

Gall, Carlotta. 2003. "2 Afghan Soldiers Slain in Heavy New Outbreak of
Clashes." *New York Times*, April 24, 2003. http://www.nytimes.com/2003/04/
24/international/middleeast/25 AFGHAN.html.

Gelb, Leslie H. and Richard K. Betts. 1979. *The Irony of Vietnam: The System
Worked.* Washington DC: The Brookings Institution Press.

Gellman, Barton. 2003. "Al Qaeda Near Biological, Chemical Arms Production."
Washington Post, March 23, 2003.

———. 2003. "Banned Iraqi Weapons Might Be Hard to Find." *Washington Post*,
April 5, 2003.

———. 2003. "Hunt for Iraqi Arms Erodes Assumptions." *Washington Post*, April
22, 2003.

George, Alexander. 1980. *Presidential Decisionmaking in Foreign Policy.* Boulder, CO: Westview Press.

Gerges, Fawaz A. 2003. "Muslims Called to Jihad." *Los Angeles Times*, March
26, 2003. http://www.latimes.com/news/opinion/commentary/la-war-oegerges
26mar26,1,6066432. story?coll=la%2Dnews%2Dcomment%2Dopinions.

Gerstenzang, James. 2003. "New Air Strikes Hit Targets in Baghdad." *Los Angeles Times*, March 20, 2003. http://www.latimes.com/news/nationworld/iraq/
battle/la-032003bombing_lat,1,31327.story?coll=la%2Dhome%2Dheadlines

Gerth, Jeff. 2003. "Officials Who Failed to Put Hijackers on Watch List Not
Named." *New York Times*, May 15, 2003. http://www.nytimes.com/2003/05/
15/international/worldspecial/15INTE.html.

Gettleman, Jeffrey. 2004. "U.S. Officials in Iraq Vow to Avenge Killings in Falluja." *New York Times*, April 1, 2004. http://www.ny-times.com/2004/04/01/in-
ternational/middleeast/01CND-IRAQ.html.

Gettleman, Jeffrey, and Douglas Jehl. 2004. "Fierce Fighting With Sunnis and Shiites Spreads to 6 Iraqi Cities." *New York Times*, April 7, 2004. http://www.nytimes.com/2004/04/07/international/middleeast/ 07CND-IRAQ.html.

Glanz, James. 2004. "Report Says Number of Attacks by Insurgents in Iraq Increases." *New York Times*, February 9, 2006. http://www.nytimes.com/2006/02/09/international/middleeast/09attacks.html.

Goldwater-Nichols Amendment. 1986. U.S. Code, Title 10, Subtitle A, Part I, Chapter 5, § 151, a, b, and c. http://www.jcs.mil/goldwater_nichol_act1986.html (accessed March 19, 2006).

Gordon, Michael B., and Bernard Trainor. 2006. *Cobra II: The Inside Story of the Invasion and Occupation of Iraq.* New York: Pantheon.

Graham, Bob. 2003. "Joint Intelligence Report—Post 9/11." Congressional Record, July 24, 2003: S9887-S9888.

Graham, Bradley. 2003. "November Deadliest Month in Iraq." *Washington Post*, November 29, 2003.

———. 2005. "At Pentagon, Less Ideology, More Balance." *Washington Post*, August 22, 2005. http://www.washing-tonpost.com/wp-dyn/content/article/2005/08/21/AR2005082100800.html.

———. 2006. "U.S. Looks to Baghdad to Deal With Violence." *Washington Post*, February 24, 2006. http://www.washingtonpost.com/wp-dyn/content/article/2006/02/23/AR2006022302193.html.

Graham, Bradley, and Thomas E. Ricks. 2006. "In a New Book, Bremer Defends His Year in Iraq." *Washington Post*, January 10, 2006. http://www.washingtonpost.com/wp-dyn/content/article/2006/01/09/AR2006010900614.html.

Greenberg, Maurice R., and Richard N. Haas, eds. 1995. *Making Intelligence Smarter: The Future of U.S. Intelligence.* New York: Council on Foreign Relations, the Federation of American Scientists. http://www.fas.org/irp/cfr.html (accessed March 17, 2006).

The Guardian. 2003. "Muslim Cleric's Treason Trial Begins." April 23, 2003. http://www.guardian.co.uk/ indonesia/Story/0,2763,941986,00.html.

———. 2004. "No Good Choices."December 30, 2004. http://www.guardian.co.uk/leaders/story/0,3604,1380690,00.html.

Haldeman, H. Robert. 1994. *The Haldeman Diaries: Inside the Nixon White House.* New York: G. P. Putnam & Sons.

Head, Richard G., Frisco W. Short, and Robert C. MacFarlane. 1978. *Crisis Resolution: Presidential Decision Making in the Mayaguez and Korean Confrontations.* Boulder, CO: Westview Press.

Hearing of the National Commission on Terrorist Attacks upon the United States. Ninth Public Hearing. 2004. Witness Dr. Condoleezza Rice, Assistant to the President for National Security Affairs. Hart Senate Office Building, Washington, DC: April 8, 2004. http://www.9-11commission.gov/archive/hearing9/9-11Commission_Hearing_2004-04-08.pdf (accessed on July 30, 2004).

Hendren, John. 2003. "Tape Claims Al Qaeda Is at Work in Iraq." *Los Angeles Times*, July 14, 2003. http://www.latimes.com/news/nationworld/world/la-fg-raids14jul14,1,6143435.story?coll=la-headlines-world.

———. 2004. "Uprising Could Signal a Second War for Iraq." *Los Angeles Times*. April 8, 2004. http://www.latimes.com/news/nationworld/iraq/la-fg-turn 8apr08,1,7881902.story ?coll=la-home-headlines.

Hendren, John, and Josh Meyer. 2003. "A Suspected Operative of Al Qaeda Is Held in Iraq." *Los Angeles Times*, August 30, 2003. http://www.latimes.com/news/nationworld/world/la-fgqaeda30aug   30,1,2023828.story?coll=la-headlines-world.

Hendren, John, and Azadeh Moaveni. 2003. "Anti-U.S. Sentiment Festers as Order and Calm Prove Elusive." *Los Angeles Times*, May 24, 2003. http://www.latimes.com/news/nationworld/world/la-fg-ambush24 may24,1,3136853 .story?coll=la%2Dheadlines%2Dworld.

Hermann, Charles F. 1969. *Crises in Foreign Policy*. Indianapolis, IN: Bobbs Merrill Publishing.

———. 1969. "International Crisis as a Situational Variable." In James Rosenau. Editor. *International Politics and Foreign Policy*. New York: The Free Press.

Hersh, Seymour M. 1983. *The Price of Power: Kissinger in the Nixon White House*. New York: Summit Books.

Hoff, Joan. 1994. Nixon Reconsidered, New York: Basic Books.

Holley, David. 2003. "Russia to Beef up Tajikistan Presence." *Los Angeles Times*, April   28,   2003.   http://www.latimes.com/news/na   tionworld/world/la-fg-tajik28apr28,1,6602189.story?coll=la %2Dheadlines%2Dworld.

Hong, Peter Y. 2004. "Iraqi Militias to Disband, Join Official Forces." *Los Angeles Times*, June 8, 2004. http://www.latimes.com/news/nationworld/world/la-fg-militias8jun08,1,736213.story?coll=la-headlines-world.

Horwitz, Sari. 2006. "Old-School Academy in Post-9/11 World: New Focus Is on Terrorism, but Training Is Struggling to Keep Up." *Washington Post*, August 17, 2006. http://www.washingtonpost.com/wp-dyn/content/article/2006/08/16/AR2006081601622.html.

Hosenball, Mark, Michael Isikoff, and Evan Thomas. 2003. "Cheney's Long Path to War." *Newsweek*, November 2003. http://www.msnbc.com/news/991211.asp.

Ignatius, David. 2006. "The CIA at Rock Bottom." *Washington Post*, May 7, 2006. http://www.washing-tonpost.com/wp-dyn/content/article/2006/05/05/AR2006050501660.html.

———. 2006. "The Defense Secretary We Had." *Washington Post*, November 9, 2006. http://www.washingtonpost.com/wp-dyn/content/article/2006/11/08/AR2006110802084.html.

Inderfurth, Karl, and Loch Johnson. 2003. Editors. *Fateful Decisions: Inside the National Security Council*. Oxford: Oxford University Press.

Intelligence Reform and Terrorism Prevention Act. 2004. Public Law 108-455. 108th Congress, 2nd Session, December 17, 2004. http://frwebgate.access.gpo .gov/cgi-bin/getdoc.cgi?dbname=108_cong_public_laws&docid=f:publ458 .108.pdf (Adobe Acrobat Copy obtained February 2005).

Jehl, Douglas. 2004. "Terror Memo Disregarded, Report Says." *New York Times*, April 15, 2004. http://www.nytimes.com/2004/04/15/politics/15INTE.html.

———. 2005. "After a Year Leading C.I.A., Goss Is Struggling, Some Say." *New York Times*, September 23, 2005. http://www.nytimes.com/2005/09/23/ politics/23intel.html.

———. 2006. "North Korea and Iran Win Special Notice at Spy Center." *New York Times*, January 12, 2006. http://www.nytimes.com/2006/01/12/politics/ 12intel.html.

Johnson, Jeff. 2002. "Congressional Inquiry into 9/11 Will Look back as Far as 1986." *New York Times*, June 5, 2002. http://www.nytimes.com/2002/06/05/ politics/05INQU.html.

Johnston, David. 2006. "C.I.A. Director Will Lead Terror Center." *New York Times*, January 29, 2003. http://www.nytimes.com/2003/01/29/politics/ 29TERR.html.

Johnston, David, and James Risen. 2003. "New Signs of Terror Not Evident." *New York Times*, April 6, 2003. http://www.nytimes.com/2003/04/06/international/ worldspecial/06SECU.html.

Jordan, Mary. 2006. "Britons Urge Arrest of Protesters Advocating Violence." *Washington Post*, February 7, 2006. http://www.washingtonpost.com/wp-dyn/ content/article/2006/02/06/AR2006020601571.html

Karnow, Stanley. 1983. *Vietnam: A History*. New York: Penguin Books.

Kelly, David. 2003. "Regime's Priority Was Blueprints, Not Arsenal, Defector Told U.N." *Los Angeles Times*, April 26, 2003. http://www.latimes.com/news/ nation-world/world/la-war-kamel26apr26,1,4372842.story?coll=la%2D headlines%2Dworld.

Kessler, Glenn. 2003. "State-Defense Policy Rivalry Intensifying." *Washington Post*, April 22, 2003.

Kessler, Glen, and Philip P. Pan. 2003. "Missteps With Turkey Prove Costly." *Washington Post*. March 28, 2003: A1

Kessler, Glenn, and Peter Slevin. 2003. "Rice Fails to Repair Rifts, Officials Say: Cabinet Rivalries Complicate Her Role." *Washington Post*, October 12, 2003.

Khalil, Ashraf. 2004. "Top Sunni Party Quits Election." *Los Angeles Times*, December 28, 2004. http://www.latimes.com/news/nationworld/world/ la-fg-iraq28dec28,1,6933324.story?coll=la-headlines-world.

Kirkpatrick, David. 2005. "Congress Approves Financing to Fight Wars and Terrorism." *New York Times*, May 11, 2005. http://nytimes.com/2005/05/11/ politics/11spend.html.

Knickmeyer, Ellen, and Jonathan Finer. 2003. "Insurgent Leader Al-Zarqawi Killed in Iraq." *Washington Post*, June 8, 2006. http://www.washingtonpost.com/wp-dyn/content/article/2006/06/08/AR2006060800114.html.

Knowlton, Brian. 2003. "Top General Says Iraqi Resistance Is Far From 'Monolithic,'" *New York Times*, July 6, 2003. http://www.nytimes.com/2003/07/06/international/worldspecial/06CND-POLI.html.

Kohut, Andrew and Carroll Doherty. 2005. The Pew Research Center for the People and the Press, "Bush Approval Rises Modestly: Tempered Public Reaction to London Attacks." July 11, 2005. http://www.pewtrusts.com/pdf/PRC_terror_0705.pdf (accessed May 18, 2006).

Kraul, Chris. 2003. "U.S. Soldiers Fire on Iraqi Family." *Los Angeles Times*, August 12, 2003. http://www.lat-imes.com/news/nationworld/world/la-fg-shoot12aug12,1,2595297.story?coll=la-headlines-world.

Kristof, Nicolas D. 2006. "Talking to Evil." *New York Times*, August 13, 2006. http://select.nytimes.com/2006/08/13/opinion/13kristof.html.

LaFraniere, Sharon. 2003. "How Jihad Made Its Way to Chechnya." *Washington Post*, April 26, 2003.

Lamb, Christopher Jon. 1989. *Belief Systems and Decision Making in the Mayaguez Crisis*. Gainesville, FL: University of Florida Press.

Leonnig, Carol D. 2006. "Surveillance Court Is Seeking Answers: Judges Were Unaware of Eavesdropping." *Washington Post*, January 5, 2006. http://www.washingtonpost.com/wp-dyn/content/article/2006/01/04/AR2006010401864.html.

Lichthblau, Eric. 2006. "With Power Set to Be Split, Wiretaps Re-emerge as Issue." *New York Times*, November 10, 2006. http://www.nytimes.com/2006/11/10/us/politics/10nsa.html.

Lichthblau, Eric, and James Risen. 2005. "Eavesdropping Effort Began Soon After Sept. 11 Attacks." *New York Times*, December 18, 2005. http://www.nytimes.com/2005/12/18/politics/18spy. Html.

Lichthblau, Eric, and Scott Shane. 2006. "Files Say Agency Initiated Growth of Spying Effort." *New York Times*, January 4, 2006. http://nytimes.com/2006/01/04/politics/04nsa.html.

Linzer, Dana. 2005. "Iran Is Judged 10 Years From Nuclear Bomb: U.S. Intelligence Review Contrasts With Administration Statements." *Washington Post*, August 2, 2005. http://www.washingtonpost.com/wp-dyn/content/article/2005/08/01/AR2005080101453.html.

Lippman, Thomas W. 2003. "Iraqi Muslims Protest Against Foreign Troops." *Washington Post*, April 18, 2003. http://www.washington-post.com/ac2/wp-dyn/A50762-2003Apr18.html.

The Literature of Intelligence. *A Bibliography of Materials with Essays, Reviews, and Comments*. Muskingum College, New Concord, OH. http://intellit.muskingum.edu/cia_folder/ cia70s_folder/cia70sinvu-z.html [accessed May 2006].

The Los Angeles Times. Editorial. 2005. "One step at a time in Iraq." *Los Angeles Times*, December 15, 2005. http://www.latimes.com/news/opinion/editorials/la-ediraq15dec15,0,7559925.story?coll=la-news-comment-editorials.

The Los Angeles Times. Editorial. 2003. "Silence Feeds 9/11 Theories." *Los Angeles Times*, October 28, 2003. http://www.latimes.com/news/opinion/editorials/la-ed-withhold28oct28,1,1355905.story?coll=la-news-alert.

Lynch, Colum. 2003. "Brahimi to Be U.N. Adviser on Iraq." *Washington Post*, January 12, 2003.

MacFarquhar, Neil. 2003. "Rising Tide of Islamic Militants See Iraq as Ultimate Battlefield." *New York Times*, August 13, 2003. http://www.nytimes.com/2003/08/13/international/worldspecial/13ISLA.html.

MacFarquhar, Neil, and Kirk Semple.2003. "Blast in Iraq Kills a Leading Shiite Cleric." *New York Times*, August 29, 2003. http://www.nytimes.com/2003/08/29/international/worldspecial/29CND-IRAQ.html;

Markoff, John. 2006. "Questions Raised for Phone Giants in Spy Data Furor." *New York Times*, May 13, 2006. http://www.nytimes.com/2006/05/13/washington/13phone.html.

Markon, Jerry, and Timothy Dwyer. 2006. "Moussaoui Says He Was to Fly 5th Plane." *Washington Post*, March 28, 2006. http://www.washingtonpost.com/wp-dyn/content/article/2006/03/ 27/AR2006032700148.html

Marshal, Tyler, and Edmund Sanders. 2003. "Iraqi Advisors Are Left Cooling Their Heels." *Los Angeles Times*, May 27, 2003. http://www.latimes.com/news/nationworld/world/la-fg-expats27may27234427,1,5796003.story?coll=la%2Dheadlines%2Dworld.

McManus, Doyle, and Peter Spiegel. 2006. "Spy Czar, Rumsfeld in a Turf War" *Los Angeles Times*, May 6, 2006. http://www.latimes.com/news/nationworld/nation/la-na-ciaassess6may06,0,1094951.story?coll=la-home-headlines.

McNamara, Robert S., with Brian VanDeMark. 1996. Reprint Edition. *In Retrospect: the Tragedies and Lessons of Vietnam*. New York: Vintage.

Mead, Walter Russell. 2003. "Battlefield Europe: Fight for EU's Future Is on, with U.S.-German Relations at the Middle." *Los Angeles Times*, March 30, 2003. http://www.latimes.com/news/opinion/commentary/la-war-opmead30mar30,1,4767155.story?coll=la%2Dnews%2Dcomment%2Dopinions

Melanson, Richard A. 2004. *American Foreign Policy since the Vietnam War: The Search for Consensus from Richard Nixon to George W. Bush*. New York: E.H. Sharpe.

Meyer, Josh. 2003. "Hezbollah Vows Anew to Target Americans." *Los Angeles Times*, April 17, 2003. http://www.latimes.com/news/nationworld/iraq/world/la-warhezbollah17apr17,1,4681007.story?coll=la% 2Dhome%2Dheadlines.

———. 2004. "Terror Not a Bush Priority before 9/11, Witness Says." *Los Angeles Times*. March 25, 2004: http://www.latimes.com/news/nationworld/nation/la-na-commish25mar25,1,7704823.story?coll=la-headlines-nation.

Meyer, Josh, and Patrick J. McDonnell. 2004. "U.S. Says It Has Captured Suspected Terrorist Leader's Aides in Iraq." *Los Angeles Times*, January 24, 2004. http://www.latimes.com/news/nationworld/world/la-fg-terror24jan24,1, 7632365.story?coll=la-headlines-world.

Meyers, Steven Lee. 2006. "Strong Rebuke for the Kremlin From Cheney." *New York Times*, May 5, 2006. http://www.nytimes.com/2006/05/05/world/05cheney .html.

Milbank, Dana. 2006. "On the Subject of Leaks a Talkative President Runs Dry." *Washington Post*, April 11, 2006. http://www.washingtonpost.com/wp-dyn/ content/article/2006/04/10/AR2006041001500.html.

Milbank, Dana, and Walter Pincus. 2004. "Rice Defends Refusal to Testify." *Washington Post*, March 29, 2004. http://www.washingtonpost.com/ac2/ wp-dyn/A31904-2004Mar28.html.

Miller, Gregg. 2006. "E-Mails Show FBI Agents Fretted about Prisoner Abuse." *Los Angeles Times*, February 24, 2006. http://www.latimes.com/news/nation-world/nation/la-na-abuse24feb24,1,5488026.story?coll=la-headlines-nation.

Miller, Gregg, and Joseph Menn. 2006. "President Backs Off Wiretap Secrecy." *Los Angeles Times*, May 17, 2006. http://www.latimes.com/news/nationworld/ nation/la-na-nsa17may-17,1,7523163.story?coll=la-headlines-nation.

Miller, Judith. 2003. "Illicit Arms Kept Till Eve of War, an Iraqi Scientist Is Said to Assert." *New York Times*, April 21, 2003. http://www.nytimes.com/2003/04/ 21/international/worldspecial/ 21CHEM.html.

Mohammed, Arshad, and Terence O'Hara. 2006. "NSA Program Further Blurs Line on Privacy." *Washington Post*, May 13, 2006. http://www.washingtonpost .com/wp-dyn/content/article/2006/05/12/AR2006051202048.html.

Morely, Jefferson. 2003. "The Fallout from Fallujah." *Washington Post*, May 1, 2003. http://www.washingtonpost.com/wp-dyn/articles/A64971-2003May1 .html.

Murphy, Kim. 2003. "Ladies' Tea Boils over as Saudis Rail at U.S." *Los Angeles Times*, March 27, 2003. http://www.latimes.com/news/nationworld/world/ la-war-saudi27mar27002426,1,614041.story?coll=la%2Dheadlines%2Dworld %2Dmanual.

———. 2003. "Saudis Tighten Oil Security." *Los Angeles Times*, April 18, 2003. http://www.latimes.com/news/nationworld/world/la-war-oil18apr18003423,1, 7852868.story?coll=l a%2Dheadlines%2Dworld%2Dmanual.

Murray, Shailagh. 2005. "House Approves War Funding." *Washington Post*, March 17, 2005. http://www.washingtonpost.com/wp-dyn/articles/A40248-2005Mar16 .html

The National Commission on Terrorist Attacks upon the United States. The 9/11 Commission's Ninth Public Hearing. 2004. "Testimony of Condoleezza Rice." April 8, 2004. http://www.9-11commission.gov/archive/hearing9/9-11Com-mission_Hearing_2004-04-08.pdf.

Negroponte, John D. 2006. "Intelligence Reform: Challenges and Opportunities." Remarks by Ambassador John D. Negroponte, Director of National Intelligence. Georgetown University, February 17, 2006. http://www.dni.gov/dni_remarks_georgetown_20060217.html (accessed on February 18, 2006).

Neilan, Terrence. 2004. "C.I.A. Chief Defends Agency but Allows 'We Made Mistakes,'" *New York Times*, April 14, 2004. http://www.nytimes.com/2004/04/14/politics/14CND-PANE.html.

New York Times. 2003. "Rumsfeld Denies the U.S. Has Plans for Permanent Iraq Bases." April 22, 2003. http://www.nytimes.com/2003/04/22/international/worldspecial/22PENT.html.

——. 2004. "Names of the Dead." August 12, 2006. http://www.nytimes.com/2006/08/12/us/12list.html.

——. 2006. "Full Panels to Get Surveillance Briefing." May 17, 2006. http://www.nytimes.com/2006/05/17/washin-gton/17intel.html;

Nixon, Richard M. 1978. *The Memoirs of Richard Nixon*. New York: Grosset and Dunlap.

Oppel, Richard A., Jr., and Khalid al-Ansary. 2004. "Iraqi Rebels Set Trap for Police, Killing at Least 32." *New York Times*, December 29, 2004. http://nytimes.com/2004/12/29/international/middleeast/ 29cnd-iraq.html.

Oppel, Richard A, and Khalid al-Ansary. 2004. "25 Insurgents Are Killed Trying to Overrun U.S. Outpost in Mosul." *New York Times*, December 30, 2004. http://nytimes.com/2004/12/30/international/middleeast/30iraq.html.

Oxford English Dictionary. 2006. Online Edition.

Paddock, Richard C. 2003. "Muslim Terrorists Tied to 2 Blasts." *Los Angeles Times*, April 18, 2003. http://www.latimes.com/news/nationworld/world/la-fg-phil18apr08002429, 1,3716068.story?coll=la %2Dheadlines%2Dworld.

——. 2003. "Violence Surges Again in Indonesian Province." *Los Angeles Times*, April 8, 2003. http://www.latimes.com/news /nationworld/world/la-fg-phil8apr08002429, 1,3716068.story?coll=la %2Dheadlines%2Dworld.

Pasley, Jeffrey L. 2006. "An Old Debate on Presidential Power." *New York Times*, April 2, 2006. http://www.nytimes.com/2006/04/02/weekinreview/02read2.html.

Perry, Tony. 2004. "Fallouja Neighborhood Suddenly Turns Fierce." *Los Angeles Times*, April 7, 2004. http://www.latimes.com/news/nationworld/iraq/la-fg-fallouja7apr07,1,6602210.story?coll=la-home-headlines

Pew Charitable Trusts, 2006. "Analysis: The Iraq-Vietnam Difference." May 17, 2006. http://www.pewtrusts.com/ideas/ideas_item.cfm?content_item_id=3368&content_type_id=18&issue_name=Public%20opinion%20and%20polls&issue=11&page=18&name=Public%20Opinion%20Polls%20and%20Survey%20Results.

Pillar, Paul R. 2006. "Intelligence, Policy, and the War in Iraq." .Foreign Affairs, March-April, 2006: http://www.foreignaffairs.org/20060301faessay85202/

paul-r-pillar/intelligence-policy-and-the-war-in-iraq.html (accessed April 3, 2006).

Pincus, Walter. 2004. "Al Qaeda Figure Captured." *Washington Post*. January 24, 2004.

———. 2005. "CIA to Remain Coordinator of Overseas Spying." *Washington Post*, October 13, 2005. http://www.washingtonpost.com/wp-dyn/content/article/2005/10/12/AR2005101202174.html.

———. 2005. "Intelligence Panel's Findings Criticized: Experts Call Suggestions Uniformed." *Washington Post*, March 31, 2005. http://www.washingtonpost.com/wp-dyn/articles/A14104-2005Mar30.html.

———. 2006. "Corralling Domestic Intelligence: Standards in the Works for Reports of Suspicious Activity." *Washington Post*, January 13, 2006. http://www.washingtonpost.com/wp-dyn/content/article/2006/01/12/AR2006011201852.html.

Pincus, Walter. 2006. "Gates May Rein In Pentagon Activities." *Washington Post*, November 14, 2006. http://www.washingtonpost.com/wp-dyn/content/article/2006/11/13/AR2006111301135.html

———. 2005. "Ex-CIA Official Faults Use of Data on Iraq." *Washington Post*, February 10, 2005. http://www.washingtonpost.com/wp-dyn/content/article/2006/02/09/AR2006020902418.html.

———. 2006. "Ex-Iraqi Official Unveiled as Spy." *Washington Post*, March 23, 2006. http://www.washingtonpost.com/wp-dyn/content/article/2006/03/22/AR2006032202103.html.

———. 2006. "Negroponte's Battle for Authority." *Washington Post*, March 6, 2006. http://www.washingtonpost.com/wp-dyn/content/article/2006/03/05/AR2006030500817.html.

———. 2006. "NSA Gave Other U.S. Agencies Information from Surveillance." *Washington Post*, January 1, 2006. http://www.washingtonpost.com/wp-dyn/content/article/2005/12/31/AR2005123100808.html

———. 2006. "Some Lawmakers Doubt DNI Has Taken Intelligence Reins." *Washington Post*, February 2, 2006. http://www.washingtonpost.com/wp-dyn/content/article/2006/02/01/AR2006020102215.html.

Pincus, Walter, and Mike Allen. 2003. "Terrorism Agency Planned." *Washington Post*, January 29, 2003: A12.

Pincus, Walter, and Peter Baker. 2005. "Data on Iraqi Arms Flawed, Panel Says" *Washington Post*, April 1, 2005. http://www.washingtonpost.com/wp-dyn/articles/A15184-2005Mar31.html.

Pincus, Walter, Bob Woodward, and Dana Priest. 2003. "U.S. Thinks Hussein, Sons Were In Bunker." *Washington Post*, March 21, 2003: A1

Powell, Michael, and Dale Russakoff. 2003. "In New York, Roll of Names Is Part of Quiet Remembrance." *Washington Post*, September 11, 2003. http://www

.washingtonpost.com/ac2/wp-dyn?pagename=article&contentId=A59167-2003Sep11.

Prados, John. (1991). *Keepers of the Keys: A History of the National Security Council from Truman to Bush*. New York: William Morrow and Company.

Priest, Dana. 2004. *The Mission: Wagging War and Keeping Peace with America's Military*. New York: W.W. Norton and Company.

——. 2004. "Panel Says Bush Saw Repeated Warnings." *Washington Post*, April 14, 2004. http://www.washingtonpost.com/ac2/wp-dyn/A9642-2004Apr13.html.

Princeton University. "Ferdinand Eberstadt Papers." http://infoshare1.princeton.edu/libraries/fires-tone/rbsc/finding_aids/eberst/eberstlist1b.html (accessed November 12, 2005).

Project for A New American Century (PNAC). 1997. "Statement of Principles." June 3, 1997. http://www.newamericancentury.org/statementofprinciples.htm (accessed July 25, 2005).

The Public Discourse Project. 2005. "Final Report Card on 9/11 Commission Recommendations." The 9/11 Commission. December 5, 2005. http://www.9-11pdp.org.

Reuters. 2003. "Baghdad Residents Protest U.S. Troops." *New York Times*, April 18, 2003. http://www.nytimes.com/reuters/international/international-iraq-demonstration.html.

——. 2003. "Muslim Cleric Urges Iraqis Not to Resist." *New York Times*, April 3, 2003. http://www.ny-times.com/reuters/international/international-iraq-fatwa.html.

——. 2003. "29 Tourists Are Missing in Algeria." *Los Angeles Times*, April 8, 2003. http://www.latimes.com/news/nationworld/world/la-fg-missing8apr08,1,7766978.story?coll= la%2Dheadlines %2Dworld.

——. 2004. "Iraq Blast Kills U.S. Soldier." *Los Angeles Times*, December 28, 2004. http://www.latimes.com/news/nationworld/world/la-fg-deaths28dec28,1,2206638.story?coll=la-headlines-world.

——. 2004. "U.S. Seizes Terror Suspect." *New York Times*, January 24, 2004. http://www.nytimes.com/2004/01/24/politics/24ANSA.html.

Reynolds, Maura. 2003. "Bush Commitment Is Key to 'Road Map' for Mideast." *Los Angeles Times*, April 30, 2003. http://www.latimes.com/news/nationworld/nation/la-fg-bush30apr30001423,1,2491552.story?coll=la%2Dheadlines%2Dnation.

——. 2004. "A Chance to Erase Doubts, or Raise Them." *Los Angeles Times*, April 7, 2004. http://www.latimes.com/news/nationworld/nation/la-na-rice7apr07,1,3642779.story?coll=la-headlines-nation.

——. 2004. "Testimony Paints Image of Passive Inner Circle." *Los Angeles Times*, April 8, 2004. http://www.latimes.com/news/nationworld/nation/la-na-assess9apr09,1,3756594.story? coll=la-headlines-nation.

Rice, Condoleezza. 2000. "Life after the Cold War." Foreign Affairs (January/ February 2000), 79(1): Council of Foreign Affairs Website. http://www .foreignpolicy2000.org/library/issuebriefs/readingnotes/fa_rice.html (accessed September 2002).

Richter, Paul. 2005. "Cheney Still in Background, but Not Unscathed." Los Angles Times, October 29, 2005. http://www.latimes.com/ news/nationworld/ nation/la-na-cheney29oct29,1,3843933.story?coll=la-headlines-nation.

Richter, Paul, and David Holley. 2006. "Cheney Has Harsh Words for Moscow." Los Angeles Times, May 5, 2006. http://www.latimes.com/news/nationworld/ world/la-fg-cheney5may05,1,41783.story?coll=la-headlines-world.

Ricks, Thomas E. 2006. "Rumsfeld Rebuked by Retired Generals: Ex-Iraq Commander Calls for Resignation." Washington Post, April 13, 2006. http://www .washingtonpost.com/wp-dyn/content/article/2006/04/12/AR2006041201114 .html.

Risen, James. 2003. "Prewar Views of Iraq Threat Are Under Review by C.I.A." New York Times, May 22, 2003: A1.

———. 2006. "The War on Terror, Under New Scrutiny." New York Times, December 3, 2006. http://www.nytimes.com/2006/12/03/weekinreview/03risen .html.

Risen, James, and Eric Lichtblau. 2005. "Bush Lets U.S. Spy on Callers without Courts." New York Times, December 16, 2005. http://nytimes.com/2005/12/16/ politics/16program.html

Rosenau, James N. 1966. "Pre-Theories and Theories of Foreign Policy." In R. Barry Farrrell, ed. Approaches to Comparative and International Politics. Evanston, IL: Northwestern University Press.

Rotella, Sebastian. 2003. "Terror Suspect Linked to Hamburg Cell." Los Angeles Times, April 11, 2003. http://www. latimes.com/news/nationworld/world/ la-fg-terror11apr11,1,7321973.story?coll=la%2Dhead-lines%2Dworld.

Rothkopf, David J. 2005. Running the World: The Inside Story of the National Security Council and the Architects of American Power. New York: Public Affairs.

Rubin, Alissa J. 2004. "12 Marines Are Killed as Violence Spreads in Iraq." Los Angeles Times, April 7, 2004. http://www.latimes.com/news/nationworld/ world/la-fg-iraq7apr07,1,2052657.story?coll=la-headlines-world.

Rubin, Alissa J., and Jesús Sanchez. 2003. "Iraqis Protest U.S., Demand Islamic State." Los Angeles Times, April 19, 2003. http://www.latimes.com/la-war-iraq 19apr19,1,3329182.story?coll=la-headlines-world.

———. 2003. "Thousands in Baghdad Protest Occupation." Los Angeles Times, April 18, 2003. http://www.latimes.com/news/nationworld/iraq/inside/la-iraq-041803iraq_lat,1, 3180485.story?coll=la%2Dhome%2Dheadlines.

Rubin, Alissa J., and Carol J. Williams. 2004. "U.S. Transfers Sovereignty to Iraq." *Los Angeles Times*, June 28, 2004. http://www.latimes.com/news/nationworld/iraq/la-062804iraq_lat,1,3085056.story?coll=la-home-headlines.

Rutenberg, Jim, and David Sanger. 2006. "Bush Aides Seek Alternatives to Iraq Study Group's Proposals, Calling Them Impractical." *New York Times*, December 10, 2006. http://www.nytimes.com/2006/12/10/world/middleeast/10prexy.html

Sanders, Edmund. 2004. "Cleric's Militia Has Surprised American Forces." *Los Angeles Times*, April 18, 2004. http://www.latimes.com/ news/nationworld/world/la-fg-najaf18apr18,1,6880460.story?coll=la-headlines-world.

———. 2004. "Iraqi Mob Kills 4 Americans." *Los Angeles Times*, April 1, 2004. http://www.latimes.com/news/nationworld/world/la-fg-iraq1apr01,1,7300126.story?coll=la-headlines-world.

———. 2004. "28 Die in Wave of Insurgent Attacks in Iraq." *Los Angeles Times*, December 29, 2004. http://www.latimes.com/news/nationworld/world/la-fg-iraq29dec29,1,7392078.story?coll=la-headlines-world.

Sanger, David. 2005. "In Speech, Bush Says He Ordered Domestic Spying." *New York Times*, December 17, 2005. http://nytimes.com/2005/12/18/politics/18bush.html.

Sanger, David E., and David Johnston. 2006. "White House Memo." *New York Times*, April 11, 2006. http://www.nytimes.com/2006/04/11/washington/11leak.html.

Sanger, David, and John O'Neil. 2006. "In 1st Major Shift of 2nd Term, Bush Looks to Inner Circle." *New York Times*, March 28, 2006. http://www.nytimes.com/2006/03/28/politics/28cnd-bush.html.

Sanger, David E., and Eric Schmitt. 2004. "Hot Topic: How U.S. Might Disengage in Iraq." *New York Times*, January 10, 2005. http://nytimes.com/2005/01/10/politics/10policy.html.

Savage, David G. 2006. "Phone Firms Questioned." *Los Angeles Times*, May 13, 2006. http://www.latimes.com/news/nationworld/nation/la-na-nsa13may13,0,7842766.story?coll=la-home-headlines.

Schlesinger, Arthur, Jr. 1967. *Bitter Heritage: Vietnam and American Democracy, 1941–1966*. New York: Houghton Mifflin Co.

———. 2003. "Good Foreign Policy a Casualty of War." *Los Angeles Times*, March 23, 2003. http://www.latimes.com/news/opinion/commentary/la-war-opschlesinger23mar23,1,7925658.story?coll=la%2Dnews%2Dcomment%2Dopinions.

Schmitt, Eric. 2006. "Pentagon Contradicts General on Iraq Occupation Force's Size." *New York Times*, February 28, 2003: A1.

Semple, Kirk. 2003. "Ceremonies Nationwide Commemorate Sept. 11 Attacks." *New York Times*, September 11, 2003. http://www.nytimes.com/2003/09/11/national/11CND-ATTA.html.

Shadid, Anthony. 2003. "In Basra, Worst May Be Ahead." *Washington Post*, August 12, 2003: A1.

——. 2003. "Battle Reveals New Iraqi Tactics." *Washington Post*, December 2, 2003: A1.

——. 2003. "Unfulfilled Promises Leave Iraqis Bewildered." *Washington Post*, May 27, 2003: A1.

——. 2004. "Shiites March for Elections in Iraq." *Washington Post*, January 20, 2004: A1.

Shadid, Anthony, and Daniel Williams. 2003. "Blast Kills at Least 95 at Iraqi Shrine." *Washington Post*, August 30, 2003: A1.

Shane, Scott. 2005. "Official Reveals Budget for U.S. Intelligence." *New York Times*, November 8, 2005. http://www.nytimes.com/2005/11/08/politics/08budget.html.

——. 2006. "Iraqi Official, Paid by C.I.A., Gave Account of Weapons." *New York Times*, March 22, 2006. http://www.nytimes.com/2006/03/22/politics/22intel.html

——. 2006. "In New Job, Spymaster Draws Bipartisan Criticism." *New York Times*, April 20, 2006. http://www.nytimes.com/2006/04/20/washington/20intel.html.

——. 2006. "Year into Revamped Spying, Troubles and Some Progress." *New York Times*, February 28, 2006. http://www.nytimes.com/2006/02/28/politics/28terror.html.

Shane, Scott, and Eric Lichtblau. 2006. "Cheney Pushed U.S. to Widen Eavesdropping." *New York Times*, May 14, 2006. http://www.nytimes.com/2006/05/14/washington/14nsa.html.

Shanker, Thom. 2006. "Bremer Says He Sought Rise in U.S. Troop Strength in Iraq." *New York Times*, January 10, 2006. http://www.nytimes.com/2006/01/10/politics/10bremer.html.

Shanker, Thom, and Eric Schmitt. 2003. "Rumsfeld Seeks Consensus through Jousting." *New York Times*, March 19, 2003: A1.

Shawcross, William. (1979). *Sideshow: Kissinger, Nixon, and the Destruction of Cambodia*. New York: Simon and Schuster.

Shenon, Philip. 2003. "9/11 Commission Could Subpoena Oval Office Files." *New York Times*, October 26, 2003. http://www.nytimes.com/2003/10/26/national/26KEAN.html.

——. 2004. "Senators to Request Extension for 9/11 Panel." *New York Times*, January 30, 2004. http://www.nytimes.com/2004/01/30/politics/30TERR.html.

Shmitt, Eric. 2003. "Iraqi Informants' Tips Grow After Brothers' Deaths." *New York Times*, July 26, 2003. http://college3.nytimes.com/guests/articles/2003/07/26/1103045.xml.

Shrader, Katerine. 2005. "WMD Commission Releases Scathing Report." *Washington Post*, March 31, 2005. http://www.washingtonpost.com/wp-dyn/articles/A15184-2005Mar31.html.

Sidoti, Liz. 2005. "Senate Votes to Give Bush More War Funds." *Washington Post*, October, 7, 2005. http://www.washingtonpost.com/wp-dyn/content/article/2005/10/07/AR2005100700202.html.

Silverstein, Ken. 2003. "Congress Presses White House for 9/11 Papers." *Los Angeles Times*, October 27, 2003. http://www.latimes.com/news/nationworld/nation/la-na-commish27oct27,1,6597578.story?coll=la-headlines-nation.

Simon, Richard. 2005. "House Approves $82-Billion War Spending Bill." *Los Angeles Times*, May 6, 2005. http://www.latimes.com/news/nationworld/nation/la-na-spend6may06,1,5546810.story?coll=la-headlines-nation

Sipress, Alan. 2002. "Policy Divide Thwarts Powell in Mideast Effort." *Washington Post*, 26, 2002: A1.

———. 2003. "Bomber Wounds 58 Troops in Iraq." *Washington Post*, December 10, 2003: A21.

———. 2003. "Iraqis Exact Revenge on Baathists." *Washington Post*, December 20, 2003: A1.

Smith, Craig S., and Don Van Natta Jr. 2004. "Officials Fear Iraq's Lure for Muslims in Europe." *New York Times*, October 23, 2004. http://www.nytimes.com/2004/10/23/international/europe/23france.html.

Spiegel, Peter. 2006. "Perle Says He Should Not Have Backed Iraq War." *Los Angeles Times*, November 4, 2006. http://www.latimes.com/news/nationworld/nation/la-na-neocons4nov04,1,1461704.story?coll=la-headlines-nation.

Spiegel, Peter, and Paul Richter. 2006. "Anti-Rumsfeld Chorus Grows." *Los Angeles Times*, April 13, 2006. http://www.latimes.com/news/ nationworld/nation/la-na-general13apr13,0,3539237.story?coll=la-home.

Spinner, Jackie. 2004. "26 Die in String of Attacks on Iraqi Forces." *Washington Post*, December 29, 2004. http://www.washingtonpost.com/wp-dyn/articles/A30605-2004Dec28.html.

Spinner, Jackie, and Khalid Saffar. 2004. "At Least 28 People Killed by Explosion in Iraq." *Washington Post*, December 29, 2004. http://www.washingtonpost.com/wp-dyn/articles/A32855-2004Dec29.html

Stack, Megan K. 2003. "Beirut Rioters Attack Church." *Los Angeles Times*, February 6, 2006. http://www. latimes.com/news/nationworld/world/la-fg-muslims6feb06,0,4694855.story?coll=la-home-headlines

———. 2004. "U.S. General Sees Al Qaeda Evidence in Iraq." *Los Angeles Times*, January 30, 2004. http://www.latimes.com/news/nationworld/world/la-fg-iraq30jan30,1,6933323.story?coll=la-headlines-world.

———. 2006. "Sectarian Violence Sweeps Iraq." *Los Angeles Times*, February 24, 2006. http://www.latimes.com/news/nationworld/world/la-fg-iraq24feb24,0,7711680.story?coll=la-home-headlines.

"Statement of the Family Steering Committee for The 9/11 Commission." March 8, 2004. http://www.911citizenswatch.org/modules.php?op=modload&name=News&file=article&sid=110&mode=thread&order=0&thold=0 (accessed July 27, 2004).

Stolberg, Sheryl Gay and Jim Rutenberg. 2006. "Rumsfeld Resigns as Defense Secretary After Big Election Gains for Democrats." *New York Times*, November 8, 2006. http://www.nytimes.com/2006/11/08/us/politics/09BUSHCND.html

Stout, David. 2003. "New Air Strikes Hit Targets in Baghdad." *Los Angeles Times*, March 20, 2003. http://www.latimes.com/news/nationworld/iraq/battle/la-032003bombing_lat,1,31327.story?coll=la%2Dhome%2Dheadlines

———. 2004. "Bush Understood Threat Posed by Al Qaeda, Rice Tells Panel." *New York Times*, April 8, 2004. http://www.nytimes.com/2004/04/08/politics/08CND-PANE.html.

———. 2006. "C.I.A. Director Porter Goss Resigns." *New York Times*, May 5, 2006. http://www.nytimes.com/2006/05/05/washington/05cnd-cia.html.

Strickland, Daryl. 2004. "Iraq Council Disbands." *Los Angeles Times*, June 1, 2004. http://www.latimes.com/news/nationworld/iraq/la-060104iraq_lat,1,4465904.story?coll=la-home-headlines.

Struck, Doug. 2003. "Korean Peninsula on Edge as U.S. and S. Korea Stage War Games." *Washington Post*, March 23, 2003. http://www.washingtonpost.com/ac2/wp-dyn/A13984-2003Mar23.html.

Suarez, Ray. 2002. "New Hour" Online. "George W. Bush, Presidential Debate, between Vice President Albert Gore and Governor George W. Bush." Hosted by Ray Suarez. http://www.pbs.org/newshour/bb/politics/july-dec00/for-policy_10-12.html (accessed February 23, 2006).

Sullivan, Kevin, and Rajiv Chandrasekaran. 2003. "Hussein's Two Sons Killed In Firefight With U.S. Troops." *Washington Post*, July 23, 2003: A1.

Telhami, Shibley. 2004. "Arabs See Danger, not Hope, in Iraq." *Los Angeles Times*, March 14, 2004. http://www.latimes. com/news/opinion/commentary/la-op-telehami14mar14,1,293521.story?coll=la-news-comment-opinions

Trebilcock, Craig T. 2000. "The Myth of Posse Comitatus." October 2000. http://www.homelandsecurity.org/journal/articles/Trebilcock.htm (accessed April 16, 2006).

Truman, Harry S. (1947). "Suggested draft of the President's message to Congress on the Greek Situation, March 7, 1947." Truman Presidential Museum and Library.   http://www.trumanlibrary.org/histlestop/study_collections/doctrine/large/documents/index.php?pagenumber=6&documentid=39&document date=1947-03-07&studycollectionid=TDoctrine&groupid= and http://www .trumanlibrary.org/whistlestop/study_collections/doctrine/large/documents/ index.php?pagenumber=5&documentid=39&documentdate=1947-03-07& studycollectionid=TDoctrine&groupid= (accessed February 2005).

———. 1956. *Years of Trial and Hope*. New York: Double Day and Company.

USA Today. 2002. "Intelligence Agencies Close Minds to Suggested Reforms." Editorial. December 12, 2002. http://www.usatoday.com/news/opinion/editorials/2002-12-12-13-edit-usat_x.htm (accessed August 4, 2004).

U.S. Department of Defense. "Official Biographies." http://www.defenselink .mil/specials/secdef_histories/bios/ (accessed March 17, 2006).

U.S. Department of Defense, Comptroller. 2006. National Defense Budget Estimates, for FY 2006. http://www.dod.mil/comptroller/defbudget /fy2006/ (accessed July 24, 2006).

U.S. Department of Defense, Defense Intelligence Agency. "History." http:// www.dia.mil/history/index.htm (accessed March 17, 2006).

U.S. Department of State. "Official Biographies." http://www.state.gov/secretary/ former/ (accessed March 29, 2005).

U.S. Department of State, Office of the Inspector General. 2005. "Inspection of the Bureau of Intelligence and Research." http://oig.state.gov/oig.state.gov/ documents/organization/58019.pdf (accessed on March 18, 2006).

U.S. Department of State. 2005. "Supporting Human Rights and Democracy: The U.S. Record 2004–2005." March 28, 2005: http://www.state.gov/g/drl/rls/shrd/ 2004/ (accessed March 29, 2005).

U.S. House of Representatives, Committee on Armed Services. 1947. *The National Security Act of 1947*, Public Law 253, 80th Congress, 2nd session, July 26, 1947.

U.S. House of Representatives, Committee on Armed Services. 1973. Amended. *The National Security Act of 1947*, Public Law 253, 80th Congress, 1st Session, Sec. 101. [U.S.C. 402] (a)7. Washington, DC: Government Printing Office, 1973. September 30, 1973.

U.S. House of Representatives. 2004. "Intelligence Authorization Act for Fiscal Year 2003." H.R. 4628, 107th Congress, 2nd Session, 116 Statute 2383, Public Law 107-306.

U.S. House Permanent Select Committee on Intelligence and the Senate Select Committee on Intelligence. 2002. *Report of the Joint Inquiry into the Terrorist Attacks of September 11, 2001*. 107th Congress, 2nd Session, December, 2002.

U.S. House Permanent Select Committee on Intelligence and the Senate Select Committee on Intelligence. Senate Report Number 107-351, House Report Number 107-792. 2002. 107th Congress, 2nd Session, December 20, 2002: http://intelligence.senate.gov/iraqreport2.pdf (accessed December 29, 2002).

U.S. Office of the Director of National Intelligence. 2005. "Declassified Key Judgments of the National Intelligence Estimate 'Trends in Global Terrorism: Implications for the United States Dated April 2006.'" September 26, 2006. http://dni.gov/press_releases/Declassified_NIE_Key_Judgments.pdf.

U.S. Office of the Director of National Intelligence. 2005. "Establishment of the National Clandestine Service (NCS)." ODNI News Release No. 2-06.October 13, 2005. http://www.dni.gov/release_letter_101305.html (accessed December 5, 2005).

U.S. Office of the Director of National Intelligence. 2006. "ODNI Announces Mission Managers and Senior Leadership Position." News Release. January 11, 2006. http://www.dni.gov/release_letter_011106.html (accessed January 20).

U.S. National Archives of the United States. 2003. "The Federal Register." Executive Order 12863 Section 1.2: http://www.archives.gov/federal-register/executive-orders/pdf/12863.pdf (accessed September 19, 2004).

U.S. National Commission on Terrorist Attacks Upon the United States. 2004. The 9/11 Commission Report. July 24, 2004. http://www.9-11commission.gov/report/911 Report.pdf (accessed July 24, 2004).

U.S. National Geospatial-Intelligence Agency. "Fact Sheet." http://www.nga.mil/portal/site/nga01/index.jsp?epicontent=GENERIC&itemID=31486591e1b3af00VgnVCMServer23727a95RCRD&beanID=1629630080&viewID=Article (accessed March 18, 2006).

U.S. Senate Select Committee on Intelligence. 2006. "The Nomination of General Michael V. Hayden to Be The Director of The Central Intelligence Agency." 216 Hart Senate Office Building, Washington, DC: May 18, 2006. http://dni.gov/testimonies/20060518_testimony_2.pdf (accessed on May 19, 2006).

Vick, Karl. 2004. "Muslim Rivals Unite In Baghdad Uprising." *Washington Post*, April 7, 2004: A1.

Von Drehle, David. 2004. "Zeroing In on One Classified Document." *Washington Post*, April 9, 2004. http://www.washingtonpost.com/ac2/wp-dyn/A62481-2004 Apr8.html.

Warrick, Joby. 2003. "Lacking Biolabs, Trailers Carried Case for War: Administration Pushed Notion of Banned Iraqi Weapons." *Washington Post*, April 12, 2006. http://www.washingtonpost.com/wp-dyn/content/article/006/04/11/AR2006041101888.html.

——. 2005. "Warnings on WMD 'Fabricator' Were Ignored, Ex-CIA Aide Says." *Washington Post*, June 25, 2006. http://www.washingtonpost.com/wp-dyn/content/article/2006/06/24/AR2006062401081. html.

Washington, George. 1796. "Transcript of President George Washington's Farewell Address (1796)." OurDocuments.gov. http://www.ourdocuments.gov/ doc.php?flash=true&doc=15&page=transcript (accessed on December 22, 2005).

Washington Post. 2006. "Operative's Role Unclear." March 28, 2006. http://www .washingtonpost.com/wp-dyn/content/article/2006/03/27/AR2006032702056 .html.

Washington Post. 2006. "Pentagon Official to Resign." Washington in Brief. December 2, 2006. http://www.washingtonpost.com/wp-dyn/content/article/ 2006/12/01/AR2006120101471.html.

Washington Post. 2006. "Pentagon Wrongly Kept Reports in Threat Files." Washington in Brief. April 6, 2006. http://www.washingtonpost.com/wp-dyn/ content/article/2006/04/05/AR2006040502102.html.

Wayne, Leslie. 2005. "Contractors Are Warned: Cuts Coming for Weapons." *New York Times,* December 27, 2005. http://www.nytimes.com/2005/12/27/ business/27weapons.html

Weisman, Weisman, and Shailagh Murray. 2005. "Congress Approves $82 Billion for Wars." *Washington Post,* May 11, 2005. http://www.washingtonpost .com/wp-dyn/content/article/2005/05/10/AR2005051001145.html

White House. 2002. National Security Council. National Security Strategy of the United States, December 2002. http://www.whitehouse.gov/nsc/nss.pdf

———. 2005. "Protecting the Homeland." News Release. December 5, 2005. http://www.whitehouse.gov/news/releases/2005/12/20051205-5.html (accessed January 6, 2005).

———. 2005. "Personnel Announcement." October 31, 2005. http://www.white-house.gov/ news/releases/2005/10/print/20051031-2.html (accessed May 5, 2006).

———. 2005. "President Addresses Nation, Discusses Iraq, War on Terror." Fort Bragg, North Carolina: June 28, 2005. http://www.whitehouse.gov/news/ releases/2005/06/20050628-7.html.

———. 2006. National Security Council. The National Security Strategy of the United States, March 2006. http://www.whitehouse.gov/nsc/2006/nss2006.pdf.

———. "Bibliography of George W. Bush." http://www.whitehouse.gov/ president/gwbbio.html (accessed on February 12, 2006).

———. National Security Council. "Clinton Administration, 1993–1997." http:// www.whitehouse.gov/nsc/history.html#clinton (accessed March 17, 2006).

———. National Security Council. "NSC History." http://www.whitehouse.gov/ nsc/history.html (accessed multiple times since 2001).

———. "The Introduction," "The History of the Board," and "The Role of the Board." President's Foreign Intelligence Advisory Board. http://www .whitehouse.gov/pfiab/ (accessed in August 2005).

———. "Bush Administration Implements WMD Commission Recommendations: Actions to Implement WMD Commission Recommendations." Press Release. June 29, 2005. http://www.whitehouse.gov/news/releases/2005/06/20050629-2.html.

White, Josh. 2004. "Calm Is Broken in Hussein's Home Town." *Washington Post*, December 29, 2004: A15.

———. 2006. "FBI Interrogators in Cuba Opposed Aggressive Tactics." *Washington Post*, February 24, 2006. http://www.washingtonpost.com/wp-dyn/content/article/ 2006/02/23/AR2006022301813.html.

———. 2006. "Rumsfeld Challenges Rice on 'Tactical Errors' in Iraq." *Washington Post*, April 6, 2006. http://www.washingtonpost.com/wp-dyn/content/article/2006/04/05/AR2006040502269.html.

Wilkerson, Lawrence B. 2005. "Weighing the Uniqueness of the Bush Administration's National Security Decision-Making Process: Boon or Danger to America?" New America Foundation, American Strategy Program Policy Forum. October 19, 2005. http://www.newamerica.net/Download_Docs/pdfs/Doc_File_2644_1.pdf (accessed November 12, 2005).

———. 2005. "The White House Cabal." *Los Angeles Times*, October 25, 2006. http://www.latimes.com/news/opinion/commentary/la-oe-wilkerson25oct25,0,7455395.story?coll=la-news-comment-opinions.

Wilkinson, Tracy. 2003. "U.S. Troops Clash With Insurgents, Kill 18 Iraqis." *Los Angeles Times*, December 17, 2003. http://www.latimes.com/news/nationworld/world/la-fg-iraq17dec17,1,5884744.story?coll=la-headlines-world.

Will, George W. 2006. "The Triumph of Unrealism." *Washington Post*, August 15, 2006. http://www.washingtonpost.com/wp-dyn/content/article/2006/08/14/AR2006081401163.html.

Williams, Carol J. 2003. "62 U.S. Troops Injured in Iraq." *Los Angeles Times*, December 10, 2003. http://www.latimes.com/news/nationworld/world/la-fg-iraq10dec10,1,2673466.story?coll=la-headlines-world.

———. 2004. "U.S. Ambassador Takes His Post." *Los Angeles Times*, June 30, 2004. http://www.latimes.com/news/nationworld/world/la-fg-iraq30jun30,1,4176230.story?coll=la-headlines-world.

Williams, Carol J., and Patrick J. McDonnell. 2003. "31 U.S. Soldiers Hurt in Iraq Blast." *Los Angeles Times*, December 9, 2003. http://www.latimes.com/news/nationworld/world/la-fg-blast9dec09,1,5477784.story?coll=la-headlines-world.

Williams, Daniel. 2004. "Fallujah Insurgents Find a New Focus." *Washington Post*, February 8, 2004: A20.

———. 2004. "As Kurds Mourn, Resolve Hardens." *Washington Post*, February 3, 2004: A13.

——. 2004. "Kurds Press for Independence." *Washington Post*, January 30, 2004: A18.

Wittkopf, Eugene R., Charles W. Kegley Jr., and James M. Scott. 2003. *American Foreign Policy: Pattern and Process*. 6th ed. Wadsworth/Thomson Learning. Belmont, CA: Wadswoth/Thomson Learning.

Wolfowitz, Paul. 2002. Deputy Secretary of Defense. "Standup of U.S. Northern Command." Peterson Air Force Base, Colorado Springs, CO: October 1, 2002. http://www.dod.gov/speeches/2002/s20021001-depsecdef1.html (accessed January 13, 2006).

Wong, Edward. 2004. "Iraq Is a Hub for Terrorism, However You Define It." *New York Times*, June 20, 2004. http://nytimes.com/2004/06/20/weekinreview/20wong.html.

——. 2004. "U.S. Tries to Give Moderates an Edge in Iraqi Elections." *New York Times*, January 18, 2004. http://www.nytimes.com/2004/01/18/international/middleeast/18BAGH.html.

——. 2006. "More Clashes Shake Iraq; Political Talks Are in Ruins." *New York Times*, February 24, 2006. http://www.nytimes.com/2006/02/24/international/middleeast/24iraq.html.

——. 2006. "As Violence Ebbs, U.S. Envoy Warns of Danger to Iraq's Future." *New York Times*, February 24, 2006. http://nytimes.com/2006/02/24/international/middleeast/24cnd-iraq.html.

Wong, Edward, and Ian Fisher. 2004. "Wary Iraqis Welcome the Handover but Ask, Now What?" *New York Times*, June 28, 2004. http://nytimes.com/2004/06/28/international/middleeast/28CND-REAC.html.

Woods, Kevin M., Michael R. Pease, Mark E. Stout, et al. 2006. "The Iraqi Perspective Project: A View of Operation Iraqi Freedom from Saddam's Senior Leadership." Joint Forces Command. Joint Center for Operational Studies. May 2006. http://www.jfcom.mil/newslink/storyarchive/2006/ipp.pdf (accessed March 25, 2006).

Woodward, Bob. 2003. *Bush at War*. New York: Simon and Schuster.

Wright, Robin. 2003. "Cheney Was Unwavering in Desire to Go to War." *Washington Post*, April 20, 2004. http://www.washingtonpost.com/wp-dyn/articles/A25550-2004Apr19.html.

——. 2003. "U.S. Ends Talks with Iran over Al Qaeda Links." *Los Angeles Times*, May 21, 2003. http://www.latimes.com/news/nationworld/world/la-fg-usiran21may21,1,3914095.story?coll= la%2Dheadlines%2Dworld.

——. 2003. "White House Divided over Reconstruction." *Los Angeles Times*, April 2, 2003. http://www.latimes.com/news/nationworld/iraq/homefront/la-war-postwar2apr02,1,7358865.story? coll=la%2Dhome%2Dheadlines.

——. 2004. *Plan of Attack*. New York: Simon and Schuster.

———. 2004. "U.N. to Consider Request to Study Earlier Elections in Iraq." *Washington Post*, January 20, 2004: A15.

———. 2004. "U.S., Iraq Reach Security Accord." *Washington Post*, June 7, 2004: A18.

———. 2006. "Bush Initiates Iraq Policy Review Separate From Baker Group's" *Washington Post*, November 15, 2006. http://www.washington-post.com/wp-dyn/content/article/2006/11/14/AR2006111401095.html

Zegart, Amy B. 1999. *Flawed by Design: The Evolution of the CIA, JCS, and NSC*. Palo Alto, CA: Stanford University Press.

Index

About the Author

M. **Kent Bolton** is a professor of political science and global studies at California State University, San Marcos. He has a degree from the Ohio State University (Ph.D. in political science, 1992) as well as baccalaureate (political science) and master's (international relations) degrees from Brigham Young University. M. Kent Bolton was awarded an academic fellowship with the Foundation for the Defense of Democracies (2005) where he traveled to the Middle East to study with some of the world's preeminent experts on the issue of how democracies may effectively counter global jihadis and other transnational threats. His publication record and expertise include both U.S. foreign and national security policy. Bolton has previously published a book on post-9/11 foreign policymaking, *U.S. Foreign Policy: George W. Bush, 9/11, and the Global-Terrorist Hydra* (Prentice Hall, 2005).